Working Knowledge

For the Trowbridge Family

With gratitude

Catherine Fisk

STUDIES IN LEGAL HISTORY

Published by the University of North Carolina Press

in association with the American Society for Legal History

Daniel Ernst and Thomas A. Green, *editors*

Working Knowledge

EMPLOYEE INNOVATION *and the* RISE *of*

CORPORATE INTELLECTUAL PROPERTY,

1800–1930

Catherine L. Fisk

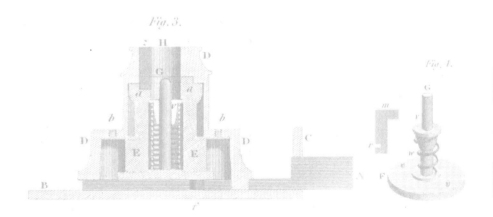

THE UNIVERSITY OF NORTH CAROLINA PRESS *Chapel Hill*

Designed by Courtney Leigh Baker and
set in Whitman by Rebecca Evans

The paper in this book meets the guidelines for permanence
and durability of the Committee on Production Guidelines for
Book Longevity of the Council on Library Resources.

The University of North Carolina Press has been a member
of the Green Press Initiative since 2003.

Library of Congress Cataloging-in-Publication Data
Fisk, Catherine L., 1961–
Working knowledge : employee innovation and the rise of
corporate intellectual property, 1800–1930 / Catherine L. Fisk.
p. cm.— (Studies in legal history)
Includes bibliographical references and index.
ISBN 978-0-8078-3302-5 (cloth : alk. paper)
1. Inventions, Employees—United States—History.
2. Intellectual property—United States.
3. Patents and government-developed inventions—
United States. I. Title.
KF3135.F57 2009
346.7304'86—dc22
2009009385

13 12 11 10 09   5 4 3 2 1

[F O R   E R W I N]

CONTENTS

ACKNOWLEDGMENTS

In the twelve years I have been working on this book, I have accumulated debts so many and so great that it is impossible to acknowledge them all here. Nevertheless, in a book about the relationship between individual authorship and collaborative work, I would be remiss if I did not try. First, I thank Dan Ernst for believing this was a book, for reading the manuscript several times and offering penetrating editorial suggestions, and for seeing it through to publication. I am grateful for financial and material support from the deans, librarians, and staff of the law schools of Loyola Marymount University, the University of Southern California, Duke University, and the University of California, Irvine, and from the Hagley Museum and Library. An embarrassingly large number of law students at Loyola, USC, UCLA, and Duke did research: Amin Aminfar, Geoffrey Moore, and Katherine Scott made extraordinary research and editorial contributions; Kim Kisabeth got the manuscript in shape at the end; and Richard Allen, Kristin Beattie, Michael Blacher, Eric Compere, Robin Diem, Laura Durity, Kelly Firment, Ian Fried, Jennifer La Macchia, An Le, Michael LeBoff, Lin Lee, Max Rieger, Mary Roccapriore, and Kathrin Weston all helped with the research.

Some parts of the book were published in article form, as "Removing the 'Fuel of Interest' from the 'Fire of Genius': Law and the Employee-Inventor, 1830–1930," 65 *University of Chicago Law Review* 1127 (1998); "Working Knowledge: Trade Secrets, Restrictive Covenants in Employment, and the Rise of Corporate Intellectual Property, 1800–1920," 52 *Hastings Law Journal* 441 (2001); "Authors at Work: The Origins of the Work-for-Hire Doctrine," 15 *Yale Journal of Law and the Humanities* 1 (2003); and "Credit Where It's Due: The Law and Norms of Attribution," 95 *Georgetown Law Journal* 49 (2006). I am grateful to the staff and editors of these law reviews for their assistance at the time the articles were published and for permission to include portions of them here.

Many people read and commented on earlier versions or parts of this work. I particularly wish to thank Erwin Chemerinsky, Clyde Spillenger, and Fred Konefsky for reading and commenting on the entire manuscript multiple times at different stages. I am also grateful for excellent suggestions from Dirk Hartog, Ariela Gross, Ellen Aprill, Craig Joyce, Matt Stahl, Paul Saint-Amour, Mary Dudziak, Nomi Stolzenberg, Hilary Schor, Mark Rose, Stephen Siegel, Kenneth Sokoloff, Naomi Lamoreaux, Zorina Khan, Deborah Malamud, Greg Mark, David Lange, Jeff Powell, Roger Horowitz, Gillian Lester, Richard Ross, Stuart Banner, Oren Bracha, and Dan Klerman. Members of the Los Angeles law and humanities reading group and workshops and discussions at conferences and universities all over the country helped refine my thoughts, and my friends and colleagues Carrie Hempel and Doriane Coleman offered sustenance of every kind.

And then there are the debts to my family that I can never repay: to Winston Mills Fisk and Margaret Wilcox Fisk, who taught me to believe that I could write a book but didn't live to see it; to Laura Buck Dennison for being the one who both believed *and* saw me through; and to Jeff, Adam, Alex, and Mara Chemerinsky, without whose unwavering energy and affection this book might have been finished in half the time but wouldn't have given me the same joy. Most important, I am grateful to Erwin Chemerinsky for reading almost everything I write, offering the wisest editorial advice, and making it all worthwhile. The dedication hardly begins to cover it.

Working Knowledge

INTRODUCTION

A foundation of the modern intellectual property regime, and of the business strategy of innovative firms throughout the economy, is the right of firms to the intellectual property produced by their employees. Today's corporate employer typically insists on contracts claiming the copyrights and patents to works produced both during and after a term of employment by employees and independent contractors. In addition, under the law of trade secrets, firms control current and former employees' use of a wide range of unpatented information, and employers can buttress the protection offered by trade secret law through a noncompete or nondisclosure agreement preventing the employee from working in certain occupations or from using or disclosing certain knowledge. Through the contract of hiring, workers are deemed to sell not only their physical labor and its products but also their intellectual labor and its products, and sometimes even the products of intellectual labor done after the term of employment. In short, corporations own workplace knowledge.

In 1800, "ownership" of workplace knowledge was dramatically different. Most knowledge was not something that could be owned. American employers had very few legal rights to control the creative products of their employees or to protect themselves from competition by current or former employees. The law presumed that the employee-inventor owned his patents and the employee-author owned his copyrights. There was no law of trade secrets. Nor would courts readily enforce agreements that would circumvent these legal presumptions. Workers considered themselves at liberty to make the most of whatever knowledge they possessed. Most employers believed they had few ways to prevent the loss of information entailed in employee mobility because knowledge and skill were widely considered to be attributes of skilled craftsmen rather than assets of firms. Of course, there was a market for ideas, but inventors and authors (and not their employers) were envisioned as the primary entrepreneurs in that market.

This is a history of the origins of corporate ownership of employee knowledge as a legal construct and as a business practice. It examines the nineteenth-century origins and development of myriad legal doctrines that allocate employees' ideas, inventions, creative works, and talent to their employers. The central argument of the book is that corporate ownership of workplace knowledge came into existence as employment shifted from being a relationship where legal obligations were determined primarily by status (as family relationships are today) to being one where legal obligations are determined primarily by contract (as business relations are today). The rise of the corporate form of business organization and the early twentieth-century dominance of laissez-faire contract played a crucial role in expanding employer rights. Responding to the opportunities of industrialization, to new markets for intellectual property, and to the new theory of "scientific management," lawyers for firms used the newly emerging rhetoric and rules of contract to expand their clients' rights over workplace knowledge and employee-generated intellectual property. Law, particularly the law of contract, was a catalyst, a means, and, eventually, a product of the change. The movement from status to contract was not the movement from bondage to freedom that used to be imagined by apologists of nineteenth-century liberalism. For highly skilled, talented, and innovative workers, the move from status to contract was one from entrepreneurship to dependence.

The gap between inventors or authors and patent or copyright owners is more pronounced than at any time since the creation of patent and copyright law in Europe and America in the eighteenth and nineteenth centuries. Labor and property theorists since Marx have thought a great deal about the consequences of the alienation of labor from ownership of the physical property and the wealth that are labor's products. Theorists of intellectual property, innovation, and cultural production are beginning to think about the significance of the alienation of creative work from intellectual property. Copyright and patent ownership have until quite recently been equated with authorship and invention, which in turn are often conflated with the notions of originality, plagiarism, and credit (or blame) that go with being the author or inventor of a work. In public discourse, the moral standing earned by the hard work and creative genius of the author and the inventor is still mobilized by corporate intellectual property owners to expand and protect intellectual property rights, by lengthening the term of copyright, campaigning against unauthorized Internet distribution of movies and music, or arguing against compulsory licensing of patented pharmaceuticals in poor nations. But the connection between inventors and patents and authors and copyrights has become attenuated and mediated by corporations.

Both legal doctrines and business practice institutionalized the separation between the human creators of innovations and the intellectual property right owners. Though that separation is now an accepted part of our popular and legal culture, our workplace relationships, and our labor market, its development and enforcement in the nineteenth century reflected a prolonged and sometimes painful contest between the perceived exigencies of economic development and the ideology of free labor. The conflict pitted norms of artisan production—independence, entrepreneurship, and economic democracy—against the felt needs of the emerging industrial system—bureaucracy, efficiency, and hierarchical control. These economic and legal struggles were fought out partly at the highly abstract level of competing habits of legal discourse and partly in the daily lives of workers. [3]

This is both an intellectual history of legal doctrines and a social history of ideas, especially the ownership of ideas. It weaves together the methods and insights of the history of law, labor, business, and technology to show how workplace knowledge, which Frederick Winslow Taylor described as the "principal asset or possession of every tradesman," became the intellectual property of the corporate employer.[1] I aim to bridge an occupational, bibliographic, and social divide between legal history, labor history, and the history of technology. The dominant approach to the study of the history of innovation has been history of technology and history of business. Not surprisingly, scholars in these fields tend to envision the change from the workshop of the mid-nineteenth century to the corporate research and development facility of the mid-twentieth century in managerial and scientific terms. One may expect to see photographs of Edison's increasingly sophisticated laboratories, machine shops, and ever-larger research staff, and illustrations of the increasingly complex devices contained in patent specifications filed by company lawyers. Law enters these stories only peripherally: patent applications made and granted; copyrights registered; patent and copyright litigation won and lost; antitrust suits threatened and resolved. Historians of business and technology have largely failed to see the salience of legal categories and the formative influence of legal discourse and legal rights in analyzing company practices regarding innovation. Labor historians have missed the fertile ironies in this area, where the hierarchical norms of the nineteenth-century master-servant relationship collided most forcefully with the respect accorded the ingenious tinkerer and clever author.[2]

The aim of this book is to show how thoroughly the law and norms of the workplace were intertwined with the business practices that eventually generated the modern regime of corporate intellectual property. This book weaves together discussion of judicial opinions, lawyers' pleadings,

legal treatises, law review articles, and other conventional sources for legal history with the records of business practices gleaned from company archives and from social and business histories of the sectors of the economy that
[4]   produced significant changes in the law. My claims are based on a reading of every published judicial decision between 1800 and 1930 having anything to do with competing employer and employee claims to workplace knowledge and intellectual property, as well as on a comprehensive reading of legal treatises and articles of the period. I make no claim of comparable comprehensiveness in the study of corporate archives; that Herculean task would pose an insuperable obstacle to the author or the reader finishing this book. I can say that the selection of corporate archives for study was deliberate, intended to be representative of different industries, economic sectors, and approaches to innovation and to provide context for understanding the areas of the economy that produced the most reported judicial decisions on disputes involving workplace knowledge.

The book aims to fill another gap in the literature as well. Contemporary accounts of the relationship between particular legal regimes and the rate and direction of innovation and economic development seek to determine which legal regimes best foster innovation. A substantial body of work by economic historians has demonstrated the importance of intellectual property law in directing the path of economic and industrial development in the nineteenth century. What has not been as thoroughly studied, however, is the significance of rules allocating ownership as between innovators and their employers and collaborators. Corporate control of employee-generated intellectual property is often said to have become the legal rule because it was economically efficient. It prevented holdups and other opportunistic behavior. Yet the rules cementing employer control of intellectual property were solidly in place only in the 1920s, a generation after the development of the large corporation and the corporate research lab. The lag between the development of the factory, the corporate research lab, and the large corporation suggests that there can be robust economic development, rapid innovation, and valuable workplace-generated intellectual property even without default rules or contracts allocating intellectual property to the firm.[3]

Not only was there robust economic development during a period of weak and uncertain rights to intellectual property and innovation (as between employer and employee); this book also suggests that management of technology (and, perhaps, the nature, pace, and direction of technological change) varied depending on the form of business organization and the relationships among people working within it. Attitudes toward employee innovation and toward the diffusion of innovation entailed by employee mobility varied widely among firms. E. I. du Pont de Nemours & Company, the Delaware manufacturer of explosives, was from its founding in 1802 careful to guard its technology from its competitors and was acutely aware of the relationship between intellectual property protections, its employment policies, and its strategy for market dominance. Du Pont's methods to achieve its goals, however, changed as the firm grew and as the law offered tools for the firm in the twentieth century that had been unavailable in the nineteenth. Railroads and steel companies approached innovation and the relationship between employment practices and technological innovation quite differently than Du Pont did. Copyrights were handled differently in different sectors, with great variance depending on whether the enterprise was theater production, map publishing, or law publishing.

Although the transformation of legal doctrines, business strategy, and employment practices that I describe here was both dramatic and foundational to modern law, the story should not be read as an instance of what E. P. Thompson called the "Pilgrim's Progress orthodoxy" of history, in which the past is "ransacked for forerunners" of the dominant categories, concepts, or institutions of the present.[4] Such narratives downplay the roads not taken, the contingent, the serendipitous. I most definitely do not invite the reader to assume that the onward march of history is a depressing chronicle of how judges and industrialists, or, more vaguely, law and industrialization, steadily squashed the working person, turning self-reliant, skilled, and inventive artisans into unimaginative drones who clock into their R & D jobs from nine to five just like their colleagues at assembly lines or desks. Both as a transformation of work narrative and as a transformation of law narrative, the story I tell is more complex and the path of legal change more rambling. The creative employee fared considerably better in court than one familiar with nineteenth-century labor and master-servant law might expect. Creative employees enjoyed substantial legal control over the patents, copyrights, and other economically valuable ideas and knowledge they generated or possessed. Not until the 1920s did courts routinely conclude that most economically valuable workplace knowledge was corporate property rather than an attribute of the skilled employee. Some companies declined to exert the legal rights they eventually gained, while others tried and failed in the face of employee opposition. Some legal battles over knowledge ended in stalemate, while others resulted in settlements favorable to the enterprising employee even though courts filed opinions favorable to the employer.

Although the course of legal change did not run smoothly, it did run. One goal of this book is to explain why the path of the law changed, and why it changed as late as it did. I have been urged repeatedly to make a provocative and elegant monocausal explanation, but I cannot because it would be wrong. Many legal, economic, and social forces contributed to the change. First, there is the complex and evolving relationship between the ideology of free labor and rising corporate power. The historiography of work in the nineteenth century has shown the pervasiveness and variety of meanings attached to the concept of free labor both before and after the Civil War. Free labor—as distinguished from slave labor in the South and factory labor ("wage slavery") in the industrializing North—was widely considered both a defining characteristic and an essential precondition of American democracy. Courts adjudicating conflicting claims to control of workplace knowledge saw the connection between what I loosely call employee intellectual property ownership and the freedom of labor. U.S. Supreme Court Justice Joseph Philo Bradley, sitting by designation as a circuit judge, declared in 1887: "A naked assignment or agreement to assign, in gross, a man's future labors as an author or inventor,—in other words, a mortgage on a man's brain, to bind all its future products,—does not address itself favorably to our consideration."[5] Another court protested against issuing an injunction preventing a chemist from disclosing a formula for wallpaper backing, on the ground that to do so would mean "that hereafter no man can work for one and learn his business secrets, and after leaving that employment engage himself to a rival in business, without carrying on his back into that business the injunctive mandate of a court of equity."[6] Restrictions on the use of knowledge and on intellectual property ownership were characterized in quasi-slavery terms, as if they deprived the employee of his freedom and independence.

As will become apparent, I do not believe the evidence supports any single or elegant theory of the relationship between legal, social, and economic change. At some points, material change clearly aided—catalyzed if it did not precipitate—legal change. The expansion and popularization of corporate research laboratories after 1900 helped judges see invention and patenting in collective terms in the 1920s. In other ways—and even at the same time—law was clearly endogenous. The use of contracts in corporate research laboratories illustrates the complex relation between the possibilities of legal rules, their limits in practice, and the ways in which law is described by lawyers to corporate clients, then filtered through the web of relationships in the workplace, and then redescribed by lawyers and judges. There is, in short, heavy traffic back and forth across the bridge of causation between the legal and the material.

The free labor imagery of the mid- and late nineteenth century fit well with a notion of employee control of workplace knowledge and intellectual property. Intellectual property discourse often treated the relationship be- tween a person and her idea as if the copyright, patent, or trade secret were the external manifestation of the creator's soul, and as if protecting the bond between them were not merely a matter of economic rights but also neces- sary to human flourishing. Courts embraced the idea—often attributed to Diderot—that no one is so clearly the master of his goods as a person is the master of the labor of his mind. The dilemma of intellectual property from the beginning has been to reconcile that vision of freedom (which is often seen to demand robust protection for intellectual property) with another, articulated by Thomas Jefferson, that locates freedom in much less protec- tion for intellectual property rights. Jefferson wrote, "It would be curious . . . if an idea, the fugitive fermentation of an individual brain, could of natural right, be claimed in exclusive and stable property. If nature has made one thing less susceptible than all others of exclusive property, it is the action of the thinking power called an idea. . . . He who receives an idea from me," Jefferson explained, "receives instruction himself without lessening mine, as he who lights his taper at mine receives light without darkening mine."[7] Law has struggled to accommodate both views of the nature of knowledge. While reconciling these two views of property rights in knowledge was and remains a dilemma when the competing claimants were the intellectual property creator and an alleged infringer, there was no dilemma when the competing claimants were employer and employee. When an employer ar- gued that the relationship of employment gave it the exclusive right to the employee's intellectual property, both Diderot's vision and Jefferson's pointed toward protecting employees' rights to use the fruits of their creativity.

American democracy was believed to be dependent upon the existence of a substantial and financially independent middle class. The reluctance of courts throughout the nineteenth century significantly to limit employee use of workplace knowledge and intellectual property was attributable to the perception of the employee litigants' middle-class status; employee in- dependence was an essential bulwark against the tyranny that characterized both chattel slavery and the degraded wage labor of the factory system. John Stuart Mill proposed in *On Liberty* (1859) that a contract of slavery was a labor contract that was "legally binding beyond a limited duration of time" and that could not be retracted; "there are perhaps no contracts or engage- ments, except those that relate to money or money's worth, of which one can venture to say that there ought to be no liberty whatever of retraction."[8] An employee's agreement to relinquish the products of his mind struck courts as the sort of contract that should be subject to retraction for it restricted future freedom and constrained creativity. In the labor unrest after the Civil

War, courts and legal treatises insisted that it was the contract that made wage labor free. Christopher Tiedeman's famed treatise on government power insisted that "liberty of contract" was "the badge of a freeman."[9] The challenge for courts in employment cases during contentious decades of industrialization and the rise of employer control associated with managerial capitalism was to create a legal definition of contract that preserved enough freedom to satisfy this ideological frame while allowing management the control over its workers that it insisted was necessary. One line courts could easily draw was to protect the rights of the inventive worker to control the use of his knowledge and its products.

Class and status figured in the law in other ways as well. As will become apparent, very rarely did a factory hand litigate workplace knowledge issues. Most of the disputes that form the backbone of this book involved highly skilled workers. Some involved people who then and now would be considered professionals (including lawyers). Some involved "machinists," a category that today might encompass many engineers. Many were on the porous border between entrepreneur and skilled labor.[10] The legal relations between the workers and the firms also varied. Some were what today would be deemed independent contractors: workers who were hired by the job and who worked with little supervision or control from their employer. Some were clearly what today would be deemed employees: workers who were hired for an extended period and who were subject to extensive control as to the manner of their work. Some were stockholders in the small enterprises that employed them. When workers demanded and courts granted legal rights to their knowledge to protect their independence and capacity for entrepreneurship, they operated in a culture and a legal regime that recognized the importance and the possibility of freedom of contract, and free labor, in real terms—not just as legal abstractions or political slogans.

Over the course of the nineteenth century, notions about the middle classes and their independence changed, of course, and so changed the courts' view that employee control over workplace knowledge was an essential feature of middle-class status. In the mid-nineteenth century, the economic independence enabled by control over one's own creative products was seen as a foundation of the kind of social independence that would reconcile democracy with economic development. By the second decade of the twentieth century, middle-class independence connoted steady and respectable corporate employment rather than entrepreneurship, and freedom to consume rather than to produce. Courts revised nineteenth-century notions about the relationship of control of knowledge to social and economic respectability. Intellectual property ownership and legally unrestrained mobility were no longer regarded as necessary to protect the innovative or entrepreneurial worker from the social decay of downward mobility.

Evolving ideas about freedom and work were shaped by the role of contract and property law in regulating it. The cases reveal a tension between two different discourses: one about contract and work relationships and a second about property. Early in the nineteenth century, the employment relationship was a status relationship in which the rights and obligations of employer and employee inhered in their status. Certain terms were contractual, of course—particularly compensation and the worker's responsibilities. And in the 1830s and 1840s, courts sometimes used the rubric of "implied contract" to describe the rights and obligations that were imposed by law rather than consciously and voluntarily assumed by the parties. Later in the century, the employment relationship came to be seen as *only* (or at least overwhelmingly) a matter of contract. The role of the law was ostensibly limited to identifying and enforcing the agreement of the parties. Courts redefined the contract between the creative employee and his employer with regard to ownership and control of the process and products of creativity. The growth of contract concepts, and particularly the development in the late nineteenth century of implied contractual terms that replaced the earlier status-based obligations of employment, facilitated a substantial expansion of the firm's rights to employee creative products.

The independence guaranteed by intellectual property ownership that courts had guarded for creative employees in the nineteenth century was washed away in a tidal wave of contract changes after the turn of the twentieth century. It is often imagined that contract was the legal engine that liberated Americans from the hierarchy of constraints imposed by the nearly immutable status relationships described by Blackstone (master and servant, husband and wife). The conventional story of nineteenth-century American work relations imagines "a movement from Status to Contract" as a movement from constraint to liberty, in the felicitous terms of Sir Henry Maine's book.[11] I argue that, when it came to creative employees, the movement from status to contract was a movement from independence to dependence.

As legal conceptions of property changed over the nineteenth century from a notion of absolute dominion over things to a fragmented relationship among people concerning intangibles, American legal thinkers began to associate certain forms of property rights with commerce and with the continual expansion of human freedom. As Gregory Alexander explained, James Kent's influential 1836 treatise on American law found the fundamental policy of property law to be marketability; Kent associated commerce with freedom from an archaic and repressive legal, political, and social order.[12]

Entrepreneurial activity benefited society and the law of property should foster it. While Whigs and Jacksonians famously disagreed about whether law should protect vested property rights against competition, their shared view of the importance of property rights in liberating individual talent for entrepreneurial activity meant that there could be a dominant view that the talents of the innovative worker should not be constrained by legal rules that would prevent his ability to better his position through the careful development of his industry. Fostering the talent and industry of the skilled worker was of the keenest interest to the courts.

By the end of the nineteenth century, as the discourse about property and its role in promoting American freedom changed again, property no longer concerned itself primarily with ownership of land or tangible things at all, but included corporate trust indentures, debentures, stock, and a host of other investment devices. The definition of property, as John R. Commons explained, had changed from "physical things having only use-value to the exchange value of anything."[13] These changes in property theory influenced how courts perceived workplace intellectual property claims as well. Property rights supported massive accumulations of wealth and unprecedented concentrations of private ownership and power, and the growing popular rebellion against them represented the most serious challenge to the democratic political order. With this new view both of the nature of property and of its relationship to freedom, the terms in which courts described the ownership or control of workplace knowledge changed as well. The relationship between property rights and entrepreneurship came to be seen less in terms of individual control over talents and resources and more in terms of the difficulty of coordinating a complex undertaking involving many inputs to production, protecting the return on an investment in a large enterprise, while ensuring an acceptable standard of living for the growing armies of factory and office labor. As cases involving corporations and their property disputes came to dominate the dockets of federal courts at the turn of the twentieth century, and as the power of concentrated labor and capital seemed to pose a greater threat to social stability and political democracy than ever before, the legal imagination of property and its relationship to freedom changed. The employee entrepreneur seemed a relic of the past. Workers' freedom would be ensured by a legal and economic regime that provided stable and sustaining corporate employment, not by protecting the right of workers to become entrepreneurs.

Moreover, the modern intellectual property theory that defines originality by linking it to property arose in the same period in the nineteenth century during which modern labor economics and theories of value became dominant.[14] In particular, theories that root the value of an object in the scene of its production developed at the same time in economic theory and in aesthetic theory, and common arguments about value arose in legal debates about copyright law and in literary debates about originality and plagiarism. [11] Over the course of the late nineteenth and early twentieth centuries, as labor theories of value gave way to consumption theories of value, views about originality changed. Today the value of a copyright, or an idea, or a patent, or information, is not the quantity or value of the labor that produced it but rather the value to consumers of it. The divorce of the value of the creator from the value of the creation was made possible in part because of widespread corporate ownership of intellectual property. As the actual creators faded from view, the relationship between the marketers and the consumers became dominant. Corporate control of workplace knowledge was facilitated by advertising and the massive consumption of mass-produced goods. The realization of Thorstein Veblen's worst nightmare—a society dominated by idle consumers—enabled the transition from the nineteenth century's monopoly view of patent and copyright to the twentieth century's property view.[15] The consumer's relationship to the product, which is partly constituted by corporate advertising creating an imagined affinity between the consumer and the corporate brand, determines the value of an innovation.

The field of intellectual property has been expanding in multiple dimensions for at least a century. The outer boundaries of the field have grown, as more forms of information (such as computer programs, photographs, and recorded music) and previously disparate causes of action came within the ambit of what is now called intellectual property. In addition, the boundaries of the constituent parts enlarged, as if each subfield of intellectual property were an expanding universe or solar system of its own. Copyright, for example, now covers not merely books and maps but all sorts of expression in a constantly expanding range of media. Even the depth and density of the parts are growing. The length of copyright protection, the claims to ownership of works created by others, the forms of derivative use that are prohibited, and the remedies available to stop infringements of intellectual property rights—all have expanded. Not only have legal categories grown, so too has the web of institutions that create and define intellectual property, including the patent office, legislatures, corporate and university research labs and law offices, the Internet, high-technology districts, advertisers, and workplaces. The institutional behavior that we understand to be relevant to or constitutive of intellectual property shades into a web of relationships, including those among inventors, investors, manufacturers, marketers, consumers, employees, corporations, universities, and even, most amorphously,

Introduction

networks.[16] The transformation in ownership of workplace knowledge was an essential aspect of the expansion and transformation of intellectual property generally.

[12] The various doctrines allocating ownership of creative products evolved over the course of nineteenth-century American industrialization in similar ways during roughly contemporaneous time periods. This book is organized chronologically in three parts in order to capture the similarities across legal doctrines within historical periods. Within each of the three parts, the chapters are divided by economic sector and type of knowledge. One or more chapters in each part focuses on what are today considered technology or industrial sectors, in which patents and trade secrets are the dominant forms of intellectual property. One chapter in each part addresses what are today considered cultural or entertainment industries, in which copyright is the dominant form of intellectual property. Each chapter attempts to bridge the legal-labor-business history divide by offering both analysis of legal rules and a narrative about how the law was used, ignored, and created by workers in their daily interactions with each other, with their supervisors, and with the fictional entity—the corporation—that eventually came to stand in for the concept of collective ownership of innovation.

A Note on Intellectual Property Law and Terminology

This book does not aim to be a history of intellectual property law generally. It examines the history of certain aspects of patent law, copyright law, and other areas now included within the ambit of intellectual property from the perspective of the work relationships that created it. I do not assume knowledge of intellectual property law, which is complex and full of technical terms. The following explanation may serve as an aid to those unfamiliar with the basics.

"Intellectual property," as noted above, was not used to refer to patents, copyrights, trade secrets, and trademarks collectively until the middle of the twentieth century. In the nineteenth century, these were all distinct and disparate bodies of law, with different origins, and lawyers did not think of them as forming a coherent field. Today, they are regarded as forming a field because each establishes a legal right in information.

Patent Law and Terminology

A *patent* is an exclusive right to make, use, or sell an invention for a term of years (now twenty years). A patent cannot be renewed, so the exclusive right expires after the end of the twenty-year term. A patent is granted upon application to the United States Patent Office. The application must contain a *specification* describing the invention and how it works. The application also makes one or more *claims* showing that the invention is *new, useful, and nonobvious* in one or more respects. Novelty is judged by whether the invention makes advances beyond the *prior state of the art* of which the invention is a part. Patent applications are public documents. The purpose of treating applications as public documents is to disclose all advances in the art to those who practice it.

The Patent Office *examines* the application and conducts a search of past patents and relevant technical literature to determine whether the invention meets the novelty, utility, and nonobviousness requirements imposed by the patent act. If an application appears to resemble too closely an existing patent or application, the Patent Office will declare an *interference*. The applicant may then litigate the novelty of the proposed patent before the Patent Office and subsequently in the courts.

A patentee may sue for *infringement* anyone who uses, makes, or sells any part of the patented invention without authorization. In defense, the user may show that the Patent Office erred in issuing the patent (for example, that the invention was not new or useful or nonobvious) or that the patentee engaged in certain kinds of unfair conduct before or after the issuance of the patent.

A number of technical terms arose over time to describe the ways that an employee-inventor might transfer patent rights to his or her employer. One was an *assignment*, which is a permanent sale or transfer of all rights in the patent. Another was a *license*, which is like a rental: a right to use the patent on certain terms. A third was a *shop right*, which was a compulsory and uncompensated (i.e., *royalty*-free) license that occurred not by agreement but by force of law.

Copyright Law and Terminology

A *copyright*, like a patent, is an exclusive right for a term of years to make certain uses of a *work*. The term of copyright today ranges from the life of the author plus 70 years to 120 years after creation, depending on the type of work. Works that are subject to copyright were originally limited by federal statute to books, maps, and maritime charts. Over the course of the nineteenth and twentieth centuries, Congress amended the statute to provide for copyrights in other written, recorded, or *fixed* texts, sounds, and images, including recorded music, performed dramas, photographs, moving pictures, paintings, sculpture, and computer software.

One requirement for securing a copyright is that the work be *original*, which is not the same thing as the novelty required of a patent. Originality requires only that the *author* created the work himself or herself without copying from someone else, and not that the idea expressed in the work be novel. Another requirement is that the work be *fixed* or expressed: an idea cannot be copyrighted, only a particular expression of it.

Formalities for obtaining a copyright are now almost nonexistent, and the procedure has always been much simpler than for obtaining a patent. There is no office that examines the copyright to determine eligibility before a copyright is granted. The validity of the copyright is legally determined only if there is infringement litigation. For some of the nineteenth century, all that was required was registration (filing a document and paying a small fee), deposit of a small number of copies of the work with a designated government office (initially the federal courts and later the Library of Congress), and inclusion of a notice in the work that it was subject to copyright. The deposit requirement was eventually abandoned and today it is not necessary even to *register* the work or to include a copyright notice (the customary © symbol).

Because the validity of a copyright is determined largely by the originality of a work by the author, ownership of copyrights rests significantly on *authorship*. From the beginning, it was possible for an *author* to sell or "*assign*" a work to someone else who would register the work as its *proprietor* and thus be deemed the exclusive copyright owner. Legal complexity arises when there are multiple possible claimants to the role of author. When a work is composed of material created by more than one person (such as a co-authored book), or when it consists of various components (such as melody and lyrics), it is a *joint work*. A joint work must be a "unitary whole" consisting of "inseparable and interdependent parts." If two or more authors contribute to a work without intending to merge them into a single work at the time of creation, the work is likely to be a *compilation*, such as an encyclopedia or an anthology. If two or more authors create a work in which one builds upon copyrightable work originally created by another, the later work is likely a *derivative* work; the second author will be the owner of the derivative work and the first author will be the owner of the original. Finally, and most important for this book, there is the category of a *work for hire* or a *work made for hire*. This book tells the story of the creation of that category of ownership. Today, the copyright statute defines a work for hire as being one either created by an employee within the scope of his or her employment, or specially commissioned. In either case, the employer (also known as the *hiring party*) is deemed the author. An *employee* is one who is subject to the direction and control of the employer in the creation of the work. Only works created *within the scope of employment* are owned by the employer; the employee remains the author and owner of works created during the employee's free time and not related to the employee's employment. Specially commissioned works are generally those created by persons working for pay but not under the direction and control of the hiring party, a category of worker that today is called an *independent contractor*. Whereas any type of work may be a work for hire if created by an employee, only nine types of works may be deemed works for hire as specially commissioned works: contributions to collective works; parts of motion pictures or audiovisual works; translations; supplementary works (forewords, illustrations, etc.); compilations; instructional texts; tests; answers to tests; and atlases.

[15]

Both copyright and patent law are, in the United States, exclusively a matter of federal law; states cannot issue copyrights and patents (although, as we will see, state courts can adjudicate some forms of contract disputes over ownership of copyrights and patents). The law of trademarks is largely federal law today, although there is some state regulation. The law of trade secrets is almost entirely state law.

Unfair Competition Law and Terminology
TRADE SECRETS

A *trade secret* is information that derives independent economic value from the fact that it is not generally known to people who could put it to use in some aspect of business or trade. One of the more famous contemporary trade secrets is the recipe for Coca-Cola. Almost any kind of knowledge or information could be a trade secret, including recipes, lists of customers, or knowledge about manufacturing or business techniques, or even knowledge about what kinds of processes do *not* work to achieve certain goals. There is no requirement that a trade secret be novel or original to the person or firm that possesses it. Nor is a trade secret owner required to register it. All that is required is that the information be secret, be valuable because of its secrecy, and be subject to reasonable efforts to maintain its secrecy. Because of the requirement that information be secret in order to be protected, a firm usually must choose between patenting (which requires public disclosure of the information in the patent application) and claiming trade secret status. The law of trade secrets, like the law of trademarks (explained below), derives from nineteenth-century unfair competition law; the common theme was that it was unfair for a business to seek competitive advantage by using secrets or marks belonging to other merchants or manufacturers. As a consequence, even if a product is composed of a trade secret, if the secret information can be independently derived (as by disassembling the product), the person who learns the information through this "reverse engineering" is free to use it. The permissibility of reverse engineering is an important distinction between trade secrets and patents (independent derivation is no defense to patent infringement).

[16]   Trade secret protections are created and enforced under state law. The law is violated if a person who owes a duty to guard the secret (such as an employee) reveals it to anyone who has no right to know it, or uses it for his or her own gain. It is for that reason that the law of trade secrets was and remains an important part of the law of workplace knowledge. The law is also violated if a person acquires the trade secret through what used to be known as "industrial espionage," as by posing as a delivery person or a prospective employee for purposes of gaining access to the secret, or by illicit photography or recording.

NONCOMPETE AGREEMENTS

A contract by which two people or businesses promise not to engage in certain business in competition with one another is known as a *restrictive covenant* or a *noncompetition contract* or *noncompete agreement*. Like most contracts in the United States, their validity is determined under state law. As contracts designed to require a person or entity to refrain from competitive business, however, noncompetition agreements have also come under scrutiny under both state and federal antitrust law, which is a body of law that regulates anticompetitive business practices such as price-fixing and monopoly. Noncompetition agreements are not generally regarded as an aspect of intellectual property, but primarily as a matter of unfair competition law. Unlike patents, copyrights, trade secrets, and trademarks, a noncompetition agreement does not necessarily reflect an effort to treat certain knowledge, information, technology, or an image or symbol as a species of property. Nevertheless, as applied to the relation of employer and employee, the principal use of a noncompetition agreement is to restrain the employee from using information (often a trade secret) that the employer deems valuable. Thus, enforcement of noncompetition agreements gives property-like protection to certain business information.

TRADEMARKS

Historically, a *trademark* was a distinctive mark (usually that of a guild) placed by artisans on goods to identify the goods as the product of a particular group of craftsmen. Today, the federal trademark statute, the Lanham Act, provides the owner of a *federally registered mark* the right to prevent use of similar marks by others if any confusion might result as to the origin or manufacture of the goods. Trademark law originated in the United States as a branch of the state law regulating various forms of unfair competition and remains part of the general law of unfair competition. Thus, its origins lie in the same area of law and the same notion of "unfair" competition as the law of trade secrets and noncompetition agreements. The enactment of the Lanham Act in 1946 (and its precursors in 1881 and 1905) provides a structure for federal registration of marks and for enforcement of the common law of trademark in federal courts. Eventually the federal trademark statute was amended to allow the registration and enforcement of service marks (which identify a service rather than a good). The essential requirements of modern trademark law are that the mark be *distinctive* and that use of that mark by another person or entity be likely to *confuse* customers or, even, to affect the value of the trademark. Eventually, as advertising grew, trademarks came to have independent value reflecting not just the origin of the goods, but also and more important the embodiment of the owner's reputation and *good will*, a legal term referring to customer loyalty.

INNOVATION SELDOM OCCURS and never spreads by one person working alone. Who profited and who lost, and in what amounts, and why; who received credit even if not money and who faded into obscurity; and how creative collaborations occurred, how they succeeded, and how they disintegrated—all these are absolutely crucial parts of the inquiry into the nature of workplace innovation. This book shows the importance of the opportunity for individual entrepreneurship within collaborative social structures. As we reflect on the rapid innovation associated with computers, the Internet, and the so-called information revolution of the late twentieth century and early twenty-first, in which most of the revolutionaries are people working for corporations, it behooves us to contemplate the experiences of those who worked on the innovations of earlier industrial, market, and information revolutions. Where the risk of loss and the possibility for profit are placed matters a great deal in providing incentives to create. Where the power to allocate profit, loss, credit, and blame is abused, innovative communities do not thrive.

PART I

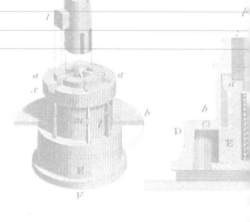

WORKPLACE KNOWLEDGE
AS A PERSONAL ATTRIBUTE,
1800–1860

At the turn of the nineteenth century, the United States was a predominantly agricultural economy with little manufacturing. Most people worked in household or small-scale family or kin-based enterprises. Mainly they worked on farms, but some worked in town or village households, making things for their own use or for trade or sale on a small scale. The typical manufacturer was a master artisan or mill proprietor and the typical manufacturing workplace was a room or rooms in the artisan's home or in a small building. The typical manufacturing employee was a handicraft worker. Businesses were very small, involving the effort and collaboration of a few people, perhaps related by kinship. Except in textiles and armaments, there was almost no factory production in the United States before 1840. Wage labor was neither predominant nor permanent. Opportunities for entrepreneurship among artisans and small shop owners were significant. Wage labor was not a lifetime prospect for most people, both because it was possible to move west and claim land and because the small scale of manufacturing and commerce allowed entrepreneurship for those with access to even a modest sum of capital.[1]

Both skilled labor and technology were scarce. The United States was a developing nation and, as in developing nations today, individuals and governments pursued the introduction of technology by invention and importation. Secretary of the Treasury Alexander Hamilton in his *Report on Manufactures* (1791) recommended a concerted governmental effort to encourage domestic manufacturing, including the imposition of tariffs on imports, the granting of patents and copyrights to inventors and authors, and the awarding of pecuniary benefits to those who introduced technologies to the United States. The *Report* also advocated the creation of a government fund "to defray the expenses of the emigration of artists, and manufacturers in particular branches of extraordinary importance; to induce the prosecution and introduction of useful discoveries, inventions, and improvements."[2] Manufacturers recruited skilled artisans to immigrate to the United States and to bring detailed and recent technological knowledge, sketches, working models, and machinery with them. Textile manufacturing techniques were especially sought after, but a variety of other forms of knowledge were imported as well. While Americans devised elaborate schemes to evade English mercantilist restrictions on the emigration of artisans and the exportation of technology to the colonies, Parliament enacted statutes prohibiting the export of machines and the emigration of artisans, mechanics, or manufacturers for the purpose of carrying on their trade. Enforcement of these prohibitions was not terribly effective, and when machinery was imported into America it was common to import as well a skilled worker to operate it, as the primitive state of most written materials on technology meant that most machinery could not be assembled or operated without someone skilled in its design and use. As a consequence, the emigration of artisans was the crucial factor in technology transfer from Britain to America.[3]

[20]

From the early nineteenth century, invention was understood as a foundation and catalyst of economic development. Admiration of inventors and faith in the power of technological development to enrich the nation became part of American culture. The patent system was designed to be democratic, and to a substantial extent the operation of the system achieved the goals of the design by enabling ordinary people to patent their inventions. While invention as opposed to importation did not early emerge as distinct or superior, innovation and technological development by whatever means were much lauded. A central aspect of the early American enthusiasm about the benefits of invention and industry was the awareness of the need to cultivate knowledge and creativity among as wide a swath of the population as possible. As Hamilton said, encouraging manufactures and rewarding the ingenuity of people would give employment to "classes of the community not originally engaged in the particular business," as well as allow "greater scope for the diversity of talents and dispositions which discriminate men from each other." Invoking the already familiar notion of "Yankee ingenuity," Hamilton argued: "If there be anything in a remark often to be met with, namely, that there is, in the genius of the people of this country, a peculiar aptitude for mechanic improvements, it would operate as a forcible reason for giving opportunities to the exercise of that species of talent, by the propagation of manufactures."[4] Beginning in 1824 with the Franklin Institute in Philadelphia, mechanics' institutes were founded to bring the contents and methods of science directly to artisans and mechanics.[5] Alexis de Tocqueville wrote of what he observed in the 1830s that the knowledge cultivated in America was of the "practical" sort, and he discerned in American democracy a desire to put knowledge to immediate and practical use. "In America the purely practical part of science is admirably understood, and careful attention is paid to the theoretical portion which is immediately requisite to application. On this head the Americans always display a clear, free, original, and inventive power of mind. But hardly anyone in the United States devotes himself to the essentially theoretical and abstract portion of human knowledge."[6]

The workplace was the primary site of technical education and innovation. Most innovators learned their technology by doing rather than by study in an academic setting. The breakdown in America of traditional craft organization meant that individual workers were responsible for obtaining their own technical education. Most found it in the workplace. The tremendous mobility of skilled labor—spurred in part by general mobility in early America and also by labor shortages and the great demand for machinists and those with valuable knowledge—ensured that technical knowledge spread rapidly from one early industrial or manufacturing center to another. Many found it in the mechanics' institutes during the 1820s and 1830s, which further reduced the authority of masters in the transmission of knowledge. Thus, practical education and entrepreneurship were linked in the early nineteenth century, as craft workers were encouraged both by the institutes and by their economic circumstances to see the acquisition of technical knowledge as a business strategy.[7]

The small scale of most enterprises at the turn of the nineteenth century contributed to the relative obscurity of disputes over control of knowledge. While there were some joint-stock companies for land, water supply, mining, and other ventures, most productive enterprises were sufficiently small that they could be financed by individuals or small partnerships. Corporations were rare. When there were few participants in a business, and those who put up the investment capital were often those who worked in the shop, there were fewer claimants to the workplace knowledge and to any intellectual property rights they produced. Moreover, the persistence of craft production by families or under the fluid and, by European standards, lax American norms of the master-journeyman-apprentice system meant that most issues regarding the control of workplace knowledge could be resolved with reference to traditional status obligations or interpersonal negotiations among kin.[8]

From the vantage point of today's thoroughly market-dominated society, in which mass-produced, brand-name consumer goods protected by patents, copyrights, trademarks, and trade secrets litter every home and shape our sense of self and our status in the world, it is hard to imagine early nineteenth-century cultural attitudes toward what we today call intellectual property. Markets were discrete events occupying distinct places and times, and many homes had few purchased goods, no mass-produced items, and relatively few things period. Society before the "market revolution"—and before the consumer goods revolution—had a dramatically different relationship to things and to the intellectual property that today permeates things and our perceptions of things. People cooked food on a fire, made their own clothes and tools, spoke to the people nearby and wrote letters to those far away, and rode horses for transport; ordinary life was not filled with items that embodied patents, copyrights, or trademarks. Patents and copyrights were not something with which ordinary people had much personal experience; they were a nearly alien concept to the vast majority of people, including lawyers. Of course, inventors, writers, and mapmakers, and those who sought to manufacture or sell inventions, books, or maps, were keenly interested in patents and copyrights.[9] But there was no law of trade secrets or trademarks, only patents and copyrights, and the kinds of innovations that could be patented and copyrighted were much more limited then than now. The mass-production consumer-goods economy of today shapes our understanding of the value of ideas, of names, and of the role of intellectual property in commodifying ideas, names, and information, and it also obscures from our view the smaller role of idea ownership in the economy of 1800.

Across the spectrum of workplace knowledge and legal rules governing it, judges and lawyers, skilled workers and those who hired them, acted as if they believed that workplace knowledge was a valuable possession, or more likely an attribute, of the individual worker. This belief was largely unchallenged before the Civil War. But it came under a number of challenges beginning around 1860. The following two chapters illustrate the legal treatment of workplace knowledge between roughly 1800 and 1860. The first takes up equipment and technology and the allied field of patent law; the second, printing and publishing and the allied field of copyright law.

1

Stealing in the Dark the Improvements of Others

In 1808, the Wilmington, Delaware, powder manufactory of E. I. du Pont de Nemours & Company was a sophisticated operation by the standards of American explosives manufacturing of the day. On account of its founders' superior knowledge of the chemistry of gunpowder and its employees' careful development of techniques for its composition, the firm had established a favorable position in the market even in the six short years of its operation. The employees' know-how was one of the firm's most precious assets. When a competing powder maker sought to recruit Du Pont workers to learn from them the company's techniques, Du Pont found it had no legal remedy for the harm inflicted by the departure of its skilled workers. Skilled employees bound by no contract were free to quit and to take whatever knowledge they learned on the job with them. And even if Du Pont had attempted to bind its employees through agreements not to compete or not to disclose its secrets, the courts would not have enforced them. If both lawyers and businesspeople appreciated the value of knowledge, why did the law provide no remedy?

This chapter begins with an explanation of the nature and reasons for the early American legal commitment to mobility of labor and to the courts' refusal to regard workplace knowledge, whether unpatented secrets like Du Pont's or patented inventions by employees, as the virtually inalienable attribute of the individual employee. Against the context of the antebellum legal commitment to free mobility of skilled labor and individual entrepreneurship protected by patent law, the chapter then examines how Du Pont's business strategy and choices for managing its skilled workers reflected and adapted to the American insistence that workplace knowledge was the attribute of skilled workers, not an asset of the firm that employed them.

American law of the workplace, like the rest of American law in 1800, was
[24] in a state of uncertainty. There were few treatises, catalogs, digests, or even
reports of American law.[1] American law was, by design and by necessity,
heavily reliant on English law, both as a matter of individual precedents and
as a matter of an entire structure and philosophy. According to Edmund
Burke, Blackstone's *Commentaries* sold as many copies in the colonies before
the Revolution as in England. As Daniel Boorstin argued, it played a greater
role in the history of American institutions than any book save the Bible,
in part because it was a highly readable and succinct summary of an entire
body of law that came in handy for lawyers and judges who often had little
formal legal training and no access to a complete law library.[2]

The English law of work relations was largely common law, based primarily on the status relations associated with the guild system of master, journeyman, and apprentice; the household model that dominated agricultural work;
and some adaptations thought necessary to respond to the emerging factory
system. There was some statutory regulation (beginning with the Ordinance
of Labourers of 1349) that fixed wages, regulated certain other terms of the
labor contract, compelled able-bodied persons to accept employment, and
prohibited enticing away another's servants. The English law of patents and
copyrights was largely statutory, as the U.S. law later came to be. Both the
patent and copyright statutes provided for exclusive rights for limited terms
and only upon compliance with the statutory requirements.[3]

Lawyers in the new United States showed reasonable reluctance to borrow the English law of master and servant wholesale. A country governed
by lawyers committed to a republican form of government, to obliterating
the status hierarchies of Europe, and to developing a free and economically
independent citizenry would not unthinkingly embrace the law of work relations that existed in England. The American law evolved from a variety of
different legal relations, including those of master and apprentice, head of a
household and his staff, and principal and agent. As a number of nineteenth-
century legal historians have shown, American workers strenuously resisted
the notion that they were servants, and lawyers did not use the term to refer
generally to people who worked for others until well into the century. The
category of persons whom the law called "servants" was quite small in the
colonial period, consisting mainly of indentured servants and household
help. The nineteenth-century treatises, following Blackstone's lead, typically
treated master and servant as a species of the law of domestic relations, and
originally it referred to household servants only, thus making the domestic

relation seem a logical category.[4] A 1699 English book, *Instructions for Masters, Traders, Laborers, &c.*, separately cataloged the obligations of masters toward servants; traders toward customers; buyers toward sellers; workmen and laborers toward those who hired them; lawyers, physicians, and surgeons both toward clients and toward those whom they hired; and "governors, overseers of colleges, hospitals &c., trustees, overseers of the poor, masters of schools, debtors, masters of families, [and] gentlemen of estates."[5] An 1857 English volume, David Gibbons's *Rudimentary Treatise on the Law of Contracts for Works and Services*, treated contracts of master and servant as a distinct category from contracts for hiring "workman or contractor."[6] It was over the course of the nineteenth century that the term "servant" came to be applied to all who worked for others.[7]

The legal rights to control the talents and products of creative people who worked with and for others fell into something of a legal and intellectual lacuna at the turn of the nineteenth century. The legal questions associated with the control of workplace knowledge and its products arose at the intersection of diverse bodies of English and colonial common law and early American state and federal statutes. Among these diverse bodies of law were two dominant strands, each of which rested on a distinct philosophical perspective on the role of artisans, mechanics, and inventors in society. First, there was a patchwork of common law and statutory regulation of the relations of master, journeymen, and apprentices and the closely related but distinct legal traditions arising from English hostility to restrictions on trade, the craft regulation of trade monopolies to ensure quality goods, and English concern about the export of technology to the colonies. Second, the intense American interest in fostering economic development through technological innovation spurred the enactment of patent and copyright legislation and ongoing efforts throughout the colonies to recruit skilled artisans and workers from abroad, regardless of English mercantilist prohibitions on the emigration of skilled labor and the export of technology. When, in the 1830s, courts began to confront cases involving the rights of workers and their employers over workplace knowledge, they had to reconcile the hierarchical and status-oriented intellectual habits of master-servant law with the very different entrepreneurial and democratic republican culture of early patent and copyright law.

American law at the dawn of the twenty-first century imagines the employment relationship as entirely contractual. While attitudes on this point have fluctuated greatly over the last century, much of the contemporary common law of employment tends to assume that the terms of the employment relationship are freely negotiated between parties who either have equal power and rights or, to the extent that they do not have equal bargaining power, there is either a scarcity of labor for the job in question or a scarcity of jobs for the employee in question. This thoroughly contractarian view of the nature of the employment relationship was not prevalent at the dawn of the nineteenth century. Contract experienced the rise to its contemporary prominence only in the nineteenth century.[8] Blackstone's *Commentaries*, for example, devoted hundreds of pages to property and to status relations like family but relatively few pages to the individual, negotiated bargain that in the nineteenth century became the paradigmatic contract.

Master-servant law in the early nineteenth century was premised on a dramatically different vision of the nature and source of rights and obligations. As Professor Steinfeld described it, early modern English and American law conceived of the employment relationship in two distinct ways. One was "a form of jurisdiction that masters enjoyed over the persons of their workers." The second was as a kind of property right that the master enjoyed in the services of the servant.[9] Even free blacks who were skilled mechanics and artisans suffered under legal regulations designed to protect whites in similar trades from fair competition with them. Under English law, masters had rights to the labor, and to the produce of the labor, of apprentices and servants. The rights to the labor were good not only against the servant or the apprentice but also against the world.[10] But for many skilled workers—those most likely to possess the knowledge that would enable them to develop valuable innovations—the law was quite favorable to their control of their workplace knowledge because courts did not regard the issues of ownership of patents or copyrights through the framework of master-servant law. The workers who litigated disputes with employers over creative property and knowledge generally speaking were not apprentices or servants. As a consequence, courts were likely to ignore the master-servant law and its hierarchical and property-based assumptions, and instead to regard creative workers as mechanics, artisans, or partners in an enterprise who should enjoy the legal status of entrepreneurs.

At the beginning of the nineteenth century, the law recognized few ways that employers could restrict their employees' use of knowledge in subsequent employment. Enticement prohibited hiring away another's employee—reflecting awareness of the costs of labor mobility—but it did not prevent a free employee from leaving and taking his knowledge with him. Enticement protected the employer's right to the employee's labor, not to his or her knowledge, and was actionable irrespective of whether the employee possessed any valuable knowledge. Absent an express contract, employees could, at the end of a term of employment, freely depart with whatever skill and knowledge they had acquired; there was no legal protection for the value of employee knowledge. Similarly, although colonial laws prohibited servants from engaging in business apart from their work for their masters and prohibited unauthorized trading with other people's servants, the focus of these laws was to prevent workers from cheating their masters by selling the masters' goods, working for themselves on their masters' time, or making contacts that might tempt them to desertion.[11]

Restrictions on the use of workplace knowledge were enforced in the eighteenth century by local regulation tied to the guild system, which protected the right of artisans and skilled workers to practice their trade by prohibiting outsiders from practicing certain crafts. In the pre-industrial economy, craft knowledge was transmitted through families or from master to apprentice. The secrecy of recipes and techniques that passed from generation to generation enabled a family or a firm to gain a reputation and to retain exclusive control of production. Apprenticeship indentures recognized the value of guarding secrecy while ensuring the passage of knowledge by specifying that the master was to instruct the apprentice and to reveal his knowledge (commonly called his "mystery") to him, and, in return, the apprentice pledged to keep these techniques secret during the term of the apprenticeship. The duty of the apprentice to guard the master's secrets was a standard term in apprenticeship agreements as early as the fifteenth century, when an apprentice promised to "well and faithfully serve the aforesaid John Gibbs and Agnes his wife as his masters and lords" and "keep their secrets" and "everywhere willingly do their lawful and honourable commands." The standard term about secrets in form apprenticeship agreements had changed little by the early nineteenth century. One such form agreement, executed for a boy apprenticed in 1829 to William Whittaker & Sons of Philadelphia, a textile mill, stated that the boy "doth covenant and promise his said master faithfully to serve, his secrets to keep, and his lawful commands every where readily to obey." For his part, the master "doth covenant and promise to use the utmost of his endeavours to teach, or cause to be taught or instructed, the said apprentice in the trade or mystery of [here was written in the blank 'a cotton spinner']."[12]

Legal regulation of artisanal work relations explicitly contemplated that the apprentice eventually would become a journeyman or a master and, as such, would be free to use all knowledge that he had acquired. Courts enforced covenants not to compete in connection with the sale of a business, but did not allow masters to extract them from apprentices. Although the apprentice was obliged to guard the master's secrets of the trade, courts were hostile to the efforts of masters to restrict competition from persons who had completed apprenticeships and were thus fully entitled under the guild system to make full use of the "mystery" in which they had been instructed. Studies of litigation of apprenticeship indentures note disputes over a master's failure to train or failure adequately to educate or support the apprentice but not efforts by masters to restrict apprentices from using their knowledge in subsequent employment.[13]

Some American states enacted legislation regulating apprenticeships by including prohibitions on contracts that restricted competition by former apprentices. Chancellor Kent's *Commentaries on American Law* (1826) described a New York statute that "specially and justly provided, that no person shall take from any journeyman or apprentice any contract or agreement, that, after his term of service expired, he shall not set up his trade, profession, or employment in any particular place; nor shall any money or other thing be exacted from any journeyman or apprentice, in restraint of the place of exercising his trade."[14] The St. George Tucker edition of Blackstone's *Commentaries* from 1803—the first American edition of the famed treatise—explicitly distinguished between English and American law on apprenticeship. Blackstone discussed the English statutes restricting the practice of a trade to those who had served an apprenticeship in it and noted that Virginia law, unlike English law, did not so restrict entry into a trade.[15] There were a number of pre-industrial efforts of the colonies and states to regulate the artisan relations so as to prevent monopoly and encourage training and quality manufacturing.[16]

Nevertheless, when the knowledge seemed less like the skills of a trade and more like discrete information or objects, employers sometimes tried to claim control of it. An example is an English case, *Makepeace v. Jackson* (1813), which came to be a common citation in American trade secret cases in the late nineteenth century. It was a fight between a textile mill owner and a dyer over control of the dye recipes. A calico printer's shop fired its head dyer. The dyer sued to recover a book of dye recipes. The employer contended that the book was his: "it was written on paper which he had furnished; and all the entries were made by the Plaintiff while he was the Defendant's servant; and the Defendant could not conduct his business of a calico printer without the book." In addition, the opinion emphasized the uniqueness of the book to each shop: "Every printer has a standard color, consisting of certain ingredients, to which standard every color that he compounds is preferred; and whenever any color is mixed, the history of the process and ingredients is entered in a book, and when the mixture is made, and a piece of calico is dyed accordingly, a small strip is cut off and pasted into the book; and all future orders for goods are received, and the goods prepared, with a reference to that book, and to the standard color of that shop, every color having a different standard color."

The dyer sought to prove that some of the entries in the book were his own invention and claimed entitlement to the book on that basis. The judges rejected the claim. Judge Heath said that "the book was the property of the master, and though there might be inventions of the Plaintiff in it, yet they were the property of the master." Judge Chambre said: "The master has a right to something beside the mere manual labour of the servant in the mixing of the colours; and though the Plaintiff invents them, yet they are to be used for his master's benefit."[17] *Makepeace* was cited later in the nineteenth century not only in cases involving early trade secrets but also in early patent treatises on disputes to ownership of inventions.[18] Although the mill owner won the dispute in England, the custom of dyers controlling color books persisted throughout the nineteenth century in the United States. [29]

Prior to the mid-nineteenth century, only a few distinct employment relations were characterized as confidential and, therefore, incorporated an obligation not to divulge workplace secrets. As noted, the relationship of master to apprentice explicitly incorporated a duty of confidence. In Britain, guilds shored up this restriction by prohibiting the dissemination of knowledge outside the guild. The household servant's obligation to keep family confidences affected a significant number of workers in a pre-industrial economy in which the boundaries among family, household, and workplace were quite indistinct. Under certain circumstances, an agent might have had a fiduciary responsibility that would include guarding the confidences of a principal. Skilled workers would have been bound by none of these obligations. The superintendents, partners, skilled chemists, and machinists whose work was crucial in early industrialization were not deemed analogous to apprentices, household servants, or fiduciaries. Not until the creation, in the latter half of the nineteenth century, of a homogeneous law of "master and servant" applicable to workers of all stations would there have been any basis to apply to all work relationships the limited duties of confidence that existed in a few such relationships.

Lawyers today regard covenants not to compete and contractual restrictions on disclosure of knowledge as crucial aspects of a firm's overall legal right to prevent competitors and former employees from using valuable workplace information. In the nineteenth century and before, however, such contracts were not a legally permissible device to protect workplace secrets. English law allowed the use of noncompetition agreements in connection with the sale of a business or the formation or dissolution of a partnership to enable the buyer of the business or partnership effectively to acquire the business goodwill, but not against employees. The English hostility to restrictive covenants was a response to the guild tradition that skilled artisans could practice only a single trade in a single area. If an artisan promised not to practice his trade, he gave up his livelihood. The hostility persisted in America well into the nineteenth century.[19] In an 1837 Massachusetts case in which the defendant, in connection with the sale of stock in an iron foundry, covenanted never to work as an iron founder or caster, or even to be "interested . . . directly or indirectly" in the iron foundry or casting business,[20] the court declined to enforce the covenant, stating in very broad terms the evils associated with restrictive covenants—the deprivation of the capacity to earn a livelihood, the loss to the public of the services, the diminution of competition.[21]

[30]

That courts would not enforce the agreements did not always stop employers from asking mill hands to sign them. In the 1810s, for example, a mechanic at a New England textile mill agreed for a term of seven years not to disclose "the nature, construction, properties, [or] operation . . . of the machinery of the said cotton manufactory," or to "avail myself or take advantage of my knowledge of the same machinery." The contract specifically exempted the mechanic from compliance with its terms if he found employment "in the New England states" at a mill using "any cotton machinery of the same peculiarities of construction as the machines that [his employers] are constructing or may construct within the said term of years. . . ."[22] These contracts may very well have constrained the behavior of mechanics and others bound by them even if there is no evidence that courts did or would enforce them.

Moreover, when firms sold or licensed patented machines to other firms, the terms of the sale sometimes included an obligation of the buyer not to "communicate to others, or for the interest of others, such information as they may receive under this agreement," and a promise to "adopt such measures as the [seller] shall communicate for the purpose of preventing publicity to such things as the said parties shall require not to be made public."[23] Either such provisions were rare or they were ineffectual because they did not appear to stem the flow of information from one firm to another. The machine technology imported from England and developed by Samuel Slater spread from New England into New York, New Jersey, and Pennsylvania, carried along by workers who had learned their trade in Slater's mills.[24]

Restrictions on the use of workplace knowledge were treated with suspicion and were difficult to enforce over the objections of skilled labor in a culture of easy mobility. As the concentration of production associated with early nineteenth-century industrialization eliminated the possibility of owning a workshop in most trades, the master-apprentice relationship eroded, and with it went the traditional way that knowledge had been transmitted among generations and within trades.[25] The class of employees whose knowledge and experience made them especially valuable were the first-generation descendants, not of the apprentices, but of the more middling sort—journeymen in the crafts, as well as mechanics, machinists, and people with some education in chemistry or drafting. This class of employees historically had not been bound by the apprentice's duty of confidence. The independence and the entrepreneurial spirit of these men were recurring images in the republican antebellum culture and the developing commercial and manufacturing economy.[26] The development of one unified law of master and servant and the rise of factory production during the second industrial revolution after 1870 were necessary before courts would obliterate the legal distinctions among different statuses of working men and assert a duty of confidentiality and an employer's prerogative to restrict post-employment competition for all employees ranging from factory laborers to research chemists.

Early American Patent and Copyright Law

During the colonial era and the period of the Articles of Confederation, a number of the colonies and then states granted patents and, to a lesser extent, copyrights according to their own law. In this period, when neither the term "intellectual property" nor a legal category of ownership of ideas yet existed, both patents and copyrights were regarded as a state-granted exclusive right as opposed to a species of property. As a form of monopoly, patents were regarded with some suspicion, though many people were less hostile to patents than to other forms of monopoly.

Copyright and patent laws varied from state to state and did not exist at all in some, and the rights granted in one state were not enforceable in another. Madison noted "the want of uniformity in the laws concerning . . . literary property" as a (minor) defect of the law that the constitutional convention might want to address. The framers of the Constitution empowered Congress to enact national patent and copyright laws, but the debate on this clause was not reported.[27] Nor is there much evidence from the state ratifying conventions or The Federalist. Little is known other than that the framers ultimately agreed on language in Article I, section 8, empowering Congress to enact laws "to promote the Progress of Science and useful Arts, by securing for limited Times to Authors and Inventors the exclusive Right to their respective Writings and Discoveries."[28] Given the greater importance and salience of the many other issues addressed in the Constitution, it is hardly surprising that the intellectual property clause did not generate much attention.

Now that intellectual property looms large in the public (or at least legal) imagination, an outpouring of recent scholarship has speculated about what the framers' views might have been. Not surprisingly, contemporary histori-

ography, influenced by contemporary debates about the desirability of broad versus narrow intellectual property rights, has generated dueling views about the views of the people of the framers' generation. On the one hand, many look to Thomas Jefferson and Benjamin Franklin as exemplars of an ethos of broad sharing of new knowledge and skepticism about aggressive claiming of intellectual property rights. Franklin quite famously declined to seek a patent for his new wood-burning stove, instead publishing a pamphlet to explain to the world how to make one, and how and why they worked well. All he sought, evidently, was reputation as an inventor, not a monopoly on the profits associated with the invention. Thomas Jefferson is also often cited as an intellectual property skeptic, though his views on the benefits of granting patents and copyrights changed over time. Those emphasizing Jefferson's doubts about the wisdom of broad intellectual property rights often cite his famous 1813 letter to Isaac MacPherson: "If nature has made any one thing less susceptible than all others of exclusive property, it is the action of the thinking power called an idea, which an individual may exclusively possess as long as he keeps it to himself; but the moment it is divulged, it forces itself into the possession of everyone, and the receiver cannot dispossess himself of it." Some also note the fact that in 1815 Jefferson declined to patent a device he had invented for "braking and beating" hemp. As Lewis Hyde has noted, Jefferson explained in a letter to a friend that he wanted to publicize his invention anonymously in a pamphlet to make it available to the public, and by publicizing it he would also "forestall the prevention of its use by some interloping patentee."[29]

On the other hand, there is plenty in the writing of the framers and their generation to support an argument that patents and copyrights liberally construed and vigorously enforced were precisely what the framers had in mind. Alexander Hamilton famously argued the importance of patents in the *Report on Manufactures*, and indeed suggested that the Constitution should perhaps have been written to allow for patents on imported technologies rather than just on inventions. Madison wrote in *The Federalist* that "the utility" of the power to grant patents and copyrights "will scarcely be questioned. The copyright of authors has been solemnly adjudged, in Great Britain, to be a right of common law. The right to useful inventions seems with equal reason to belong to the inventors. The public good fully coincides in both cases with the claims of individuals."[30]

Not long after the ratification of the Constitution in 1789, Congress enacted a Patent Act and a Copyright Act (in April and May of 1790) to supplement or, as it turned out, to replace the patent and copyright laws of the individual states. The first federal patent act was designed to ease the patenting process through a relatively affordable application process. Fees for filing patent applications were low as compared to England, and it was easier in the United States than in England for prospective applicants to review existing patents to determine the state of the art. Applications could be mailed free of postage, which contributed to the accessibility of the patent system to ordinary people. As Zorina Khan has argued, the American patent system, especially after 1836, was designed to encourage patenting and to disseminate knowledge of innovations throughout the country speedily and quickly.[31]

Given how few people worked for others outside agricultural employment, it is not surprising that neither the Patent Act nor the Copyright Act contained any reference to what rules might apply when an inventor or author either worked for others or had others working for him at the time he created a new invention or copyrighted work. That the law did not specifically address the phenomenon of the employed inventor or author, however, does not mean that it did not exist.[32] Long before courts and the public finally realized that many or even most major inventions were the result of organized collective effort, inventors had been aided by or had collaborated with mechanics, chemists, machinists, and other workers. Which individuals ultimately got credit as the inventors and received the patent may have been determined as much by interpersonal or political skill and economic power as by inventive genius.

Among the most significant nineteenth-century changes in legal thinking about patents and copyrights was the switch from *monopoly* to *property*. The Constitution and statutes use the term "exclusive right," not "monopoly." From the early years of the republic American courts perceived patents as a species of property that was in the public interest to protect broadly, rather than, as in England, as a form of monopoly that was in the public interest to construe narrowly. The monopoly granted by the patent law in the English tradition was justified because of the courage and industry of the inventors and because innovation thus encouraged was "a great public blessing," as it would improve the quality of life for all. As the Supreme Court said in *Pennock v. Dialogue* (1829), a case that ultimately laid the foundation for the law governing ownership of patents created by one who was not the actual inventor, the difference between the monopoly view and the property view mattered. "In the courts of the United States, a more just view had been taken of the rights of inventors. The laws of the United States were intended to protect those rights, and to confer benefits; while the provisions in the statute of England, under which patents are issued, are exceptions to the law prohibiting monopolies. Hence, the construction of the British statute had been exceedingly straight and narrow, and different from the more liberal interpretation of our laws."[33]

The American tendency to regard patents as property rather than as monopoly did not immediately prompt courts to see them as transferable from inventor to employer. At first, courts insisted that an employee's property rights in patents should be safe from the control of the employer because patents, like other forms of property, were what made men independent. Widespread property ownership was thought to promote social and political stability, to protect against the sharp class divisions and political antagonisms that had rocked France, and to ward off the miseries of urban poverty associated with early industrialization in Britain. Property, mainly real property, was the enabler of republican democracy. Property was a dominant subject in American law in the early nineteenth century, and remained so until the rise of contract and tort concepts late in the century. Over the course of the nineteenth century, there was massive transformation in thinking about the relationship of property to good governance and civil society. But there was a ready supply of images and rhetoric to draw upon to link all sorts of legal and policy prescriptions to the tradition of property theory.[34] Once ideas were conceived in legal terms as property, rather than in the eighteenth-century British and European terms of state-granted privileges and state-sanctioned monopolies, there was a rich store of rhetoric upon which to draw in arguing that ownership of intellectual property occupied a unique place among American freedoms. While patents and copyrights were thought of as monopolies, they were seen as a reward for individual endeavor; when they became just another form of property, it became easier to see them like any other product that a person or firm might create, and just as transferable from employee to employer.

Today, a sophisticated lawyer asked to name the first thing that popped into her head at the mention of the word "property" might say copyrights or trademarks, in addition to real estate, personal property, or financial assets. But in the early nineteenth century, ideas were not easily assimilated to the concept of property. Rather, the focus was on physical things. Not until late in the nineteenth century were trade secrets characterized as property in either legal or popular parlance.[35] Until the twentieth century, thing-ness was necessary for knowledge to be conceived in legal terms as property. Of course, patents and copyrights were understood as being not quite a thing, as they still retained some of their former association with monopoly privilege, but even they could be considered as specific things rather than as inchoate knowledge—the patent specification made clear that the thing patented was quite particular, and the copyright was an exclusive right to some uses (printing and selling) of a particular text, not to an idea. Courts ordered the return of trade secrets if they were things but did not enjoin the use of the knowledge expressed in those things. Judges emphasized the presence of physical things in part because they did not understand inchoate knowledge to be a firm's asset. Antebellum courts focused on protecting the physical property rather than the idea. For example, in an early Pennsylvania case, *McGowin v. Remington* (1849), a surveyor in Pittsburgh had left his maps and surveying instruments with his former assistant while he started a new business elsewhere. When he returned to Pittsburgh, the assistant refused to relinquish the maps and instruments and was busy copying the maps for his own use. The court ordered the defendant to return the maps and instruments, along with the copies he had made.[36]

Of course, even in the early nineteenth century, there were property rights in intangible things, especially future interests in property. (A future interest is a right to possess property in the future, such as upon the death of the current owner.) Focusing only on the tangible objects certainly had the advantage of allowing courts to avoid a problem that was both practically and ideologically difficult. It obviated the need to distinguish knowledge that courts were willing to prevent employees from using in subsequent employment from that which was an inalienable aspect of a person's skill, intelligence, or life experience. Granting the employer the physical things, rather than the right to control the former employee's use of knowledge, was also a more acceptable legal remedy in a society struggling with the meaning of free labor.

Although Americans may have been more willing than the English to regard patents and copyrights as property rather than as monopolies, the conceptual legacy of the English view proved to be advantageous to early American employees. It encouraged courts' belief that employee control over workplace knowledge was a necessary bulwark against monopoly. Had patents, copyrights, and other forms of workplace knowledge been seen only in terms of property, courts might have been more likely to analogize them to other workplace products and materials and to protect them against employee "theft." The analogy between employees' mental output and other forms of employee work product was sometimes drawn. For example, as Clare Pettitt points out, in debates over reforms in English copyright law in 1842, *Chambers's Edinburgh Journal* editorialized that authors' rights should be analogized to labor's rights: "Authors stand here in precisely the condition of labourers: they do a piece of work, and receive their wages. Although the mental faculties are the instruments, and the labour is a most honourable one, the materials used are common property, and the workman has no bet-

ter grounds for any subsequent claim on the result of his exertions, than a mason has on the house which he helped to rear, or a coachmaker on the vehicle he constructed."[37] As Chancellor Kent explained the basis for the law of personal property in his 1826 *Commentaries on American Law*, there were three ways that a person could become entitled to personal property by "original acquisition": occupancy, accession, or "intellectual labor." The third category, "intellectual labor," reflects the labor theory of property with regard to idea ownership rather than the earlier monopoly theory.[38]

Two hundred years ago, the term "intellectual property" did not exist.[39] It first appeared in 1845 in the opinion of a federal court in *Davoll v. Brown*, a case that arose from a Fall River, Massachusetts, textile business involving an improvement in mechanized cotton spinning.[40] The issue was whether the description of the invention in the plaintiff's patent, which claimed to be an improvement over the English technology then in use, was sufficiently specific. In rejecting the defendant's contention that the description was too general, Justice Woodbury, sitting as a circuit judge, said that "a liberal construction is to be given to a patent, and inventors sustained, if practicable." The opinion used the term "intellectual property" in eloquent defense of broad patent rights. Strong intellectual property protection, Justice Woodbury insisted, was necessary for "[o]nly thus can ingenuity and perseverance be encouraged to exert themselves in this way usefully to the community; and only in this way can we protect intellectual property, the labors of the mind, productions and interests as much a man's own, and as much the fruit of his honest industry, as the wheat he cultivates, or the flocks he rears."

Rejecting the archaic view that patents are monopolies and thus to be narrowly construed, Justice Woodbury continued, "the patent laws are not now made to encourage monopolies of what before belonged to others, to the public,—which is the true idea of a monopoly,—but the design is to encourage genius in advancing the arts, through science and ingenuity, by protecting its productions of what did not before exist, and of what never belonged to another person, or the public." Intellectual property was thus distinguished from monopoly, the crucial rhetorical move of nineteenth-century law. John Locke's moral justification for property was alluded to in the analogy to rearing sheep and crops, and the utilitarian theory that emphasizes the importance of incentives to encourage genius in advancing the arts through science and ingenuity is there, too.

The expansion of property rights to include workplace knowledge rested on the way courts understood the phenomenon that they came to describe as property. The use of "intellectual" as a modifier for the word "property" is crucial. In the nineteenth century, copyright was sometimes referred to as "literary property" and patent as "industrial property." Both terms seem rather limited. An advertisement may, by a stretch, be literary, as Justice Oliver Wendell Holmes argued in a famous case in which he compared a poster advertising a circus to works by Goya and Velázquez. But it's hard to call a computer program literature. A mechanized cotton spinner or a vacuum cleaner may be "industrial," but a product design may not. Use of the umbrella term "intellectual" avoided the limits of the categories "literary" and "industrial," enabling any product of anybody's mental effort to be a plausible candidate for intellectual property protection. It also legitimated the expansion of property rights by emphasizing the aspect of thought, creativity, and mental effort or acuity associated with the term "intellect." Intellect connotes something uniquely human and uniquely personal. Of course, it was also quite possible to own intellectual as well as physical products made by another person. *Davoll*, the Fall River cotton spinner case, assumed that the plaintiff patentee was in fact the inventor of the spinner in question. But even if he was not, if one accepts the court's analogy of a patent to crops or flocks of sheep, it sounds quite as benign to own someone else's patent as to own the wheat or the sheep someone else raised. [37]

But there were also rather dodgier associations to the idea of owning another's intellect, or the products of it. It was, after all, a bedrock of American slavery. When I began hunting up old cases discussing property rights in intellectual products, an even earlier case than *Davoll* was an 1836 decision of the Supreme Court of Tennessee, a will dispute about whether a widow who had a life estate in a plantation and the slaves on it could take the slaves to her new home in Mississippi. The court was asked to enjoin the removal of the slaves from the "humane and healthful" conditions in Tennessee to the "more oppressive" legal and meteorological climate of Mississippi in order to protect the rights of the person who would inherit the slaves on the death of the widow. The court remarked on the need for full protection of "the peculiar nature and character of slave property." Slave property, the court said, encompassed "a property in intellectual and moral and social qualities, in skill, in fidelity and in gratitude, as well as in their capacity for labor."[41]

Cases such as this, however, were not regarded as intellectual property cases; they were property cases. Or they were cases about the power of a chancery court to enjoin the removal of slaves from one state to another, or whether an adequate remedy could be had at law for someone whose future interest in a slave might be jeopardized by abuse of the slave. And, in any event, ownership of the slave's intellectual product was not an issue in the case. But if ownership of intellect, skill, and fidelity are the "peculiar character" of slave law, the notion of *intellect* as alienable *property* is problematic.

[38]   The transformation from privilege to property in reference to the right to control knowledge reflected and enabled a significant change in thinking. People invent new categories because they have an agenda; they invent new legal categories when necessary to make new legal claims. Intellectual property claimants wanted to expand and deepen their rights. They wanted a stronger market position and they got it by shifting from using the language of monopoly and privilege to using the language of property and loyalty. The eighteenth-century "monopoly," which derived from patent law's origins in the seventeenth-century English Statute on Monopolies, helped to reinforce a substantive position. As long as patents and copyrights were described as monopolies, they were dangerous devices that should be granted only when truly necessary to advance knowledge. Once "monopoly" fell out of use in favor of the more benign "property," there was less to fear.[42]

Furthermore, once worker knowledge or talent, or the right to control it, was characterized as property rather than monopoly, the firm's claim to control it through an array of legal and equitable restraints on employee mobility seemed as compelling as the firm's claim to the machines, textiles, or iron that the employees produced. Characterizing as corporate intellectual *property* the right of an employer to force an opera singer to perform her contract by preventing her from singing for anyone else initially reminded courts too much of the property right in a slave. Eventually, the courts stopped thinking as much about slavery and started thinking about how record companies could recoup their investment in identifying, refining, and promoting new musical talent.

Apart from the monopoly-property distinction, early nineteenth-century judges and lawyers had a ready vocabulary drawn from the republican political economy of the era with which to characterize the labor, know-how, and entrepreneurial endeavors of craft workers. The concepts of virtue, independence, and industry filtered down through law to the idea that creators of new and useful things should be entitled to a just reward for their industry and their contribution to the common good. In the early republic, the interlocking concepts of virtue, independence, and industry loomed large in the pantheon of morally worthy and socially indispensable qualities of humans governed by the better angels of their nature. Virtue connoted wisdom, judgment, diligence, patience, and an absence of narrow self-interest. Independence, as both a political and an economic term, meant that people must not subordinate themselves to the political will of others in order that all might work for the common good, or commonwealth. Industry connoted hard work, an enterprising spirit, some degree of cleverness, diligence, and productivity.[43] The products of their virtuous industry were the rightful property of those who possessed them, not those who might have employed them. [39] Over the course of the late nineteenth century, it became less controversial for Americans to profit from the physical or mental work of others than to profit from their own. Courts, lawyers, and commentators began to see as productive, morally worthy, and decidedly unparasitic the work of coordinating the labor and creativity of others, of investing money in their efforts and reaping the lion's share of the profit from it.

Knowledge and the Workplace Inventor

Inventors of the earliest patented U.S. inventions doubtless included persons employed by others, but their status as employees does not appear from the available records because the Patent Office did not record the employment status of patentees. The courts' first published efforts to sort out claims to ownership of employee inventions involved cases where the parties had nothing the court identified as a contract regarding ownership of the inventions. When the courts first approached competing claims to ownership of inventions in the 1840s, the employment status of the inventor did not appear to the court or to the lawyers to be the most relevant characteristic of the inventor. Rather, the question was whether the worker was an inventor. If he was, the patent must be his. Godson's 1823 treatise on English patent law did not deal with the rights of employee inventors.[44] Phillips's influential 1837 patent law treatise made no mention of the problem of determining patent ownership when the inventor was an employee. It said only that "evidence that the plaintiff's patent was for an invention made by a journeyman in his shop, with his consent" would be "doubtless a good defence against a claim for damages for an infringement," but he cited no cases for this proposition.[45] Hindmarch's 1847 patent treatise said simply that law "permits an inventor in the prosecution of his discovery to avail himself of the labour of servants, they being in fact considered as mere tools or instruments working by his directions, and carrying out the views which he has formed in his own mind."[46] Curtis's 1849 patent treatise said that "[t]he person who suggests the principle of the invention is the inventor," whether master or servant.[47]

Why was no dispute between an employer and employee decided in a published opinion during the fifty years after the first Patent Act? It is surely not that no employee had invented anything. Nor is it that no employer had obtained a contract from an employee promising to assign the patent to the employer. The Boston Manufacturing Company, a leading New England textile mill, obtained a written agreement from a mechanic promising: "Should I be fortunate enough to make or suggest any improvement for which it might be thought proper to obtain a patent, such patent or patents are to be the property of the Company."[48] Similarly, individual inventors assigned patents to companies that employed them. Paul Moody, a mechanic, prolific inventor, and salaried employee of the Boston Manufacturing Company, patented either by himself (with the firm proprietor Francis Lowell) or with others a substantial number of improvements in textile machinery between 1816 and 1824, and all the patents seem to have been treated as the property of the company, without controversy.[49] Yet, when opportunities for investment and mobility arose, Moody was able to switch employers; he left the Boston Manufacturing Company in 1823 to go to work at—and to become an investor in—the newly founded Merrimack Company, which became the foundation of the calico manufacturing business in Lowell, Massachusetts.[50] The Merrimack Manufacturing Company purchased licenses to use Boston Manufacturing Company patents as well as Moody's services. There is additional evidence from firsthand accounts of the developments of the textile industry that other mechanics also sold patterns or drawings of machines they had designed for one employer to others, or marketed themselves as employable to establish new mills based on expertise working at other mills.[51]

Some former employees who attempted to use or to patent improvements to patented technology were sued for patent infringement, but the issues addressed in the suits had nothing to do with their status as former employees. For example, the Boston Manufacturing Company brought eight patent infringement suits between 1820 and 1822 involving Paul Moody's patents, but won only one—*Moody v. Fiske*, an action against three former Boston Manufacturing employees who built copies of a dresser that Moody had patented and assigned to the company in 1819. Fiske had worked with Moody in developing the patented machine before leaving the company's employ. *Moody v. Fiske* focused on the novelty and therefore the validity of Moody's patent; the right of the defendants to build the allegedly infringing machines based on knowledge gained through their employment was nowhere mentioned in the litigation. The company ceased bringing patent infringement suits after 1822, perhaps concluding that settling for a license was more economical than suing.[52]

Disputes between employer and employee that could not be resolved through resort to informal agreements were probably settled by the party whose name was not listed on the patent paying the patentee to use the invention. The patent law's requirement that the inventor must be named on the patent, and the practice of recording the issuance of the patent to the patentee or assignee, provided a presumptive legal entitlement to the invention that probably helped resolve those disputes which might otherwise have been litigated to a published disposition.

The earliest reported opinions on the rights of employers in their em- ployees' inventions involved infringement disputes between the employer and third parties, in which the third party defended against the alleged infringement by asserting that the employer's workman was the real inventor and the employer's claim to the patent was therefore invalid. Judging from the opinions' recitations of the facts, this defense was conjured up by the infringer searching for any conceivable basis for challenging the validity of the patent, because in no case did the infringer seem to have known at the time of the infringement that the patentee was not the actual inventor. Not surprisingly, the courts rejected this *post hoc* excuse for infringement and accepted the employer's characterization of the employee as just a workman who simply executed the instructions the employer gave.[53] In these early cases, the employer successfully laid claim to the invention by showing that the idea was his own, not because he was the employer. But in none of these cases did the court confront an employer's claim that he owned the product of the employee's creative mind as opposed to the products of his hands. And in none of them did the court address a dispute *between* an employer and employee over an invention they both claimed.

The patent law both reflected and reinforced the notion of invention as a product of individual genius. Applicants for patents had to state the name of *the* inventor; the law both assumed the existence of and required the patent applicant to identify the person(s) who were the true inventor(s). The 1836 Patent Act required an inventor to make an oath or affirmation that he believed he was "the original and first inventor" and that "he does not know or believe that the same was ever before known or used."[54] Patent litigation further stimulated the search for the individual inventor because one of the common grounds for attacking either the Patent Office's decision to award a patent or the validity of a patent in defense of an infringement action was to assert that the patentee was not the true or first inventor. The legal structure thus invited patentees to identify, in their legal documents as in their own minds, an invention as the product of one person's genius, rather than as the product of a collaborative process.[55]

Correspondingly, patent users had reason to argue that the patent was not based on the patentee's own idea. As a result, many patent decisions from the early period attempted to develop a set of rules about when the suggestions or contributions of a worker were so significant as to vitiate the patentee's claim to be the true inventor. In an influential English case of the era, two judges spoke of the need to protect employer-inventors from the risk that the men they employed to assist them would wrongfully claim to be the inventor. One said: "It would be very dangerous to employ any workman in matters of this sort, if the inventor were precluded from adopting any slight and subordinate improvement suggested by him." Another judge added, "I think it is too much that a suggestion of a workman, employed in the course of the experiments, of something calculated more easily to carry into effect the conceptions of the inventor, should render the whole patent void."[56] American courts stated a rule that, so long as the contributions of the employee "required no more skill or ingenuity than that possessed by an ordinary mechanic skilled in the business," the employer was entitled to the status of inventor.[57]

Because of the requirement in patent law that the actual inventor be named on the patent, when the employee was the inventor it was necessary for an employer to seek an assignment of the patent at the time of issuance or thereafter in order to prevent the employee from using the patented invention. In the antebellum era when skilled labor was scarce and ingenuity was at a premium, it is possible that employers preferred to avoid alienating their inventive employees by demanding patent assignments and to resolve any disputes about the employee's right to use the patent through a settlement and license arrangement when and if the patent proved valuable enough that a dispute arose.

A reasonable reluctance to demand a contractual assignment and the relative ease of licensing the patents that proved valuable may explain why the first published opinion resolving a dispute between an employer and an employee over their rights to the employee's invention did not appear until 1843, when the U.S. Supreme Court handed down *McClurg v. Kingsland*. In *McClurg*, the Court held that, because the employee had freely allowed his employer to use an invention that he had developed at work before patenting it, the employer had a "shop right," which was a license to continue to use the invention after it was patented.[58] The license right that *McClurg* recognized did not rest on the employment relationship. Rather, it rested on the notion that an inventor (who happened to be an employee) who allowed someone (who happened to be the employer) to use the invention for a period of years could not later, upon patenting the invention, sue that user for infringement. This rule was simply an application of the established equity doctrine of estoppel: one who knowingly allows or encourages certain conduct cannot later object to it; his earlier forbearance "estops" him from complaining. The employer's license was based on the employee's consent. Every case from 1843 to 1886 that granted a license to an employer to use an employee's invention did so on the basis of this estoppel rationale.

Both the Court's reasoning in *McClurg* and the cases on which the Court relied (none of which involved employment) make clear that the license to a patent based on pre-patent use was justified by the public interest in the dissemination of new technology rather than individual fairness as between the employer and employee. American patent law at the time restricted the ability of people to patent things that had either been used elsewhere or had not been invented in the United States. An inventor could not first allow public use of an invention in order to create a market for it and then seek a patent monopoly in order to guarantee a high price. In this context, one sees that *McClurg* was a novel interpretation of the public use provision of the 1839 Patent Act, not an employment law case. Indeed, it is still sometimes cited as a leading early case on the public use bar to patents.

The notion that *McClurg* stated a principle regarding how an inventor's employment status affected the inventor's rights to a patent stemmed from the Supreme Court Reporter of Decisions' interpretation of the case, not from the opinion of the Court. The headnote to the case was probably drafted by Benjamin Howard, the Reporter of Decisions who was then in his first year on the job. The headnote read: "If a person employed in the manufactory of another, while receiving wages, makes experiments at the expense and in the manufactory of his employer; has his wages increased in consequence of the useful result of the experiments; makes the article invented and permits his employer to use it, no compensation for its use being paid or demanded; and then obtains a patent, these facts will justify the presumption of a license to use the invention."[59]

The headnote diverged a bit from the facts recited in the opinion and, more significantly, from the Court's reasoning. The inventor-employee, James Harley, had in fact invented an improved way of casting iron rollers while employed by the week at the defendant's foundry in Pittsburgh. One of the defendants, Kingsland, a partner in the firm that employed Harley, said in the trial court that "in the making of this discovery I believe I had as much hand in it as James Harley had," because the two men worked together experimenting with different ways of pouring the iron, "consulted together on all occasions, and I know of nothing made towards this improvement without my approbation," although he conceded that Harley was the first to suggest the method (using an inclined gate) that was ultimately patented. Kingsland said that "Harley did not at any time to me alledge [sic] any expectation of additional profit to himself, or care for the discovery succeeding well, nor during the progress of the attempts did he express any intention of making an application for a patent should he succeed. Mr. Harley was a workman entitled to, and did receive, the highest wages which was going about the foundry as a moulder." Kingsland said that Harley's wages were increased after the invention proved successful. Eventually, Harley suggested that the company should take out a patent on the invention; according to Kingsland, Harley "said nothing about upon what terms they should do so, I never heard Harley say that he was the whole inventor of this improvement until after he left to employ of K.L. and Cuddy."[60]

Harley then went to work for the plaintiffs, obtained a patent for the invention, and assigned the patent to his new employer. Harley's new employers sued the former employer for infringement. Kingsland, Lightner & Cuddy had not sought a license to use the invention; they had claimed that the patent was invalid because Harley's method of casting rollers was in use in England and, alternately, that Kingsland was the joint inventor of the patent. Although the headnote emphasized that Harley had devised the invention at work and had received a raise on account of it, the Court's reasoning did not. In the Court's opinion, Harley's status and compensation were irrelevant. The employer was just like any member of the public whom Harley might have allowed to use the invention; neither Harley nor the new employer to whom he had assigned his right could claim infringement or demand compensation for use of an invention that Harley had allowed to be used for free before obtaining a patent.

Prior to the 1860s only a minute number of published decisions addressed disputes over ownership or validity of patents in which a lawyer raised the relevance of the fact that the invention had been developed in the employment context. In none of the cases did the court address a dispute *between* an employer and an employee over an idea they both claimed. Absent an express assignment, the employee was assumed to own the patents to inventions he developed at work and elsewhere; an employer owned an invention developed by an employee only if the employer convinced the court that the idea for the invention was the employer's and that the employee had simply executed instructions given.

If ideas or technology were neither patented nor copyrighted, they were essentially part of the public domain before the Civil War. Apart from the obligation of apprentices not to reveal secrets of the master's household or his methods and the obligation of certain professions (then as now) to maintain the confidences of clients, in the absence of an express nondisclosure agreement there was no legal obligation for employees to guard secrets, processes, or other forms of workplace knowledge. Rather, what workmen learned in their employment was considered neither property nor proprietary. It was just know-how, and it was freely usable by the worker who learned it.

Two episodes from the early history of the Du Pont company illustrate how few legal methods employers had to control workplace knowledge. For the [45] first hundred years of its existence, E. I du Pont de Nemours & Company was a family-controlled manufacturer of explosives. Most of the economically valuable knowledge about the chemistry and manufacture of gunpowder was developed or possessed by the Du Pont family members and their close associates. For the most part, the Du Ponts managed the company and supervised its research throughout the nineteenth century.[61] Thus, the company's approach to employee intellectual property depended on close family control supported by informal sanctions and self-help. The legal rules that now form the principal weapons in the employer's arsenal for protecting economically valuable knowledge—nondisclosure and noncompete agreements and trade secret litigation—were either unavailable or unknown to the Du Ponts. Early nineteenth-century firms had no choice but to rely on secrecy and reputational sanctions to make it difficult for employees to take company secrets to competitors. Antebellum business proprietors whose superior technology gave them a competitive edge carefully guarded their secret processes by restricting access to the mills and discouraging employee mobility. The Du Ponts did so, as did Samuel Slater of Massachusetts, who himself had built a successful textile business based in part on machines whose designs he had copied from machines in England. Like the Du Ponts, Slater swore employees to secrecy about "the nature of the works" and paid key operatives well to prevent their "aiding and assisting another Mill." In addition, Slater and the Du Ponts were "very cautious of admitting strangers to view" their operations.[62] On the rare occasion when the Du Ponts resorted to legal proceedings, they relied on the law of criminal theft and an action for enticement.

Eleuthere Irenee du Pont de Nemours, a French aristocrat who prided himself on having studied the chemistry of gunpowder under the famous chemist Lavoisier, came with his family to the United States in 1800 to start a business (and, not incidentally, to escape the difficult situation confronting aristocrats after the French Revolution). The family bought land along the Brandywine River near Wilmington, Delaware, to build a powder mill and commenced the business in 1802.[63] Du Pont correctly believed that his chemical knowledge would enable him to manufacture gunpowder superior to any then made in the United States.[64] It was not long before others tried to discover what accounted for Du Pont's superior product. The chronicle of Du Pont's efforts to guard his secrets and to marshal both law and public opinion in his defense reveals a great deal about early nineteenth-century attitudes toward ownership of knowledge in the workplace.

[46]   The Brandywine mills consisted of a number of stone buildings along the bank of the river that supplied power, water, and security from unwanted visitors. The mills were part of a remote and self-contained enclave, with a blacksmith shop to make parts and separate buildings for the multiple steps of the gunpowder refining process. Du Pont regulated working conditions closely to ensure continuous production, to produce quality powder, and to reduce the risk of explosion. In many respects, therefore, the organization of work was more like the factories that later would develop in textiles than the artisanal, worker-controlled, small-shop mode of production that was more typical in the first decades of nineteenth-century America. Du Pont's early mills thus seem to resemble some of the rural, moderately financed, and proprietor-run mills of Massachusetts in that era.[65]

A Virginia firm, Brown, Page & Company, sought to build a powder mill in Richmond. Eager to learn the secret of Du Pont's success, they sent an agent, Charles Munns, to Wilmington in the autumn of 1808 to recruit powdermen from Du Pont's Brandywine mills. Munns set himself up at The Buck, a local tavern, where he entertained Du Pont employees. He offered to pay them wages far more generous than Du Pont paid if they would agree to go to Richmond to work for Brown, Page.[66] He inquired about the machines that Du Pont used in the different parts of the powder mills and asked Du Pont powdermen to make or steal drawings of the machinery. Munns was especially keen to get a brass pounder and some parchment sieves that were used to mix powder. He asked an assistant millwright, Joseph Baughman, to make a copy of the pounder, but Baughman was afraid to do so in the Du Pont blacksmith's shop, so he took one instead.[67] Munns also obtained a number of the parchment sieves from the mill.[68] He then arranged to meet the workmen at The Buck to sign contracts, boasting that he would "destroy" the Du Pont firm.

Du Pont and his partner, Peter Bauduy, learned of the meeting and went to the tavern determined to break it up. They beat Munns severely and ordered him to leave the neighborhood.[69] Du Pont and Bauduy were later indicted for assault and battery and fined fifteen dollars each. Munns and two Du Pont workmen subsequently left for Richmond. When Du Pont discovered that the brass pounder was missing, he tracked Munns and Baughman down and had them arrested and returned to Delaware for trial on theft charges.[70] The alderman who searched Munns at the time of his arrest found parchment sieves, a detailed description of the brass pounder, and the letters between

Munns and Brown, Page describing Munns's escape from Wilmington after the altercation with Du Pont and Bauduy.[71]

The letters formed the basis of Du Pont's unsuccessful legal proceedings against Munns. They also reveal something of Brown, Page's attitude toward Du Pont's works. In the first place, the correspondence leaves no doubt that Brown, Page's goal in sending Munns to Wilmington was to get information about Du Pont's processes. Munns promised that he could deliver, boasting that "we shall be upon a par with the Brandywine mills."[72] Brown, Page urged both Munns and Du Pont's erstwhile powder mixer, Hans Peebles, to get to Richmond as soon as possible so they could complete their own mill.[73]

Brown, Page argued to Du Pont that the millwright whom Munns had contacted "like any other mere mechanician . . . was perfectly at liberty to dispose of his own time & services as his interests might suggest."[74] Yet their correspondence with Munns suggests that they knew their efforts were questionable, at least as a matter of custom or morals if not as a matter of law. Brown, Page told Munns: "[T]he severe drubbing inflicted on you by Mr. Du Pont & his associates [was excusable]. . . . Mr. D has no doubt acted very rashly & improperly, but taking all circumstances into consideration, we think it will be prudent to take no notice of what is past—He certainly had cause to irritate him, in as much as you were endeavoring to obtain secrets appertaining to *his* business from his men *employed by him*."[75] The tone of the letter suggests both a desire to insulate the firm from responsibility for whatever injury Munns had suffered in the course of his employment and, perhaps, annoyance at Munns's complaining about the injuries.

Du Pont's outrage at the efforts to entice away workers was hardly noteworthy, as the law prohibited enticement. What was significant was the special concern Du Pont and Bauduy exhibited about the theft or copying of their technology and their dismay to learn that the law offered no remedy. They advised Brown, Page by letter that they would institute litigation "under the impression that laws are intended to protect laborious innocence against the machinations of envious malevolence."[76]

Privately, however, Du Pont doubted whether that law did, in fact, protect "laborious innocence." In a letter to the firm's lawyer, a Du Pont partner wondered whether Munns could be guilty of enticement. (It is unclear why Munns and Brown, Page would not be liable for enticement, inasmuch as Baughman and Hans Peebles, a refiner, had left Du Pont's employ.) Du Pont hoped that even if there was "a defect in the tenor of the law" through which this conduct might slip, "we presume the Judge has it left to his discretion to extend the said law in some measure when convinced that the injury done is extremely prejudicial to the party injured, and aware that the case had not been foreseen at the time the laws were enacted."[77]

Du Pont inquired of a Richmond lawyer, Daniel Call, whether the company could sue Brown, Page and was disappointed with the answer. Du Pont could maintain an action, Call said, against any of the partners of Brown, Page who "were privy to the enticing away of your workmen."[78] But, since they had no patent right to the design of the mills or to the machinery taken or copied, "I rather think no action can be sustained for taking the copies, it being what the law calls 'damnum absque injuria.'"

By the spring of 1810, Munns had landed on his feet. He was the superintendent of a powder mill at Frankford, near Philadelphia. Not content to let success in business be his revenge, he sued Du Pont and his partners for malicious prosecution, claiming the astronomical sum of $100,000 in damages.[79] The suit alleged that Du Pont and Bauduy lacked probable cause to have Munns arrested in Virginia and to institute the criminal charges in Delaware. U.S. Supreme Court Justice Bushrod Washington, riding circuit, presided. Munns brought the suit at least in part to recoup the funds he had spent in his defense against Du Pont's civil and criminal proceedings against him, as he still owed his lawyers fees for the defense.[80]

Munns lost his suit. Justice Washington's charge to the jury exhaustively summarized the evidence and suggested that Du Pont had sufficient proof that Munns was involved in the effort to steal the brass pounder and the sieves. The judge also noted the care that Du Pont had taken to preserve the secrecy of his powder mills.[81] The issues he posed for the jury were (1) whether Du Pont had probable cause to have Munns criminally prosecuted for arranging the theft of his equipment and copying his machines and (2) whether Du Pont lacked malicious intent in pressing the charges.

In rejecting Munns's suit, the jury—composed of grocers and other merchants of Wilmington[82]—must have determined both that Du Pont had cause to prosecute Munns and that he lacked malicious intent. The evidence as the judge presented it to the jury was undisputed; their only task was to apply the law to it. If the law were clear that Munns had done no wrong, the jury could not have returned the verdict that Du Pont had probable cause to have him arrested and, probably, would not have concluded that Du Pont lacked malice. Conversely, if the law were clear that Munns was not entitled to learn Du Pont technology by the means that he chose, one would think that Du Pont's action against him would have been successful. In Munns's malicious prosecution suit, the judge informed the jury that Munns had been acquitted of the criminal charges. However, the judge also stated that the prosecution had sought to require Munns to pay the costs of the prosecution pursuant to a Delaware law that evidently required the accused to pay the costs of a prosecution for which there was probable cause. Munns agreed voluntarily to do so in order to forestall the court from making a formal finding that the prosecution had been supported by probable cause. No record remains in the Du Pont archive of the civil proceeding that Du Pont instituted against Munns. Munns's malicious prosecution suit was based entirely on the criminal proceedings.

The various pieces of litigation involving Du Pont and Munns thus reveal the ambivalence of the law—at least as represented by a few courts at that time in Wilmington—toward Du Pont's right to restrict the dissemination of the company's secrets. If it were indeed undisputed, as a matter of fact, that Du Pont employees took the pounder and sieves with them when they departed for new employment, either Du Pont had cause to seek criminal prosecution for their theft, or the employees were entitled to take them.

The Du Pont company's difficulties with competitors trying to learn its methods by recruiting away its employees may have prompted it to take even more care to exclude strangers from its mills. In 1811, shortly after the Munns litigation drew to a close, the company posted a list of rules in the powder mills. The rules forbade "strangers of any description" to enter the powder yard and required the men to eject any strangers who entered.[83] The problem of employee mobility, however, remained.

Learning that the law offered no protection for the information itself was an important lesson for Du Pont and his partners. For some years thereafter, the firm chose to rely heavily on informal sanctions and public opinion, rather than on legal remedies, to protect the secrecy of its technology. A Du Pont partner, Raphael Duplanty, complained about Brown, Page in a letter to Du Pont's lawyer: "[W]e will at least satisfy our selves by publishing their transaction with their own letters and exposing to light their infamous conduct. We hope that publication will be sufficient to prove [to] every man of honor that they do not deserve the appellation of *Gentlemen* by which they have hitherto been qualified."[84]

That Du Pont and his partners did not share the modern sensibility about the harm of employee mobility is obvious from how they conceptualized the injury the company suffered from the Munns affair. Du Pont seemed especially alarmed that the prospect of high wages the firm's competitors offered to get those secrets would make the workman "unruly." Raising their expectations, Duplanty lamented, would leave "no possibility for us to maintain under the same severe regulations persons persuaded that other people will treat them better than we do." The danger of powdermen becoming resentful seemed especially great because powder mills were hazardous, and discontented workmen were likely to be careless. He observed, "The safety of our family, the safety of the families in our employ, the safety of the farmers who live in our neighborhood has imposed upon us the absolute duty of making choice of steady, sober men and of establishing the most rigid discipline among our workmen." Time and again, Du Pont and his partners described their competitors' overtures to their employees not only as dishonorable but also as likely to promote unjustified unrest among workers who should otherwise be satisfied with their position at the Brandywine mills.

The same year, Thomas Ewell, who owned considerable real estate in Georgetown and Washington, wanted to establish himself as powder maker for the U.S. government. Du Pont jealously watched this potential competitor and, being unwilling to share company secrets, rejected Ewell's overtures to form a partnership of sorts, ostensibly because the market for gunpowder was already oversupplied.[85] Du Pont also rejected Ewell's request to borrow one of the superintendents from the Brandywine mills.[86] Du Pont sought to convince Ewell that he would learn nothing valuable by hiring away Du Pont workers: "[O]ur manufactory is entirely superintended by our E. I. Du Pont and his brother and . . . the hands employed under them are nothing but common labourers who understand nothing of the principles and nature of the work they are set about."[87] As in the Brown, Page dispute, Du Pont was concerned about the possible loss of company secrets. However, Du Pont was also concerned that Ewell's "bribes" to the workers, "offering them two or three times as much wages as they [were] worth" to get Du Pont company secrets, would cause unrest.

Ewell replied and protested his innocence of "brib[ing] your hands to desertion from you." He attempted again to persuade Du Pont to join him in his new mill. Anticipating the rejection of that overture, Ewell offered to pay Du Pont in cash to provide specified information and technical assistance. Interestingly, he sought the most basic of information about making gunpowder: "the rule for adding water to the composition—for pounding—the rule for judging when the composition is sufficiently mixed."[88] He also wanted to hire one of Du Pont's "hands acquainted with the mechanical part" along with "a complete set of punches for making holes in the various sifters for granulating the powder." Finally, he requested the opportunity "to attend a month at your mill for improvement in the mechanical operations."

While Ewell was trying to persuade Du Pont to collaborate with him, he was, at the same time, trying surreptitiously to get information about Du Pont methods. Ewell wrote to one of Du Pont's powdermen, professing that "Honor & gentlemanly feeling prohibit my holding out any inducements to you to quit those with whom you now are. And I am sure you wd. not yield—were I to wish you—to act contrary to engagements existing."[89] But, he added, "you possess information—and I want it immediately. There is no impropriety in yr. parting with this. It is your right—all men sell it—and the man must be a fool who will complain of your doing it." It is interesting [51] that Ewell thought (or at least claimed) that "honor & gentlemanly feeling" prohibited him from getting his competitor's knowledge by enticing away an employee but allowed him to buy the information from the employee outright. At the time, this was a correct statement of what the law permitted, whatever it reflects about prevailing notions of honor and "gentlemanly feeling."

Du Pont regarded Ewell's overtures to his powdermen as "villainy," and it led to a protracted dispute between them. In April of 1812, Du Pont fired off an angry missive, complaining that Ewell's efforts to recruit away Du Pont's employees were "raising the pretensions" of his workman.[90] He proclaimed, "More than twenty other hands who know very well that they possess as much information as the ones you wish to bribe must naturally suppose they ought to receive the same exorbitant wages." As with Munns, Du Pont feared the destructiveness of raising the pretensions and the price of manual labor. Here, however, he asserted as well his property rights in his employees' knowledge: "[T]he proportion of skill and knowledge which we may have acquired by continual study and repeated experiments is a private property upon the possession of which depends our existence in the manufacturing line, and for the communication of which no pecuniary consideration, or *cash* as you called it, could be an adequate compensation." He concluded by appealing to a distinction between honorable and despicable competition: "[A] fair competition is certainly useful in every branch of Industry, it compels every one to improve: to such competition . . . we never will object, but to be stealing in the dark the improvements of others is a mean unworthy action which inevitably annihilates all kind of useful exertion."

The letter closed with a threat, not of litigation (perhaps the episode with Charles Munns and Brown, Page had convinced Du Pont of the futility of resorting to the law) but of humiliation. If Ewell were to entice away any Du Pont hands or, indeed, if he so much as employed any man who had ever worked for Du Pont, Du Pont would "expose" that conduct by publishing a letter Ewell had written to a Du Pont employee, Hugh Flannigan, attempting to entice him away.[91]

Ewell's response recast the claim of moral right in the dispute by suggesting that Du Pont was a grasping foreigner who refused to contribute to the improvement of American manufactures or to reward the talent of American workmen. (Ewell's claim to being the true American evidently was based on

Stealing in the Dark

his having emigrated from England in 1794 and marrying a granddaughter of Martha Washington.)[92] He accused Du Pont of exploiting his labor and protested his own innocence in driving up wages, as he said he would pay only

"common wages" to all but the most skilled. Ewell also scoffed at Du Pont's claim to have a right to protect his secret knowledge:

> There is no truth in your declaration that cash could not pay you for your property in the skill in making gun powder. It is for that article you have with peculiar caution erected a french manufactory at Brandywine not with the slightest claim to originality more than myself. . . . You display the falsehood of your estimation of your "common laborers" by complaining, as a great grievance, of their loss, from bribing and by the advance of wages. . . . Your men have a little knowledge of the practical part for which I would pay well, and it is infamous in you to keep them in slavery, and from the benefit you know their knowledge is worth to them, gained by experience in the greatest danger. . . . Any but a miserable, narrow minded and selfish wretch, would promote their success after faithful servitude.[93]

Ewell responded to Du Pont's threat of humiliation by suggesting that, if Du Pont would open his workmen's private letters, he was the sort of vile foreigner who would stop at nothing to injure his competitors: "You forget it was an American you were addressing. You fancied it was one of those animals, overbearing in prosperity, servile in adversity, commonly called frenchmen. Know then, if I ever hesitate to give employment to one of your men, it will not be from fear of you or of publicity to your wrath; because I prefer your open enmity to your friendship, as most sensible men do that of your nation."[94]

The tone of the correspondence, along with subsequent events, suggests that both Du Pont and Ewell anticipated making their letters public. In this context, Ewell's invocation of American chauvinism was a clever rhetorical move. Ewell had emigrated to the United States from England only four years before Du Pont arrived from France. He was hardly more "American" than Du Pont. In 1812, a low point in U.S.-British relations, an erstwhile Englishman who wanted to sell gunpowder to the United States no doubt needed every shred of patriotic legitimacy he could get if his competitor was a man who came from France. Ewell's insistence that he was the true American should be understood as an effort to prove his loyalty, which might have seemed particularly important as Du Pont was about to embark on manufacturing the gunpowder essential to a war against England.

Ewell fired the opening shot in the war for public opinion by publishing an advertisement in the Wilmington newspaper addressed "To Powder Makers" seeking "an able superintendent of character."[95] By promising "regular promotion in the establishment from the more laborious work and low wages to better situations; so that all will have the prospect of reward for faithful and diligent attention," Ewell undoubtedly meant to suggest that Du Pont failed to give his own employees the chance to profit from their skill and ability. Ewell had copies of the advertisement posted at the homes of powder workers in Wilmington and distributed to the workmen at Du Pont's mills.[96]

[53]

Meanwhile, Ewell kept up his correspondence with Hugh Flannigan, offering a generous salary and asking him to bring more hands. Flannigan found another powder mixer, Quigg, who was willing to quit Du Pont's employ, but he wanted assurances that Ewell really would provide better conditions than he had at Du Pont's mill. Ewell reassured him both about working conditions and that Flannigan and Quigg would be paid well above the market. Ewell also sought to assure Flannigan that he and Quigg would be the only powdermen in the mill being so well paid, apparently because Flannigan was as concerned about his relative status as he was about his absolute compensation. Ewell impressed upon him the dire need he had for his "skills & management."[97]

Not to be outdone in the public opinion battle, in June 1812 Du Pont wrote and published a pamphlet called *Villainy Detected*. The pamphlet accused Ewell of incompetence in the manufacture of gunpowder and of "villainy" in his efforts to get Du Pont knowledge by offering "extravagant wages" to workmen.[98] The pamphlet announced Du Pont's intention "to enter a suit at law against Dr. Ewell, in hopes of obtaining redress and in order to put a stop to such unjustifiable proceedings." However, "in the mean time," the pamphlet continued, Du Pont considered it "a duty towards the government who have been deceived & to themselves who have been injured" to reveal Ewell's perfidy in attempting to pass himself off as a competent powder maker only by enticing away someone else's workman. And the pamphlet then published the letter Ewell wrote to Flannigan.

The episodes involving Munns and Ewell reveal that Du Pont understood the value of the secrecy of the firm's powder-making techniques and that the law offered what he deemed inadequate protection for them. They also reveal an attitude about the social and economic costs of employee mobility that was steeped in moral notions of loyalty and duty. Enticing employees to get their knowledge was as dishonorable as it was unfair. It was destructive partly because it reduced the incentive to invest in research, but also because it made the powdermen dissatisfied with their position. The dissatisfaction might harm the firm because it would cause dangerous carelessness, but also because labor turnover would reduce production. Only one concern among others was the fear that departing workers would disseminate information about Du Pont's technological advantages to other employers.

[54] Interestingly, Du Pont did not appear to make any effort to restrain an early nonfamily partner in the firm, Peter Bauduy, from using the firm's techniques when he started a competing mill on his estate near Wilmington. This was not because Bauduy left Du Pont on good terms; the dissolution was acrimonious and led to protracted litigation. The extant correspondence about Bauduy's methods from E. I. du Pont's father to a French investor in the firm confidently stated: "Even though he has taken many of our workmen, though he uses almost the same machinery and methods of mixing—no powder compares with ours—all because of Irenee's skill and his marvelous industry."[99] Not only did courts regard the status of a gentleman, or at least of a skilled artisan, as requiring the independence that would come from being able to control one's own knowledge through switching jobs and to be an entrepreneur in the use of workplace knowledge to start a competing firm, this episode suggests that men of business did too. Nevertheless, Bauduy could not and would not be accused of theft in departing the company with the latest Du Pont chemical techniques, for it was the legal right of a man of his status to do so.

As the Du Pont story illustrates, the principal claim outside of patent and copyright that might have enabled an employer to control the dissemination of workplace knowledge was an action for enticement. An enticement claim could be brought against anyone who persuaded an employee to quit his job before the term of service had ended.[100] Enticement protected the obligation of service, not the value of the employee's knowledge or skill. Thus, if the term of service had ended, there was no action. As Du Pont discovered, that was a significant limitation on the utility of the law.

From "Villainy" to Trade Secrets

About twenty years after Du Pont's troubles with Munn and Ewell, the proprietors of a Boston glass manufactory brought an enticement action against the proprietors of a rival factory. The plaintiffs charged their rivals with enticing away and employing "certain workmen skilled in several departments of glass-making" and proved that some of the workers had been their employees up until the day they went to work for the defendant. The plaintiffs also sought to prove that proprietors of a number of the glass manufactories in the area had all agreed that, for a period of five years, they would not employ any workers "who might be in the service of either of the others, unless such workman first produced a written discharge," and that they had also agreed

"to keep the others advised of the names of the workmen in his employment."
One worker testified that the day after he had given two weeks' notice of his
intention to quit, he had been offered a job by the defendant. The trial judge
instructed the jury that an offer of employment could not legally be made to [55]
one who was employed by another, even if the offered employment was to
take effect at a future time. Nevertheless, the jury found for the defendants
and the Massachusetts Supreme Court upheld the verdict.

In that case, *Boston Glass Manufactory v. Binney*, the Massachusetts high
court held that skilled workers had a right to switch jobs and to take their
skill and knowledge with them. "The defendants had a legal right to make
a contract with the plaintiffs' laborers to take effect after the expiration of
their term of service with the plaintiffs." Implicitly recognizing that the loss
of skilled workmen was a hardship, the court nevertheless labeled it *damnum
absque injuria*, concluding in the final sentence of the opinion, "If the law
were otherwise, it would lead to the most mischievous consequences, and
would operate injuriously both to laborers and their employers." Although
the mischief of such a rule is not stated, the implication is that without mobility of labor, economic development would be retarded.[101] William Nelson
explained the case as a refusal of American courts "to extend the concepts of
property with which the courts analyzed cases involving apprentices, children, and other servants to a new legal category—that of industrial laborers."[102] One can also see in the opinion a refusal to recognize that enticement
protected a monopoly on a firm's valuable know-how. The skill of glassmakers
enhanced their status and thus rendered implausible the analogy to children
and household servants, who had been the traditional subject of actions for
enticement. It also made their mobility seem more desirable than the stability emphasized by the enticement action.

Across the Atlantic, the seeds of modern trade secret law were being sown
in a few English cases that looked at ownership of workplace knowledge
from the standpoint of a duty to protect secrets rather than ownership of
specific items. But it was not until the Civil War that any such legal principle was recognized in American law. Joseph Story's *Commentaries on Equity
Jurisprudence*, first published in 1836, was the first treatise to discuss the
principles that later became the law of trade secrets, and it remained the
only commentary on that subject until after the Civil War. His discussion was
extremely brief. One sentence stated simply that "a person may lawfully sell a
secret in his trade or business, and restrain himself from using that secret."[103]
Interestingly, this statement had no citations to support it, although *Yovatt
v. Winyard* (Ex. Ch. 1820) and *Bryson v. Whitehead* (V.C. 1822), the latter of
which Story cited elsewhere, would have been apt citations.[104] When Story

first published the *Commentaries* in 1836, there were no American cases on this issue; the first, *Vickery v. Welch*, was decided by the Massachusetts high court a year later.[105] A more fertile statement came in the discussion of

[56] injunctions to enforce copyrights, in which Story said that equity would "restrain a party from making a disclosure of secrets communicated to him in the course of a confidential employment. And it matters not, in such cases, whether the secrets be secrets of trade or secrets of title, or any other secrets of the party important to his interests."[106] The cases cited as support for this sentence suggest that Story may have intended it as nothing more than a description of the obligations owed in the few employment relations that were already recognized as being confidential. Courts later used Story's propositions, however, as a basis for expanding the number of employment relations that incorporated a duty of confidence.

Story cited three English cases for the proposition that equity would restrain the disclosure of secrets learned in confidential employment. The first, and most analogous, was *Yovatt v. Winyard* (1820),[107] in which a veterinarian's journeyman had surreptitiously copied his employer's medicine recipes that he had been explicitly forbidden to see or use. The Lord Chancellor concluded that the journeyman had breached a duty of trust and confidence and, on that basis, enjoined the former employee from using or publishing the purloined recipes.[108] According to the court's description of the employment agreement, the defendant was "to be instructed in the general knowledge of the business, but was not to be taught the mode of composing the medicines." The plaintiff's counsel conceded that the court might not protect the secret if the proprietor had himself communicated it. Here, since the defendant had first learned of the secret in breach of duty, he could be enjoined from using the knowledge.

Later English cases, often cited by American courts and by later editions of Story's treatise, repeated the same point. If the employee "was permitted to acquire, and did acquire, a full knowledge" of the trade secret to enable him to perform his duties, the employer could not afterward "restrain him from using any knowledge so acquired or any secret so disclosed."[109] At its origins, therefore, the law prohibited employees from illicitly learning secrets, but not from using knowledge that they acquired through their work.[110]

The other two cases Story cited had even less to do with what later became the law of trade secrets. One, *Cholmondeley v. Clinton* (1815), held that a solicitor's clerk, who later became a solicitor for an adversary of his former employer's client, could not use for the benefit of his new client any knowledge that he had acquired while working as a clerk. The former clerk, Montriou, had worked as clerk and then as solicitor for a firm that represented Lord Clinton in matters concerning his landholdings. In that employment, Montriou prepared abstracts and deeds and developed considerable knowledge about the titles to Lord Clinton's estates. During that time Earl Cholmondeley claimed title to one of Lord Clinton's estates by virtue of some defect in Clinton's title. About a year after dissolution of the law partnership, Montriou became solicitor to Cholmondeley to represent him in litigation concerning the estate. The court enjoined Montriou from using for Cholmondeley knowledge he had acquired while representing Clinton.[111] In contemporary parlance, the case concerned attorney-client privilege and conflicts of interest; the court simply stated the unremarkable proposition that an attorney cannot switch from representing the defendant to the plaintiff in the same or a related case. Story's third citation, *Evitt v. Price* (1827), held that a firm of attorneys could get an injunction forcing an accountant to return their account books after the accountant refused to relinquish their books until he received payment due him.[112] Neither of these cases is wholly unrelated to the ownership of information, of course. However, a lawyer's duty to guard client confidences, which was well established by the Middle Ages,[113] is a far cry from a general duty of all employees to protect all secrets of every employer.

Story's own creativity played a role in the invention of trade secret doctrine. Story did not single-handedly invent the trade secret rule; his overstatement of the principle recognized in the precedents should be understood as the nineteenth-century treatise writer's tendency toward abstraction and generalization. Not every later trade secret case cited Story, which suggests that the trade secret concept developed for reasons other than Story's influence. Furthermore, that a treatise states a legal principle that does not find solid support in the cases cited does not mean that the author conjured the principle out of thin air. Anyone who has written footnotes after weeks of laborious research knows the sometimes-attenuated relationship between what one knows to be the law or fact and the sources one can find ready at hand when the time comes to polish the notes. If that can be a problem in the modern age of easily accessible libraries and electronic research, imagine the difficulties confronting a treatise writer in the early nineteenth century.[114] More important, the synthetic and systematizing work of treatise-writing revealed the possibilities that had not been apparent before. Yet the absence of any other treatise asserting that employees had a duty of confidence suggests that Story's comments were about the available remedies for breach of an existing duty of confidence, not a description of all employment as confidential relationships. Other early treatises contained no mention of the duty to guard secrets, and there was no published American decision stating such a duty. Chancellor James Kent's *Commentaries on American Law* described the relationship of principal and agent as one in which the principal confides the management of some business to the agent, and the agent undertakes the "trust"; however, that treatise mentioned nothing of a duty to guard secrets.[115] Tapping Reeve's *The Law of Baron and Femme* (1862) contains no such mention.[116] Neither do other treatises that discuss the law of master and servant or equity mention anything of a duty to guard secrets.[117]

The other early antecedents of trade secret doctrine were an 1822 English decision, *Bryson v. Whitehead*, and an 1837 American case, *Vickery v. Welch*, both of which granted specific performance of an agreement for the sale of a secret recipe in connection with the sale of the business (a dye recipe in *Bryson* and a chocolate recipe in *Vickery*).[118] Both of these cases established a novel rule that the recipe, a discrete thing reflected in a written form, was an asset of a business that could be sold; once sold, however, the seller lost the right to use that recipe. Interestingly, in *Vickery* the defendant had argued that the seller's obligation to refrain from selling the recipe to anyone else was void as a restraint of trade, citing *Mitchel v. Reynolds*, the leading case on agreements not to compete.[119] The court was unpersuaded: "The public are not prejudiced" by the plaintiff obtaining the chocolate recipe. "If it were worth any thing, the defendant would use the art and keep it secret, and it is of no consequence to the public whether the secret art be used by the plaintiff or by the defendant."[120]

WHEN THE DU PONT COMPANY tried to prevent the dissemination of its secret methods of manufacturing gunpowder, it sought to prosecute the theft of the drawings of its machinery and of some devices for refining powder. It did not, because it could not, prosecute the misappropriation of the knowledge embodied in them or the efforts of its competitors to obtain the knowledge by hiring former Du Pont employees. Antebellum courts simply did not regard the obligation to keep secrets to be a feature of an ordinary employment relationship.[121] Patent was the only legal protection for technology, and employee-inventors were entitled to their patents, even when created for hire. At most an employer could resort to an equitable rule allowing the users of an invention to continue using it after a patent had been issued if the patentee had previously allowed it. Law offered no way to prevent workers from using knowledge they acquired in previous employment or to prevent them from capitalizing upon their own industry as authors and inventors. In other words, workplace knowledge and skill remained, in the eyes of the law, an attribute of each worker, not an asset of a firm.

PERSONAL ATTRIBUTE

The Genius Which Conceived & the Toil
Which Compiled the Book

Just as both patents and unpatented workplace knowledge were regarded as an asset of skilled labor, so too did antebellum law treat copyrights as the property of the individual author regardless of whether the work was created for hire. Although employee-authors, like authors everywhere for centuries, routinely assigned their copyrights to those who would pay for them (including their employers), the law required there to be an express assignment of the copyright before it would divest an author of the right to his work over his objection. Judges found very good philosophical and economic reasons for this rule, at least in the context of the few cases that litigated authorship.

In this chapter, I examine the law and practice of copyright ownership in the three sectors of the antebellum American economy where copyright disputes arose: law publishing, theater, and map publishing. These were also the three sectors that continued to produce the majority of the employer-employee copyright disputes for much of the nineteenth century. Judges developed rules to protect employee-authors because they were persuaded by the morality of saving creative geniuses from improvident bargains. Judges also considered it economically expedient for a new country that wished to cultivate its own homegrown culture industry to protect the rights of the author who worked for hire. Later in the century, the arguments of economic expedience seemed to favor the employer, but in the antebellum period the moral claims of the author coincided perfectly with the economic incentives for protecting the author's rights to the fruits of creative work.

The first federal copyright act had the avowed purpose of "the encouragement of learning, by securing the copies of maps, charts, and books to the *authors and proprietors* of such copies," for a term of fourteen years from the date of registration of the copyright plus a renewal term of an additional fourteen years.[1] At that time, a copyright had to be registered by depositing a specified number of copies of the work in the appropriate government office; today, registration is no longer required. That both authors and proprietors could own a copyright recognizes the fact that authorship for hire was nothing new. For centuries, people had been employed to create texts and maps, the works that qualified for copyright protection. Literary histories of copyright and authorship note that prior to the Renaissance the collective nature of the creation of texts was widespread. If texts were divinely inspired, or if texts were written versions of stories that had a long oral tradition, original creation was not understood to be the essential characteristic of authorship. And the reproduction of texts involved copying rather than conjuring. Artists had been working in the employ of others for centuries as patronage had been an important source of new music, opera, and theater. Patronage had worked well as a stimulus or support for the exercise of artistic creation. Moreover, artists had worked in what today would be considered freelance relationships. Artistic and literary production had thus been collective and involved short- and long-term employment relations for centuries.[2]

Notwithstanding substantial evidence of collective authorship, the early nineteenth-century intellectual justifications for copyright protection imagined authorship as highly individual. Evolving notions of authorship, together with Lockean labor theories of value, gradually created the Anglo-American ideas that the author is the one who does the original and creative work of imagining and writing, and that property rights are justified by the labor expended in the creation.[3] An early nineteenth-century court looking for analysis of the relationship between copyright and author's rights would likely have begun with Blackstone's individualist and Lockean defense of copyright in the *Commentaries*: "When a man by the exertion of his rational powers has produced an original work, he seems to have clearly a right to dispose of that identical work as he pleases, and any attempt to vary the disposition he has made of it, appears to be an invasion of that right [of property]."[4] Blackstone was both an author and a lawyer for a copyright claimant in a famous English case on copyrights. In Blackstone's treatise, Locke's labor theory of property "united easily with an emerging aesthetic of books as products of a creative mind and as manifestations of an individual's personality."[5]

The author as creative genius and the author as proprietor simultaneously described the nature of literature and justified the existence of legal rights in ideas. The labor theory of property, which formed an enduring synthesis with the romantic vision of authorship, offered courts an appealing reason to [61] protect the property rights of employee authors for much of the nineteenth century. Writers from Defoe to Dickens embraced the theory, joining forces with publishers to advocate the moral, cultural, and economic benefits of protecting the authors' proprietary rights in their works. From the eighteenth century onward, celebrity authors proved themselves effective lobbyists for a set of copyright rules that ultimately benefited corporate publishers as much as individual scribblers.[6]

The hegemony of the individual author as owner of the product of his or her intellectual labor made courts skeptical of employer claims to the creative products of their employees. Published cases determined that employees were entitled to the copyrights in their works, even though the works had been done during the course of employment or on commission. Nevertheless, data on copyright registrations show that employers sometimes copyrighted work prepared by their employees. As Zorina Khan has demonstrated, between 44 and 49 percent of copyright registrations between 1790 and 1800 were by a person other than the actual author.[7] A significant number of registrations were for works other than the kinds of books that typically would have an individual author; they included maps and charts, dictionaries, and directories.[8] It is reasonable to suppose that among these, some employers were registering the copyright to works that persons in their employ had created, at least in part. Then as now it was not unusual for an author to assign his rights in advance of the issuance of a copyright to a publisher and for the publisher to be identified as the proprietor of a work in the initial copyright registration. One simply cannot know from examining registrations what percentage of the copyright proprietors may have been employers. A number of the works copyrighted might well have been produced either by multiple people working in concert or by one or more people working for others. As Khan shows, some of the early works were the sort of work that typically requires the labor of more than one person to produce. About 7 percent of registrations between 1790 and 1800 were for maps or charts and about 4 percent for directories and dictionaries. It is also quite possible that the other sorts of works copyrighted—textbooks (which composed 17 percent of total registrations) and scientific and medical texts (which composed 10 percent of registrations)—are obviously the sorts of works that might involve multiple authors.[9] It is unclear whether all those registrations were pursuant to an express assignment by the employed author.

Absent an express assignment, the scant case law suggests employers might not have been able to obtain a copyright for a work prepared by an employee if the employee chose to object. In *Binns v. Woodruff* (1821), Justice Bushrod Washington, sitting as a circuit judge, held that one who employed others to create an elaborately decorated print of the Declaration of Independence could not obtain a copyright because he had neither designed, drawn, nor engraved the work and thus was not an author as required by the statute.[10] A well-advised employer in that situation would have obtained an assignment from the actual authors and then registered the copyright as a "proprietor" rather than as an "author." Although where authorship was communal, as in map publishing, actual practices of copyright ownership were complicated, the rules articulated by courts in cases where employers and employees disputed copyright ownership were not. Courts were quite clear that, absent an express and clear contrary agreement, the employee-author was entitled to the copyright.

The available legal and business archival evidence of how antebellum firms handled employee copyrights suggests two somewhat contradictory facts. First, compared with today, relatively few kinds of works were subject to copyright (the first Copyright Act of 1790 provided for copyright only in maps, nautical charts, and books) and there were relatively few copyright registrations in the antebellum period.[11] Second, copyright played a relatively minor role even in those few employment settings in which people were paid by others to create material subject to copyright protection. Although case law did not recognize an employer's right to employee works until the late nineteenth century, people other than the authors frequently registered copyrights, and it is reasonable to infer that they were registering the copyright in works created by their employees. Thus, employers may have contracted around the default rule or may simply have assumed that the default was precisely the opposite of what it was. Although courts acknowledged the legitimacy of express contracts assigning the copyright to the employer, without knowing whether early copyright registrations by employers were pursuant to an express agreement, it is difficult to know the extent to which the practice of employer registrations diverged from legal doctrine.

Three distinct sectors of the American economy generated litigation over employer and employee claims to copyrights in the antebellum period: law publishing, theater, and map publishing. Collaborative work practices produced works of substantial economic value. Authorship was ambiguous and work relations tended to be short-term, and copying was both relatively easy and potentially lucrative, which made copyright litigation likely. In each of these areas, courts clung to a rule of individual employee authorship, not-withstanding the collaborative work relationships.

Law Publishing

One of the most pressing needs of the early American legal community was to develop an adequate system for the reporting and publication of the new American law. It was a struggle to find enough competent people to report the decisions of the various state and federal courts. Even more difficult was finding printers willing to print and sell the reporters' work at a price that lawyers would pay and to develop a plan for distributing the books once printed. A system, if one can call it that, emerged whereby lawyers interested in the work of the court obtained permission from the judges (and, in some states, the legislature) to report the decisions of the court. It was then up to the lawyer to find a printer who would print the reports at a price and quantity to fulfill the reporter's obligation to the court and to enable the reporter to sell enough to make a profit to support himself. The court reporters in these years were not exactly employees of the court; neither the court nor the government paid a salary. They were independent contractors in the modern parlance, although in some jurisdictions they were also officeholders.[12]

The fact that a substantial number of early employer-employee copyright disputes involved reporters of appellate decisions probably played a role in shaping the law. Although judges no doubt understood reporters as public servants, they were not the judges' or the court's own employees, nor were they "servants" in the conventional sense. They were entrepreneurs, men of stature and education, whose diligence, analytic skills, and attention to detail were crucial in the dissemination of the law. Their work was also essential to the edification of the bench and bar. They were far too important for judges to see them as servants or to compromise their independence by restricting their claim to copyright. Their copyright disputes involved persons who would not be governed by the hierarchical rules of master and servant, and so it would not have occurred to the judges to invoke the law of master and servant to decide the respective rights of the reporter and those who claimed a right to republish their work. As a result, the relatively pro-employee rules became settled doctrine, only to be changed at the beginning of the twentieth century once the distinction between employees and independent contractors emerged.

The first published American copyright decision in which the author might even remotely resemble someone hired to write was the famous dispute between the third and fourth reporters for the U.S. Supreme Court,

Henry Wheaton and Richard Peters.[13] More accurately, *Wheaton v. Peters* was a dispute between the publishers of the reporters, for Wheaton the author had assigned his copyright to his publisher, and it was the publisher who [64] litigated the suit.[14] Although it is famous for its rejection of the notion that courts could confer common law copyrights in circumstances where the statutory requirements were not met, an equally significant aspect of the opinion was its assumption that reporters of judicial decisions were entitled the copyright in their work.

Henry Wheaton was the reporter of decisions of the Supreme Court from 1816 to 1827, the third reporter in the Court's history. After serving, like his predecessors Alexander Dallas and William Cranch, in an uncompensated capacity, Wheaton became the Court's first official reporter in 1817 following Congress's enactment of a statute providing for an official reporter of the Supreme Court's decisions.[15] After Richard Peters became the reporter in 1827, he published and sold a volume called *Condensed Reports of Cases in the Supreme Court of the United States* containing all the Court's decisions from its founding until 1827, including those reported by Wheaton. Wheaton sued Peters for copyright infringement. Peters argued that Wheaton's copyright was void because he had not complied with the statutory procedures for registering a copyright. Remanding for factual findings on the adequacy of Wheaton's efforts to register the copyright, the Court assumed that if his efforts were sufficient, he would have a valid copyright, notwithstanding his employment or appointment as reporter for the Court. His status—whether employee or appointed officer of the Court or of the United States—was, in the Court's view, irrelevant to his copyright claim. Nor did the Court mention whether Wheaton's claim to the copyright was based on a contract, on the Reporters' Act of 1817 (which said nothing about copyright), or on other terms of his appointment as the reporter. His right to the copyright was simply assumed.[16]

Wheaton was not unreasonable in supposing he owned the copyright in his reports. The members of Congress who supported the Reporters' Act of 1817, and those who opposed it on the ground that it was unnecessary to pay a salary to the reporter, presumably thought so too. The first Term during which Wheaton was the reporter ended in March 1816, and by early May, Wheaton had the volume ready to publish. But he could find no publisher willing to print it. He finally was forced to sell the copyright to the Philadelphia bookseller Matthew Carey, who paid only $1,200 in notes for all the rights. The Reporters' Act of 1817 provided for a payment of $1,000 per annum, but Wheaton had received no compensation before that, so if he had no copyright to sell he had no way to get paid for his work. As to every year after 1817, Wheaton argued that the $1,000 was "unequal to the labour and time" and was, in any event, compensation for the eighty volumes that the statute obliged him to deliver to the government, not a salary for his work. The compensation was indeed measly for the work involved. Moreover, [65] his first volume contained 487 pages of abstracts, arguments, and opinions and 46 pages of notes; the abstracts, arguments, and notes were, of course, largely Wheaton's writing rather than that of the Justices. Although some of the supplemental material was penned anonymously by Justice Story, Story gave it to Wheaton to add value to the reports and thus to assist Wheaton in publishing them.[17]

The Court stated that "no reporter has or can have any copyright in the written opinions delivered by this court; and . . . the judges thereof cannot confer on any reporter any such right."[18] The Court assumed Wheaton could copyright whatever he added: headnotes, a summary of the decision, arguments of counsel, pagination, and perhaps even his report of opinions rendered orally. He simply could not secure a copyright in the Justices' own work. As to the parts of the reports that were not opinions, the Court surely had no doubt that Wheaton's work was "authorship" in the sense that would ordinarily entitle him to copyright protection. Wheaton's industry and erudition in writing the marginal notes and the appendices on admiralty and prize law were plain to all. The Court recognized these as his valuable work. And, inasmuch as he was not being compensated for writing them, it would be inconceivable to say that the copyright was not his. Besides sympathy for him, there would also be the instrumental concerns—if he could not sell the copyright to the printer, there would be no printer willing to print, and the opinions would never be disseminated.

The Justices had institutional reasons to insist that Wheaton was the "author" and therefore the initial copyright owner of his reports. The Justices thought it mattered a great deal whether they, the people of the United States, or Wheaton had the initial entitlement to copyright, for only Wheaton was in a position to negotiate with printers like Matthew Carey to publish and distribute the reports. There would also be the matter of the Justices' respect and affection for Wheaton. He was a personal friend of Story's; indeed, they were roommates at the Washington boardinghouse where all the Justices stayed during the Term.[19]

It was obvious to the Court why Wheaton could not copyright the Justices' opinions without their consent, but the Court went further: the Justices could not confer a copyright on the reporter. The Court did not explain why, although later courts explained that judges could not copyright their written opinions because they were public servants.[20] But so, arguably, were reporters. What was the difference? Two rationales are possible, though neither was offered in the Court's opinion in *Wheaton v. Peters*. One was that law reports, like judges' opinions, could not be copyrighted because, as the work of

employees and officers of a democratic government, they were not a proper subject of private property. In this view, the nature of the written product as law makes it unfit for copyright—the law must be in the public domain so that it is free for all to use, quote, reproduce, and disseminate widely.

A second rationale might be that judges could not obtain copyright and thus could not assign it to reporters because they were public servants and their "employer," the U.S. government, could be the only proper owner of the copyright. As public servants, the judges could not acquire the copyright in the work they were employed to do—the preparation of opinions—and thus had no rights to confer upon the reporter. If that were the rule the Court adopted, then it might mean more generally that employment to create copyrighted works should be deemed to constitute an implied assignment of the copyright to the government. Such an implicit rationale, however, would be inconsistent with the Court's assumption that Wheaton owned the copyright, unless the Court thought there had been an implicit rejection of an implicit assignment.

Neither of these rationales was stated in *Wheaton v. Peters*, but an 1852 decision of a New York federal court adopted the second one based both on an express contract and on a statute providing that the reporter of decisions of the New York Court of Appeals would not obtain a copyright to his notes, to his reports, or to the references he compiled. The court's decision that judges, as public servants, could secure no copyright in their opinions to assign to the reporter because the judges' employer—the state government—should own the copyright was premised on a particular statute and contract; it was not a general rule applicable to all writers.[21] The contract between the reporter and the New York secretary of state contained an assignment of the copyright to the secretary of state, which suggests that both the reporter and the secretary of state may have believed that the reporter would, absent the contract, have a copyright to assign.

Judges probably also understood more clearly in the case of reporters than in the case of almost any other occupation how crucial allocation of copyright ownership was to the economics of law publishing. Securing the copyright for the reporter was in lieu of paying a more generous compensation from the public fisc. In an era in which government was quite limited in its ability to raise revenue to fund a judicial bureaucracy, judges doubtless were reluctant to interfere with the scheme by which reporters could be compensated from sources other than a full salary paid from the treasury. Perhaps judges understood that the willingness of competent, educated men to take on the task, and to ensure speedy publication and distribution of the developing law, depended upon the reporter's industry, spurred on by the profit motive.

Although law publishing cases dominated the early development of employee copyright law, one other decision from this era took a similar position. *Pierpont v. Fowle* (1846), a Massachusetts federal case between an author who had been commissioned to write schoolbooks and the person who hired him, presented the question of whether the author or the employer had the right to renew the copyright. The court concluded that the renewal rights did not pass with the contract assigning the initial copyright to the employer. In explaining the result, the court emphasized the importance of authors' rights to protect "genius" from bad bargains: "It was the genius which conceived and the toil which compiled the book that is to be rewarded." If "a hirer of others" is entitled to a copyright, "how does this act encourage and aid genius? It rather aids those kinds of patrons, who fatten on the labors of genius."[22] The restriction on the assignment of renewal rights, so as to protect authors from improvident bargains made when the value of a copyrighted work was unknown, was a pervasive concern in copyright law into the twentieth century. The case was not uniquely concerned with protecting employees, but illustrates that judicial solicitude for authors extended to employee-authors and certainly transcended the specific concerns about law publishing.

Theater

Theater also generated a substantial number of nineteenth-century copyright ownership disputes between employer and employee. This is not surprising, given the great commercial value of a successful play or opera and the collaborative nature of theater productions. One of the earliest reported decisions involving a dispute over a commissioned work was *Atwill v. Ferrett* (1846), which stated a general rule that the writer of an opera was the author, even if the work was commissioned by another. The opinion also stated, however, that since the theater manager who had commissioned the work had been involved in modifying the opera, he was entitled to a copyright in the version performed in his theater.

The plaintiff, an impresario named Atwill, wanted to mount a New York production of an opera, *The Bohemian Girl*, that had been composed and performed in Europe. He commissioned an unnamed third party to compose an arrangement of the opera, and Atwill copyrighted the new arrangement in his own name. At the time, this form of appropriation was not illegal under U.S. copyright law because the Copyright Act did not protect foreign works, which continued to be imported, copied, printed, and published without regard to European copyright laws throughout the nineteenth century. Today it would be regarded as blatant piracy. When Atwill's pirated but copyrighted arrangement was in turn pirated by someone else, Atwill sued. The defendants argued that the copyright was void because Atwill was not the composer. Atwill argued that, under English law, one could secure the copyright in a work he had commissioned another to create.

The court rejected the contention that an employer could acquire the copyright in an employee's work simply through the act of commissioning it. In the court's view, the English cases "recognize the right of authorship, although the materials of the composition were procured by another, and also an equitable title in one person to the labors of another, when the relations of the parties are such that the former is entitled to an assignment of the production. But, to constitute one an author, he must by his own intellectual labor applied to the materials of his composition, produce an arrangement or compilation new in itself."[23] The cases cited, according to the court, related to "new productions arranged or compiled from materials before known, or obtained by others for the author, and not to the appropriation by copyright of those materials in the same state in which they are furnished."[24] The opinion mentioned in passing that "[t]he title to road-books, maps &c., rests upon [the] principle" that one who, by his own intellectual labor, produces a new composition may claim the copyright even if others procured the materials for him.[25] The court ultimately determined that the plaintiff's allegations of having added to and altered the music were legally sufficient to constitute him the author. It cautioned, however, that if the plaintiff's title had rested only on his having commissioned the composition, he would have lost. In short, although the court was prepared to recognize as a matter of equity that an author might have a duty to assign the copyright in a work he had been commissioned to create, the law of copyright recognized no principle that employment or a commission to create by itself entitled the employer to the copyright. The court insisted that, as a matter of copyright law, only intellectual labor could make one an author.

There are a number of ironies about *Atwill v. Ferrett*. First, notwithstanding the court's insistence that only intellectual labor could make one an author, both Atwill and the unnamed third-party author were pirating it from the European composer and librettist. They were not alone: American book publishers and theater managers were notorious for their liberal reprinting or use of works that appeared first abroad. Yet *Atwill* tolerated no claim to copyright simply by virtue of being an employer: one had at least to be a plagiarist. Second, when the court invoked "intellectual labor" as the moral and legal basis of copyright ownership and insisted that the playwright rather than the theater manager owned the copyright to "his" works, the court embraced the romantic notion of individual authorship in a context in which it scarcely fit. Playwrights worked in a collaborative setting quite different from the romanticized setting of the scribbler in a garret. Moreover, in the 1840s playwrights had yet to obtain the status of genius artist that people accorded authors and, later, playwrights such as Ibsen, Shaw, or O'Neill. Theater in the 1840s was hardly considered art. An evening's bill might last four to six hours and include a main piece, a curtain-raising farce, and a closing burletta. The audience expected to see comedy, melodrama, and extravaganzas with spectacular effects. In that context, the playwright was sort of a "handyman to the company. He existed to make their performance possible, rather than they to interpret his work to an audience."[26] Although the court's opinion nods toward the intellectual labor of the playwright, and the opinion was later cited for exactly that rule, the holding of the court was consistent with the "handyman to the company" view of playwrights not as genius author-proprietors but as workmen hired for their intellectual brawn.

Cartography and Map Publishing

Map-making is an important counterpoint to law publishing and theater in a study of the history of copyrighted works made for hire. The available evidence suggests that employers of cartographers may have obtained the copyrights to the works of their employees even if the legal rules described above would suggest they were not entitled to them. There is no surprise in this, for as between books and maps, the latter were more likely to be the result of many people's collective efforts. Other forms of collective work were not eligible for copyright protection until later, including printed music (1831); performed dramas (1856); photography (1865); painting, drawing, and sculpture (1870); and motion pictures (1912).[27] The making of all but the most rudimentary maps required the efforts of many people, including surveyors, draftsmen, and printers. Cartography is thus a promising area for the study of copyright and, more generally, the social construction of knowledge in the work relationship. The creative process is inherently collaborative and usually builds—explicitly or tacitly—on past work. Maps and nautical charts are created by a series of technical activities, each performed by a different "author," and cartographers debate the extent to which copyright should restrict later cartographers from using earlier maps.

Both the available archival material and the literature on the history of cartography suggest that the person or firm who managed to organize the collective effort of the surveyors, draftsmen, and printers was the one who claimed the copyright. Yet the dearth of reported litigation between collaborators suggests that proof of infringement was either so difficult or so easy as to make few cases uncertain enough to require litigation to a published disposition.[28]

[70]   For much of the nineteenth century, cartography was dominated by small enterprises: partnerships, sole proprietors, and, later, small corporations.[29] The publisher—often one or two individuals, sometimes a firm—usually claimed the copyright.[30] What the publisher did to merit such a claim varied. A single person seldom did all the actual work of surveying, drafting, and design. Although one person could map a town or village with a compass and a rudimentary odometer, larger maps would require the work of more than one surveyor. Maps frequently gave credit to the engraver or lithographer, but not to the draftsmen or surveyors. In some cases, an individual who sought to publish a map did the surveying and drafting himself and contracted with an engraver, lithographer, or printer to manufacture it.[31] In others, a publisher with no professional training or experience in cartography or surveying staked his claim to the status of publisher based on his knowledge of map reproduction and printing. A prominent example was Matthew Carey, one of the leading publishers in Philadelphia and, hardly coincidentally, the publisher of Wheaton's reports of the Supreme Court decisions.[32]

The paucity of reported decisions involving disputed claims to copyrights in maps or charts suggests that the question of map copyright ownership appears to have been resolved significantly through self-help.[33] The evidence that does exist is somewhat contradictory. On the one hand, there is the case of Abraham Bradley Jr., assistant postmaster general in the late eighteenth century, who obtained one of the earliest copyrights for a map in U.S. history.[34] Bradley obtained information from postmasters in various parts of the country, and it was their work—the fact that his map was based on new information rather than on previously published maps—that distinguished it from maps published before. Although Bradley obtained the information on which his map was based from government officials in connection with his official duties, he copyrighted it in his own name and published it privately, and evidently no one challenged his right to do so.

In some respects, Bradley was like the reporters of decisions, in that he was copyrighting a work produced during the course of his government employment, and he was even more of an "employee" (and less an "independent contractor") than they were. It may be that the Post Office concluded, just as the courts had, that allowing government employees to copyright their work would be most likely to ensure that the map would be published and distributed widely to those who might benefit from it. Although Bradley's chart became the official map of the U.S. Post Office around 1825, the nature of his understanding with the Post Office about ownership and use of the map is not known. Bradley had practiced law before his appointment to the Post Office Department, which may explain his interest in asserting his legal rights to the map. His legal experience is also likely to have given him greater sophistication in negotiating over copyright than most employee-authors had at that time.

Other sources suggest a similar phenomenon of employees who had access to government survey data using it to publish maps on their own account. According to a publication prepared by Rand McNally to celebrate a new edition of its road atlas in the 1980s, one of the earliest road atlases was published in 1789 by an engineer named Christopher Colles. Colles had done surveys of American roads during the Revolutionary War and also had access to road surveys prepared by others for General George Washington. The atlas he published, which evidently sold few copies, was a compilation of his own surveys and those prepared by others. The possibility that Colles was not entitled to claim the copyright to the atlas seems not to have occurred to anyone; if there was an agreement between him and the army regarding ownership of his surveys, it was nowhere mentioned in the records.

Other persons commissioned by the government to compile maps may also have claimed the copyright to them. The commander of the U.S. Army operations in Texas in 1849, General William Jenkins Worth, commissioned the Federal Indian Agent for Texas, Robert Simpson Neighbors, to determine whether troops could pass through Texas between the Pecos and El Paso. Neighbors recruited a former Texas Ranger, John Salmon "Rip" Ford, to accompany him. Both Ford and Neighbors prepared reports; Ford's report was incorporated into a pamphlet published in 1849 by a draftsman employed by the General Land Office named Robert Creuzbaur, who evidently sought to profit from sales of the pamphlet to the large number of people crossing Texas on their way to the California gold rush in 1849. The pamphlet was privately published in Austin and in New York in 1849.[35]

Although Bradley's and Colles's exploits suggest a principle of employee ownership, a few cases and an attorney general opinion from the 1850s suggest a different rule regarding maps prepared by government employees. An 1858 case concerning a map made by a cartographer who had gathered his materials either while conducting surveys in the employ of the commonwealth of Pennsylvania or while employed as a draftsman "of a party working at her cost" held that all rights to the map were the property of the state, as all the results of his labor while in the state's employ were state property.[36]

An 1856 opinion letter written by U.S. Attorney General Caleb Cushing to Jefferson Davis, then serving as secretary of war, concerned a man who had contracted with the government to engrave plates for a nautical chart, the original manuscript of which was the property of the United States. Cushing opined that the engraver had no right to make prints from the engravings: "The printer, who is hired to print any of the works of Irving, Prescott, or Bancroft, might, with as much sense and reason, claim a copyright in them against the author, as Seibert can set up such claim here against the United States."[37] But, unlike Bradley, he appeared to be copying an existing chart in a new medium rather than designing a new map from survey data; the different levels of originality in the mapmakers' work might, therefore, explain the result as much as their employment status.

A case decided in 1857, concerning a field related to cartography, suggests the likelihood that surveyors, engravers, and printers may have explicitly agreed that copyrights would be owned by the publisher. In *Heine v. Appleton*, an artist named William Heine accompanied an expedition to Japan and the China Sea commanded by Commodore Matthew Perry.[38] The U.S. government had funded the expedition, and Heine's drawings were included in the expedition report to the secretary of the navy, which was published by order of Congress. When Heine later sought to enjoin publication of books containing his illustrations from the expeditions, the court denied the injunction on two alternative grounds. First, the court found that Heine and Perry had expressly agreed that Heine's drawings would become the property of the U.S. government.[39] Second, the court found that, after the expedition, the defendants (publishers of the books) had paid Heine to modify several of the original drawings to make them suitable for inclusion in the books. At that time Heine had not claimed the copyright in the drawings. "It would be inequitable now to permit him, when he has been paid to aid in their publication and sale, and has thus aided in their publication, with a view to their sale, to stop their sale, even if he had a valid copyright in them."[40]

Heine cannot be read as an early work-for-hire case in the modern sense of works for hire. Neither of *Heine*'s alternative holdings recognizes that the employer would own the copyright to employee drawings simply by virtue of employment. First, the court explained that Heine was estopped from seeking an injunction against publication of drawings because he had been paid to modify them for publication and had failed to claim a copyright. Second, the court emphasized that Heine persuaded Commodore Perry to allow him to accompany the expedition only by expressly promising that the government would own his sketches and drawings. The opinion explained the negotiations with particular emphasis on Heine's express promise to give the government his drawings:

> Previous to the sailing of the expedition to Japan, the plaintiff applied [73] to Commodore Perry, to be employed as an artist, and to accompany the expedition, as such. . . . [F]inally the commodore consented to receive him in the capacity of a master's mate, on condition that he should sign the shipping articles as such master's mate, and do whatever duties might be required of him, and be subject to all the rules and regulations of the squadron. When the commodore consented that the plaintiff might join the expedition, he informed him that all the sketches and drawings which should be made by any one attached to the expedition were to be the exclusive property of the government of the United States, and that no one could appropriate to his own use any sketch or drawing that might be made. To this the plaintiff gave his assent. . . . Upon the return of the expedition to his country, the sketches and drawings which the plaintiff made, were, with his assent, incorporated in the report made by the commodore to the secretary of the navy, and were placed at the disposal of congress; . . . Under these circumstances, the plaintiff was not such author of the prints and engravings in question, as to be able to acquire an exclusive right to the same as author or proprietor, by virtue of the certificate of copyright which he obtained. The sketches and drawings were made for the government, to be at their disposal.

These negotiations were sufficient to divest Heine of his copyright. But only such an explicit promise to transfer a copyright was deemed adequate to the task.

THE EXAMPLES OF LAW PUBLISHING, theater, and cartography show that in antebellum America, the attribution of authorship and the ownership of copyright of works produced for commercial purposes depended on the nature of the work relationship and the creative process that occurred within it. Prior to the Civil War, no court recognized that an employer was entitled to copyright the works of its employees simply by virtue of the employment; indeed, courts assumed just the opposite. An English treatise on labor contracts, while discussing the right of the "master" to the products of the servant's labor, stated that a "person who employs and pays an author to write a drama or literary work, is not by virtue of the employment entitled to the exclusive right of representation or copyright, because the statutes vest such right in the author, and require the transfer of such a right to be in writing."[41] It took an express agreement to assign the copyright to the employer, as in *Heine v. Appleton*, to persuade a court to conclude that an employer owned the copyright. Yet when the arrangement to create a work for hire did not result in litigation, the pattern of copyright registrations suggests that employers did acquire works of their employees. The more likely that there were multiple creators, the more likely that copyright could be claimed by the coordinator of the creative effort rather than by one or more of the contributors. Had more of the cases that ended up in litigation involved a collaborative creative process, courts might have crafted a default rule of employer ownership at least in some cases involving the employment of creative people. But that did not happen, and an individualist model of authorship prevailed in the courts. Later in the century, when more cases involving collaborative creative processes in the workplace were litigated, courts struggled to decide whether these early precedents, which clearly articulated a rule of employee ownership, were distinguishable. The more the courts saw cases in which a number of people had contributed to the work, the more logical it was to accord the copyright to the representative of the collective—that is, the employer.

Cases involving individual authors working alone (although in the employ of another) continued to dominate the field of employee-employer copyright litigation throughout the nineteenth century, which led courts to persist in imagining authorship as individual and employees as owners of their works, absent a contrary agreement. In addition, cases reflected the elevated social status and independence of the "employees" who created the work, the judges' assumptions about the nature of the creative process, instrumental concerns about facilitating book distribution, and the powerful rhetoric of authorship as highly personal intellectual labor.

FREE LABOR, FREE ENTERPRISE, AND THE FREEDOM TO CONTRACT OVER INNOVATION, 1860–1895

In the years bracketing the Civil War, much changed in American law and society. The agrarian republic imagined by Jefferson disappeared with early industrialization and the rise of commerce in the North. The "market revolution" that began in the Jacksonian era—the growth of commerce within the settled East and the expansion of commerce into the fast-growing West—opened up new opportunities for entrepreneurship through inventing, manufacturing, and selling. Factory production developed, first in textiles and armaments in New England, and then in clocks and other goods. The construction of roads, canals, and railroads opened up new possibilities for commerce and the extraction and processing of raw materials, including iron, lumber, and all sorts of minerals. In 1860, the United States trailed Great Britain, France, and Germany in industrial output, but by 1900 American industrial production exceeded that of these three countries combined. In those four decades, freedom in the economic sense shifted from the freedom of the yeoman farmers to work their lands to the freedom of white men to use their energy, ingenuity, and knowledge to make their way, and maybe their fortune, in the expanding markets.[1]

As the early stages of industrialization transformed the landscape and lifestyle of the eastern United States on the eve of the Civil War, leading thinkers contemplated the social significance of invention and what it portended for the future of the American people. One of the most widely quoted of such assessments is Abraham Lincoln's. In a pair of speeches delivered in 1858 and 1859, Lincoln, himself a patentee,[2] suggested that invention and innovation generally and patents in particular represented a distinguishing feature of American society. As a lawyer, Lincoln put particular emphasis on the significance of patent laws; patents, he said, add "the fuel of interest to the fire of genius." In modern terms, his argument was that the prospect of financial gain promised by intellectual property rights spurs hard work and creativity. That strictly utilitarian characterization of Lincoln's meaning does not do justice to the subtlety of his thought. Without any obvious purpose of defending a particular legal regime of patents, Lincoln expounded generally upon a link between free labor, freedom of thought, protection for inventions and discoveries, and political freedom. While Lincoln himself may not have had any law reform in mind relative to patent laws, his connection between free labor, protection for inventors, and political freedom was not merely salient in the tense years before the Civil War; it was a constant undercurrent in the American law of workplace knowledge for much of the nineteenth century.

The first speech, which Lincoln delivered in April 1858 to the Young Men's Association of Bloomington, Illinois, drew the connection between the human soul and the human propensity for discovery and invention.[3] Beginning with the statement that "[a]ll creation is a mine, and every man, a miner," Lincoln elaborated on the notion that the world was God's gift to humankind for its use. The theme of the lecture was a link between divinity and creativity—Adam's "first important discovery was the fact that he was naked; and his first invention was the fig-leaf apron." Creation, as in the world, is there for creation, as in human use. The God-given distinction between humans and animals, Lincoln said, is creativity: "[M]an is not the only animal who labors; but he is the only one who *improves* his workmanship. This improvement, he effects by *Discoveries*, and *Inventions*." Lincoln associated labor, creativity, discovery, and invention with a sacred connection between the human and the divine.

In the second lecture, delivered the following year, Lincoln shifted his focus from the link between invention and divinity to the link between invention and the use and conquest of nature, particularly by the young.[4] Invention and discovery were a habit of youth and youthful countries, especially "Young America." The discovery and conquest of new lands, like the discovery and conquest of new ideas, Lincoln said, were the pursuits of youth. Young America, Lincoln said, with a note of humor tinged by irony,

> is very anxious to fight for the liberation of enslaved nations and colonies, provided, always, they *have* land, and have *not* any liking for his interference. As to those who have no land, and would be glad of help

from any quarter, he considers *they* can afford to wait a few hundred years longer. In knowledge he is particularly rich. He knows all that can possibly be known; inclines to believe in spiritual rappings, and is the unquestioned inventor of *"Manifest Destiny."* His horror is for all that is old, particularly "Old Fogy"; and if there be any thing old which he can endure, it is only old whiskey and old tobacco.

Old Fogy was the Old World—not merely Europe, but any old society. "The great difference between Young America and Old Fogy, is the result of *Discoveries, Inventions* and *Improvements."* The expansiveness of Young America, both in its territorial ambitions and in its desire to use land, were linked in Lincoln's speech with a legal regime that rewarded those who reduced land and ideas to private property and for personal profit. After cataloging some of the most significant of the inventions to the progress of the world, Lincoln summed up the most valuable inventions in the world's history "on account of their great efficiency in facilitating all other inventions and discoveries. Of these were the arts of writing and of printing—the discovery of America, and the introduction of Patent-laws." Thus he articulated the antebellum vision of the importance of invention and creativity to the betterment of America, and the intimate connection between freedom, invention, legal protection for both, and the necessity of both freedom and creativity to economic development. He said: "In anciently inhabited countries, the dust of ages—a real downright old-fogyism—seems to settle upon, and smother the intellects and energies of man." But in America, he proclaimed, we had broken the "shackles" of the "slavery of mind" and had established a "habit of freedom of thought" that was necessary to the "discovery and production of new and useful things." The patent law nourished this habit of free thought by allowing the ingenious to profit; it added, in his famous formulation, "the fuel of *interest* to the *fire* of genius."

Lincoln's quotable phrase, and the speech from which it originates, encapsulates several of the dominant strands of antebellum thought, highlighting connections between them that have been undeservedly overlooked. There is, first, novelty. America is not one of those dusty, old, anciently habited countries; it is a new and newly inhabited (or at least newly civilized) country where all is possible. In America, ideas are fresh and effervescent. And, of course, a new country will produce new ideas. Novelty—a legal requirement to obtain a patent (along with utility and nonobviousness)—is valuable in its own right, and it is necessary for economic development.

But novelty is not all. There must also be "freedom of thought" and, quite literally, freedom of work. In 1859, as for several decades before, everything could be seen through the prism of anti-slavery ideology. Not only did slavery shackle people; it shackled labor and product markets, agriculture, manufacturing, and even, Lincoln argued, inventiveness. Slavery had been

defended as part of an ancient and venerable southern tradition; Lincoln dismissed tradition, and traditional ways of thinking, as a "slavery of mind." Free labor was necessary to freedom of thought. Finally, Lincoln drew the connection between freedom of thought, technological progress, economic development, and what in the nineteenth century was known as "enterprise." Enterprise meant something akin to what today we think of as entrepreneurship. Lincoln chose the metaphor of fueling a fire, but he might also have chosen another common patent metaphor, related to cultivation: invention and discovery occur when ingenuity and genius find the fertile soil of freedom in which to blossom, but they benefit from the fertilizer of "interest." Interest—the opportunity to profit financially or through reputation—would spur creativity and hard work. This, too, was part of the stock anti-slavery ideology. Workers worked better and the economy grew faster if the workers stood to profit from their work and their commitment.

Lincoln was doing more than praising invention in the terms of the dominant ideology of the day, and he was doing more than using a discussion of invention and scientific progress as a convenient place to take a dig at slavery (although he was certainly doing both of those things). He was attempting a sociological explanation of the conditions necessary "for the discovery and production of new and useful things." Free thought, free labor, and free enterprise were the foundations of technological progress. And, Lincoln suggested, they were necessary to each other as well. Lincoln knew it, and so did most antebellum judges. Free labor ideology, grounded in a general faith in free thought (the antebellum version of today's "ideas want to be free" attack on excessive intellectual property restrictions), shaped every aspect of intellectual property law and the question of control of workplace knowledge throughout the middle third of the nineteenth century.

AFTER THE CIVIL WAR, law began to play a new role in mediating the relationship between free labor and the kind of freedom that would generate innovation. Law was to promote freedom by protecting freedom of contract. In the latter half of the nineteenth century, contract became—at least in the language of the law—an organizing principle of as many social relationships as could be shoehorned into its framework of privately negotiated social relations. While lawyers today assume that the employment relationship is a contract, and that most terms of employment (aside from minimum wages and prohibitions on status discrimination and certain unfair dismissals) should be and are negotiated by the parties, employment was not always regarded as contractual. Employment in the early days of American government was a status relationship much like marriage and parenthood are today, with the terms of the relationship dictated by law and policy. Blackstone's influential *Commentaries* in the late eighteenth century dealt with contract only briefly and examined social relations, including master-servant and work relations, through the preexisting frameworks of status and property. But by the late nineteenth century, contract concepts had come to dominate huge areas of American law, including the relation of employment.[5] Contract became the great organizing principle of the ascendant legal ideology of free labor in a free market.

Contract concepts gained a particularly strong foothold in the area of employment. Courts found contracts, especially implied contracts, everywhere in the employment relationship. The stable regime of mutual obligation that had characterized pre-industrial employment relations gave way to a contractarian regime that eliminated employer obligation while yet enforcing dependence and subservience on employees under the guise of formal equality. All sorts of employer rights were inferred from the fact of employment as courts began to find a plethora of terms favorable to management implied in every employment contract, including the right to fire at will and rights to employee ideas and inventions. Particularly in the area of ownership of knowledge and creative products, contract law facilitated and legitimated a massive transfer of autonomy from creative workers to their employers. Contract had substantial ideological advantages as a form of discourse in the employment relationship. Contract allowed courts to leave the default rules untouched, to increase the employer's rights over employee inventions, and, most significant, to make this shift in ownership of ideas appear to be the product of free choice and arms-length negotiation.[6]

Of course, employment had always been contractual in some senses. Entry into the relationship was by contract, and some obligations, including those related to training and the use of secret knowledge, were at least partly determined by contract. Prior to the nineteenth century, however, many employment obligations were prescribed by the law and custom defining the status of master and servant or master, journeyman, and apprentice. What was new in the late nineteenth century was not that law prescribed certain obligations in the work relationship. Rather, the novelty was that law defined those obligations as contractual.

Contract had of course been a significant feature of judicial analysis of labor and employment cases in the antebellum period. Massachusetts chief justice Lemuel Shaw's famous opinion in *Farwell v. Boston & Worcester Railroad* in 1842 insisted that liability of an employer to its employees for injuries sustained in the course of employment "may be regulated by the express or implied contract between them, and which, in contemplation of law, must be presumed to be thus regulated." Shaw also argued that when no express agreement existed, "it is competent for courts of justice to regard considerations of policy and general convenience, and to draw from them such rules as will, in their practical application, best promote the safety and security of all parties concerned. This is, in truth, the basis on which implied promises are raised."[7] Shaw's vision of common law relations was influential in a general way—Oliver Wendell Holmes Jr., among other judges, was a great admirer—even if not in the specifics of workplace knowledge cases. There is no evidence that judges, grappling with the question of whether an employment contract should be presumed to transfer ownership to intellectual property rights, were inspired by Shaw's presumption that an employment contract shifted the risk of workplace injury to employees, as the patent and copyright cases did not cite *Farwell*. But it is entirely possible that judges embraced the general idea that all obligations of employment should be deemed in law to be allocated by the parties' agreement. Just as Shaw imagined the employment contract to allocate the risk of injury to employees, judges could imagine the employment contract to allocate to employers the rewards of invention, and in both cases the judges might have assumed that the wages paid were compensation for the costs incurred by employees. Echoes of Shaw's generative conception of employment as entirely contractual, and of the duty and freedom of judges to imagine all rights and obligations between employer and employee as deriving from "considerations of policy and general convenience"—which is to say implied contract—can be heard in a wide array of cases after the Civil War.

The law of contract was embraced by postbellum judges and treatise authors as a vehicle to effectuate the wishes of private persons regarding their business dealings. Thus law would liberate the productive energies of society, even in property ownership and employment relationships, which had not previously been defined primarily in contractual terms.[8] The idea that democracy would be advanced if legally prescribed obligations were replaced by "freely" negotiated ones—that status should give way to contract—was both influentially and cogently stated by John Chipman Gray with respect to privacy rights in his treatise on restraints on the alienation of property. "The process of civilization consists in the courts endeavoring more and more to carry out the intentions of the parties."[9] Contract was the legal vehicle to carry out the intentions of the parties as the courts imagined them. A core tenet of the late nineteenth-century regime of laissez-faire contract was that there should be few restraints on what parties might wish to achieve through their contracts. Courts, Gray said, should restrain them "only by rules which have their reason for existence in considerations of public policy."[10] The [81] vision of public policy that had been the chief justification for employee control of workplace knowledge came under attack. Elisha Greenhood, a proponent of the view that contract rather than legislatively imposed rules ought to govern private relations, argued in his influential treatise *The Doctrine of Public Policy in the Law of Contracts, Reduced to Rules* (1886) that the "capacity of an individual to produce constitutes his value to the public." While the product of a worker "belongs immediately to him who employs him," Greenhood said, it belongs "mediately to the State, and goes to swell the aggregate of public wealth."[11] In other words, the law of contract should protect the ability of the individual to produce and the right of the employer to own the product.

Contract emerged in the 1870s as a unified body of law with the particular purpose of facilitating the formation of productive exchanges that would enrich the parties to the contract and, therefore, society as a whole. The development of laissez-faire contract, and its particularly enthusiastic embrace by judges confronting employment cases, was the dominant feature of the intellectual landscape of the late nineteenth-century law of the workplace. The rise of a scientific view of law and highly formalist approach to contracts, especially in the areas of master-servant, intellectual property, and equity, changed the perspective of judges and legal treatises on the employment relationship. Employment was a contract whose terms were determined by the employer and freely accepted by the employee.

While the primacy of contract as an agreement between people was celebrated in general terms, in particular terms the employment contract that was actually enforced was an "objective" one whose terms were supplied, as often as not, by judges rather than the parties themselves. An objective contract provided uniformity and predictability to legal arrangements, freeing them from the uncertainty of jury determinations about the actual intent of the parties.[12] Once courts embraced the notion that idea ownership was governed by contract, and accepted the objective theory of contract under which courts could imply contract terms, as Holmes said in *The Path of the Law* in 1897, "because of some belief as to the practice of the community or of a class, or because of some opinion as to policy," it was a relatively simple process to determine that the implied contract allocated most rights to the employer.[13] Across the spectrum of the law of the workplace—most notably the rights to fire without cause, to prevent employees from joining unions, and to control workplace knowledge and intellectual property—courts used the legal fiction of implied contract to shift rights from employees to firms.

The law had always prescribed some terms of employment; calling them implied contract terms simply affixed a new label to an old phenomenon. But the new label was significant, as it suggested equality and free assent, rather than hierarchy and imposition. More important, the rights and obligations that were implied changed as courts adapted their vision of an employee's proper duties to the factory model. As courts became aware of the value of employee knowledge to firms, they sought an expanded role for the law in facilitating economic development by allocating rights in that knowledge. As the persuasive force of status-based obligations of confidentiality associated with the notion of honor and the traditional incidents of craft work disappeared, contract law provided an alternative foundation for the employee's obligation of secrecy and a justification for employer control of workplace knowledge. Contract rhetoric also suggested that employees voluntarily assumed and were compensated for whatever loss of mobility they suffered when the new law of trade secrets and pre-invention patent assignment agreements prevented competitive employment. When the popularity of Frederick Winslow Taylor's scientific management made rationalization and corporate control of every detail of employment and production seem imperative, contract provided the most powerful legitimating discourse for the significant loss of workplace autonomy that Taylorism entailed.[14]

In sum, during the latter half of the nineteenth century, a muscular new law of contract redefined the obligations of the employment relation for skilled craft workers. As the growing manufacturing firms sought ways to wrest control of the production process from their skilled workers and to expand their market power through control of patents, their lawyers found a sympathetic ear in judges who considered employee control of workplace knowledge "a reprehensible practice," as one put it,[15] or not a "good custom," as said by another.[16]

Liberty of contract discourse enabled courts to reconcile the emerging hierarchical control and loss of entrepreneurial opportunity entailed in the managerialism of factory and office work with the free labor ideology that had long dominated American thinking on the subject of labor. As Charles McCurdy observed, the roots of the liberty of contract discourse that dominated laissez faire–era labor cases may be found in the free labor ideology that suffused political and legal discourse during Reconstruction.[17] There must have been a certain cognitive dissonance facing judges who believed in free labor and yet found themselves enforcing draconian noncompete agreements, effectively restraining craft workers from working for others by preventing them from using their knowledge, and ruling that creative employees had lost the right to dispose of their patented works. Believing that workers had freely contracted for employment on these terms helped remove the dissonance.

Eventually, critics like Roscoe Pound gained traction with the argument that the freedom of contract doctrine rested on a notion of equal rights between employer and employee that was a "fallacy to everyone acquainted at first hand with actual industrial conditions." But the realist criticism of laissez-faire formalism did not surface in elite circles until after the turn of the twentieth century.[18] In making every resource a commodity that could be bought and sold, contract law did not necessarily liberate people who found themselves constrained by economic necessity to sell their land, labor, or personal property at times or on terms that felt brutal, unfair, or humiliating. Moreover, law prescribed many terms of employment, and penal sanctions were occasionally imposed to enforce prescribed contract terms against poor or vulnerable workers.[19] The notions of exchange and consent that underlay contractarian legal reasoning of the late nineteenth century tapped into the remnants of the free labor ideology and legitimated, when it failed to obscure, the harsher aspects of laissez-faire contractual legal rules as applied to the emerging class of poorly paid factory and clerical workers.

Master-servant treatises and treatises on intellectual property approached the question of employee-generated intellectual property in distinct ways. Each type of treatise tried to assimilate the phenomenon into categories that were intelligible according to the organizing structure of that field of law. While patent and copyright treatises regarded employee inventions and copyrights as an adjunct of ownership, dealing with the topic briefly and as a special case and generally according employees significant rights over products of their creativity, master-servant treatises treated intellectual property like all other products of employee work, tending to allocate to employers broad rights over intellectual as well as material work product. The potential of master-servant treatises thus to expand employer rights was tempered by the fact that they gave intellectual property short shrift, as the significance of the issue was not apparent to many authors even fairly late in the nineteenth century.[20]

Contract concepts were eagerly embraced by treatise writers seeking to rationalize all employment obligations, and courts and treatise authors used an objective theory of contract to divorce rights and obligations from the particulars of a contracting party's status (e.g., sales agent, household servant, mechanic) in favor of a generalized notion of servant applicable to all who worked for others.[21] Wood's *Treatise on the Law of Master and Servant*, for example, described the employee's duty to maintain the employer's secrets as a species of express or implied contract applicable to all "servants," not just those in traditionally confidential relationships, even before that proposition was clear in the case law.[22] Wood also listed the employee's failure to protect his employer's secrets as grounds for discharge because it was "a breach of an implied condition of the contract."[23] Wood's statement of the law did not actually find solid support in the cases until some years after the treatise was first published in 1877, as the basis for confidentiality was still grounded fairly clearly either in express contract or in defined confidential relationships, such as "attorneys, agents, or in other confidential relations."[24] Wood's habit of generalizing about *all* employment relations based on cases describing the customary duties of a particular relationship—a typical generalizing tendency of nineteenth-century treatise authors—was the mechanism by which the new implied contract of employment came to encompass a duty to guard the secrets of the trade. Through this process of abstraction and generalization, workplace secrets were assumed to be the employer's property rather than, as earlier cases had held and skilled labor still insisted, the employee's "stock in trade."

Intellectual property treatises made a similar move in adopting contract concepts to create a default rule of employer ownership, but were more ambiguous in doing so. Eaton Drone's influential 1879 *Treatise on the Law of Property in Intellectual Productions in Great Britain and the United States*, for example, could be and was read to support three contradictory propositions: a default rule of employee ownership of intellectual property rights; a default rule of employer ownership; and a rule that ownership should be assessed in each case from the express or implied agreement of the parties. The treatise began its analysis of employee ownership of copyrights with the uncontroversial proposition that a "literary production is primarily the property of the author who has created it." Drone then struggled to assimilate conventional individualist notions of authorship into a situation of collective creation. "When a person has conceived the design of a work, and has employed others to execute it, the creation of the work may be so far due to his mind as to make him the author." But, cautioned Drone, "he is not an author who 'merely suggests the subject, and has no share in the design or execution of the work.'"[25] Yet, "[t]he produce of labor may become the property of him who has employed and paid the laborer. Literary labor is no exception to this universal rule. When an author is employed on condition that what he produces shall belong to the employer, the absolute property in such production vests in the employer by virtue of such employment and by operation of law." In 1879, when Drone's treatise was published, there were no cases to support this assertion and the treatise cited none. As Drone conceded a few pages later, this time citing a case, employees who litigated retained ownership of their copyrights, absent a clear contractual promise to assign the copyright. "The mere fact of employment does not make the [85] employer the absolute owner of the literary property created by the person employed. Where there is no agreement or *implied understanding* that what is produced shall belong to the employer, it is clear that the latter acquires no title to the copyright." So the treatise compromised between what the author evidently considered the rational view (employer ownership) with the antiquated position of the cases (employee ownership) by simply saying the law was unsettled: "Whether a complete legal title to the copyright will vest *ab initio* in such employer without the necessity of a written assignment, is a point on which the law has not been expressly declared by the courts of law."[26]

As we will see, at the turn of the twentieth century courts of law began to declare exactly that.

3

If These Mill Owners Desire to Cripple a Man's Enterprise & His Energy & Intelligence, They Must Contract to That Effect

By 1860, industrialization had transformed England and was making serious headway in the United States. The transformation was both material and cultural. The Crystal Palace Exhibition of 1851 showed the British public, and the many visitors and exhibitors from America, the marvels of modern technology that would affect every aspect of modern life, but especially work. The displays featured not only the genius of great inventors but also the accomplishments of firms. It offered the public a way to associate innovation with companies rather than just with individual inventors. And the complexity of the technology exhibited drove home the idea that many modern inventions could not have been the work of one person alone. The contrast between the displays of painting, sculpture, and the other fine arts and the displays of steam engines and other mechanical marvels also served as a striking illustration of the difference between individual and collective invention. It began to be imaginable that technological development involved collective invention, whereas cultural creations still seemed to emanate from individual genius.

As the economy industrialized, more people—including inventors and authors—worked as employees of others. Once the small factories and workshops turned from war production to other enterprises, the question of who would own technological advances became quite pressing. Consequently, the 1860s and 1870s were a watershed for legal doctrines concerning workplace knowledge about technology. Courts decided major cases having to do with the kind of knowledge that was neither patented nor copyrighted but had major significance for the control of technology. In the late 1860s, a court in Massachusetts invented a new cause of action against an employee for misappropriation of trade secrets. Courts in Pennsylvania and Massachusetts explored the use of agreements not to compete as a legal device to protect manufacturing techniques. These legal changes represented an important break with the past and began a fundamental rethinking of the nature and ownership of workplace knowledge. In the late 1880s, the pace of change accelerated in favor of corporate control. After examining the importance of a particular vision of entrepreneurship to the law governing skilled white workers in the early postbellum years, this chapter describes the changes in the law regarding employee trade secrets and noncompetition agreements and examines what it meant for craft workers in a number of industries.

Entrepreneurship, Technology, and the
Law of the Workplace in the 1860s

In 1837, the Supreme Court articulated a vision of the value of competition and the desirability of encouraging new enterprise even at the expense of existing rights in the *Charles River Bridge Case*. Although the case had nothing to do with labor law—the issue was whether to protect the monopoly enjoyed by the promoters of a bridge or to allow the Massachusetts legislature to charter a competing bridge—the Court's approach to economic policy was influential in areas far removed from the issue in the case.[1] Entrepreneurship was to trump stability, and the economic, legal, and social culture of American white male work and commerce embraced the entrepreneurial spirit. The independence of the skilled worker that courts touted was the freedom to use knowledge entrepreneurially, not the freedom promoted by maintenance of artisan relations of the founding era. Courts embraced a new role for property in facilitating commerce.[2] The imagination of lawyers began to include all sorts of intangibles as valuable and important forms of property, alongside land and buildings that had previously been regarded as the property upon which civic strength was built. Once property encompassed the intangible and the commercial, it was a short step to seeing workplace knowledge, ideas, and inventions as the kind of property that could be, and should be, sold in commerce.

The established tradition in the workplace, which was reflected in law, was that each free man controlled his own labor and owned the fruits of his labor except to the extent that he had contracted away both the labor and the results thereof. For example, in *Barnes v. Ingalls* (1863), the Alabama Supreme Court declined to find that an ordinary employment contract meant that all work done during the term of the employment must have been done on the employer's behalf. The case thus recognized the right of employees to work for themselves except during the hours they had agreed to work for another or on the projects they had agreed to complete for hire.[3] Both the law and the shortage of skilled labor meant that there was still plenty of room for employees to claim the right to use their knowledge as well as their nonworking time to advance their own interests.

Inventive and entrepreneurial workers made the most of the absence of known legal restrictions on their use of their talent. Even after the British lifted prohibitions on the emigration of artisans in 1824 and relaxed the prohibitions on the export of machinery in 1842, it remained difficult to find a supply of appropriately skilled labor sufficient to meet the demand.[4] Engineering education expanded to meet the growing need. The Rensselaer Polytechnic Institute was among the first institutions to establish an engineering curriculum in 1825, followed by a number of other colleges. In 1861 the Massachusetts Institute of Technology opened a school of "industrial science" that aimed to provide a "complete course of instruction and training, suited to the various practical professions."[5] Many individuals and firms eagerly shared their knowledge and technology and tirelessly participated in networks of learning, and certain sectors of the economy flourished precisely because employers and skilled craftsmen freely shared information about the latest techniques.[6]

Skilled workers and practical men of learning also participated in societies that were important institutions in the dissemination of technical knowledge. Then as now, some firms considered it advantageous to have free access to the technical improvements devised by others, even at the expense of losing a monopoly on some of their own. Also, some firms wanted to advertise to their customers their own technological superiority. The widespread practice of sharing technological advances documented in publications, in societies, in trade schools, and in periodic expositions suggests that many companies preferred to publicize their technological advances (probably relying on patents to protect their monopoly) rather than to guard them as secrets.

Entire publications were dedicated to the dissemination of technological advances. Magazines such as *Practical Machinist*, *American Machinist*, and *Scientific American* popularized the wonders of the early industrial age by publishing detailed drawings and chemical formulae along with descriptions of machinery, factories, and processes. *Scientific American*, which was established as a weekly journal in 1845, brought to the attention of a large readership of inventors and mechanics a wide range of scientific information that the magazine's editors believed would be helpful to their work. *American*

Machinist often published articles focused on the technicalities and perils of the patent application process. *Practical Machinist* ran regular columns on patent law and occasional columns on other relevant legal issues, including termination of employment contracts, the law of unjust dismissal of employees with stated term contracts, enticement of employees with stated term contracts, and a discussion of the developing law of patents when the patentee had employed "a servant" to assist in the development of the invention.[7] Its editors aimed to inform the readership of the relevant law both with respect to work relations and with respect to protecting economically valuable technology. The focus was entirely on the termination of employment contracts on the one hand and patent rights on the other. The connection between the emerging law of master and servant and the need to protect intellectual property was not discussed.

In the 1860s disputes over workplace knowledge often centered on control of drawings of machines. It was impossible to prevent skilled machinists from switching jobs and taking along their know-how—what today is called tacit knowledge—but it was possible to prevent them from taking detailed drawings with them. The efforts of a leading Philadelphia machine tool firm, which had been founded by a machinist trained in New England textile firms, illustrates how the firm's proprietor, William Sellers, maintained control over the knowledge of the engineers and draftsmen whom the firm employed without making their subordination so apparent that they would no longer exert themselves. The Sellers firm in Philadelphia used a drawing office staffed by a cadre of trained engineers and draftsmen to manage innovation and control quality, a common business strategy before the widespread adoption of corporate research facilities. Beginning in the 1850s, the firm claimed authorship of all mechanical drawings produced by employees of the firm. The claim was made in the legend on each drawing; each legend included a drawing title, a draftsman's name, and the date of completion of the drawing. The typical format of the signature, "William Sellers & Co. per Theodore Berger," credits authorship to the firm, using attribution to establish the drawing as firm property, while also giving individual credit (and responsibility for errors) to the draftsman.[8]

The firm claimed credit to advertise its "endowments of technical knowledge." The firm's senior partner "would not let individual employees presume any ownership rights to those endowments, especially in the case of employees who contributed to that pool with ideas they developed in their plans." William Sellers the person and William Sellers the firm were thus to be merged in the eyes of the customers such that the talents of Sellers the man were supplemented by those of the firm's employees. It is no longer possible to distinguish the contributions of William Sellers himself from those of the firm's employees. Sellers filed a number of patents during that time, which suggests his involvement, but the patent record shows his signature on none of the surviving plans. It was important to the firm that the [91] draftsmen not see themselves as "mere subordinate agents in a hierarchical organization" because the firm needed them to exercise judgment and creativity. Accordingly, draftsmen were allowed "a substantial measure of autonomy." They could "compose all the elements of their plans, selecting which views (plan, elevation, and sectional) were necessary to delineate form and function adequately. They were free to place those views as it suited them. Their legend placements also show no consistency, an issue that may appear inconsequential, but is suggestive of some larger issues."[9] The larger issues had to do with the delicate balance between encouraging individual creativity to maximize innovation while maintaining control, imposing uniform standards, and protecting the firm's claim to ownership (by virtue of its authorship) of its drawings.

How should one characterize the power structure revealed by the legends on these mechanical drawings? One common way was by analogy to the fine arts. Sellers "used the drawing room as a design studio, analogous to the studio of a leading artist whose commercial success had outstripped a single person's capacity to execute the work."[10] Corporate ownership of blueprints is analogized to the studio practices of the great Baroque or Renaissance painters: the master (here the firm) puts his name on each work, but we all know that much of the painting is the work of the students in his school or *atelier*. The legitimacy of the corporate authorship is asserted by the analogy to a great artist; the reader is led to believe that the firm, like the great artist, is responsible for the overall creative vision and the genius of the product. In this story, the firm itself contributes genius and creativity, rather like an artist composing a painting and doing the difficult bits but leaving to students the task of filling in the background.

Beautiful, clever, and accurate mechanical drawings reflected well on a firm if they were disseminated, but their dissemination created problems too. The practice of sharing information sometimes collided with the desire of some firms to obtain comparative advantage through secrecy. In 1866, the English magazine *Engineering*, which like *Scientific American* published technical and scientific articles of interest to the growing sector of engineers and educated machinists, published mechanical drawings of a "floating workshop." The publication sparked a dispute between the draftsman who submitted the drawings for publication and the firm that previously employed him and claimed ownership of the drawings. The editor of the magazine then published an essay musing on the propriety of draftsmen keeping copies of drawings they did at work:

> Even to privately copy and thus carry away any drawing is regarded, in most offices, as a species of larceny, punishable by at least a certain withdrawal of confidence, if not by reprimand or even dismissal. That most clever draughtsmen habitually make and secrete sketches for all, or nearly all, they do or see done in the range of their employment is, of course, known to every one, although employers must affect not to know it, in order that they may the more severely visit their indignation upon the offending culprit when once they catch him at it.[11]

The editors then explained that they believed when the magazine published the drawings that the draftsman "[h]ad designed the floating shops . . . on his own account; at least, out of office hours at whatever establishment he might have been engaged. We should not otherwise have received them for publication at all, nor shall we knowingly ever allow our columns to be turned to account in this manner." Finally, the magazine editors noted the "moral reason" why draftsmen should not claim authorship of drawings made for their employers: "Had anything gone wrong with either design" the firm, "and not their draughtsman-designer, would have borne the whole responsibility." Credit for the creativity should be linked to responsibility for failure.

A subsequent issue of *Engineering Magazine* printed a list of "rules and conditions under which all draughtsmen are employed" by a new firm of ironworks. Among the rules for hours of work and procedures for work was the following: "All draughtsmen before being employed by J. and H. Gwynne must sign a paper that they will not copy or make use of any drawing, tracing, estimate, or calculation, the property of the firm, or make sketches of any machinery in the works, except for the benefit of the firm, without having first obtained the written consent of one of the principals." In addition, the rules specified that "[a]ll notes, drawings, memoranda, &c., made during working hours must be considered the property of the firm, and must not be removed from the offices without permission."[12]

The Advent of Noncompetition Agreements in the 1870s

The Pennsylvania Supreme Court's 1866 decision in *Keeler v. Taylor* was the first American case to consider whether covenants not to compete could legitimately be used to protect employers' rights in knowledge and information possessed by former employees. The court rejected the employer's effort. *Keeler* involved a "mechanic" who had agreed, in consideration for the nominal sum of one dollar plus training in the manufacture of platform scales, never to make platform scales for anyone else or to convey the information he learned to anyone else. The mechanic agreed that he would pay his former employer $50 for any scales made in violation of the agreement. [93] He worked for the plaintiff for seven years and then set up for himself in the manufacture of scales. Under the norms of the artisanal relationship, the mechanic would have been free to leave at the end of the customary seven-year apprenticeship and to take his knowledge and skill with him. The employer, however, chose to litigate to repudiate the old way of doing things.[13]

The court held the agreement unenforceable because it "restrained the industry of the defendant, not in a particular locality, but everywhere, not for a specified period, but for a lifetime. . . ." The contract was also objectionable because it levied "a tax or duty" upon "the industry of all who may derive their information from" the employee. The employer had no entitlement to monopolize the method because he was neither the inventor nor the patentee of the scales, but simply had taught his employee "his handicraft." Finally, the court concluded that an equity court should "regard the hardship of the bargain, and the prejudice to the public." Although the court did not press the point, the employee must have argued that the contract lacked consideration: Why would anyone regard training in the manufacture of platform scales as valuable if the knowledge could not be used elsewhere? Implicit in the court's reasoning is that, in the absence of a patent, an employer could not restrain his employees' subsequent use of the knowledge of the trade they had learned, just as master craftsmen could not restrain their apprentices from setting up for themselves once they had learned the trade and completed the term of apprenticeship.

In 1869, the Massachusetts Supreme Court became the first state to report a decision on a post-employment restraint on soliciting customers. The court enforced the noncompetition agreement but limited the reach of its rule. Morse Twist Drill Company was formed in order to manufacture and sell a twist drill that the company's founder had invented, but for which he had assigned the patent to the firm. When the founder sold the company, moved to another state, and began soliciting his old firm's customers, the court enjoined him on the ground that the competition effectively appropriated "a part of that which he has sold to the plaintiffs."[14] *Morse Twist Drill & Machine Co. v. Morse* did not squarely establish that such covenants would routinely be enforced, for the case was more akin to a sale of business than a simple employment relationship, but it did open the door to use of noncompete agreements.

Both *Keeler* and *Morse Twist Drill* used the existence of a patent as marking out the boundaries of knowledge that employees could be enjoined from using. To the extent that Morse was enjoined from soliciting customers, it was because he was trying to sell the same thing to new people after he had already sold his patent rights and business. By and large, employees remained free to use all knowledge acquired during the course of their employment.

The Advent of Trade Secrets

The Massachusetts Supreme Court in the year before its 1869 restrictive covenant decision in *Morse* became the first American court to articulate a duty of employees who were neither apprentices nor traditionally in a relationship of confidence (like a household or an attorney) to guard secrets. In the influential 1868 decision of *Peabody v. Norfolk*,[15] the defendant machinist had been employed as an engineer in the plaintiff's factory, which manufactured gunny cloth from jute. Norfolk had agreed in writing not to reveal information about machinery used there. Upon allegations that Norfolk had quit Peabody's employment and aided others in constructing a factory with machines like Peabody's (and had provided them copies of the original drawings of Peabody's machines), the court enjoined Norfolk from revealing the secrets to those with whom he was involved in building the other factory.

The potential importance and evident novelty of the case was not even hinted at in the pleadings. Obviously, it was not in Peabody's interest to note that the relief sought was unprecedented, nor would a lawyer in that era likely think it his role to advocate major change. So, Peabody's lawyer adopted the rhetorical strategy of making the claim seem so obvious as to be a matter of common sense. In the bill of complaint, he portrayed his client as a small-time entrepreneur-inventor who had begun by conducting "experiments" to develop the machinery on his farm and had employed Norfolk as a machinist to assist "in originating, inventing, adapting, and perfecting" the machinery.[16] When the trials of the machinery were successful, Peabody employed Norfolk to aid in the construction of a factory that would house the equipment and manufacture gunny cloth on a larger scale. Although the pleadings emphasized the misappropriation of the drawings themselves, Peabody sought and received an injunction requiring Norfolk to return the drawings and to refrain "from communicating . . . any knowledge of the said machinery or of the models and plans of the same," from "building any such machinery for any other person or persons," from "communicating said secret process of manufacturing Jute cloth from Jute butts as aforesaid," and "from using said process in company with any other person or persons or by himself."

Norfolk's new employer, James Cook, demurred to the bill. In his brief in support of the demurrer, Cook contended that the promise was void as a re-straint of trade because it "restrains him from ever using during his life at any time or place the skill acquired in this employment." He also argued that the machinery's design and operations were not secret because all who worked in or visited the factory could observe the machinery in operation.[17]

Given that Norfolk had copied drawings of the machines, *Peabody* cannot be read as stating a rule prohibiting employees from using general knowledge of machine design. Further, Justice Gray's statement of the case emphasized that it was the plaintiff who designed the machinery, not Norfolk's new em-ployer, and thus the injunction was solidly in the tradition of patent law: to protect the right of one who "invents or discovers, and keeps secret, a process of manufacture . . . against one who in violation of contract and breach of confidence undertakes to apply it to his own use, or to disclose it to third persons."[18] Although Norfolk had agreed that he would "not give any parties information, directly or indirectly, in regard to the machinery, or any por-tions of it,"[19] the court was not asked to and did not allow an employer to control *all* employee knowledge. Rather, it was only the drawings that were protected.

Moreover, *Peabody* and its subsequent interpretations grounded the duty to guard secrets in an express promise by the employee; the duty was not implicit in all employment relationships. For example, in 1873, James High's treatise on injunctions described *Peabody* in narrow terms that equity would protect the inventor or discoverer of a secret from revelation by "one who, in violation of his contract and in breach of confidence, undertakes to apply the process to his own use or that of third persons."[20] High considered the existence of the express contractual promise of secrecy to be the foundation of the *Peabody* holding.

Use of the New Rules by Businesses in the 1870s

Although by 1870 law offered two new tools to control workplace knowl-edge, American firms appeared to make little effort aggressively to use either noncompete agreements or trade secret policies. Du Pont company manag-ers remained critically aware of the competitive advantage of technological superiority. The company grew rapidly, as the Civil War was good business for a gunpowder manufacturer. The scarce surviving evidence of its policies with regard to creative employees shows a company that was keen to learn as much as possible about everyone else's methods while taking few legal steps to protect its own. The company wanted to avoid conflict over recruitment and, therefore, refused at least through the 1840s to hire employees from competitors as a matter of policy.[21] Nevertheless, it eagerly acquired technology by whatever methods seemed least likely to provoke litigation—whether by buying up competitors, purchasing patents, or touring competing mills.[22] Company officials toured powder mills in Europe to learn the latest methods.

[96] Like many firms, Du Pont purchased patents from independent inventors and often contracted with the inventor to provide services in developing and improving the patent.[23] In common with many British manufacturers, Du Pont restricted entry to its plant to workers and those with permission to enter, and it did attempt, until the 1860s, to prevent the dissemination of knowledge (as well as to maintain quality control) by building only as many powder mills as members of the firm could personally supervise. Even that changed when Lammot du Pont developed a way to make powder from soda instead of saltpeter (soda was cheaper and easier to obtain). The increased demand for the new, improved Du Pont powder led the family to expand the business and to abandon the tight family-only supervision of the production process.[24]

Du Pont may also have protected itself from the loss of employees by being somewhat benevolent (or at least paternalistic) toward its employees. Whereas early in the century E. I. du Pont seemed most concerned with the physical, social, and economic dangers of raising the pretensions of his pow-dermen, later du Ponts painted a more benevolent picture of du Pont sons and cousins, with their sleeves rolled up, working alongside their men. These retrospective accounts of the family and the business emphasized respect for the workmen and the company's support for the widows and children of men who had died in powder mill explosions (along with a number of du Ponts).[25] While one may discount the self-congratulatory aspects of these company histories, the relatively close community they describe—the du Pont family house, along with housing for some powder mill workers, a school, and a church all nestled along the bank of Brandywine River near the powder mill—enabled a degree of control that law could not.

Possible uses of the new cases on patents, trade secrets, and noncompeti-tion agreements evidently were not brought to the attention of Du Pont man-agers. There is no record that the Du Pont company tried to bind employees through restrictive covenants or nondisclosure agreements. Of course, there were no reported trade secrets cases other than *Peabody* until the 1890s, and none was decided in Delaware. Later scholarship portrayed *Peabody* as a watershed, but there is no evidence that it was so perceived in its day. It is possible, given the difficulties of legal research and the sketchy treatment of it in treatises, that lawyers for other firms did not run across it.

In sum, by the 1870s, Du Pont could have obtained, but did not seek, legal protection for the drawings of its powder mill machinery and particular chemical formulae if it had expressly contracted with its employees not to divulge specified information that the company regarded as secret. Not until the end of the century would the company likely have succeeded in protecting the full range of its employees' know-how about powder making, such [97] as techniques for mixing powder so as to minimize the risk of explosions, the advantages of using one sort of mixing device as opposed to another, or the rules of thumb for preserving or mixing powder in different weather conditions.[26] Yet the company did not claim trade secret protection for any of these. There is no evidence that Du Pont could have obtained protection for its knowledge by restraining all competitive employment by its employees, as courts had not yet accepted the use of restrictive covenants to protect technology. The major expansion in the doctrine and the dramatic changes in company practice occurred in the years that followed.

Du Pont's attention to the value of maintaining the secrecy of its methods is not typical of all nineteenth-century firms. The surviving records of the Pennsylvania & Reading Railroads, the Lukens Steel Company, and a few mid-Atlantic textile mills and machine shops reveal sporadic efforts to obtain employee patents in particular cases. None showed an awareness of the value of protecting employee knowledge from their competitors and of the possible uses of the law in doing so. Attitudes about ownership or control of employee knowledge clearly varied among sectors of the nineteenth-century economy. The difference may be attributable to the fact that Du Pont's chemistry-based industry used knowledge that was most easily characterized as tangible secret information rather than as general skill or technique, as in an industry where employee skills are mechanical. The difference may also be attributed to the Du Pont view that they were more likely to be innovators than imitators, and thus they were generally likely to be more at risk from others learning their methods than from being unable to learn methods of others. Whatever the reason, other sectors of the economy reveal a much more forthcoming group of manufacturers eager to share their recent developments with their customers and competitors.[27]

The Demise of Craft Worker Control of Workplace Knowledge

The transformation of craft knowledge into trade secrets occurred relatively quickly in a series of cases in the late 1880s and early 1890s. Using implied contract, courts revised traditional workplace norms while insisting that they were simply enforcing a bargain. Trade secret law grew from a relatively limited obligation to guard a particular and highly confidential piece of information or to convey a secret recipe along with the sale of a business, into a general prohibition on using a wide range of firm-specific information in subsequent employment. As courts expanded trade secrets and used non-compete agreements to protect employer control over workplace knowledge, they transformed the nature and ownership of what had been regarded as artisanal knowledge. It ceased being an attribute of skilled craft workers and became an asset of corporate employers.

[98]

The rejection of the artisanal tradition of knowledge transmission was stated most clearly in *Merryweather v. Moore*, an English case of 1892 that was widely cited by American courts. A draftsman, an apprentice of a firm that designed fire engines, copied dimensions of his employer's designs shortly before leaving their employment. When the former employer sought to enjoin him from using or revealing the information, the defendant argued that he was simply using the knowledge of fire engine design that he had legitimately acquired, and that his copying was not wrongful because the plaintiffs, as employers of an apprentice, had a duty to instruct him. The court rejected the core obligation of apprenticeship—the obligation to train—by redefining the contract of employment. It was, the judge said, "a matter of bargain. I cannot imply from that relation any obligation on the part of the employer to instruct the clerk." Although the court thus revised the traditional obligation of a master-apprentice relationship by invoking a supposed bargain between them, the court also insisted that a duty of confidence existed wholly apart from the bargain: "[I]s not this an abuse of the confidence necessarily existing between him and his employers a confidence arising merely out of the fact of his employment, the confidence being shortly this, that a servant should not use, except for the purposes of service, the opportunities which that service gives him of gaining information?"[28]

American courts in the 1880s similarly blended the emerging notions of trade secrets and implied contracts to reject the tradition of worker control of craft knowledge in favor of the factory production model. The most articulate defense of the new legal regime was offered by William Howard Taft during his first year on the bench as a state trial judge in Cincinnati. Taft, who was the son of an Ohio judge and later became president and then chief justice of the United States, loved being a judge. He took very seriously the judicial task of crafting the law, and so took the unusual step for a young state trial judge of writing a self-consciously pathbreaking opinion that clearly aimed to redirect the law toward greater employer controls on workplace knowledge.[29] The opinion in the case, *Cincinnati Bell Foundry Co. v. Dodds*, reads like the early handiwork of the man who later was popularly regarded as "a stubborn defender of the status quo, champion of property rights, apologist for privilege, inveterate critic of social democracy—the gigantic symbol of standpattism."[30] As Taft himself described his judicial philosophy in labor matters, in a graduation speech at the University of Michigan Law School in 1894, it was necessary that judges fight "the present movement against corporate capital" so that "every laborer, and every man of moderate means" will see "the truth" that it was in their interest "to preserve the inviolability of corporate property."[31]

In *Cincinnati Bell Foundry*, the issues were whether the technique for making bells was a trade secret and whether employees could be enjoined from using or disclosing it even in the absence of an express contract not to disclose or use the employer's secrets. The employee, Dodds, denied that he had been instructed to keep the process secret, and Judge Taft conceded that the evidence showed that the employers had not "attempted to enjoin secrecy upon their many subordinate employees, but preferred rather to rely upon the difficulty there would be in acquiring such a complete knowledge of the bell-making as to enable them to communicate it or use it if they wanted to." There was, therefore, no basis for finding Dodds to have breached a trust in using his knowledge. Neither was there a basis for a finding that he breached an express contract. Nevertheless, Judge Taft concluded that, because Dodds had learned the technique in the course of his employment, "I am inclined to think that his obligation to preserve such secret as the property of his employer must be implied, even though nothing was said to him on the subject."[32]

Cases such as *Cincinnati Bell* and *Merryweather v. Moore* signified the demise of the craft tradition of employee control of workplace know-how and the rise of the modern notion that an implied term of the employment contract is corporate control of economically valuable information. Taft mixed old notions of duties of trust and breach of confidence with the new concept that all employment rights and obligations were a matter of contract. The contract concept was used to reject the old tradition that a master was obligated, by his relation if not by express agreement, to instruct his apprentice. One might argue about whether the traditional training in an apprenticeship included the right to copy specific information, but that was not the approach the courts took. Rather, the courts redefined an old status-based relation as entirely bargained for, and then, regardless of what the actual bargain between the parties may have been, prescribed an implied term that prohibited the employee from carrying away certain information. The rhetoric of contract was used to redefine the rights of employment while making the redefinition seem to be a matter of consent, not prescription.

The expanding definition of trade secrets increased the possible uses of covenants not to compete. Courts extending the horizon of contractual restrictions on employment faced rhetorical challenges that both resembled and differed from those of the trade secret cases. The effort to articulate the employer's legitimate interest in restricting competition from former employees was complicated by the challenge of fitting the rules into the liberty-of-contract jurisprudence. A covenant not to compete is both a contract in its own right and a restriction on future freedom to contract. Not surprisingly, the laissez-faire jurisprudence of the Gilded Age made interesting appearances on both sides of the courtroom debates, as lawyers and judges would cite liberty of contract and property rights in labor as the basis for both granting and declining injunctive relief to employers.[33] The malleability of the freedom of contract concept in this context, however, made it an unreliable rhetorical move for the courts and the litigants.

Taft returned to the conflict between the freedom of the skilled worker and the employer's property and contract rights to control workplace knowledge several years after *Cincinnati Bell Foundry* while a judge on the federal court of appeals. In the later case, which became an influential defense of noncompetition agreements, Taft again laid out a vision in which private agreement was taken as the apotheosis of public freedom. In *United States v. Addyston Pipe & Steel Company* (1898), Taft stated that an agreement not to compete would be valid if it was ancillary to the main purpose of another lawful contract, such as a sale of business or an employment contract.[34] Although enforcement of noncompetes against employees was still quite rare at that time, Taft stated the rule as if it were settled law and the articulation of a basic freedom. The *Addyston Pipe* decision, in the words of Herbert Hovenkamp, "fused the neoclassical model of competition with the legal doctrine of combinations in restraint of trade" and in the process "created the illusion that the law of combinations in restraint of trade had always been concerned with 'competition,' neoclassically defined."[35] In reality, of course, the content of the contract was imposed by courts (as Taft had done in inventing a contractual duty to guard trade secrets in the absence of any such contractual provision) if not by powerful firms. Taft seamlessly blended a laissez-faire defense of freedom of contract with a deliberate effort to accord as many rights as possible to the firm.

Opinions like Taft's enforcing restrictive covenants against employees obscured the novelty of the legal doctrine by relying on eighteenth-century cases having little to do with employment. Since the question was whether to enforce a contract, the cases compelled judges to reconcile liberty of contract values with other values, including the value of restricted labor and trade and that of freely usable knowledge. Courts had to determine explicitly whether the employee's knowledge was alienable. Courts also brushed aside old doubts about whether or how much value must be paid for a monopoly on employee knowledge, whether employers were likely to exploit employees in seeking to control the use of knowledge, and whether the employer's interest justified the restriction on an employee's freedom (or obligation) to work.   [101]

Given the increased uses of restrictive covenants and the difficulty of justifying their enforcement simply by reference to liberty of contract, courts sought a new rationale. One of the most persuasive was that the contract was necessary to prevent an employee's "abuse of confidence."[36] As the trade secret concept became a settled part of the late nineteenth-century tort doctrine, courts could justify restrictive covenants as an unobjectionable contractual expression of the obligations that tort law imposed already. Ironically, just as contract discourse was on an ascending arc in trade secret cases, tort concepts popped up in cases involving contracts not to compete. Of course, the distinction between "contract" and "tort" was itself new and not yet clear, so it should come as no surprise that the concepts blurred in the area of trade secrets and restrictive covenants.[37]

The Demise of Craft Worker Control in the Factories of the 1890s

The transformation of artisanal knowledge into corporate intellectual property was resented by some craft workers who experienced the change in law as a significant loss of workplace autonomy and possibilities for entrepreneurship associated with the threat of job mobility. The impact of the new law can be seen most clearly in looking at the story behind the famous Pennsylvania Supreme Court decisions in *Dempsey v. Dobson*, which arose out of the Philadelphia textile business. Philip Scranton's careful history of the industry tells the story behind the litigation, which was covered extensively in the Philadelphia textile trade press. Until the late nineteenth century, dyers had a practical monopoly over technical knowledge of the chemistry and mechanics of dying fabrics and yarns. For generations, dyers had relied on traditional organic dyestuffs and methods handed down from father to son and from master to apprentice, and thus maintained effective control over craft knowledge and enjoyed considerable labor market autonomy. The German advances in the chemistry of synthetic dyes associated with the so-called aniline revolution prompted American textile manufacturers to attempt to modernize their methods in the 1880s.[38] As Scranton noted, "[t]he Philadelphia trade journal *Textile Colorist* inveighed relentlessly against by-guess and by-golly dyers throughout the 1880s, calling for the application of science to textile processing and an end to craft secrecy."[39] The case of *Dempsey v. Dobson* represented a legal rejection of the tradition of craft knowledge in favor of corporate control over economically valuable workplace knowledge. Modern dye chemistry was to replace old craft knowledge, and dyers were to be brought under corporate control.

[102] *Dempsey* was a final skirmish in a legal battle that textile employers and dyers had been fighting for centuries over control of the chemical knowledge of dyes. The leading English case on noncompete agreements, the *Dyer's Case* (1414), which had declined to enforce a noncompete agreement, had been an early effort of a master to control knowledge by preventing a dyer from setting up shop for himself.[40] A later English case involving dyers, *Makepeace v. Jackson* (1813), was a common citation in early American trade secret litigation. In *Makepeace*, as explained in chapter 1, a calico printer's shop fired its head dyer, who sued to recover the color book. The dyer sought to prove that some of the entries in the book were his own invention and that on that basis he was entitled to some of the book. The judges held that the book was the property of the employer, even though some of the colors were devised by the dyer, because "[t]he master has a right to something beside the mere manual labor of the servant in the mixing of the colors; and though the Plaintiff invents them, yet they are to be used for his master's benefit."[41] *Makepeace* was cited not only in cases involving early trade secrets but also in early patent treatises on disputes to ownership of inventions.[42] Nevertheless, as illustrated by the Philadelphia dyers' view of the story underlying *Dempsey v. Dobson*, the custom of dyers controlling books persisted, notwithstanding *Makepeace*.

It was no accident that the Dobsons, whose extensive operations represented the modernization of mass factory production of textiles, should have been the driving force behind what they (and the courts) perceived as a badly needed modernization of the law. Brothers James and John Dobson owned and operated a successful textile business comprising several mills on the Schuylkill River. John W. Dempsey, the plaintiff in the case, was a well-compensated and skilled British color mixer who had learned the dyer's trade in Britain before coming to Philadelphia and the Dobson mills in 1873. Dempsey worked with the Dobsons' carpet designer to match pattern colors, and he created batch lots of dyes for each design and for use in tinting yarns for both initial and repeat orders. Dempsey recorded each dye formula in his "color books," along with notes to facilitate duplication of the shade at a later time. After twenty years at the Dobson mills, Dempsey gave notice in August 1892 of his intention to quit their employ in September. According to Scranton, although Dempsey "had routinely taken his books home with him for study and updating, Dempsey was stopped August 30 by the mill watchman and was 'informed that he could not quit the mill until he gave up his recipe books . . . by order of the Dobsons.'" Dempsey offered to stay the night in the mill with his books, but "he was after a few hours forced out of the factory, the books remaining behind." The Dobsons kept the books for almost four weeks while they were copied in their entirety for the firm, "and even then, only a portion of the volumes were returned."[43]

Among the facts proved at trial were that Dempsey had purchased the blank ledgers himself and that of the 2,300 recipes in the books, he had recorded 1,800 in England before coming to the Dobson mills. When the trade press, sympathetic to the mill, reported on the decision, the article neglected to mention that the majority of the recipes in the books predated Dempsey's employment in the United States. Perhaps in their view it was not relevant who had originated the recipes. The textile manufacturing firms that controlled the trade press might well have deemed all employee knowledge to be corporate property, not merely the knowledge developed on the payroll of the firm.

The trial court focused substantially on the ownership of the books as objects, rather than on the knowledge in them, and a jury returned a substantial verdict for Dempsey. The Pennsylvania Supreme Court overturned the verdict in 1896, saying that although Dempsey might keep copies of his recipes, the books containing the recipes and yarn samples were the property of the Dobsons. The court emphasized that the firm purchased, through wages, the product of Dempsey's skill. "The designer and the color mixer, like the printer and the weaver, are employed, and their wages adjusted with reference to their skill and experience." The court emphasized that Dempsey was an employee whose skill is owned by the firm that paid him. Dyers like Dempsey "are not independent contractors, producing designs or shades of color by a secret process of their own, which they sell, as patterns or colors to the manufacturer, for a fixed price; but they are employés, bringing their skill and experience, in the use of the materials furnished by their employers, into his service, for his benefit in the production of his goods."[44]

On remand for a new trial, Dempsey offered evidence to prove that the custom in the industry was that the carpet mixer's recipes and sample books belonged exclusively to the employee. Dempsey testified that "color mixers and dyers keep color books for their private use" and that neither in the United States nor in England would a dyer "give his books up, because they are the tools of his trade." In addition, he offered the testimony of an experienced dyer who had worked both in England and in Philadelphia that the dyers' possession of color books was a custom of the trade, and the testimony of the proprietor of a Philadelphia textile firm to the same effect. The trial court excluded the evidence.

They Must Contract to That Effect

On appeal, the Pennsylvania Supreme Court upheld the exclusion of this evidence and again ruled for the Dobsons. Given Dempsey's evidence, the court could no longer rest on its earlier stated view that the implicit contract between dyers and their employers was that the dyer sold his talent to the firm. Rather, the court insisted that whatever custom of dyer control of workplace knowledge that might exist was not a "good custom" and was not "reasonable" because it was contrary to what the court imagined to be the employees' duty of loyal service to the employer. "The color mixer, like the designer and weaver, is employed because of his supposed ability to serve his employer in the particular line of labor which he is expected to follow. . . . The employer has an equal right to the faithful service of each, and is equally, so far as his own business is concerned, entitled to the results of the labor of each." Moreover, continued the court, a custom of employee ownership of the dye books must be illegal because it would give the employee excessive power over the firm. "If a color mixer could at his pleasure carry off the recipes and color books from his employer's factory, and refuse to permit their further use except upon his own terms, it would be in his power to inflict enormous loss on the manufacturer at any moment, and not merely to disturb, but to destroy, his business. Such a custom would not be reasonable, and could not be sustained."

Finally, insisted the court, the custom of dyer ownership of recipes and dye samples was contrary to the shop-right rule that had begun to emerge in the area of employee patents, and it was "against the law" for that reason as well: "Even if his employee had obtained letters patent for his formula, protecting himself thereby against the public, still the employer's right to continue its use in his own business would be protected by the United States courts."[45] Although the court cited the 1843 edition of Curtis's treatise on patent law for this proposition, the court's characterization of the strength of the employers' shop right was an overstatement of the law that existed at the time. With respect to the recipes developed before Dempsey began at the mills, the firm would have had no interest, and with respect to the others the firm would only have had the right to use the recipes, not to keep the books so as to prevent Dempsey from using them. But the court did not bother to state the law of patent ownership correctly, and simply assumed that employers *would* own employee patents because they *should*.

The reasoning in *Dempsey* reveals a view of employee knowledge that is at once both quaintly archaic and strikingly modern. The court believed that Dempsey had developed the recipes and color samples while employed and therefore anticipated the modern rule that the Dobsons were entitled to "the results of the labor" for which their firm had paid.[46] Of course, the court overlooked the fact that most of the knowledge in the books was not the result of the labor for which the Dobsons had paid. The early nineteenth century's emphasis on "faithful service" merged seamlessly with the employer's right to "the results of the labor" for which it paid. Employee control of knowledge would give "power to inflict enormous loss on the manufacturer," a very modern concern. Fear of that power provided the basis for rejecting evidence that employee ownership was the custom—part of what would otherwise be described as the implied contract of employment. But it could not be an implied contract term because—as the court quaintly stated—it is not a "good custom"; it was unreasonable and must, therefore, be "against the law." It was common in the nineteenth century for judges and lawyers, following William Blackstone, to use custom as a source of common law; a rule was valid only if it was a "good custom."[47]

The reaction of Philadelphia dyers to the *Dempsey v. Dobson* opinions as recounted by Scranton reveals that the dyers understood exactly why the company would insist upon ownership of the recipes: it would enable the company to gain the economically valuable knowledge of dyes and therefore to substitute cheaper, less skilled workers for the expensive labor of skilled and experienced dyers. As one dyer said, the dye recipes were his property, "handed down (as in my case) from father to son (my grandfather having used some of them a hundred years ago)." To claim as corporate property the skill that he regarded as both a personal attribute and a family tradition was an injustice. "By what right should an employer demand these formulae to put into the hands of an inexperienced and cheaper man, after I had worked for some time?" The dyer imagined a very different employment contract than the one described by the Pennsylvania Supreme Court. In modern terms, dyers described themselves as highly trained professionals like doctors, lawyers, or accountants who are retained, like independent contractors are today, by the job and for their expertise. "The goods are sent to him to be colored, and the result of his efforts is what he is paid for, not how he does them. If his formulas are incomplete, or have not been compiled with skill, the result will be poor, and his services of no value. If, on the other hand, the colors are good, by his skillful mixing or his peculiar knowledge of the process, he is of value to the concern employing him."[48]

NO PROCESS OF COMMON LAW change is perfectly orderly and linear, and not all cases in the 1890s came down so heavily on the side of management. The expansion of trade secret and noncompete law met resistance as many litigants and some courts remained anxious to protect the right of the employee to use "mechanical skill and experience."[49] Some courts refused to prevent engineers, mechanics, salespeople, and office workers from divulging or using alleged trade secrets in subsequent employment, often reasoning that the information was common knowledge in the trade.[50] A New Jersey equity court refused to enforce an express agreement not to divulge information about the employer's suppliers and customers. The court held that, after the term of the employment, the employee remained free, "notwithstanding such agreement" to "use the knowledge he had obtained" to do business with his former employer's customers.[51] Horace Gay Wood's influential 1886 treatise on master-servant law conceded that customer lists or relationships—which by 1930 were widely regarded as information that an employer could control as trade secrets or through a noncompetition agreement—were open to use by a former employee. As Wood said, an employee "may solicit trade from his master's customers for himself, when he shall set up in the same business for himself, after the term has expired."[52]

At the turn of the twentieth century, as law recognized the validity of corporate control of some workplace knowledge, courts struggled with the boundaries of what could be owned. Did firms own only the drawings or objects that embodied the secrets or, more broadly, the ideas contained in them? In an Ohio case about an engineer who went to work for a competitor to build a mill identical to the one he had built for a prior employer, the court held that the former employer owned just the drawings and patterns, not the idea of the design. The court emphasized that the employee, not the former employer, had conceived the idea for the design and although the patterns themselves were trade secrets, the court rejected the notion that "when I employ a man who has skill, knowledge, and experience in a particular line, ask him to furnish me the knowledge . . . and he then supplies me an article, . . . the idea or ideas he evolves become the property of the employer as a trade secret." Rather, the court thought that "the only property interest that the employer can claim is the product of his skill, the industry, and the intelligence of that workman, i.e., he owns the pattern, but he does not own the idea." The narrow definition of a trade secret followed from what the court termed the "natural rule of right": "That a man shall have the benefit of all his intelligent thought and enterprise, of all that he may discover by industry and ingenuity. . . . Therefore, if these mill owners desire to cripple a man's enterprise and his energy and intelligence, to hamper him in his future employment by requiring that he shall not give to that future employer the benefit of his skill or the things that he has developed for the former master, they must contract to that effect."[53]

By contrast, a Pennsylvania case, decided only two years later, stated quite emphatically that the employer owned "property in the design, in the idea, and in the mental conception, as well as in the piece of paper on which it is expressed." Although the court ordered the defendant only to return the [107] misappropriated blueprints, it obviously envisioned that the remedy would preclude the defendant from using the plaintiff's design. As in *Dempsey*, the court rejected the notion that the employee had breached no duty because it was the custom in the industry for draftsmen to make blueprints of their work and to retain them for their own use. The court said: "If there be such a practice, it is a reprehensible one."[54]

4

An Ingenious Man Enabled by Contract

Just as the law and culture of the workplace in the early postbellum years embraced worker control of craft and mechanical knowledge as part of the antimonopoly conception of entrepreneurship, so too did the law and culture of patenting. In 1860, the law presumed that the inventor should own his patents unless or until he assigned or licensed them to others. Leading thinkers on American political economy from Hamilton to Lincoln viewed technological development as crucial to American progress, and the patent system was widely believed to be integral to it. The general faith in patenting and technology included a particular veneration for inventors, and courts would not lightly divest an inventor of his possibilities for enterprise.

Moreover, the fact that patents could be seen as distinct things separable from general workplace or craft knowledge facilitated courts in seeing patents as employee property. Even as the growth of factories and offices in the 1870s might have prompted courts to realize that control over the production process—and thus craft knowledge—was essential to the employer's right to manage, judges remained reluctant to reject an employee's ownership of an innovation, distinct from the general craft knowledge. The shop-right doctrine recognized that when the innovation or invention was incorporated in the employer's normal processes of production over an extended period, to grant the employee an exclusive right to the invention would be too great an interference with the employer's interest in controlling the business. Indeed, the core of the Supreme Court's reasoning when it invented the shop-right doctrine in *McClurg v. Kingsland* in 1843 was that the employee who left to go work for a rival overreached if he attempted to deny the former employer the right to use the process and to deny to the public the benefits of competition. Whereas in the early twentieth century courts would emphasize the employer's investment in labor and materials as a rationale for employer ownership of patents, in the 1860s and 1870s courts still regarded patents as being presumptively the creation, and *ipso facto* the property, of the named inventor whose brain they imagined had conceived of the idea.

[109]

The Hero-Inventor and the Courts

The importance of innovation was conveyed through a mythologizing of the lives and personalities of the "great inventors." Popular accounts of inventors beginning with two books published in 1863 marveled at their individual genius and at the miracle of their accomplishments.[1] This popular literature, which tended to be "retrospective in scope and nostalgic in tone," contributed to a "national myth of heroic invention" that influenced how judges perceived employee-inventors.[2] In the books as in the law, inventions were typically credited to individuals rather than to collective efforts, thus underscoring the legitimacy of individual (as opposed to firm) ownership of patents. The popular and even the academic vision of invention that prevailed in the nineteenth century was that of the genius alone in his workshop, tinkering away until suddenly a bright idea came to him in a flash (what was sometimes called a "Eureka moment").[3] In addition, inventions, especially those that were patented and exploited by the companies that grew up to market them, were credited as the catalyst of "man's slow ascent from barbarism to civiliza-tion." One breathless account insisted "it is to inventors mainly that we must look for all that civilization can be made to be."[4] Invention, said another, was the most important factor in "the evolution of that social pattern which produced a nation from the United States."[5] This perspective cast inventive-ness in moral rather than strictly instrumental tones, lending support to the arguments that inventors—whether employed or not—had a moral claim to legal protection for their enterprise. It was also quite significant that the literature emphasized the cleverness of new technology and the mystery of how people conceived of new ideas, rather than the tedious process of building and testing and the incremental rather than revolutionary nature of most patents. The hero-inventor books presented readers with elaborate descriptions of the great inventions of the early industrial revolution, such as the power loom, accompanied by diagrams of strings, gears, and wires. As one critic quipped, "the whole discussion left a cloudy impression that somehow the eighteenth century in England must have been an especially brainy period, when inventors suddenly abounded and, by their cerebrations, brought the marvelous new machines of the age into being."[6]

The conventional account of Eli Whitney's invention of the cotton gin is illustrative. While visiting a southern plantation, Whitney was said to have learned from his hosts that it was difficult to remove the seeds from cotton. As the story goes, Whitney pondered, tinkered, and in a few days produced the cotton gin that revolutionized cotton processing, guaranteed the South a lucrative cotton crop, sealed the fate of thousands of black people as slaves, and ultimately brought on the Civil War.[7] The involvement of others in Whitney's conception, design, and development of the cotton gin tended to be neglected in the literature in favor of emphasizing his genius and the novelty and importance of his inventions.

Even companies, which in the long run might have benefited from emphasizing the collective nature of product development, tended to emphasize the pioneering work of the individual men whose inventions formed the basis of the company's success. The companies that were built on the new technologies had every reason to burnish their own image by lionizing their founders. Glorified life stories of Alexander Graham Bell, George Westinghouse, Cyrus McCormick, Henry Ford, and Thomas Edison were important assets of the corporations that bore their names because the genius of the founders suggested quality of the products and the familiarity of their names was a way to create a brand. As one critic of the hero-inventor explanation of the industrial revolution explained, "[T]he American popular belief that McCormick invented the reaper may be worth millions to the International Harvester Co., the fame of Bell certainly is to the telephone company, Fulton is the hero of the Hudson River Day Line, Edison and Marconi of various companies, and the Wright Brothers of the Wright Aero Corporation, while the rival Curtis Interests set dead Langley on an airplane, like the Cid on his horse again, to fight their battle."[8] Not until the middle of the twentieth century did published accounts of invention emphasize the significance of organized collective or corporate research and development.[9]

Legal doctrine of the 1860s and 1870s remained largely as oblivious to the importance of collective invention as was the heroic invention literature that emerged in the same era. The paradigm of individual invention inspired judges to cling to rules of individual patent ownership even as technological complexity and industrialization were rendering the individual inventor-entrepreneur increasingly rare. When the courts in the 1860s saw the first few patent disputes between firms and employee-inventors, they brought to the law the notion that inventiveness was a personality trait more than an organizational task, and sought to determine ownership of an invention by assessing the character and abilities of the employee and employer.

The Supreme Court's influential 1868 decision *Agawam Woolen Co. v. Jordan* was a leading example of the phenomenon. In the absence of an express patent assignment agreement, the Court held patent ownership was to be determined by who originated an idea: the employer or the employee. *Agawam* was a patent infringement suit in which the alleged infringer sought to invalidate the patent on the basis that the employee, not the employer-patentee, was the true inventor. The case involved John Goulding, a "machinist and a manufacturer of textile fabrics," who in 1824 hired a blacksmith to help him devise a modification of the machinery for spinning yarn from wool. The invention devised by Goulding and his blacksmith, Edward Winslow, which was patented in 1826, proved to be quite significant; as the Court said, "The patented improvement soon came into universal use, and worked a revolution, both here and in Europe, in the art of manufacturing fibrous yarns."[10] The patent was quite valuable and had been licensed by Goulding and his assigns to numerous firms for substantial sums of money. When the litigation raised the question whether Goulding was the true inventor, Goulding testified in the form of a lengthy deposition about his extensive efforts over a period of years to invent improved spinning and textile machinery.

In his testimony, Goulding drew a distinction between what he called "experiments done while I was in the employment" of a firm and experiments done "on my own account." He explained that the invention in dispute was perfected after he had ceased working for others and had leased a textile mill in Dedham, Massachusetts, where "I carried on my experiments on a large scale, having no one to interfere when machines were stopped to try experiments."[11] Goulding took care in his testimony to make clear that the alleged employee-inventor "did not claim to be a finished machinist" (meaning a fully trained machinist), "did not profess any skill in wood work," and was only "a workman" and was not an investor or otherwise "interested" in the business. Goulding also insisted that every aspect of the patented machines, "except the clothing and castings and wrought iron," "was done in my shop by me and my hands." As Goulding recalled the operations,

Said Winslow might have had and probably did have something to do with some parts of the iron work about the machines; there was no one hand that went through with building all parts of any machine, or machines that I built; workmen have their different parts to perform on each machine, such as blacksmithing, turning of iron, filing, cutting screws, and the wood work in the different stages would all be performed by different hands, as a general thing; it would take too long if one hand was skilled sufficient to go through all those branches, to bring out those improvements as fast as I wanted them done, therefore I kept hands to fill all the different branches that I wanted to carry on. I would set such hands to work on the different parts that I knew they could perform; it is very difficult to tell what hands, or who, or what names of hands might have worked on those above parts named. Said Winslow had nothing to do about the invention any more than any other hand; he suggested nothing to me in relation to the business.[12]

Winslow's son, who provided evidence for the defendant, recalled it quite differently, of course, emphasizing his father's indispensable contributions to the invention and conversations he had had with Goulding (which Goulding denied) about how the invention would make them rich men.[13] The resolution of the suit essentially came down to resolving disputed issues of fact based on voluminous evidence, and the courts accepted Goulding's version rather than that of Winslow's son.

Assuming that an invention could be traced to a single great mind in a workshop, the Court said that if an employee was hired to work on an invention, the employer owned the right to the resulting invention, at least if the employer supplied the initial idea that formed the basis of the employee's invention. The Court determined that the employer had been the true inventor—the one who had supplied what the Court imagined as the single brilliant idea—and the employee was deemed to be a mere assistant. Therefore, the employer was entitled to the patent.

Agawam was a case in which there was no express agreement regarding ownership of workplace inventions. In those cases where there were such agreements, courts faced a different task of interpreting and enforcing the contract. Courts regarded as perfectly permissible and sensible that a patentee would assign rights to a patent to someone or to a firm and then go to work with or for the assignee to manufacture and sell the patented item. All recognized that through an assignment an inventor might obtain the capital necessary to bring a new invention to market and that the inventor might seek employment with the firm to which he assigned the patent.[14] Yet courts remained reluctant to enforce contracts by which employees agreed to assign *future* inventions to their employers. Although the law was settled by 1855 that contracts to assign existing patents were enforceable, courts used a variety of rules of interpretation to make employees' pre-invention assignment agreements difficult for employers to enforce.

The earliest reported cases about such arrangements involved partnerships; thus the legal framework was established as a phenomenon of patent law, or the law of partnerships, not as an aspect of master-servant. This was the period in which courts decided that patents were assignable and even that agreements to assign future patents were enforceable. Although the Patent Act imposed a variety of procedural requirements on patent assignments,[15] courts enforced assignment agreements that did not comply with the statutory requirements under a variety of equitable doctrines.[16] Thus, [113] when courts first confronted employees' invention assignment agreements, there was an established tradition of enforcing assignments. Yet in the beginning the courts were wary of employer efforts to enforce such agreements against employees. The challenge was to protect the inventor from exploitation and bad bargains but to avoid making patent assignments of uncertain legal force.

Courts developed essentially two strategies for declining to enforce employees' patent assignment agreements. First, they would decline to find the existence of an agreement to assign in the absence of a clear, written contract. Second, even when there was a written contract, the courts would construe the coverage of such agreements narrowly against the employer so as to exclude all inventions that were not either directly related to the employee's work or clearly made during the term of the contract. By this means, they protected the employer that clearly negotiated for ownership of patents but did not allow overreaching by employers that had not. When this strategy worked, employees were adequately compensated for the assignment of the patent.

A leading example of these interpretive approaches was the Pennsylvania Supreme Court's pioneering decision in *Slemmer's Appeal* (1868), an internecine struggle among the partners in a family business. Henry Slemmer, a partner with family members in oil drilling and refining, developed and patented an improved petroleum refining process. The other partners sued to require him to assign the patent to them jointly as partners and to force him to share the profits from the patent. The court declined to require assignment of the patent because it found that Henry had been the inventor. It held, however, that under the shop-right doctrine of *McClurg* the former partners had a license to use the invention because Henry had agreed to let them use it while he had been part of the partnership.[17] (Through the 1880s, every decision that granted an employer a license to use an employee invention did so on the basis of facts like these showing that the employee had permitted or encouraged his employer to manufacture his invention or to manufacture with his invention during his employment.) The decision rested on a factual determination about the nature of the parties' understanding, but it created a stringent standard for establishing an enforceable contract to assign ownership because it gave decisive weight to the inventor-partner's testimony.

Inventing for the Farm in the 1870s and 1880s

Organized invention and the devotion of focused energy to product improvement and innovation occurred in the midwestern agricultural implements business in the latter half of the nineteenth century. From 1870 on, hired inventors (as opposed to firm owners) constituted the majority of inventors who both repeatedly innovated and made their inventions available to firms. The hiring of inventive talent was an important aspect of business strategy in agricultural implements. Yet the courts approached workplace intellectual property disputes arising out of the efforts of agricultural equipment manufacturers to institutionalize product development in a way that suggests the companies' lawyers had failed to convince the judges of the significance of the recent efforts. Courts insisted that substantial formality with regard to assignment of inventions and a narrow reading of the shop right (the employer's nonexclusive, royalty-free license to manufacture and use the patented item) were necessary to protect the rights of inventive employees to have the opportunity for entrepreneurship.

The judicial insistence on a model of individual invention even in the face of efforts to institutionalize product development reflected a persistent belief in the importance of individual employee entrepreneurship with respect to innovations. But even as courts adhered to a legal rule of employee ownership, they began to embrace the emerging law of contract as the framework for analyzing disputes over workplace knowledge. Although the idea that workplace knowledge and intellectual property rights could be sold in a contract of employment was gaining some traction in the cases, the story of a valuable invention in railroad locomotive design shows that some employers had not yet taken advantage of it. Through a study of the Reading Railroad's willingness to allow its superintendent to own the patent to a locomotive firebox, we see how technology firms negotiated a delicate balance between controlling valuable technologies, encouraging inventive activity by employees, and advertising the employees' endowments of technical knowledge to competitors and customers by identifying individual employees with important innovations.

In 1886, the U.S. Supreme Court decided a seminal case on contractual assignment of employee inventions, *Hapgood v. Hewitt*, which grew out of the same innovation boom in the agricultural equipment industry. It was the high-water mark of the nineteenth-century judicial solicitude for the rights of employee-inventors, reflecting a profound belief in the necessity of upward mobility flowing from patent ownership in a democratic economy.[18]

The story of the case is drawn from the allegations of the Hapgood Company's complaint filed in equity in a federal court in Indiana in February 1880. The case never went to trial and was decided solely on the legal insufficiency of the company's allegations; thus all we know of the story is the version that the frustrated employer chose to tell. In 1873, the Hapgood Company, a Missouri corporation, hired Horace Hewitt, "a man of large experience in mechanical pursuits" who had worked for some years making plows in Kentucky.[19] Hewitt was "to devote his time and services to getting up, improving, and perfecting plows and other goods, and to introducing the same." The next year, Hewitt purchased half the shares of the Hapgood Company then owned by the company's president, took the title of vice president, and also agreed orally to "fill the position of superintendent of the manufacturing department." As the Supreme Court described the company's structure (based, evidently, mainly on the allegations of the bill in equity), Hewitt was management but not top management (even though he had purchased half the president's shares in the firm). Below him, "[t]he corporation employed a large number of manual laborers." Hewitt was one of "various employees of higher grades, among them a superintendent, a secretary, a foreman, and a traveling salesman, all of whom had charge of different departments, but were under the control and direction of the president, as chief executive officer." As superintendent, Hewitt had "general charge of the manufacturing department, subject to the discretion of the president."[20]

During his working hours, using the materials of the company and the manual labor of employees of the company, and incorporating design suggestions made by the company salesman and the company president, Hewitt devised an improved iron riding plow. He left the company in 1877, sold his shares of stock back to the president, and in 1878 applied for and received a patent in his own name on the new plow. Shortly thereafter, the Hapgood Company dissolved and reincorporated under the laws of another state as the Hapgood Plow Company. Hapgood Plow Company and Hapgood sued Hewitt in equity seeking an injunction requiring Hewitt to assign the patent to the Hapgood Plow Company (or to its stockholders who were trustees of the dissolved Hapgood Company). Both the circuit court and the Supreme Court rejected the employer's claim on the ground that the allegations amounted only to an assertion of general employment, which would entitle only the original employer (Hapgood Company), and not its successor (Hapgood Plow Company), to a license to make and sell the patented invention as part of its business. The dissolution of Hapgood Company extinguished the shop right, which could not be transferred to the new company. The allegation that Hewitt had been hired precisely for his expertise in the design and manufacture of plows was held insufficient to establish that he had agreed that the company would have title to his inventions.

[116] The circuit court started from the premise that "[p]ersons are not deprived of their right to their inventions while in the service of others, unless they have been hired and paid to exercise their inventive faculties for their employers." And the court accepted the contention that Hapgood Company had contracted for Hewitt's "knowledge and experience" as well as his "time, labor, skill." The court recognized that inventive talent could be hired as distinct from labor or skill, but because the contract did not *expressly* require Hewitt to "exercise his inventive faculties for the benefit of the company," the company was not entitled to the patent. The court also rejected the company's contention that the invention should belong to the firm because other Hapgood employees had assisted in developing the patented plow; the court remarked simply that perhaps the other employees might be the joint inventors, and thus Hewitt might not be entitled to a patent in his name alone, but their contributions did not entitle the firm to the patent.[21]

The Supreme Court's brief opinion mainly adopted the reasoning of the circuit court. The Court found nothing in the allegations concerning the employment agreement between Hapgood Company and Hewitt to indicate "that the former was to have the title to his inventions, or to any patent that he might obtain for them. The utmost that can be made out of the allegations is that the corporation was to have a license or right to use the inventions in making plows."[22] To characterize the employment agreement as if it gave the employer only a license is a fiction. According to the employer's allegations, there was no actual agreement, in the sense of a meeting of the minds, one way or another on patent ownership or licenses. It may or may not have been desirable to establish a default rule of employee ownership that could be altered only by an express agreement that the employer would get the patent for its employees' inventions. But it was a fiction to say, as the Court did, that the parties had agreed to that allocation.

In *Hapgood*, the Court established a presumption that even employees who invented within the scope of their employment and were hired because of their ability to do so would own their own intellectual property unless they specifically contracted away their rights. A man of stature like Hewitt would not be presumed to have given up his right to profit from his ingenuity. It was considered unjust to enforce anything but a clear contract to assign future patents to employers. As Justice Bradley, sitting by designation as a circuit judge in 1887, put it: "A naked assignment or agreement to assign, in gross, a man's future labors as an author or inventor,—in other words, a mortgage on a man's brain, to bind all its future products,—does not address itself favorably to our consideration."[23] Although Justice Bradley enforced an express agreement to assign an employee's patent for an improved potato planter, he suggested that such contracts must be limited.

[117]

Inventions and the Law of Implied Contracts

It might be thought that the courts' unwillingness to enforce assignment agreements they found vague was simply an application of a general rule that courts would not specifically enforce contracts that were vague or indefinite.[24] But it was not. In the first place, the general rule about specific performance was shot through with exceptions that would have encompassed employees' assignment agreements, yet courts never mentioned these exceptions. For example, courts would decline specific enforcement only where the contract was so vague or indefinite that the court could not discern what to order the defendant to do,[25] and courts would supply missing terms by reasonable inference.[26] The agreements to assign inventions were not so vague or indefinite as to be unenforceable under the traditional rule, because the uncertainty was not about this or that term—what invention, when to assign it—but rather about whether the contract existed at all.[27] Moreover, the courts seemed no more inclined to grant a damages remedy than to order assignment, so the rule was not just the equity court's traditional reluctance to order performance.[28] The rule declining enforcement of assignment agreements was a presumption against the existence of a contract in case of doubt, not a rule about specific performance. It was a rule for employees' patent assignment agreements, not for all contracts.

Even as courts construed invention assignment agreements narrowly, the fact that they insisted all rights must be determined by reference to a contract was quite significant. It paved the way for a radical shift in employee rights only a decade later when courts changed their view about whether an implied term of an employment agreement included an obligation to transfer all inventions to the employer. The judicial reinterpretation of the implied contract appeared in cases in which employers gained only a license or right to use an employee invention rather than ownership of the patent itself.

The late nineteenth-century change in the law was not the sudden emergence of contract where it had never existed before. On the contrary, judges had enforced explicit agreements covering patents to employee inventions.[29] However, express contracts were rare until the early to mid-twentieth century, and courts had seldom invoked a notion of implied contract. The interpretation and enforcement of patent assignment contracts was not even mentioned in the patent treatises that began to be published in the 1830s and 1840s. Nor did courts conclude that the ordinary employment contract contained any implied term that an employee hired to improve a business had been hired to invent. Only if the parties had an explicit agreement cover-

ing ownership of inventions (as opposed to a general understanding that an employee was hired to develop a line of business, a product, or a machine) would a court hold that an employee had been hired to invent and award the resulting invention to the employer.[30] As late as 1895, in a case in which the employer alleged it had hired the inventor, a machinist, for the express purpose of building an improved power press based on the machinist's rough idea, a federal court awarded only a license because there was no express agreement that the employer would own the resulting patent.[31]

The new approach to the implied terms of employment contracts regarding the control of workplace knowledge was not limited to patent assignment agreements. It also emerged in the area of the employer's shop right to patented inventions where it manifested itself in a subtle shift in the legal justification for the employer's entitlement. From the 1840s through the 1870s, the shop right had been based on the employee's having allowed the employer to use the invention. In the mid-1880s, courts began to justify the shop right on the ground that the employer had invested in the development of the invention by paying the inventor's salary and providing the workshop where the employee-inventor perfected the patented device. Of course, in every shop-right case, the employee devised the invention on the job using the employer's materials; by definition, that is the only time a shop right exists. The circumstances of inventing did not change, but the facts the courts emphasized did.

The courts redefined the implied contract of employment for inventive people to transform the shop-right doctrine from the noncontractual idea that employees owed a basic obligation of fairness to allow firms to use inventions developed at work into an investment-based contractual right to use employee innovations. An 1886 federal circuit court decision from New Hampshire was the first to conceptualize the shop right entirely as an implied term of the employment contract. An overseer in a mill who installed a number of his patented devices in the mill's machinery sued the mill for patent infringement. The company's witnesses claimed that the overseer allowed the company free use of his inventions in order to test and obtain publicity for them. The inventor testified that he allowed it only because the company officials told him that his status as employee gave them a right to the uncompensated use of his inventions (at trial the officials did not deny having said this). He also proved that when he protested, they agreed to pay him $250 per year. The company claimed it was an increased salary;

the plaintiff asserted it was a license fee that was intended to be continued so long as the company used the patents. Accepting the employee's version of the contract, the court stated that, where an employee's invention was installed in the employer's factory, "a license from the patentee was to be presumed."[32] [119]

In sum, through the 1880s, employees retained significant legal rights to their innovations, and employer lawyers failed—at least in the short term—in their efforts to redefine the contract of employment so as to recognize corporate investment in workplace knowledge as a presumptive basis for corporate ownership. But employers did succeed in reorienting the courts' thinking about the nature of the relationship as being contractual. The vessel of implied contract was one that could easily be, and eventually was, emptied of its employee-friendly content and refilled with a view that employers should control the rights to workplace inventions.

Inventing for the Railroad in the 1870s and 1880s

The Philadelphia & Reading Railroad in the 1870s allowed at least some employees substantial control over their patents. The Reading's treatment of the patented locomotive firebox developed by its employee John Wootten in 1877 illustrates how some firms that were acutely aware of the value of innovation nevertheless considered it both expedient and inevitable that they should allow employees significant control over workplace-generated intellectual property.

Railroads, "the first modern business enterprises," were the first to employ a significant number of salaried managers to control their far-flung operations from a central office commanded by top managers. Railroads created an internal organization with "defined lines of responsibility, authority, and communication between the central office, departmental headquarters, and field units" and methods for monitoring the work of each manager and the performance of each department. They were, in short, the first thoroughly bureaucratic employers.[33] They were also among the most sophisticated in terms of technology. The shopworkers and skilled mechanics employed in the railroad's machine shops and maintenance facilities were "the 'high-tech' community of the nineteenth century."[34] Yet, although full-time, salaried, career managers had enormous say on the organization and growth of the railroads,[35] they paid scant attention to the relationship between innovation and employment policy. Because employee control of inventions did not threaten the railroads' strategy for growth, they did not see employee control of intellectual property as a problem.

John Wootten was part of that "high-tech community." Wootten worked in a variety of capacities for the Reading Railroad from 1864 to 1886. He served as the Reading's superintendent of the Mine Hill & Schuylkill Haven Branch in the 1860s, then rose through the ranks of the central technical offices of the railroad in the 1870s, serving as engineer of machinery and assistant general superintendent, as general superintendent, and eventually as the general manager of the railroad from 1877 to 1886. Wootten was unusually involved, for a railroad superintendent, in the technological aspect of his job. Railroad general managers typically delegated the role of master mechanic to subordinates. Not Wootten; he himself closely monitored railroad technology and patents and was both a manager and a technical employee. At the Reading, in contrast to some technology companies, especially after the turn of the twentieth century, invention and technological development had not yet been divorced from firm management.[36]

Over the course of the 1870s, Wootten sought to design a locomotive that would burn coal dust, which the collieries considered waste. As he explained in a letter to Franklin Gowen, the president of the Reading: "There are hundreds of thousands of tons of culm (waste coal) piled up at our breakers. It's just sitting there, doing us no good and getting in the way of operations."[37] Working with the shopworkers, enginemen, and firemen of the Reading, and with the permission of the company president, in 1876–77 Wootten designed and built a firebox that would burn coal dust to power a locomotive. The firebox was patented in Wootten's name. The Reading invested heavily in the development and promotion of Wootten's firebox. Besides paying his salary, allowing Wootten to use the staff and facilities of the Reading in his inventive work, and paying for all the materials used in developing the firebox, the Reading paid to have a locomotive with Wootten's firebox displayed at the Paris Exhibition in 1878. Reading lawyers probably also applied for the patent, as they applied for patents for other employees of the Department of Machinery.[38] Wootten's locomotive won a silver medal at the Exhibition, which garnered Wootten the praise of the Reading's leaders; one wrote to Wootten: "Dear Sir, I beg to congratulate you on the success of your locomotive. We are awarded the Silver Medal." Highlighting Wootten's technology expertise by professing none of his own, he continued, "I never realized what a fool I was until I ran across the Rail Road experts on the Jury. Every one on the Jury was a rail road manager or chief Engineer." The firebox's success was publicized in trade journals. The Reading installed Wootten's firebox on many locomotives. Wootten sold his firebox to many companies and personally supervised the initial runs of locomotives with the firebox.[39]

Wootten evidently became so involved in the development of the firebox and the Reading invested so much in it that the railroad's receivers became suspicious. The Reading, like many railroads in the late 1870s, had filed for bankruptcy and was therefore operated under the supervision of receivers appointed pursuant to the bankruptcy law. According to the historian of railroad innovation Steven Usselman, the receivers "accused Wootten of pursuing his own inventive activities at the expense of the company and even brought in technical experts in an unsuccessful effort to discredit the locomotive." Usselman explained: "These charges lacked merit, however, not just because the locomotives performed admirably, but also because Wootten's efforts often were directed not at furthering his personal fortune but at developing theoretical insights into the performance of heat engines."[40] Yet Wootten did appear to make some personal profit off his inventions, although it is not clear who received the profits from the sale of the firebox to other railroads. Although there is no evidence to suggest that Wootten ever charged the Reading for use of his inventions, he sold some of his smaller inventions having to do with a boiler and a nut lock for his own benefit.

In 1889, three years after Wootten retired, the railroad's management evidently became concerned about the legal status of the railroad's right to use Wootten's patented technology. The Reading's general counsel drafted an assignment for Wootten to sign "granting to the Philada. & Reading R.R.Co. and its allied lines, the use of all his machines, devices and patents." Wootten's reply indicated that he was perfectly willing to execute the assignment, but stated that he had assigned the patent to the firebox to the Baldwin Locomotive Company of Philadelphia, which built most of the Wootten locomotives. Wootten reported that he had requested a copy of the assignment from Wharton Basker, the president of the Baldwin company, "in order that I may be assured of the agreement of terms of the respective papers." A few months later, Archibald McLeod, the vice president and general manager of the Reading, wrote pleadingly to Wootten that one of the Reading's "allied roads wishes to build two or three engines, and I have induced them to adopt yours. They tell me that some one asks them $750 for the patent. Is there any way by which a reduction from that can be secured?" Obviously, the Reading did not have full control of the patent. Wootten replied that he would, "with pleasure, endeavor to meet your views with relation to the sum to be charged for patent license to construct the several locomotives to which you refer." He said that he would meet with Wharton Basker regarding the matter and would report to McLeod.[41] Today's corporate chief executive would, of course, be shocked at the idea of a company pleading and offering to pay for permission to use an invention that an employee had developed at work entirely at the company's expense.

Throughout the nineteenth century, the Reading appears to have had no formal policy regarding patent assignments by employees who developed inventions in the course of their employment. The absence of a contemporaneous agreement with Wootten regarding his firebox thus was not anomalous. None of the company's surviving law department records indicate that the railroad contracted with its employees in writing on anything having to do with patents or development of technology. The Reading's records do suggest, however, that periodically employees did devise improvements to various aspects of railroading technology and that the firm's lawyers advised on patenting them.[42]

The casual approach to ownership of employee patents cannot be explained by indifference either to innovation or to the significance of patents, for the Reading was plenty concerned with both during that era. But railroads did not adopt a competitive strategy of attempting to monopolize innovation. The basic technologies of the railroad—the steam locomotive, steel rails, and wheels—were widely considered to be part of the public domain. Nor did even the major railroads use the scientists whom they had on staff to develop new knowledge to enable the company to move into new fields or radically new innovations to gain competitive advantage in existing fields. As Usselman has explained, railroads sought territorial monopolies by ensuring that a corporate charter for operating a road was granted only to one company. Patent monopolies and controlling the diffusion of technology were not part of their strategy. Along with this went openness about experimental technologies; railroads generally exchanged technical information quite freely.[43]

The spread of the Wootten firebox to other railroads was not atypical. Master mechanics at the various roads tinkered with various approaches to particular technical problems such as fuel efficiency and water use. Once mechanics on a railroad or in a region reached a consensus about the best technology, news of the development traveled to other railroads and other regions through informal channels. Moreover, railroads did not jealously guard innovations from one another. Master mechanics of the railroads regularly exchanged information with mechanics all over each railroad's line and with mechanics at locomotive building firms, such as Baldwin, and at other railroads. They corresponded and frequently visited shops at other lines and at supply firms. General journals such as *Scientific American, Engineering*, and, after the Civil War, the specialized journal *Railroad Gazette* were another forum where they shared technological information.[44]

The railroads' attitude toward innovation had significant consequences for how they regarded innovation by employees, and, therefore, for how they regarded their technically skilled employees more generally. Many railroads relied on employees rather than outsiders to develop technology because the complexity and expense of the systems made it difficult for outsiders to develop and test their inventions without access to the railroads themselves. After all, only railroad employees would have a locomotive and a few miles of track at their disposal for testing inventions. Railroads encouraged employees to innovate within a certain range—the Pennsylvania Railroad's Board of Directors requested "the able mechanics employed at the various shops of the Company to exercise their wits and talents to produce such improvements as may be of service to this company which pays them so well for their time and attention to its interests."[45] In 1875, the Pennsylvania Railroad employed a chemist with a Ph.D. to establish a laboratory for the testing and analysis of materials produced by suppliers, and the laboratory was quite involved in the study of the properties of steel when railroads began to replace iron rails with steel. Yet the Pennsylvania's laboratory, complete with its staff of thirty-plus trained chemists, did not produce major innovations.[46] Like the Reading, most railroads adopted rather casual policies regarding ownership and control of employee patents.

At the end of the nineteenth century, as Usselman has shown, the railroads' approach to patents and innovation changed. The threat of infringement suits by outside inventors presented a greater risk of substantial liability than had been encountered up to that point. Many railroads reorganized their mechanical and technical operations to create an executive-level superintendent of motive power to oversee all technical matters on all equipment in the entire system. The push was to standardize, not to innovate; innovation made it more difficult to standardize, and standardization was thought to lead to efficiency. Superintendents of motive power "did not view themselves as inventors, nor did they especially value the inventive ability of their master mechanics and skilled operators. In many cases, the new superintendents of motive power actively sought to limit the freedom of employees to tinker and invent."[47] Thus, when the railroads established organized laboratories and testing facilities at the end of the nineteenth century, the agenda for such work was quite different than the bureaucratized invention that was beginning to occur at companies like Du Pont, Bell Telephone, General Electric, and Eastman-Kodak, which set up research laboratories around the turn of the twentieth century. The railroads' goal was to bureaucratize testing and to develop standards for devices and materials, not to come up with dramatically new technologies. The testing facilities came to be regarded as "ideal entry points on the path to careers in management."[48] But they were not centers of radical innovation, and their employment policies reflected that fact.

An Ingenious Man Enabled by Contract

It is ironic that in the mid-nineteenth century, when railroads zealously sought to innovate, they did not have the legal tools to enable them readily to claim their employees' inventions. Late in the century, when the legal tools became available, railroads no longer had the occasion to use them. By the time that judges interested in spurring innovation no longer regarded corporate ownership of employee patents as anathema, railroads were no longer centers of organized innovation and thus lacked the institutional incentive to push for legal change. Thus, an employee like John Wootten could comfortably occupy a position of inventor and manager and the social and economic status that accompanied that combined position without the railroad perceiving his independence as untenable for its legal and economic position. After the turn of the twentieth century, by contrast, most companies would have seen his ownership of his inventions as a threat to their business model.

It is also significant that John Wootten was a superintendent, not an ordinary employee. Railroad managers were men of stature in their business communities, and Wootten was no exception.[49] In 1877, shortly after Wootten became general manager and just as the firebox was being put into operation, it fell to Wootten to host a lavish reception in a private railway car for a White House delegation sent to investigate the bloody strike in which the militia fired on the workers, killing ten in one night. It had been Wootten's job as general manager to keep the trains running, and he directed the militia to turn on the strikers. (He claimed to have been haunted for years afterward by feelings of guilt for having set the killings in motion.)[50] As general superintendant and general manager, his job was no doubt to improve the Reading's business overall, and certainly the development of a locomotive powered by otherwise useless coal dust was a significant improvement in the business of a railroad that traveled through the coal mining regions of Pennsylvania. He used the time, materials, and manpower of the Reading to develop his locomotive. Because his job was to manage rather than primarily to invent, the Reading did not see that an implied term of his employment agreement included the obligation to assign to the employer any inventions he might make.

The story of Wootten and his locomotive suggests that the railroad managed to secure employee innovations by not being unduly focused on who owned them. Wootten was encouraged in his inventive efforts and received ample credit both within the firm and outside it for his successes. By being somewhat casual about control of the invention, and by supporting Wootten in his work, the railroad created an attitude of goodwill that made Wootten perfectly willing to allow his employer and other railroads freely to use the invention. Railroad executives, as Usselman said, "recognized that patents were an important source of personal esteem and potential reward for their mechanics," which may explain why they allowed employees to control them. As in the case of John Wootten, they sometimes offered assistance in obtaining patents and sometimes offered compensation for use of the patent, [125] but tended to rely on informal agreements that the employee would grant the railroad unlimited use of the patent while remaining free to license the invention to other railroads.[51]

The relatively high status of railroad mechanics and superintendents was both a cause and a consequence of employee patent ownership in the 1870s. Engineers like Wootten enjoyed the social status of gentlemen in the early nineteenth century. By the late twentieth century engineers were considered middle class, as fewer had the opportunity to rise to a position like Wootten's. Changes in legal rules and corporate practices regarding intellectual property rights after 1890 contributed to the decline in social status of men like Wootten and fellow engineers. The steady outpouring of scientifically trained engineers from the new technological schools, combined with industrial consolidation and bureaucratization that increasingly restricted access to top positions, led the majority of young engineers into subordinate corporate employment. The growing complexity of the machines and other technologies used in industry required greater coordination and oversight of the engineers and others who designed them.[52]

Increased managerial oversight, corporate lawyers' insistence on company control of intellectual property, and declining opportunities for entrepreneurship all contributed to the changed status of inventive men working for technology firms in the late nineteenth century. Among the things that rankled creative workers was the increasingly common practice of managers (a new breed of employee at that time) claiming credit for work done by their subordinates. Attribution as an inventor was an important determinant of social status. Wootten valued recognition as the inventor of the firebox as much as or more than whatever money he may have made in licensing the patent to the Reading or to other railroads. When the corporate management of intellectual property began to obscure proper attribution of inventions, it hurt creative workers deeply. Firms that claimed ownership of employee intellectual property—unlike the Reading—negotiated a complex balance of claiming corporate ownership where possible while also attributing individual creativity properly so as not to sap the morale of the workers.

In the 1870s and 1880s, courts largely adhered to a view of workplace innovations as the rightful property of employees, but they adopted a new contractual framework to support the conclusion. Contract became the method by which courts would assess competing claims to patents and other valuable knowledge. For those firms that made clear in their dealings with employees that the firm owned the technical knowledge, contract protected corporate intellectual property. But for the firms like the Reading Railroad and agricultural implements manufacturers that failed both in the contractual language and in workplace policy to aggressively assert corporate ownership of innovations, courts were unprepared to offer a remedy, insisting instead that a presumption of employee ownership of invention would best promote innovation, enterprise, and the independence of inventive men. It would be another decade before company lawyers figured out how to translate the systematic corporate efforts to innovate into a language and legal argument that courts would recognize as sufficient to justify corporate ownership of workplace intellectual property.

Inventing for the Factory in the 1890s

The intersection of employment contracts and the emerging law governing workplace knowledge significantly reduced the ability of inventive employees to act as entrepreneurs as well as employees. An influential 1895 federal court of appeals decision on the ownership of a patent to a cigarette-rolling machine reveals that courts realized employer control of technical knowledge was essential to the social policy of inducing innovation. The decision was a catastrophe for the career, business strategy, and self-conception of an entrepreneurial mechanic who regarded the new freedom of contract rhetoric as being directly contrary to his economic interests and to the true meaning of freedom. The episode illustrates the difference in legal rules and reasoning between the 1870s and 1890s. It also illustrates the difference between the prospects of a high-level inventor-manager like Wootten and a low-status outside inventor-mechanic.

The Bonsack Machine Company was founded shortly after James A. Bonsack, the twenty-year-old son of a wealthy woolen mill owner, patented a machine for making cigarettes in 1881. James Bonsack, his father, Jacob, a family friend D. B. Strouse, and a banker formed the company, which manufactured Bonsack machines and then leased them to cigarette companies, sending its own operators to set up and run the machines. The cigarette companies then paid the Bonsack Company a royalty based on the number of cigarettes produced.[53] William A. Hulse, a mechanic, was employed by the Bonsack Company under a contract requiring assignment to the firm of any "improvement in cigarette machines" he might develop during his employment "or at any time thereafter."[54] The Bonsack machine initially did not work very well, leading manufacturers to believe that the public was prejudiced against machine-made cigarettes. That changed in the late 1880s when a Bonsack mechanic managed to increase the daily output of cigarettes and to reduce production costs significantly at the cigarette factory owned by the Duke family of North Carolina.[55] The Bonsack Company soon sent a number of other operators to work there. One of these was William Hulse.[56]

At that time, tobacco employees were free to take their knowledge to other factories. Duke company president James B. Duke acknowledged that some employees of a firm that Duke had acquired "knew more about manu-facturing tobacco than the man that owned the business and sold it."[57] Duke considered it essential to keep the good Bonsack machine operators at his factory and objected to training employees who might take their knowledge elsewhere. Duke resented the Bonsack Company "sending any man here to learn to run the machines in our factory unless he proposes to remain in our employ." Duke complained vociferously over the years about turnover among Bonsack operators and was particularly irritated when he learned in 1889 that a Bonsack operator working in the Kinney Tobacco Company factory was trying to persuade one of the operators from Duke's factory to join him at Kinney. "[W]e don't propose to have our factory used as a school to train your operatives to be used at other factories. They can bear their own loss from training men for you just as we have done."[58]

The cigarette industry of the late 1880s and 1890s was fiercely competi-tive. Tobacco companies struggled to take control of the latest in cigarette production machinery on favorable royalty terms.[59] James Duke pushed Strouse to pursue patent infringement claims against the users of the ciga-rette-making machines in use at competitor factories, and the Bonsack and Duke companies acquired the patents to some other machines.[60] Duke also pressured Strouse to limit the introduction of Bonsack machines at new to-bacco companies, complaining about the training costs Duke would incur:

> If the machines were put into factories that have an established trade,
> I would raise no complaint. Five large factories now make, I think
> at least 90% of all the cigarettes sold in this country, and control the
> cigarette makers and it is hard for new beginners to take hands from
> an established factory where they run the risk of losing a permanent
> position.
>   Do you think it wise, under the circumstances for any of the large
> factories to put themselves in a worse position by introducing ma-
> chines that a new beginner can get and be ready to compete without
> extra expense? It cost us a large amount of money to train our hands,
> and was a great deal harder for us to build up our business than it
> would have been if all other factories used machines and we could

have gotten them at the time we started and saved this big outlay to train our hands.[61]

[128]   Finally, in 1888 and 1889, Duke got his wish: an agreement to limit Bonsack machines in the United States to the five largest factories. These five companies combined in 1890 to become the American Tobacco Company, also known as the Cigarette Trust. An 1895 newspaper reported that American Tobacco used the Bonsack machine "to crush out all competition."[62]

The litigation over employee patent rights had its origins in the activities of Richard Harvey Wright, a businessman with numerous interests who had been a partner in Washington Duke, Sons & Company in the early 1880s but had tired of "playing second fiddle" to James B. Duke.[63] Wright signed a contract in December 1888 for an exclusive agency to sell Bonsack machines to companies in Asia and Africa.[64] James Duke was angry at the prospect of international competition and threatened to hire an inventor "to get up a better machine than yours to be controlled solely by W. Duke Sons & Co." Wright's contract with the Bonsack Machine Company created a venture called "The Bonsack Oriental Affairs," from which Wright and Bonsack would share equally in the net profit. He was to procure foreign patents in his own name or the name of the Bonsack Machine Company, and they would both share ownership in those patents. Wright soon licensed Bonsack machines in Egypt and Malta, and then headed to Port Elizabeth, South Africa. William Hulse, who had worked intermittently for the Bonsack Machine Company since 1886, headed to Port Elizabeth to operate Bonsack machines on Wright's behalf. The work relationship while Hulse was in South Africa was punctuated by salary disputes, although eventually Wright paid the sums due Hulse.[65]

In July 1890, just as Hulse had returned to the United States, a Shanghai company accepted Wright's offer to license Bonsack machines. In August 1890, Hulse agreed to "make the trip to Manilla [sic] and Shanghai and remain at these two places as long as may be necessary to put up a Bonsack machine at each place and train a man to succeed me for the sum of one hundred and ten (110 dollars) per month." In the fall of 1890, Hulse went to Manila and set up a Bonsack machine. Realizing the power he had, and apparently concerned about a lack of communication from Wright, he threatened to leave Wright's employ: "The whole thing lays in my power now to make it a success. If I say the thing goes, she will go, and if I say no, she is a failure. So you will understand by this that I have got the whole thing under my thumb now, and I expect you to do the square thing by me, or she is no go. This company has made me a good offer to stay here in Manila and take charge of the machine department at a nice salary. I have almost given them a decided answer to stay. I will let you know what I am going to do when I get through at Shanghai."[66] Hulse wrote glowing reports of how well the Bonsack machine was faring. He then went on to Shanghai and then back to Manila to set up another Bonsack machine.[67] Finally, in July 1891, Hulse returned home to Rochester, New York, complaining that he was sick of Asia: "I h[a]ve had typhoons & centipedes enough to last me a lifetime without any earthquakes thrown in it."[68]

In August 1891, Hulse told Wright, "I have got something very important to talk to you about when I see you." Six days later, Wright and Hulse drew up a contract regarding "a certain invention or improvement relating to the manufacture of tobacco cigarettes, the same consisting substantially in wrapping a continuous rod of tobacco in a continuous paper strip or ribbon and folding and crimping the edges together so as to secure or seal the paper strip around the tobacco rod without the use of paste, it being his present plan to modify the tube now in use upon the Bonsack cigarette machines and apply thereto a device for folding together and crimping the edges of the paper strip after it has been wrapped around the tobacco rod so as to securely hold it in place." Hulse agreed to continue to develop this machine, which he called the "crimper," at his own expense, and to assign half his rights in the invention to Wright. In return, Wright agreed to handle and finance the patent application and licensing. A week after that, Hulse wrote, "I am getting along all right with the crimper. Am convinced more than ever that it will be a success."[69]

Hulse must have suspected at this time that his contract with his former employer, Bonsack Machine Company, might become an issue because he wrote the company to get a copy of the agreement. He wrote to Wright explaining that "it make[s] no difference whether [the company] sends it or not, as I only wanted to destroy the thing."[70] Hulse was right to worry that the 1886 employment contract with the Bonsack Machine Company was a problem. The contract stated that if Hulse made "any improvement in cigarette machines, whether the same be made while in the employment of the said company or at any time thereafter, the same shall be for the exclusive use of said company." The contract also provided that Bonsack could fire Hulse if he "shall in any way neglect his duty," but Hulse had to give 60 days notice before quitting.[71]

Such a pre-invention assignment clause was not unheard of in the industry. The American Tobacco Company used the same kind of employment contract, at least for some employees, and insisted on its ownership of inventions developed by them. As Duke explained in a 1900 letter rejecting an inquiry about licensing a machine from an inventor in New Jersey: "This company does not desire to take advantage of your offer. One, and a sufficient reason for not so desiring, is the fact that this company already owns any machine invented by Mr. A. Moonelis. Under conveyances and contracts made to and with this company, to which Mr. Moonelis is a party, this company is entitled to all inventions and patents of, or belonging to, Mr. Moonelis, on February 11th, 1895, and for a term of 20 years thereafter, which are in any way connected with machines for the manufacture of cigarettes and cigars."[72]

Hulse apparently began thinking about the crimper as early as 1890 and made a sketch or a model of it. He may or may not have been inspired by inventions he saw on his travels. While in Manila, Hulse wrote of "the machine that makes the cigarette without starch": "[T]here is one here [and] . . . you need not fear it in the least, for it makes more waste than it does cigarettes. But what work it does do is fine beyond a doubt."[73] Hulse wrote frequently to Wright giving progress updates, and Wright sent money to keep Hulse going. Meanwhile, the Bonsack Company started to press Wright for a statement of accounts, as the officers were concerned that they had not yet received any profit from the venture. Wright consulted a New York patent attorney to see whether the crimper could be patented. The lawyer eventually concluded that the crimper was sufficiently novel to be patented.[74]

To perfect the crimper, Hulse needed access to a Bonsack machine. In January 1892, he went to Lynchburg to show the machine to the Bonsack Company and briefly tested it there. He also obtained a custom cigarette tube for the crimper and charged it to Wright's account. On January 27, Hulse met with the New York patent lawyer, who advised that Hulse and Wright had "made a great mistake by letting any of the Bonsack Co. know anything about the thing at all until we had the thing patented & secured." Nevertheless, the lawyer commented optimistically to Wright, "It seems to me that the principle of his construction is all right, and I think that he will be able to make such slight improvements in this construction that it will do good work."[75]

In February 1892, Hulse briefly returned to Rochester and kept working on the crimper. His lawyer filed the patent application for it on February 12, commenting to Wright that the patent examiner was a "very cranky man," so it would be hard to predict how much trouble they would have getting the application accepted. On March 23, 1892, Hulse wrote: "I have got the thing all O.K. at last. She runs slick as greased lightning." A few days before reporting that success, Hulse and Wright sent a letter to the Bonsack Company, asking $100,000 for the rights to the crimper.[76]

Strouse responded the same day, making clear that Bonsack Company regarded the invention as covered by the invention assignment agreement in Hulse's employment contract. When Hulse found out that Bonsack insisted the invention was covered by Hulse's employment contract from years before, he was surprised and angry. In his view, Strouse was "trying to play a dirty game on us" by invoking the contract. "We will have to watch them like a hawk after a chicken. It beats the Duce—the meanness that's in that man." Bonsack decided not to insist on its right to the machine and offered "not only to pay Mr. Hulse for actual services rendered, but also to pay him what we regard as liberal for his improvement, provided it proves valuable to our company by reason of its being perfected, and letter patent be obtained covering the same." Wright replied that they would "push forward the crimping device as fast as possible, under the assurance of your board as to your liberality in the matter, if we make a success of it."[77] It is not clear what the Bonsack Company initially offered Wright and Hulse as compensation for the invention, although two years later, after litigation over the invention had begun, Hulse reminded Wright that Wright had "rejected the offer the Bonsack Co made us when they offered us the 20 thousand dollars."[78]

In April 1892, both the Bonsack Company and Hulse and Wright tried to make separate deals to sell the crimper patent to Duke. The Bonsack Company filed suit and obtained an injunction to keep Hulse and Wright from selling the machine. Hulse regarded Bonsack's litigation to prevent his using or selling the crimper as gross unfairness. "They are a slick lot of rascals, and I don't think they can be beat this side of it. I don't see what grounds they had to serve a warrant on you. Was it for infringement, or what the h—— do they mean by their rascality. I hope to god we can sell to some other Co. and burst the BokCo all to the devil."[79]

The first question Hulse and Wright's lawyer asked was whether Hulse had been an employee for Wright or Bonsack at the time he developed the invention. Upon learning of the contract Hulse had signed, the lawyer developed the arguments that the Bonsack Company had shown "bad faith," that the pre-invention assignment contract was "unreasonable" "when the circumstances of concealment are taken into consideration," and that the contract was void for lack of consideration and as a restraint of trade.[80]

The decision in the case was delayed. Wright sought to test the crimper on a Bonsack machine, but Duke's American Tobacco Company refused, and Wright tried to find other machines on which he could test the crimper at his own expense.[81]

In October 1892, the Patent Office declared an interference between Hulse's patent application and two applications from the American Tobacco

Company. (When a patent application claims the same subject matter as another application or an issued patent, the Patent Office declares an interference, a procedural mechanism to determine which is the first inventor.)

[132] Hulse and Wright's lawyer meanwhile found evidence that a "man in Durham . . . got a copy of Hulse's claims & sent them to the Amer. Tob. Co. or to J. B. Duke!" While the legal proceedings dragged on, all parties continued working on their machines.[82]

In February 1893, Strouse arranged with a factory in Montreal to allow a test of Hulse's crimper. Strouse insisted, however, that "nothing shall be known of the test or the result of the test, except to the parties directly interested in the said suit, The Bonsack Machine Company, Mr. Hulse and yourself." He justified this secrecy on the grounds of protecting Hulse's patent application from "parties who are antagonizing him in the Patent Office." Hulse and Wright's lawyer, however, feared that the test would work only to Bonsack's advantage, since Wright would be unable to use the results of a secret test to prove the value of the crimper. The lawyer would have preferred a test on another cigarette machine called the "International machine," since that would prove the crimper's value while providing less justification for Bonsack to claim ownership. Wright also did not want to take Hulse away from the packing machine project.[83] By February 1893, their lawyer seemed less optimistic about the case. He was "not at all sure" he could get the injunction dissolved, so he was intent on getting proof that the machine worked, to maximize the monetary award. He was reluctant to go to trial with the evidence available so far, but Wright pushed him to proceed.

The trial judge upheld Hulse's 1886 contract with the Bonsack Company. Judge Goff believed from the available evidence that Hulse had read and understood the contract. He found the contract to be a reasonable bargain, in which Hulse got favorable employment, while the Bonsack Company protected its interests with a narrowly tailored restriction on Hulse's subsequent inventive activities. Goff did not seriously consider the public policy argument regarding restraint of trade, since no matter who won the case, the public would not get free use of the device. Instead, the public policy concern that the judge emphasized was "freedom of contract." "To hold that he had not the right to so contract would deprive him of a privilege that might be of great value to him, and the effect of such a rule would be to discourage improvements and prevent inventions."[84]

According to Judge Goff, the contract provision requiring assignment of future inventions made it irrelevant whether or not Hulse was in Bonsack's employ when he invented the crimper, yet Goff nevertheless decided that Hulse had been employed by Bonsack at the relevant times.[85] Goff skipped over the second half of 1891 when Hulse worked on the crimper in Rochester, and described the testing that Hulse did in Lynchburg as being an "an arrangement" between Hulse and Bonsack in which "the company furnish[ed] a machine, room, labor, and material . . . with the mutual understanding that the device, when successfully tested and complete, should be the property of the Bonsack Machine Company, and that Hulse should be paid by that company liberally for his work." [133]

Goff also decided that even though the contract required Hulse to assign his interest in the crimper to the Bonsack Company, Bonsack would have to pay Hulse "a reasonable and just compensation" for the improvements made while Hulse was not on the company payroll, including the time that he had spent working on the crimper since he had left Lynchburg. It was necessary to order Hulse to assign the patent, rather than just to pay damages, since "[i]t would be impossible, from the nature of the case, to ascertain the damages the company might sustain by being deprived of the invention for which it had contracted." The case was referred to a master for a determination of what compensation Bonsack would be required to pay. The master returned his decision in late 1893, reporting unfavorably on the practicability of the crimper, and awarding $8,126.36, which was calculated based on Hulse's having spent nineteen months of labor at a rate of $5,000 per year. Although his lawyer thought this would be acceptable, Hulse was disappointed, feeling that he had been "bought by the Bonsack Machine Co."[86]

Hulse was still furious with Bonsack, but he was ready to give up the litigation, especially since he did not want to risk losing the whole settlement if Duke won the interference case in the Patent Office and his patent was rejected. "The d. dirty skunks. . . . Well, if they will settle with us, and we can get our money back and put us on even ground again, I think we had better let the buggars have it and not go to any more expense and loose [sic] the whole thing in the end, for the way things look now, I haven't the least doubt in the world but what they would beat us if we went at them again." Still, he left the decision to appeal up to Wright. The Bonsack Company, meanwhile, took the position that the crimper was not of practical use, so the award had been excessive.[87]

In spite of misgivings, Wright chose to pursue the appeal. Meanwhile, Hulse worked on Wright's new investments—an automatic tobacco packing machine and an attachment for stamping and labeling the packets—and Wright negotiated a deal for the use of the Bonsack machine, including an option to purchase a crimper, in South Africa. Wright also continued to provide instructions to his lawyers about procuring foreign patents for Hulse's crimper.[88]

Wright and Hulse settled the case with the Bonsack Machine Company on February 4, 1895, while the appeal was pending in the Fourth Circuit. Hulse and Wright assigned their interest in the crimper to the Bonsack Machine Company in exchange for a payment of $50,000, to be divided evenly between them.[89]

Settling the case turns out to have been wise, or at least extremely lucky, for Wright and Hulse. Judge Simonton's opinion for the Fourth Circuit, affirming the trial court's decision and award of $8,126.36, appeared the very next day.[90] Wright and Hulse's lawyer had telegraphed the court to advise of the settlement and speculated that the court issued its opinion anyway because the Bonsack Company wanted to set a precedent. The case was, indeed, a significant precedent.

The court first rejected the argument that Hulse's promise to assign his inventions had lacked consideration, finding that Hulse's willingness to agree to all the terms of the contract had been a necessary condition for the Bonsack Company to hire him, so consideration was present on each side of the deal. The court also decided that the contract was neither unreasonable nor unconscionable. The primitive state of the Bonsack machine had made it likely that improvements would come to mind that could not be conceived and developed without access to the Bonsack machine. "The improvement would be [the employee's] own idea. But it owed its suggestion and origin, its progressive development and perfection, to the business, the practical working, the opportunity afforded by the company." Therefore, it was "a natural and reasonable thing" for the company to require its employees to agree to assign their Bonsack-related inventions. It was necessary to include inventions that occurred after the employee left the company, since otherwise "the contract on this point could be easily evaded, and be made valueless." The opinion explained that the exchange of letters in March regarding "liberal compensation" could be seen either as a contract modification or as a mere statement of intent by the Bonsack Company, but in either case the terms of the original contract were not unconscionable.

The court of appeals agreed with the lower court that the contract was not against public policy and then elaborated further on its fairness and on the value of allowing Bonsack to protect its interests. First of all, if Hulse had not signed the contract, or if the contract had been known to be invalid, then Bonsack would not have hired Hulse, Hulse would not have invented the crimper, and "the public would have lost the benefit of his discovery." Thus, there was a significant public policy rationale in favor of upholding this type of contract. Also, the court saw the agreement as fair in light of the company's right to protect itself from the misuse of its secrets by its trusted employees. "The company lets [employees] into an intimate knowledge of its cigarette machines, affords them the opportunity of discovering any needed improvements in them, gives them at hand the means of testing any improvements which may suggest themselves. Naturally it seeks to protect itself from an abuse of these results."

Overall, the opinion's description of the equities of the situation suggested that the judges viewed the main problem in the case as being how to protect the firm's organized efforts at innovation from the depredations of this overly enterprising employee. "Here we have the case of an ingenious man, without opportunity of developing his talent, and struggling under difficulties, enabled by this contract to secure employment in a large and prosperous corporation, where he could give his inventive faculties full play."[91] The court rejected the argument that contracts assigning rights to all future inventions were against public policy because they restrained trade or stifled invention. The public interest, according to the court, lay in promoting innovation, which could best be achieved by protecting the firm, not the employee. Without the contract, Hulse would never have been hired, and "[t]hen, in all human probability, the public would have lost the benefit of his discovery."[92]

Immediately after the settlement, Bonsack's stock jumped. Bonsack hired a man to build and improve Hulse's crimper. Wright continued in his agency for the Bonsack Company, which even continued to refer employees to him. He went overseas to handle their business, which included licensing the improved crimper along with Bonsack machines.[93]

The Bonsack affair was not Wright and Hulse's only entrepreneurial effort in the area of cigarette manufacturing technology. In May 1893, Hulse had started working on a packing machine at a company in Chicago, and he later traveled throughout the United States setting up packing machines at various tobacco plants according to the customer's specific needs. In spite of his efforts to train local mechanics, Hulse was often the only one who seemed to be able to keep the machines functioning, and hence customers often pleaded for his assistance: "[I]f you cannot send Mr. Hulse here [to S. W. Venable] very soon, we will be obliged to start to pack by hand again."[94]

Hulse was well aware of his value as a skilled worker and the creativity that he contributed to his work, and he was sometimes unafraid to stand up to Wright. When Wright questioned one charge Hulse had made to the company, Hulse protested: "You had a machine here that wasn't worth a cent to you, and I went to work studied out a plan by which means you have a first class machine and now you want me to go ahead and do the same thing on another one, and more than that." Hulse recounted his other successes:

"The machines at Lorillards did not work at all until I went to work and studied out a device and attached it to the machine in order to make a success for you." If he were just a mere mechanic running machines designed by someone else, rather than an inventor and designer, Hulse insisted, "how many would you have made a success of?"[95] Hulse justified his salary by his importance to Wright's business: "You know as well as any one that you can't get a man that is reliable and that can do the work for the Co (that I have done) for any less money than you have been paying me." "And as to ordinary laborers, yes you can get plenty of them for 40 or 50 dollars per mo. But what earthly good would it do you, for you know better than I can tell you that no ordinary man can handle one of these machines. Just look what a time the Bonsack Co had trying to get men to handle their machines and what it cost them. And they got no returns for the money they layed out for 3 or 4 years and the Bonsack machine is not half as hard to handle as this machine, for it is not half so complicated."[96]

IN CONTRAST TO THE INVENTORS featured in the other stories recounted in this chapter and in the twentieth-century R & D facilities described in the chapters to come, Wright and Hulse were not regular employees of large corporations. They remained independent, by choice or by circumstance, and they were compelled to be entrepreneurial about their inventions. Contrary to the Fourth Circuit's imagined world in which Hulse was "enabled by this contract to secure employment in a large and prosperous corporation, where he could give his inventive faculties full play," Hulse never did enjoy security of employment. He remained an entrepreneur who sold his ideas piecemeal, and he was not in a position to trade the stability of corporate employment for the loss of intellectual property rights. He managed to come out of the litigation successfully only because he settled it the day before the Fourth Circuit issued its opinion divesting him of most of the ability to be entrepreneurial with respect to his patents. The change in law that culminated in such cases as *Hulse v. Bonsack Machine Company* would have the greatest impact on a person like Hulse, even though he himself did not feel the consequences. Inventors in later years would either have to negotiate for a much better contract or have to take and keep a job and pin their hopes on the security of a corporate salary.

5

They Claim to Own Him, Body & Soul

Popular entertainment looms large in the nineteenth-century picture of contractual allocations of employees' creative output. It was one of the few areas where creative people worked as employees (rather than for themselves) and where the results were sufficiently valuable commercially to make it sensible to litigate over ownership. This was an area in which courts most explicitly and self-consciously considered the line between the inalienable traits of human personality and the commodified knowledge and talent that could be sold through a contract of employment.

Litigation over control of the talent of singers, actors, writers, and others in popular entertainment from 1860 to 1895 reflected an evolving understanding of the nature of creativity and the role of employment contracts in creating property rights in employee innovation. Creativity and its products became commodities. The scope of intellectual property expanded, especially in the area of copyrights, trade secrets, and trademarks. Markets to sell intellectual property expanded in the growing consumer culture. These developments, combined with the transformation of working conditions and the rise of bureaucratic employment practices associated with factories and the emerging science of management, prompted firms to contract for ownership of employee innovations to an unprecedented degree. As such, courts were now persuaded to enforce such contracts or, if necessary, to imply contractual terms that had not been made. Judges enforcing the contracts had to define free labor to include ever-greater restrictions on employees' use of their talent. Enforcement of onerous sharecropping contracts was reconciled with free-labor ideology and came to define what freedom meant for southern black agricultural workers, and injunctions against strikes by factory and railroad workers came to define what freedom meant for industrial workers.

Similarly, enforcement of new contractual rights to employee knowledge and talent came to define the content and boundaries of free labor for those who worked with their minds, their talent as performers, and their celebrity.

[138]   The culture industries of publishing and performance offer a window not only into copyright but also into the full range of legal rules regarding workplace knowledge and employment contracts. As courts evolved an approach to employment agreements that increasingly recognized the employer's implied contractual right to own and control the knowledge and creative output of employees, they had to decide what role to play in enforcing the terms of the contract as they had defined it. The question of what remedy a court will order for a legal wrong is intimately connected to what courts are prepared to define as wrong in the first place. Thus, the extent to which the employee or the employer effectively controlled knowledge, ideas, and even celebrity or reputation—whether through a patent, copyright, trade secret, or contractual right to exclusive service—is determined by what a court will do when the parties dispute over its use. As increasingly diffuse forms of knowledge were recognized as employer-owned intellectual property, the question of enforcement grew especially acute because effective employer control would require prevention of the employee working for competitors or in certain occupations. It was in theater cases that courts first, most exhaustively, and most directly discussed whether protection of the employer's right under a personal service contract and rights to control employee intellectual property could justify a judicial order that an employee be prohibited from working. And, thus, it is in the theater context that we see most fully the conflict between the emerging law of corporate intellectual property and the freedom of labor.

In the 1860s, courts began to recognize employer rights in the copyrighted works of their employees. At the beginning, employer ownership was based on the existence of an express contract granting the employer the copyright or, in one case, on an equitable principle. It was not a copyright rule. The legal change began in the world of New York theater. This makes sense, as theater was one of the few sectors of the nineteenth-century economy where catalysts of legal change coalesced. Extensive collaboration produced a discrete work that reflected the collaboration (as opposed to something inchoate, like a technique, or something large, like a complicated piece of patented machinery). The work product was of sufficient value to make litigation sensible. There was no artisanal tradition shaping expectations of credit and ownership. As with many collaborative creative projects, it was difficult for the participants in the group project to predict or negotiate about whose contributions would be most significant and who should get what share of the benefit (if any) of being the author. Finally, it was relatively easy and often lucrative to copy a copyrighted work, so it was likely that if artistic or business differences arose, one of the collaborators would seek individual control over a joint or collective work, or indeed believe that the work was not a collective work at all.

A trio of theater cases from the 1860s, along with a few cases involving law books and other commercially valuable copyrighted works, sparked a change in the law regarding employer rights to employee-written copyrighted works. The theater cases all involved actors, some of whom also worked as playwrights and theater managers, who contracted with theater owners or managers to write a play. The cases acknowledged a general rule that the employee/actor/writer owned the copyright and the employer at most had a license to perform it in that particular theater for that particular run. Yet the courts suggested that theater managers might acquire proprietary rights based on the contributions that they had made to the changes in the plays and, as a matter of equitable principle but not copyright, based on an agreement to hire an actor to develop a play for performance in the theater. As a matter of copyright law then and now, if the playwright and the theater manager both contributed substantially to a single work, they could both be deemed authors—and copyright owners—of a "joint work." Neither the playwright nor the theater manager wished these plays to be deemed joint works, however, because each wanted exclusive rights to exploit the work.

These cases involved some of the most acclaimed actors of their day, as well as some respected legal scholars. The celebrity or academic reputation of the litigants invited the courts to consider whether reputation should influence attribution of authorship or ownership of literary property. The reputation of either the writer or the employer may have influenced the courts to see proprietary rights to these valuable theatrical literary properties as belonging to whichever party to the litigation (employer or employee) struck the court as most likely to have been the most important talent behind the production. The principle of employer ownership of works made for hire thus entered the law in a subtle way, but later became influential throughout the law of copyright.

A long-running and bitterly contested litigation of the 1880s and 1890s between a playwright and theater manager and the investors who financed his theater provided the occasion for judges to move the law away from the rules of the 1860s. The litigation produced one of the first published opinions enforcing a contract granting an employer the right to patents and copyrights created by an employee. The story reveals a sharp disjunction between the court's willingness to enforce the terms of contract and the attitudes expressed repeatedly in the popular press that the patents, copyrights, and especially the employee's reputation for having been the one to create them were inalienable. Yet, in stark contrast, in the 1870s courts adopted a rule allowing theater managers to enjoin performers from breaching their employment contracts by performing at rival theaters. Injunctions against breach of an employment contract presented a direct challenge to the long-settled notion that what defined free labor was the right to quit. If employer control over employee talent and knowledge could be protected at the expense of an employee's ability to quit her job, the newly emerging notion of corporate ownership of workplace knowledge would work a substantial incursion upon the freedom of talented employees. In the decades bracketing the turn of the twentieth century, courts expanded the remedies for employers facing the defection of valuable employees. What courts ultimately resisted, however, was a wholesale amalgamation of the law regarding injunctions to enforce employment agreements and the law governing other workplace knowledge, thus partially protecting the right of talented employees to engage in competition with their former employers.

Culture Workers and the Culture of Work in the 1860s

The first two of the trio of theater cases involved *The Octoroon*, a melodrama by the renowned playwright and actor Dion Boucicault. After his 1854 debut on the American stage, he appeared in many of his own plays and was acclaimed especially as the author of *The Poor of New York*, which opened in 1857 in New York.[1] Thus, at the time the pair of *Octoroon* cases were decided in 1860 and 1862, Boucicault was hardly the ordinary employee. He was a celebrity in American theater who ranked behind only Shakespeare as the most frequently performed playwright in Philadelphia theaters between 1856 and 1878.[2]

Boucicault was acutely aware of the significance of copyright ownership to his prospects as an entrepreneur in the emerging market of popular entertainment. He was sophisticated about legal matters and was successful in lobbying Congress to amend existing law to provide for copyright protection of plays in performance as well as in printed form.[3] Ironically, as one of his biographers tartly observed, Boucicault fought for copyright revisions and litigated to protect his rights yet was perfectly happy to take advantage of the absence of U.S. copyright protection for foreign works; "he had not the least hesitation in continuing his piratical raids on French dramatic literature and, indeed, any place that suggested a fertile idea. Sometimes he quite generously acknowledged his source, but I doubt that he usually paid any royalties." He complained bitterly about London theater managers who preferred to pay

£25 for a translation of a successful French play rather than £300 to £500 for a new but untried work. By such practices, Boucicault protested, "the English dramatist was obliged to relinquish the stage altogether or to become a French copyist."[4] Or, as Boucicault himself endeavored to do, the English or American dramatist had to make sure that his pirated versions of others' works were more successful than others' pirated versions of his. Boucicault was not alone in borrowing European plays; many American playwrights did exactly the same thing. Nor was he alone in complaining about the lack of foreign copyright protection for American works.[5] [141]

The Octoroon was the product of careful study of American theatrical taste and a deliberate effort to appeal to a wide audience. The play portrayed life on a Louisiana plantation in such a way as to offend neither North nor South by suggesting that slavery was an intolerable system while depicting southern slave owners as sympathetic characters. In the play, the plantation and the slaves who live and work there are to be sold to satisfy debts incurred by their late, spendthrift owner, Judge Peyton, on account of the mismanagement of the scheming Yankee overseer M'Closky. The plantation had been left to the judge's son, George, a charming playboy recently returned from Paris. Zoe, the judge's daughter by a slave who had been raised as a white daughter rather than a slave, must be sold as well because the judge's letter manumitting her is declared invalid on a legal technicality. Naturally, George and Zoe fall in love. M'Closky arranges to intercept a letter and a check sufficient to pay off the debts, but a faithful slave, Paul, gets the letter first. M'Closky kills Paul and blames the Indian Wahnotee (played by Boucicault) for the murder. A camera—an exciting new technology at that time—serves as the *deus ex machina* of the plot: the truth is eventually revealed when a photograph of the murder is discovered. Wahnotee then avenges the death of Paul by murdering M'Closky. Unfortunately, M'Closky's crimes are discovered too late, because Zoe, who had already been sold to M'Closky at the slave auction, swallows poison to avoid her fate. In the closing scene, Zoe dies in George's arms.[6]

According to the facts recited in the opinion, Boucicault wrote the play in 1859 while "employed as an actor and stage manager" of the Winter Garden Theater in New York City. William Stuart was the manager of the theater. A couple of years before, Stuart and Boucicault had opened the Washington Theater in Washington, D.C., but the theater was not a success. So the Winter Garden was not their first collaboration, and, obviously, Boucicault was not an "employee" in the sense of being Stuart's subordinate. Indeed, Boucicault is credited in some books as being the producer of the play. He and Stuart were more akin to partners than to employer and employee.[7]

Boucicault and Stuart orally agreed that the former would, as one court found, "write a play representing life on the Mississippi, and that it should be performed at Stewart's theater so long as it should continue to draw good audiences." Boucicault quit the Winter Garden six nights after *The Octoroon*

opened because he and his wife, Agnes Robertson, who also acted in the play, were in a dispute with Stuart over their salaries. The day before quitting, Boucicault registered a copyright on the play in his own name. When Stuart continued to run the play without him, Boucicault brought suit in Massachusetts for a preliminary injunction to prevent Stuart from running the play, and in New York for damages for Boucicault's share of the profits.[8] Although both courts found that Boucicault was Stuart's employee at the time he wrote the play, neither thought that fact entitled Stuart to the copyright.

The Massachusetts court rejected Stuart's defense that Boucicault was employed to write the play. The court determined that he was employed as an actor and stage manager, but not as an author, and that a simple agreement to write a play did not entitle the employer to the copyright.[9] The court's framing of the case left open the possibility that an employer might obtain the copyright to works by one employed for no purpose other than to write.

In the suit for damages two years later, the New York court did not emphasize the difference between employment as an actor and employment as a writer. Rather, it suggested that only an express contract would entitle the employer to the copyright in any of its employees' works because of the special nature of authorship. Boucicault's agreement to write and perform in the play, and to share half the profits from it, did not confer upon Stuart title to the drama: "The title to literary property is in the author whose intellect has given birth to the thoughts and wrought them into the composition, unless he has transferred that title, by contract, to another." Stuart lost the suit because, the court found, "[i]n the present case, no such contract is proved. The most that could possibly be said, in regard to the right of Stuart, or his trustee, in the play, is, that the arrangement entitled them to have it performed at the Winter Garden as long as it would run."[10]

The crucial reasoning begins with a metaphor of the nature of authorship that by itself is supposed to justify copyright: "the author whose intellect has given birth to the thoughts." The rights of parents in their children—the famous paternity metaphor of authorship that the work is the "brat of the brain," in Daniel Defoe's terms—is employed to justify a default rule of employee copyright ownership.[11] Authorship, like parentage, is particularly personal: "A man's intellectual productions are peculiarly his own, and, although they may have been brought forth by the author while in the general employment of another, yet he will not be deemed to have parted with his right and transferred it to his employer." If authorship is the "bringing forth" of new life, a new creation, and the creation is "peculiarly" one's own and irreducibly personal, a legal rule should not presume one has given away one's property (or one's children) in the absence of a clear intent to do so. Thus, the court articulated a clear statement rule, explaining that "producers" who employed "authors in particular literary enterprises" could easily, when they felt it in their interests, contract for employer ownership of the copyright, and that a contract transferring the copyright would be enforceable. In other words, the employee-author could give up his creation for adoption by his employer, but should not lightly be found to have done so.

A similar result was obtained in the same period in a New York federal court in a suit against a newspaper that reprinted the entirety of a copyrighted book. The plaintiff had registered a copyright in a book about the life and exploits of a pirate. Part of the book was allegedly written by the pirate himself, part was the pirate's alleged confession to a deputy U.S. marshal, and part was allegedly the marshal's description of the "phrenological character" of the pirate. Although the court's opinion has been lost, the summary prepared by the reporter of decisions stated that the plaintiff could not maintain the action for infringement because he was not the actual author: "The literary man who writes the book and prepares it for publication is the author, and the copyright is intended to protect him and not the person who employed him."[12]

The third case in the trilogy of actor/playwright cases from the Civil War period was *Keene v. Wheatley* (1861), which concerned the famous play *Our American Cousin*. The play is about a gullible English baronet whose financial advisor swindles him out of the family fortune. To save the fortune, the baronet's lovely daughter is engaged to be married to the unscrupulous advisor. An American relative (the cousin of the title) turns up on the scene and eventually everything is straightened out. The legal dispute was between Laura Keene, a celebrity actress, producer, and theater manager, and the actor who played the title role.[13]

Though most playwrights worked for the company or for the theater, some playwrights such as Boucicault were beginning to enjoy a certain celebrity status and to assert their entitlement to copyright their works (even when they plagiarized from others and were paid to do so by the theater). Court rulings favoring Boucicault established a principle of employee copyright ownership because Boucicault was in the role of employee. When—as in the case of Laura Keene, who combined the roles of playwright, actor, and theater manager—the celebrity played the role of employer and the competing copyright claimant was an actor in the company, the courts saw the entitlement to copyright very differently. Court rulings favoring Keene eroded the pro-employee rulings secured by Boucicault.

With the celebrity as the employer, the decision articulated a very different and more employer-friendly view of copyright ownership. According to the statement of facts, Joshua Silsbee, an American actor, had performed in *Our American Cousin* in Benjamin Webster's famous London theater company. Silsbee returned with a copy of the play to the United States, where he died, bequeathing the manuscript to his widow, who later sold it to two Philadelphia theater producers, Wheatley and Clark. Meanwhile, the British author of the play, the well-known playwright Tom Taylor, sold the American rights to Laura Keene, the proprietor of a theater in New York, for $1,000. With the assistance of Joseph Jefferson, an actor in her company, Keene adapted it for performance in her theater.[14] After the play's long and wildly successful run at Keene's Theater in New York, Keene and her theater company took it to Ford's Theater in Washington, D.C.

It was during the 1865 run of *Our American Cousin* at Ford's Theater that John Wilkes Booth shot Abraham Lincoln. Booth was able to plan the assassination because, as an actor, he knew both the play and the theater. After he shot Lincoln, Booth jumped from the state box down onto the stage, knocked Keene out of his way, and ran out the stage door. Keene was said to have run up to the president's box and stayed with the Lincolns after the president was carried across the street to the boardinghouse where he died. Evidently Keene's bloodstained dress became an artifact much sought after by souvenir hunters. Keene herself was briefly arrested when she and her company later left Washington, presumably on suspicion that she had been involved in Booth's plot. She was quickly released and never prosecuted.[15]

Long before the Ford's Theater run, *Our American Cousin*'s huge success in New York had already shaped taste in theater and spawned fashion trends emulating the style of some of the characters. Little wonder, then, that theater managers in other cities eagerly sought to mount their own productions and share in its success. Jefferson, too, sought to share the wealth and sold to Wheatley and Clark the additions he had developed with Keene's company. Keene and Jefferson disagreed about the extent of their own contributions in revising Taylor's version of the play for the American stage. Keene's biographer emphasizes Keene's rewriting. Jefferson's autobiography, not surprisingly, emphasizes his, suggesting that Keene initially "thought little of the play, which remained neglected upon her desk for some time." Jefferson claimed that it was only because her business manager "chanced" upon it and gave it to Jefferson, who saw "the chance of making a strong character of the leading part," that the play was recommended for production.[16]

Keene, who had a long and successful career as an actress and theater manager, was a determined adversary. In addition to acting, managing her theater, and touring, Keene also had a play-brokering business. She constantly sought out new material, revising it to suit her needs, and wrote her own plays. She copyrighted all the plays in her own name and frequently licensed them to theater managers around the country. As she wrote to one Boston theater manager offering to license "her play," "It is now the sensation of London and Paris. It has been carefully rewritten by myself to suit America. All my stage knowledge has been employed to give the two grand scenic effects the elements of such a success as will create a genuine sensation. The story is simple, yet thrilling, the piece full of good parts, incidents, and fun." It is thus not surprising that Keene litigated over the rights to the play, for she obviously thought of plays as valuable literary properties that she could license to others as well as perform herself. She regarded the company's changes to *Our American Cousin* as her property rather than as the creative property of Jefferson and the others. She copyrighted the play shortly before the premiere, and, according to her biographer, she dreamed up the title when she filed for copyright because Taylor had not titled it before selling the rights to her.[17]

There is no line-by-line comparison that parses out the various contributions of Taylor, Keene, Jefferson and others in Keene's company who contributed to the success of the play. Keene, as director, allowed an unprecedented two weeks for rehearsal before the play opened in New York, and it evidently was during that time that the work evolved to the point that she and others would dispute authorship and ownership. The two weeks "gave the cast members the unusual privilege of 'developing their characters.'"[18] Jefferson developed the American cousin character by significantly altering a stock character in nineteenth-century theater (the "Yankee"), transforming the role from a "droll, awkward, bumpkin" or "broad and extravagant boor" into someone of "stature," a "quiet, easy, natural, and at the same time excessively droll fellow."[19] Edward Sothern created many distinctive aspects of his famous role as Lord Dundreary: He devised the drooping mustache that became the hallmark of an eccentric comic as well as a variety of verbal and physical tics that became staples of nineteenth-century comedy. The cast, including Keene, collectively revised the script, and she, perhaps with others, designed elaborate new sets.[20]

All the work paid off. Sothern and Jefferson became stars and Keene's own fame grew.[21] The play was so popular that the company gave benefit performances to raise money for good causes, establishing the charity matinee tradition. Society ladies who had snubbed Keene flocked to her theater for the charity performances, and Keene found the social acceptance that eluded most actresses and theater people. She also found prosperity. Jefferson quipped that during the run Keene began "to twinkle with little brilliants until at the end of three months she was ablaze with diamonds."[22]

When Wheatley and Clark mounted a production of *Our American Cousin* based on the script purchased from Silsbee's widow and the additions purchased from Jefferson, Keene sued for misappropriation of "her" play. The court concluded that Taylor, as a British citizen, did not have a valid U.S. copyright to sell to Keene, and therefore Keene did not have a valid copyright claim to the original version of the play. Although Keene and her cast were American residents, their modifications could not be copyrighted because they were only accessions, not an independent work. Nor could she challenge the defendants' use of the script obtained from Silsbee's widow, for she owned no rights in it. But the court found Keene could seek an equitable remedy for the use of the additions procured from Jefferson: "Mr. Jefferson, while in the general theatrical employment of the complainant, engaged in the particular office of assisting in the adaptation of this play; and made the additions in question in the course of his willing performance of this duty. She consequently became the proprietor of them as products of his intellectual exertion in a particular service in her employment."[23] The court did not ground Keene's proprietary rights to the "products of his intellectual exertion" in copyright, but rather in a vague, equitable principle that employers have a right to the work product of their employees.

One way of reading the case is as a judicial expansion of the scope of copyright to fix what the judge considered a deficiency that Congress had not yet seen fit to address. Foreign works could not be copyrighted in the United States, but neither could they be significantly modified and then copyrighted in their revised form by Americans. *Our American Cousin* fell into that gap in copyright law, and its huge success served as a reminder that the gaps could cost a lot of money to those enterprising Americans who capitalized on foreign works and made them successful in the United States. As will be seen, however, the court's perception of Keene's rights as Jefferson's employer led to the recognition of a legal principle that eventually transcended the specific facts of the case.[24]

Although Keene's win in *Keene v. Wheatley* in 1861 established a principle of employer rights that later became significant, it did not accomplish for her what she had hoped. She spent several years and instituted at least three suits trying (unsuccessfully) to protect her exclusive right to *Our American Cousin*. Six years later, Keene was again trying to fend off those who sought to produce the play without her permission.[25] She learned that Edwin Booth, brother of the infamous John Wilkes Booth,[26] had purchased the Winter Garden Theater and named as manager her adversary from *Keene v. Wheatley*, John Clark. She sued Clark and, perhaps growing skeptical about the efficacy of legal remedies, made her fight public. She wrote a letter addressed to him but intended for publication in which she accused him of theft. She asserted that it was her "enterprise, industry and expenditure" that made the play a success: [147]

Sir—I see by your advertisement in the Herald that you purpose [*sic*] playing *Our American Cousin*.

No one in our profession is better aware than yourself that in all honor, honesty and fair dealing the said play is my sole property. I gave the author a large sum for it when it was an unacted manuscript. By my enterprise, industry and expenditure, I made the play a great success. You then being one of the managers of the Arch street theatre, Philadelphia, determined to act the play. You obtained a copy of it, which was proven on trial to have been stolen from the author, Tom Taylor. I brought a suit against you then and it was proved you had obtained all the original matter which had been written by my stage manager and myself from an employee of my theatre. Judge Cadwalader decided against you, and under whose decision you were compelled to pay damages. You ultimately apologized for your share of the transaction and wished to shift all the blame on others. You had made many thousands of dollars, however, while the suit lasted. Since then you have played it in Washington, Baltimore, etc., knowing full well that my professional engagements would prevent restraining you by law from so doing. In these places you have again made large sums from its production. Should not the money you have already made from my property content you? You know well this is not a case of copyright[;] it was my personal, private property, and should have been held sacred to me by every respectable member of our profession; but now, while I am absent from New York, you take advantage of that absence to play *Our American Cousin*. I am so identified with that play that I consider it one of my most valuable possessions. Why seek to deprive a woman of her honestly acquired property? Why not take the Beteran or Rosedale or any other play owned by a man?

The bad taste of seeking to deprive me of the use of this play is only equaled by your ever appearing in a comedy which ought to have only a memory of shame and horror for you and every member of your family. You cannot lift the cloud which has fallen upon our whole profession by acts which set at naught all regard for principle and right.[27]

Keene, like Eleuthere Irenee du Pont a half-century earlier, wrote the letter as a plea to the court of public opinion when pleas to the courts of law were unavailing. That strategy for dealing with infringement of literary property rights both predated these American cases and continues to this day. Entertainment companies still make public pleas urging movie viewers to avoid unauthorized copies of their products and complain vociferously about the harms caused by piracy of copyrighted works.

The letter and its subsequent history underscore the importance of claiming the moral high ground and the rhetorical force of staking that claim in authorship. Keene's letter used a number of devices to do so. Obviously, one was the characterization of the play as her property that he had stolen. Interestingly, in the ensuing litigation, *Keene v. Clark*, attorneys for both parties stipulated that she did not in fact write the letter accusing him of theft, since, as a *lady*, she could not possibly have written such a scurrilous attack.[28] Perhaps one ought not take this stipulation at face value. Lawyers for both litigants might have wanted the letter excluded from the record for other reasons. A second tactic was to remind the world that a member of the Booth family, above all people, should not have any connection with the play that Lincoln was watching when John Wilkes Booth killed him. Third, invoking chivalry and feminine prerogative, she accused him of stealing from her because she was a woman.

Keene was absolutely right that this was "not a case of copyright." Unlike the cases involving *The Octoroon*, the ruling in her favor was based on "equitable principles," not copyright. Significantly, it did not rely on copyright doctrine or on any of the copyright cases that preceded it.[29] Since the court disavowed reliance on copyright law, its opinion was nominally consistent with the Boucicault rulings. That is, Keene's claim to own the modifications to *Our American Cousin* was based not on copyright (as Stuart had tried to claim against Boucicault) but rather on the equitable principle that Jefferson had acted improperly in selling rights to a text that he did not own. Thus, although an employer may not have been entitled to a copyright as an "author," she could be entitled to equitable remedies against overreaching by her employees. But at another level, it was not at all consistent. Except for the fact that she had been involved in adapting *Our American Cousin*, and no one alleged that Stuart had been involved in the creation of *The Octoroon*, there was no more reason for her to receive legal protection to Jefferson's creative work than Stuart had to Boucicault's, so long as one adheres to the intellectual labor theory of authorship.

Keene drew on a variety of precedents having to do with ownership of inventions and trade secrets, as well as on the *Lumley* rule, which held that an opera singer who breached a contract to perform at one theater could be enjoined from performing elsewhere for the term of her contract.[30] Interestingly, the court did not even bother to try to distinguish the facts of the *Keene* case from the Boucicault case, *Roberts v. Myers*, decided by a Massachusetts [149] federal court only the year before. Nor did the second Boucicault case, decided by a New York federal court a year later, attempt to distinguish the Pennsylvania federal court decision in *Keene*. There were some distinctions. Keene was personally involved in adapting *Our American Cousin*; there is no evidence that Stuart assisted Boucicault in writing. Keene's lawyer may have made in litigation the same claim that Keene herself later made in print: the play was her "personal, private property," and the product of her "enterprise, industry and expenditure." Characterizing the play as Keene's own work made the claim of employer ownership more compelling because it did not contradict the extant justification for employee ownership of the copyrights to works that were entirely the product of their own efforts (even though they were employed to exert that effort).

Finally, there was her celebrity, the notoriety of the play, and the fact that it was well known that neither she nor Jefferson was really the "author" in the copyright sense. These facts, as well as her aggressiveness in claiming the fruits of her "industry and enterprise" in hiring Jefferson and promoting the play, combined to make her claim to ownership of the play more compelling than the theater managers' claims had been. The old rhetoric of authorship, thus, did not fit. The court created a new rhetoric of employer prerogative based on industry, enterprise, and collaborative creation.

The First Case of an Author for Hire

The rhetoric of employer ownership did not long remain confined either to cases in which the employer had contributed to the work or to "general equitable principles" as opposed to copyright. In 1869, a federal court in Massachusetts stated in dicta, without acknowledging its apparent departure from earlier decisions, that an employer would have the copyright in the literary products of its employees. The decision, *Lawrence v. Dana*, was another chapter in the long and unsuccessful copyright battles fought by or on behalf of Henry Wheaton, the erstwhile Supreme Court reporter whose litigation over copyright to Supreme Court reports had first considered the possibility of employer ownership of works created for hire.[31] Wheaton had written a respected treatise on international law, *Elements of International Law*. After his death, his widow, Catharine, contracted with William Lawrence, a friend of the family, to prepare an updated edition of her late husband's work, which came out in 1855. Catharine Wheaton copyrighted the book in her own name and received royalties from the sales. Lawrence then began to prepare a second updated edition. Catharine Wheaton registered the copyright to the second updated edition in her own name in 1863.[32]

[150] While Lawrence was still working on the second edition, he and Mrs. Wheaton learned of a Mr. Brockhaus in Leipzig who planned to publish a French version of Lawrence's annotation. In return for Lawrence's cooperation with the creation of the French edition, Mrs. Wheaton's daughter signed a memorandum granting Lawrence the rights to his annotations, but not to the text of the book. Subsequent attempts to formalize the agreement left the status of Lawrence's notes unclear, as Lawrence refused to agree to either of the express agreements offered to him concerning ownership of *Elements of International Law* and his contributions toward it.[33]

Catharine Wheaton was dissatisfied with Lawrence's work on the first two editions. Lawrence's notes were unnecessarily long. Worse yet, he expressed views sympathetic to the South in the Civil War, an egregious offense for a northerner writing on international law. His scandalous views were reported in the *New York Times*, and the *North American Review* reported that "examination of the notes of the edition of 1863 at the State Department had resulted in its condemnation for disloyalty of sentiment in those parts wherein questions arising in the pending civil war were discussed. . . . It was made evident that Mr. Lawrence had . . . intent to discredit the government of his country and to afford aid to its enemies."[34]

Mrs. Wheaton asked Richard Henry Dana, another family friend, to create another annotated edition "to rescue the honorable fame of Mr. Wheaton from this disgrace, and to restore value and authority to the work." Dana, who is today remembered by many for his 1840 memoir of his youthful adventures at sea, *Two Years Before the Mast*, had respectable credentials to take on the task. He had graduated from Harvard Law School, been active in the Free Soil movement, and run unsuccessfully for public office, though he was not eminent even by the standards of the day.[35]

Dana's edition of *Elements of International Law* was published in 1866 and favorably reviewed. Mrs. Wheaton had directed Dana to leave Lawrence's notes entirely out of the new edition, so the preface to Dana's edition stated that "[t]he notes of Mr. Lawrence do not form any part of this edition." In fact, however, Dana had used Lawrence's notes as a source; he just did not print the notes themselves. Dana's friend Thornton K. Lothrop wrote to Charles Francis Adams, Dana's biographer, that Dana "thought anybody could collect authorities, and that to do this was a day laborer's task; he used Lawrence's collections, and then despised his notes because they were mere collections of authorities, and at last thought himself under no obligation to him, because the notes were what anybody could have done, and so would not say the soft word that might have turned away wrath, but wrote instead what almost rendered a lawsuit inevitable."[36]

Neither Catharine Wheaton nor the book's publishers informed Lawrence of Dana's undertaking, so he learned of it through word of mouth. Furious and deeply offended, Lawrence wrote letters to newspapers and to international law experts accusing Dana of plagiarism.[37] The *New York Times* opined that "the aesthetic was greater than the legal error. Mr. Dana's fault in borrowing from Mr. Lawrence's learning might have been palliated by reason of the admirable and original use which he made of what he borrowed. But he should have acknowledged his indebtedness, as is the wont of professional and historical writers in such circumstances."[38]

Lawrence also sued Dana for copyright infringement. Dana defended himself by arguing, among other things, that Mrs. Wheaton's copyright in Lawrence's work was invalid, and thus Lawrence had none either. The court rejected the defense, finding that Mrs. Wheaton had the right to copyright the work because Lawrence had performed his annotation services as a gift to her and had consented to her securing the copyright. The court explained: "Although the services were gratuitous, the contributions of the complainant became the property of the proprietor of the book, as the work was done, just as effectually as they would if the complainant had been paid daily an agreed price for his labor." Therefore, Mrs. Wheaton did not need a formal assignment of rights from Lawrence in order to be allowed to copyright the work. In the court's view, Catharine Wheaton had expressly contracted with Lawrence that she would make no use of his notes in any later editions without his written consent and that he would have the right to make any use of them he wished. What is significant about the case is the dictum. The court remarked that, absent such a contract, Catharine would have owned the copyright to the notes. Finding a valid copyright in the Lawrence edition, the court submitted to a special master the question of how much Dana had copied. The master's report finally came back in 1881 finding far less copyright infringement than Lawrence had alleged, consisting only of citations and lines from sources that Lawrence had quoted.[39]

The principle of employer ownership as a default rule, recognized in *Keene* and *Lawrence v. Dana*, could be introduced relatively painlessly because in both cases the employee did not lose significant rights. In *Keene*, Jefferson lost little because he was not a party to the litigation; presumably, he had sold Wheatley and Clark his rights, and they were the ones who would stand to lose if it turned out that he had no rights to sell. In any event, he only authored certain additions, not the whole play, and the defendants had an independent source for everything in the play except his additions. In *Lawrence v. Dana*, the employee-author lost nothing by recognition of the principle because there was an express contract protecting his claim to copyright.

The novelty and importance of the work-for-hire principle were obscured because it first slipped into the cases without the usual adversary process (either because the actual employee author was not a party [as in *Keene*] or because the principle was stated in dicta [as in *Lawrence*]). These seminal cases did not actually force a court to choose between the rights of the employee and those of the employer. For a generation afterward, courts simply repeated the principle as dicta, giving it the patina of age without ever actually relying on it to decide a case. A string of cases decided in the 1880s and early 1890s persisted in finding one reason or another to recognize the copyright of the employee-author. Many acknowledged employer ownership in dicta, but no courts actually held that the fact of employment *ipso facto* entitled the employer to the copyright. The work-for-hire principle most definitely was not legal doctrine at that point—it was dicta—but it became a shadow in the corners of cases decided on other grounds.

The uncertainty of property rights was perhaps ameliorated by the importance of express contracts. The fact that most copyrighted materials in the era were produced by people who would have entered into relatively short-term contracts in which both parties contemplated the creation of copyrighted works suggests that in many cases the parties probably allocated ownership rights by contract. The extent to which parties contracted around the default rule is unclear and probably varied significantly by industry. There are reasons to believe that it was not particularly easy to contract around the uncertain defaults. The costs of transacting were high; then as now it was difficult for the parties to discuss something as touchy as authorship. Employers might have been afraid to alienate employees or to give them ideas by demanding assignment of the copyright. Some employees (probably not Lawrence, but perhaps Jefferson) may have lacked legal sophistication to realize that it was necessary to contract for copyright ownership. Moreover, the instability of the law made enforcement of any contract they did reach highly uncertain, so even those who were aware of the need for a contract may have doubted whether it was worth the trouble to negotiate one.[40]

The experience of Dion Boucicault and William Stuart bears this out. Why, when they agreed that Boucicault would write *The Octoroon* for performance at the Winter Garden, did they not agree who would own the copyright? Surely they both contemplated that their association would produce a copyrighted work and both must have hoped it would be valuable. Moreover,

Boucicault was not naïve about copyright law. Perhaps they failed to negotiate explicitly for copyright ownership for the same reasons that playwrights and those who assist them often fail to today: there may be serious costs to the relationship in raising those issues. The parties may each hope for a better result through informal resolution, or they may be unsure at the outset what each of their contributions will be and how, therefore, best to divide the credit and profit. Then as now, there may be many reasons why even those most likely to anticipate the production of a copyrighted work might not negotiate around the default rule.[41] [153]

An intriguing feature of the handful of cases decided in the 1860s involving disputes over the work product of creative employees is that some judges became *bricoleurs*, borrowing a bit of law from here and there without acknowledging the degree of creativity that they exercised. *Keene v. Wheatley* (1862) was an astonishing exercise of *bricolage*. To resolve the dispute about ownership of additions to a play that neither of them had written, the court looked to copyright law, to general principles of "equitable jurisprudence," to English equity cases involving injunctions against creative employees, to English cases on "secrets of inventors, or improper disclosures of knowledge acquired in professional relations, or in those of service or agency" to devise a brand-new American legal rule regarding workplace creativity.[42]

But still the various cases did not seem to form a self-conscious body of law. For every court that drew on a variety of sources to pull out common threads, there was another court somewhere else that approached employee copyright ownership as if it had nothing to do with patent ownership or control over workplace secrets. And, indeed, copyright and patent remained separate and distinct bodies of law until well into the twentieth century. Thus, the *Keene* court's treatment of these cognate doctrines involving ownership of workplace knowledge—the enticement rule of *Lumley v. Wagner*, the emerging trade secret rule—was virtually unprecedented. Most of the cases it cited involving employees were of recent vintage (none was more than a decade or two old), and *Keene v. Wheatley* was the first court to put them all together in a published opinion articulating a default rule of employer ownership. The court stated a general principle of employer ownership of employee knowledge or creative works at a time when very few courts had so ruled and when there were some cases stating just the opposite.

Second Generation Litigation over Ownership of
Knowledge and Free Labor in Theaters

In the ten or twenty years after *Lawrence*, *Keene*, and *Boucicault*, a number of significant legal changes had occurred outside the area of copyright law that might have changed the perspective of courts about disputes over ownership of creative employees' work product. While the law was still in flux, there were precedents that would provide a judge who was so inclined with the tools to change the law of copyright to recognize greater rights for employers. And, in 1879 the opportunity presented itself in the form of a dispute between some investors and Steele MacKaye, an accomplished actor, teacher, playwright, theater designer, and director.[43] MacKaye had long wanted to build a combination theater and theater school, and he had announced his plans to expand the theater he was currently leasing into a larger one. However, he was also so deeply in debt that he could not keep his current theater operating. Reverend George S. Mallory approached MacKaye about buying the theater from MacKaye's landlord and employing MacKaye to renovate and reopen it. As a clergyman, Reverend Mallory wanted to keep his involvement with the theater a secret, so only his brother, Marshall Mallory, was named in the contract with MacKaye.

The contract provided that MacKaye would work for Marshall Mallory, devoting "the whole of his time, energy and service" in the capacities of "an author, a manager, an actor, a director, or in any other capacity having any connection with theatrical labour." The contract also stipulated:

> And the said Steele MacKaye further agrees that the entire product of his intellectual and physical labour and skill, together with all copyrights and patents, which may be obtained or obtainable therefor, together with the whole of the income, royalties or receipts produced by the said patents and copyrights, or arising from the use of any play, . . . or of any invention of the said Steele MacKaye, . . . shall belong absolutely to the said Mallory, and be his exclusive property.
>
> And the said MacKaye further agrees, . . . that the aforesaid patents, copyright, income, royalties or receipts shall be absolutely and directly assigned, made over and paid to the said Mallory as his exclusive property.[44]

MacKaye was to receive a salary of $5,000 per year, which was to be "full compensation . . . for the whole of his time, energy and services . . . and . . . for all copyrights, inventions, royalties, income and receipts herein agreed by him to be assigned or paid to the said Mallory." MacKaye was also to receive a quarter of the profits once the theater had returned twice the amount of Mallory's investments. The contract was renewable every ten years at Mallory's option, and Mallory could terminate the agreement at the end of any year. If Mallory terminated the contract, he would have to pay MacKaye one-fourth of the current cash surplus, but only if Mallory had first recouped his investment with interest. There were no provisions to allow MacKaye to terminate the contract. Anxious to get to work and trusting the Mallorys, MacKaye signed the contract without reading it, or so he later claimed.[45] By the standards of the day, the contract was not a good deal for MacKaye, but on the other hand, it was certainly not unheard of at that time for an employee to assign in advance the rights to his future patents and copyrights. What was unusual, at least before this case, was that a court would enforce it as written.

While working for the Mallorys, MacKaye invented a mechanical "double stage" to allow changes of scenery in as little as forty seconds and with fewer stagehands, as well as a new ventilation system and an overhead lighting system. The inventions thus improved the experience for the audience while reducing labor costs by cutting the number of backstage employees that were necessary to mount a production. Pursuant to the contract, MacKaye assigned the patents for these inventions to Marshall Mallory. He also rewrote a play he had started earlier, called *Hazel Kirke*, and prepared a company to stage it.[46]

Hazel Kirke opened to favorable reviews at the new Madison Square Theatre in February 1880. MacKaye's technical innovations received the most praise. Even *Scientific American* discussed the Madison Square stage in 1884, crediting the stage machinist with an improvement upon MacKaye's original design and also noting the other technological advances in the theater, such as the ventilation system. The play was wildly successful both in New York and on the road, such that by October 10, 1882, *Hazel Kirke* had earned at least $100,000 profit for the Mallorys. The Mallorys sent *Hazel Kirke* on a worldwide tour, and they and their successors may have reaped as much as two million dollars from the play for the next thirty years.[47]

For the first year of *Hazel Kirke*'s run, MacKaye prepared road companies, acted in the play, and promoted it on the Mallorys' behalf. Conflicts arose as the play became fabulously successful, but MacKaye saw little financial reward. MacKaye believed that the Mallorys were not reporting the full profits from the show, and consequently, he was not receiving his fair share. MacKaye was also incensed at having his name removed from the advertisements for the play and at the Mallorys' ticket prices. He accused the Mallorys of deliberately driving him out of the theater. MacKaye left the Mallorys in March 1881 and assembled a company to perform *Won at Last*, a play MacKaye had written before his association with the Mallorys.[48]

The Mallorys then dropped MacKaye's name not only from *Hazel Kirke*'s publicity, but also from the playbills. One theater critic was as outraged by the denial of credit as by the enforcement of the onerous contract terms: "The

They Claim to Own Him, Body and Soul

name of the author of *Hazel Kirke* should be promptly restored to the bills! This does not affect the legal ownership of the play; but it *affects seriously every author, dramatist, composer and artist in the world.* We protest against the theory that an author's name may be suppressed because his work has been purchased. . . . The outrage perpetrated upon the author of *Hazel Kirke*, without the shadow of excuse, is an outrage upon every man who wields a pen, and should be properly resented."[49] When MacKaye announced plans to stage his own production of *Hazel Kirke*, Mallory sued to prevent him from doing so or from using the patented double stage. MacKaye counterclaimed to prevent Mallory from performing the play, to recover his share of the profits, and to prevent Mallory from using the double stage.[50]

[156]

MacKaye's complaint and the contract were published in New York newspapers, with many editorial comments sympathetic to MacKaye. The newspapers strenuously asserted that MacKaye should own the rights to his innovations and that the contract was outrageously unfair. The *Spirit of the Times* accused the Mallorys of keeping MacKaye as a "bond-servant for life, at $5,000 a year." Comparing the Mallorys to Shylock, the newspaper wondered sarcastically why "should they recklessly make him a partner by that free-handed gift of 25 per cent, after they had been paid double, with interest? . . . *Shylock*, to be sure, did not demand *two* pounds of flesh, with interest—and, at first sight, this looks like a pious improvement on the grand old speculator; but then *Shylock* would never have been weak enough to make himself a partner of *Bassanio*, by taking only 75 per cent of the profits." Switching literary metaphors, the newspaper went on to compare MacKaye to Faust and Mallory to the devil. "Now we do not mean to say that no other enthusiast, like Steele MacKaye, has ever signed an agreement like this before. Inventors, artists, and authors have sold themselves at a lower price to speculators, brokers, publishers, and his Satanic Majesty. 'Give me a fixed income,' struggling genius often cries, 'and you shall have all I can produce to repay you.' But we do mean to say that never before did a pious, religious business man, who edits a churchman paper and occasionally preaches, draw up such an agreement for any genius to sign." The paper portrayed MacKaye as "a man *in extremis* giving himself away, body and soul, to accomplish a purpose."[51]

In more restrained language, the *New York Dramatic News* focused not on the harshness of the contract but on the justness of MacKaye's claim that his creativity entitled him to own his innovations. "Whatever may be the technicalities, one thing is certain, that the great success the Madison Square Theatre has achieved is due wholly to Mr. MacKaye. He was the originator of the idea of the theatre; he baptised it; he opened it originally with one of his plays, before it was rebuilt; he wrote the present play, which has had the longest run ever known in New York; he engaged the company, built and managed the theatre." In the paper's view, the Mallorys did nothing but furnish the money. "That may be a great deal, but without MacKaye that money would have been wasted." Invoking the saying that success has many parents and failure is an orphan, the paper questioned the fairness of the Mallorys' claim. "So long as there were any doubts of the success of their scheme, the Mallorys were content to employ MacKaye as their figurehead. But the minute success dawned upon him, they . . . threw him overboard." The *Chicago Tribune* lamented that while MacKaye "has given New York a model theater," he himself had "no voice in the management, nor any voice in his own play, *Hazel Kirke*. The Rev. Messrs. Mallory claim to own him, body and soul."[52]

The constant theme in the press's portrayal of the arrangement was the appalling idea that a talented theater director should be treated like a slave ("a bond-servant for life") or like factory labor. One paper exclaimed: "The clauses concerning MacKaye's duties for service and labour would make a West India coolie contractor blush at their far-reaching stringency."[53] In the terms of the great debates of the 1880s about the relation of labor and capital, the Mallorys were extracting the entire surplus value of MacKaye's creative labor. The theater press thus came down squarely on the side of labor: investment of capital was neither morally as significant nor socially as valuable as the labor that produced a product.

The court came down squarely on the side of capital.[54] It enjoined MacKaye from performing the play or using the patented double stage and denied MacKaye's request for an injunction. The court did comment that an accounting might determine that Mallory owed MacKaye more money than he had so far been paid under the profit-sharing provision of the contract, but MacKaye had no other rights to control whether or how Mallory used the play or the stage or to demand that he do more to maximize the profits from the play. "Undoubtedly, Mackaye expected that Mallory would so employ the property that both parties would profit by it; but the contract carefully excludes the former from any right to insist upon the fulfillment of such an expectation." As the court read the contract, Mallory was "at liberty from the outset to use the drama and the patented device as he saw fit. He had the legal right to give them away or to consign them to obscurity." Whether there would be profits to be shared under the contract, the court insisted, "was to depend solely upon Mallory's option."[55]

On October 3, 1884, MacKaye opened a new theater, the Lyceum, with an associated acting school, to compete with the Madison Square Theatre. The

Lyceum featured new inventions and updates to MacKaye's earlier inventions, including an improved folding theater chair with room underneath for a man to store his hat. Key employees left the Mallorys to join MacKaye's new venture, and the press awaited the competition between MacKaye and the Mallorys with excitement.[56]

The parties went on with their careers and dropped their pursuit of the litigation, probably because MacKaye's lawyer died. After MacKaye's death in 1894, his widow revived the suit to get the copyright to *Hazel Kirke*, but the district court held that MacKaye was unjustified in abandoning his employment with the Mallorys, and therefore the contract was not rescinded. The Second Circuit reversed, holding that MacKaye was entitled to the share of profits he would have received, up to the time he breached the contract. However, the court also decided that since Mallory had not yet doubled his investment when MacKaye left, he owed MacKaye nothing. The court emphasized that the contract made MacKaye an employee of Mallory, in return for MacKaye's assumption of the financial risk of the venture. MacKaye's widow eventually received the copyright for *Hazel Kirke* and triumphed in her first royalty check of $138.[57]

MacKaye v. Mallory broke new conceptual as well as legal ground. The court treated creativity as alienable just as labor was, and even found no legal wrong in removing MacKaye's name from the work he created. MacKaye and his allies in the theater press expressed nearly as much ire over the Mallorys' failure to attribute his work to him as to the alleged financial exploitation. The case embodies all that is distinctive about the American regime of corporate intellectual property. If a contract assigns all rights to a work to the employer, the employee-creator does not have even a right of attribution. Across the Atlantic, by contrast, while corporate intellectual property developed at the same time, a regime of moral rights emerged in copyright law that was intended to prevent the buyer of a literary property from alienating the author's name from the creation. The development of a moral right of attribution in continental copyright law responded precisely to the intuitive sense, expressed so loudly by the theater press, that the right to be recognized as the author of a work ought to be inalienable.

The other significant case in the development of the law regarding employee agreements to assign copyrights in the 1880s also arose from the world of theater and involved the efforts of Gilbert and Sullivan to obtain a U.S. copyright for *The Mikado*. *Carte v. Evans* (1886) established the principle that an express agreement in which the employer should own his employee's literary product vested the copyright entitlement in the employer, even in the absence of a formal assignment. At that time, only American citizens could obtain U.S. copyrights, and then as now there was no international copyright.[58] So, as British citizens, Gilbert and Sullivan had no legal protection from those in America who sold copies of their music and lyrics, or who produced their own versions of the operas, which were often objectionably altered from the original. Gilbert and Sullivan attempted security measures, but piracy occurred anyway. Sullivan complained about the many ways in which competitors could pirate their works. "Keeping the libretto and music in manuscript did not settle the difficulty, as it was held by some judges that theatrical representation was tantamount to publication, so that any member of the audience who managed to take down the libretto in shorthand, for instance, and succeeded in memorising the music was quite at liberty to produce his own version of it." Even their practice of ejecting from the theater anyone seen to be taking notes was not enough, as "some of the members of my orchestra were bribed to hand over the band parts. Incidents of this sort became of constant occurrence."[59]

To work around these limitations in American copyright law, Gilbert and Sullivan and their manager, Carte, hired an American composer named Tracy to create a piano arrangement of the orchestral score. Their American lawyer, Alexander Browne, took out the copyright in his own name and transferred it to Carte. The court held that Tracy's consent allowed Browne, as proprietor, to take out the copyright and obviated the need for a formal assignment. The court went on to hold that Carte had a valid copyright, and the defendants, a group of Boston music dealers, had infringed that copyright by selling a book with a very similar piano arrangement. The defendants insisted that they had not used Tracy's arrangement. The plaintiffs, using a litigation tactic that became common in copyright infringement cases, called Tracy as a witness and asked him to write the notes in each arrangement upon a blackboard for purposes of comparison.[60] The court accepted the plaintiffs' view and enjoined the defendants from selling the songsheets.

The court relied on *Lawrence v. Dana* (1869), which was the first case to enforce an agreement to assign a copyright. Although, as explained below, there was a parallel line of cases involving the mobility of performers arising under the *Lumley* doctrine, neither the copyright–theater manager competition cases such as *MacKaye* and *Carte* cited the *Lumley* doctrine cases, nor did the cases that followed *Lumley* cite the copyright cases involving theater managers. At that time, employment contract disputes involving actors and those involving playwrights and composers occupied separate fields of law, as actors did not produce copyrightable materials (and thus the only legal action was for a breach of contract to perform). In contrast, playwrights and composers produced a product that could be copyrighted, which enabled courts to create rules at the intersection between copyright and equitable remedies for breach of contract to create.

Unfortunately, directors in other states ignored the ruling and continued to perform pirated productions of Gilbert and Sullivan's work. Carte was unable to gain an injunction to stop a pirated production in New York City. Gilbert, Sullivan, and Carte ultimately found that they were unable to protect their work through copyright law. As Sullivan complained, "[A]lthough the companies we sent out had a great vogue in America, the methods adopted for preservation of copyright did not really pay, mainly owing to the trouble and expense of the law-suits in which we became involved in the effort to protect our rights." They still made money by staging their own performances of the operas.[61]

From Property in the Product of Talent to Property in Talent: The Rise of Contract and the Demise of Free Labor

Thus far, we have considered disputes over the products of employee talent: the play, the book, the music, or the patented theater design. But there was also a category of cases in which talent itself, and the labor through which talent was displayed, was the thing in dispute. Those cases were litigated under the rule articulated in the famous English cases *Lumley v. Wagner* and *Lumley v. Gye*, a rule that was adopted in America in 1874.

In *Lumley v. Wagner* (1852), the English chancery court held that the opera singer Johanna Wagner, who had contracted to perform at one theater, could be enjoined from performing elsewhere when she threatened to breach her contract.[62] In *Lumley v. Gye* (1853), the Queen's Bench enjoined a prospective employer from soliciting Wagner to break her exclusive engagement.[63] The circumstances in which courts believed that the employer's interest in controlling an employee's talent outweighed the employee's interest in free labor and the public's interest in free competition reveal a deep conflict between the emerging ideology of corporate knowledge and the ideology of free labor.

The *Lumley* doctrine had some legal precedents in both the United States and England. The action of enticement recognized the power of equity courts to enjoin employees from quitting a job to work for competitors. Enticement allowed employers to control dissemination of employee knowledge or skill indirectly by preventing others from hiring away their employees.[64] Enticement, however, was a cause of action available in the United States only against indentured servants and apprentices.[65] The novelty of the *Lumley* doctrine in America was to extend the enticement action from the category of unfree labor (household servants, indentured servants, slaves, and agricultural workers) where it had been confined in the early nineteenth century into the ranks of free labor.

In the 1860s and 1870s, efforts to bind performers to their contracts found no favor in American courts. A New York court in 1861 assumed without explanation that a New York dance hall could replace a "danseuse" who went to perform at a rival theater.[66] A Pennsylvania decision from 1865, *Ford v. Jermon*, which involved a famous actress and the manager of the famed Ford's Theater, assailed the notion of barring the defendant from earning a living "by writing or by her needle." "Are such decrees to be made solely with reference to actors, or shall lawyers be held to their clients, mechanics to their employer, and servants to their masters by the same process? Is it not obvious that a contract for personal services thus enforced would be but a mitigated form of slavery, in which the party would have lost the right to dispose of himself as a free agent, and be, for a greater or less length of time, subject to the control of another?"[67] Other courts eschewed broad pronouncements on free labor and found technical reasons for denying injunctive relief.[68]

Daly v. Smith (1874) was the first American case that explicitly adopted the *Lumley* rule. It was also the first time an enticement case relied on trade secret cases as the basis for enforcing an employment contract by preventing an employee from pursuing her occupation in competition with the former employer. For the most part, American courts had yet to recognize the concept of trade secrets as constraining an employee's ability to use his or her talent or knowledge after the termination of an employment relationship. Therefore, the American court in *Daly* turned to English cases, *Yovatt v. Winyard* and *Cholmondeley v. Clinton*, for support.[69] *Yovatt* and *Cholmondeley* had first reached American shores in Joseph Story's influential 1836 *Commentaries on Equity Jurisprudence* in a passage in which Story stated that equity would "restrain a party from making a disclosure of secrets communicated to him in the course of a confidential employment."[70] In *Yovatt*, a veterinarian's journeyman had surreptitiously copied his employer's medicine recipes that he had been explicitly forbidden to see or use. The Lord Chancellor concluded that the journeyman, whose employment agreement was that he would be instructed in "the general knowledge of the business" but not "the mode of composing the medicines," had breached a duty of trust or confidence and, on that basis, enjoined the former journeyman from using or publishing the purloined recipes. In *Cholmondeley v. Clinton*, a solicitor's former clerk, who had later become a solicitor for an adversary of his former employer's client, was barred from using for the benefit of the new client any knowledge acquired while working as a clerk for the adversary's solicitor.

The court in *Daly v. Smith* very likely relied on Story's treatise on equity and simply cited two of the very few precedents in the treatise as authority to reject the notion that equity would not enjoin one party to a contract if it could not enjoin the other. Judge Freedman did not attempt to weave these precedents into a general obligation of employees with regard to economically valuable knowledge. Rather, they were simply principles about the scope of equity jurisdiction in cases involving employees being enjoined not to do specific things. Yet the opinion did draw analogies not only to the antecedents of the trade secret cases, but also to other cases involving economically valuable knowledge: "similar to these are cases of injunction, to protect legal rights, as patents, copyrights, services to mills and others."

The court then discussed *Lumley* and rejected the criticism of it. The bulk of the opinion was devoted to explaining why enjoining an employee from working was not inequitable. To do that, it was essential to rebut the charge that injunctions against working for a competitor unfairly harmed both the employee and society, who would benefit from free competition. As to the need to protect the employee, the court remarked: "Fanny Morant Smith is not only a great actress, but . . . she is also a shrewd lady of great business capacity, and mature age and judgment, and it is therefore safe to assume that, in the light of her past experience with the plaintiff, she made the best bargain for herself that could be got under the circumstances." As to the possible anticompetitive effects of the injunction against other work, or the possible analogy to cases refusing to enforce restrictive covenants post employment, the court simply dismissed the notion, evidently because her lawyer did not seriously press it.

The shock of the American adoption of the *Lumley* doctrine, and the trade secret and restrictive covenant rules that developed at the same time, was that skilled, independent, and professional workers could be compelled not to quit. As noted in chapter 1, some employers had tried to bring enticement actions against competitors as a way of protecting trade secrets, but the use of enticement for such a purpose did not catch on. Free white workers could not, through threat of suit for enticement, be prevented from quitting. Indeed, the freedom to quit, even in breach of contract, was what free labor meant for white workers.[71]

The ordinary remedy for breach of an employment agreement is an action for damages. The long-standing rule of equity courts in all cases, not just employment cases, was that they would get involved and issue injunctions only when the legal remedy of damages was inadequate to compensate the plaintiff for the harm caused by the breach. In the United States, the traditional equitable rule declining specific enforcement of employment agreements was reinforced by the Thirteenth Amendment's prohibition on involuntary servitude. Decrees forcing runaway household servants, indentured servants, and slaves to return to work were an exception to the general rule that courts would not order employees to work. After the enactment of the Thirteenth Amendment, on account of the decline in indentured servitude and apprenticeship, there were relatively few cases involving runaway employees who historically would have been subject to court orders to return to work. *Daly v. Smith* was, thus, a dramatic departure. It, along with the use of injunctions against trade secrets after *Peabody v. Norfolk* (1868), launched courts onto the difficult and often unpalatable task of deciding which sorts of employee talent or knowledge were sufficiently unique that its loss to the employer should be prevented by court order.

Essentially three lines of cases involving suits for enticement or breach of employment agreement emerged. The first were the *Lumley*-type cases involving performers and athletes. The second were a line of civil and criminal cases from southern states involving enticement of sharecroppers and black agricultural workers from 1871 to 1929.[72] The third were cases involving trade secrets. Courts tended to regard the southern cases involving sharecroppers as *sui generis*, but the cases involving performers, athletes, and trade secrets often cited each other. It was in these cases that the meaning of free labor for white nonagricultural labor proved the most vexing. These were the sorts of workers whose freedom to quit seemed most compelling to white judges. Courts found it no easy task to reconcile free labor principles with emerging notions of implied employment agreements that gave employers broad rights to restrict competition from former employees.

The cases involving performers began in the United States, as Professor Lea VanderVelde has shown, with a series of cases involving singers and actresses.[73] Because it was clear that courts would not order the defendants to perform for the plaintiff (they remarked on the impossibility of forcing a bird to sing), the question in most of the cases was whether damages were an adequate remedy for the performer's breach of her contract, or whether the theater owner/manager was entitled to an injunction prohibiting the performer from working in any other theater. The performer's reputation and the incommensurability of her talent were taken as definitive proof of the inadequacy of damages.

Upon reflection, it is not entirely clear why damages would be inadequate. Presumably, an action against the rival theater could produce an accounting of its profits that might be the basis for a reasonable estimate of the plaintiff's lost profits. And because many of the actresses and rival theater managers were reasonably well-to-do, there would be little difficulty in collecting the damages awarded. But the opinions in these cases did not address that issue.

Rather, they simply assumed that the unique talent of certain actresses, singers, and dancers was proof itself of the inadequacy of damages as a remedy.

In justifying employer control of a performer's talent, courts in the 1880s and 1890s tended to emphasize "the exercise of intellectual qualities" and "the impossibility or great difficulty of measuring damages" in such cases. They began to reject the old ideas that negative injunctions were unjust and unadministrable as part of a general change in the law across the spectrum of doctrines governing control of workplace knowledge. Recognizing the value of an employer's investment in cultivating or promoting a performer's talent and celebrity, courts began to see celebrity as an economic asset that was created through the employer's investment in advertising more than the performer's own investment of ability and effort in developing her talent. The first American judge to grant an injunction remarked on the great hardship to "theatrical managers with large capital invested in their business, making contracts with performers of attractive talents, and relying upon such contracts to carry on the business of their theaters," when they are "suddenly deserted by the performers in the middle of their season." The rhetoric shows a mixture of the modern concept of investment in an enterprise with older notions of "desertion." That investment is what justifies the injunction to protect the employers' right to "the fruits of his diligence and enterprise."[74] As in the case of MacKaye or Gilbert and Sullivan, courts recognized the importance of the investment made by the theater manager as being essential to allow talent to flourish, and they were willing to abandon earlier commitments to free labor in order to enable managers to recoup their investment.

Courts articulated in a variety of ways the nature of the employer's interest that would justify an injunction not to work. The Oregon Supreme Court said "the element of mind furnishes the rule of distinction and decision, as distinguished from what is mechanical and material."[75] Other courts identified an exclusive right to profit from an employee's celebrity—the newly recognized quality of being a "star." On this analysis, a court denied an injunction because "the defendant is not a star or attraction of the company, or even a prominent member thereof. However capable an actor the defendant may be, he has not yet achieved distinction."[76] A third view of the employer's protectable interest was not in the exclusive services of a star, but in the exclusive use of part of her repertoire. The actress was enjoined, not from performing at all, "but only from making certain imitations or mimicking other actresses and actors."[77] Her technique, as a commodity divisible from herself, was what the employer could acquire through contract.

Eventually, courts conceptualized the performer's celebrity (what courts called "personality") as the crucial factor justifying an injunction. A performer's success, as measured by reviews, by a large salary, or by some vague word of mouth, was taken as sufficient proof of the uniqueness of the performer's services, which was the basis for granting the negative injunction.[78] The identification of unique talent rested in part on the investment the manager had made in promoting the show, and in part on whether the actor played a central role "upon whom the whole action of the play depends, of any one production, prepared at great expense."[79]

What eventually became the legal standard to define when a performer's talents were so unique or extraordinary as to entitle the former employer to an injunction was as poetic as it was vague. In the often-cited case of *Philadelphia Ball Club v. Lajoie* (1902), second baseman Napoleon Lajoie argued that his talent was not extraordinary and many others could play his position. The trial court found that Lajoie "is an expert baseball player in any position; that he has a great reputation as a second baseman; that his place would be hard to fill with as good a player; that his withdrawal from the team would weaken it, as would the withdrawal of any good player," but that his abilities were not "unique, extraordinary, and of such a character as to render it impossible to replace him." The Pennsylvania Supreme Court thought otherwise. Paraphrasing Shakespeare, the court explained, "He may not be the sun in the baseball firmament, but he is certainly a bright particular star."[80] Thereafter, courts sometimes simply cited this phrase as proof that a performer was unique—a vivid quotation from Shakespeare became a legal standard.[81] One court concluded that since in a prior case an actress "who received the modest salary of ten pounds a week was restrained from rendering services to any other manager," *ipso facto* anyone earning even modest pay for performing was unique as a matter of law.[82]

Identifying talent and celebrity as commodities was only one facet of the development of the *Lumley* rule. The other was reconciling injunctions against working with notions of free labor. The conflict seems to have been felt most acutely in some of the southern states. In *Bourlier Brothers v. Macauley*, the Court of Appeals of Kentucky rejected the theory of *Lumley v. Gye*, which had found liability on the part of the employer who recruited away the employee, as an affront to the freedom of white labor.[83] Noting that the Kentucky legislature had enacted a statute prohibiting enticement, the court ruled that the statute must be the only third-party liability for inducing breach of an employment contract: "We are satisfied that [the] statute, passed soon after slavery ceased to exist in this State, and consequent change of the labor system took place, was intended to apply principally to farm laborers, and to extend application of it so as to include contracts for performance of dramatic artists would be not only fraught with much injustice, unnecessary strife and litigation, but entirely beyond the intended scope and operation of it."[84] Outside the realm of what the court variously called "farm labor" and "domestic relations," the court insisted "it is not the policy of the law to restrict or discourage competition in any business or occupation."[85] Rather, if it is the policy of law "to leave sale and exchange of property free and unrestrained," which the court took as given, then "it is no less just and expedient that, in order to have fair remuneration for labor, a person be allowed to hire the service of any one *sui juris* who offers to be hired."[86] The court drew an explicit analogy between enforcement of employment contracts by injunction and slavery: it would be "legal recognition of personal dominion, bordering on pure servitude."[87]

Underlying the rhetoric about the freedom of labor there lay a thick vein of paternalism that veered to and away from patronizing the performers, depending on the gender of the performer and the inclinations of the judge.[88] Employers made sporadic efforts to expand the principle of *Lumley* to employee knowledge, ability, or talent outside the realm of performers and athletes and to spin out of *Lumley* a general right of the firm to control employee knowledge and human capital. A dozen reported decisions between 1890 and 1916 involved athletes who sought to get out of onerous contracts, and another dozen in the same period involved salespersons and others whom firms also sought to enjoin from competitive employment. Concern about how to reconcile freedom to work with the commodification of talent was much more apparent in the cases in which baseball players attempted to get out of their contracts.[89]

Once courts began to treat *Lumley* as authority for employer ownership of *talent*, it was not a long conceptual leap to translate it to authorizing employer control of *knowledge*. But it was a leap that courts initially refused to take. One of the earliest cases that explored the possible applicability of the *Lumley* rule regarding unique talent to ordinary workers, *Wollensak v. Briggs* (1886), involved the alleged uniqueness of inventive talent. Orlando Briggs had allegedly agreed in writing to construct machines for making speaking tubes incorporating "various new and useful improvements and inventions made, and to be made, by [him]." In a series of modifications to the contracts, Briggs obtained the right to use the machines for purposes other than making speaking tubes, and his employer obtained only the right to use the machines for making speaking tubes. According to the bill in equity, Briggs nearly completed the machines but then refused to show the machines to his employer, to explain how they worked, or to apply for or to assign patents. Instead, Briggs allegedly delivered the machines and assigned his rights in them to someone else.[90] Citing *Lumley*, the court dismissed the bill and refused to order specific performance of the contract to deliver the machines or to assign the patents. The court did not even order Briggs to refrain from delivering the machines or the patents to anyone else. The opinion treated the issue as if there had been no case law on negative injunctions. It also was quite free of rhetoric about the policy reasons justifying the refusal to grant relief. All the court said was that it would be impossible for the court to know whether the machines delivered were the ones contracted for and it would be impossible to order the defendant to construct machines without knowing precisely what machine would satisfy the terms of the contract.[91]

In rejecting the first efforts to extend *Lumley* beyond entertainers and athletes, judges rejected the analogy between celebrity and talent, on the one hand, and specialized craft or technical knowledge, or an employee's reputation for them, on the other. It was not that courts could not imagine the value of specialized knowledge or of a sterling reputation; it was that, outside the realms of entertainment and sports, courts could not envision them as business assets divisible from the employee who possessed them. Thus in 1890, the Connecticut Supreme Court rejected the contention that the reputation of a company's general manager, even when he shared the same name as the firm that employed him, was a company asset protectable by negative injunction. The William Rogers company, a Hartford manufacturer of silverware, sought to enforce a twenty-five-year exclusive employment agreement with its general manager, Frank Rogers, by preventing him from going to work for or lending his name to a rival silverware firm. The case rejected the effort to meld *Lumley* with trademark protection in the firm's use of the employee's name and trade secret protection for employee knowledge. The services of the general manager were not "special, or unique, or extraordinary; nor are they so peculiar or individual that they could not be performed by any person of ordinary intelligence and fair learning." As to the harm that would be caused by Rogers associating himself and his name with a rival firm, the court pointed out that the plaintiffs did not own the trademark to the name Rogers and had not alleged that they used the Rogers name "as a stamp on the goods of their own manufacture." More important, the court found no showing that Rogers's use of his own name "would do them any injury other than such as might grow out of a lawful business rivalry." Finally, the court summarily rejected the contention that Rogers possessed knowledge of the plaintiff's business or customers that would be protectable as trade secret.[92]

Wollensak and *Rogers* reveal that before the turn of the twentieth century courts tended to articulate the free-labor opposition to injunctions most forcefully in cases involving what courts considered ordinary employment. Managers, sales employees, and craft workers, even when alleged to be especially talented, were not subject to injunctions against competitive employment.[93] In the era of industrialization and urbanization, when courts desperately feared the social ills of low-wage work, unemployment, and destitution of the urban poor, such injunctions raised the specter of reducing formerly solid citizens to a state of dependence. As the New Jersey chancery court exclaimed: "To many persons the right to labor is the most important and valuable right they possess. It is their fortune; constituting the only means they have to obtain food, raiment, and shelter, and to acquire property. To such persons a deprivation of this right is ruin, and to abridge it is to do them an injury which will very likely result in their ruin."[94]

Courts used the laissez-faire rhetoric of freedom of contract, which in other contexts was used to restrict legislation aiming to protect workers, as a basis for declining to enforce contracts through a remedy they considered too harsh. In rejecting a negative injunction prohibiting a hat trimmer from going to work at a rival milliner, an Illinois appellate court discerned a general freedom of an employee to quit her job from the U.S. Supreme Court's famous laissez-faire decision in *Allgeyer v. Louisiana* (1897), which had invalidated a statute limiting enforcement of insurance contracts.[95] "When we reflect that among the most valuable rights one possesses is the right to labor, and that this right is also a public duty, it is manifest that by reversing this decree we would destroy more than we would preserve, and would do more injustice than justice."[96] The Iowa Supreme Court rejected an injunction preventing a corset saleswoman from going to a competing firm. The court analogized specific enforcement of personal services contracts to "involuntary servitude, a condition utterly incompatible with our institutions, and the fundamental law of the land." It would be a "state of degradation," a "state of servitude as degrading and demoralizing in its consequences as a state of absolute slavery, and, if enforced in a government like ours which acknowledges a personal equality, it would be productive of a state of feeling more discordant and irritating than slavery itself." The court went on to say that "[t]he allegation that appellee is profiting by the experience and knowledge which she obtained in appellant's service alleges no legal wrong. The employee leaving an employer's service cannot leave the experience or knowledge there acquired." Her knowledge and experience, the court said, "are legitimate additions to her personal equipment which she has a perfect right to use for her own benefit."[97]

Although courts were initially reluctant to find ordinary work experience to be unique under the *Lumley* rule, after the turn of the twentieth century, as part of a general expansion in the definition of trade secrets, courts became willing to issue negative injunctions to protect proven trade secrets. Although the concept of a trade secret first appeared in 1868, courts refused to enforce them by injunction before the 1897 Michigan Supreme Court decision in *O. & W. Thum Co. v. Tloczynski*. In *Thum*, although the company sought an injunction restricting the employee from communicating secret processes and knowledge of secret machinery, the opinion suggested that the employee was enjoined from even working for a competitor. The court justified the restriction on the employee's freedom to work by a long-run interest in encouraging investment in secret technology, which would benefit the public by producing "a larger output . . . of a useful article" and employees by increasing the willingness of employers to hire.[98] The assimilation of *Lumley* cases with trade secret law is most evident in *Clark Paper & Manufacturing Co. v. Stenacker* (1917), in which a New York court granted an injunction against competitive employment, emphasizing that trade secrets presented a legitimate basis for a negative injunction. The court did not identify the basis for the trade secret claim, stating only that it was "meager" but "sufficient to sustain the injunction."[99]

Even after 1900, when the courts began vigorously to state the employer's interest in controlling employee intellectual property, they remained ambivalent about whether the employer's interest warranted an injunction against competitive employment. The ambivalence reflects the difficulty, as a practical matter, of treating worker knowledge or talent as a corporate asset. For example, in a 1907 case brought by an ironworks, the chancery court found it necessary to enjoin an ironworker from going to a competitor because a narrower injunction preventing the use of trade secrets would afford "an easy opportunity" to obtain knowledge from the employee, in spite of the injunction. The broader injunction was necessary to prevent flouting of a narrower one. On appeal, the New Jersey Supreme Court determined that the employer had not proved that all the knowledge in question was its trade secret but allowed an injunction preventing the employee from working for a competitor during the term of his contract with Taylor Iron, simply because it was a contract for exclusive employment.[100] Thus, the *Lumley* doctrine was used to protect knowledge, even though the court did not think the knowledge amounted to a trade secret.

Some courts continued to express reservations about the spread of the *Lumley* doctrine into an expansive protection for amorphous trade secrets. "If the injunction issues," one court suggested, "it means that hereafter no man can work for one and learn his business secrets, and after leaving that employment engage himself to a rival in business, without carrying on his back into that business the injunctive mandate of a court of equity." The court thought the injunction was premised on a jaundiced view of human nature: "There is nothing whatever in the facts of this case, except the opportunity to do wrong and a suspicion in the mind of the rival that wrong will be done. . . . The chancellor ought never to come into such a frame of mind that he assumes human nature to be essentially and inherently evil."[101] Evil, in that paragraph, operates in two directions. On the one hand, it demarcates use of certain knowledge in subsequent employment in the most morally degenerate terms. That was a rhetorical victory for employers who finally convinced courts that certain workplace knowledge was an asset of the firm, not an attribute of the employee. Yet the rhetorical victory was pyrrhic, for the court denied the injunction sought by the employer on the grounds of the honor and trustworthiness of the employee. The court reconciled broad employer rights to workplace knowledge with employee autonomy by denying remedies to prevent the anticipatory breach of the duty of secrecy. The tension between autonomy and servitude remained, but the most acute form of conflict was avoided.

After 1900, *Lumley* merged with trade secret doctrine; it also crossed over into some copyright and patent disputes as well. It was used to protect the employer's right to future production of copyrighted material in *Star Company v. Press Publishing Co.*, in which a New York intermediate appellate court refused to grant an injunction preventing Rudolph Dirks, the creator of the *Katzenjammer Kids* comic strip, from drawing his popular cartoon for a competing newspaper. Dirks and the *New York Star* had a three-year contract that gave the *Star* the exclusive right to publish Dirks's cartoons but did not obligate them to publish the strip or to pay Dirks unless the *Star* was satisfied with his work. The contract also stated that, for the second two years of the agreement, Dirks was not obligated to provide any cartoons. In a first appeal, the court was divided as to whether the provision that gave the *Star* the option to refuse cartoons rendered the agreement unenforceable under the contract doctrine of mutuality—a doctrine that was seldom used to protect employees. What the court did agree upon in the second appeal, however, was that during the second two years of the agreement neither party was obligated to do anything except Dirks, who was prohibited from making drawings for any publication other than the plaintiff. On the basis of that provision the court denied the injunction.[102]

The *Lumley* negative injunction concept was applied to an agreement regarding future patents in *Universal Talking Machine Co. v. English*. The defendant had been employed by the plaintiff as what today would be called a recording engineer.[103] He had also agreed to assign future inventions to his employer. At the time he signed the initial employment agreement, he dictated the formula for making the master record to an officer of the plaintiff company. Before departing the plaintiff's employ he trained his successor in the only other element of his unique knowledge, the proper placement [171] of the singer in front of the horn during the recording process. The court concluded that the defendant possessed no trade secrets, had made no inventions, and did not possess any unique talent entitling his former employer to an injunction against competitive employment. Although the employer lost the case, the opinion nevertheless reveals that lawyers had begun to roll all categories of employee knowledge into one general category of human capital that employers were entitled to control upon a proper showing.

The transition from the freedom of labor rhetoric of the 1880s, as evidenced in *Wollensak* and *Rogers*, was complete. What had begun as a limited departure from the free labor principle that was narrowly tailored to protect only an employer's particular investment in cultivating celebrity became a broader rule protecting an employer's investment in finding, supporting, and maybe even monopolizing extraordinarily valuable knowledge, talent, or even reputation. Not only would courts enforce contracts giving employers exclusive rights to particular innovations like MacKaye's stage and script; they would sometimes (but not always) enforce contracts giving employers exclusive rights to the knowledge or talent that might produce innovations.

Doctrinal uncertainty and controversy continued to surround the issue of remedies for breach of express or implied exclusive employment agreements. Courts remained skeptical about whether or the extent to which the prospect of inevitable disclosure of trade secrets justified an injunction against particular work. The full legal consequences of employer control of knowledge and talent remained contested. But by 1900 the basic principle of some employer control was clear, and that in itself was a major change.

PART III

WORKPLACE KNOWLEDGE AS CORPORATE INTELLECTUAL PROPERTY, 1895–1930

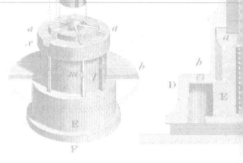

The modern law of corporate intellectual property was created during the same span of years that produced both the archetypes of reactionary legal conservatism and the probing critiques of law that laid the foundations of modern progressive legal thinking. These were the years of what Owen Fiss called, in his history of the Fuller Court (1888–1910), "the negative examples"—the cases that live in infamy among modern progressive lawyers for their heartlessness and racism: *Lochner v. New York* (which invalidated protective labor legislation); *Plessy v. Ferguson* (which approved racial segregation); *In re Debs* (which gave the president the power to use troops to end a strike); the Danbury Hatters case (which treated labor unions as illegal conspiracies to restrain trade); *Adair* (which invalidated a law granting a right to join a union); the Insular Cases (which denied constitutional rights to some people in territories annexed by the United States); and the Chinese Exclusion cases (which upheld the first racial restriction on immigration and excluded Chinese immigrants from citizenship).[1] The late nineteenth century was a period of transition from what Morton Horwitz termed the "old conservative" worldview of "Classical Legal Thought"—"one that presumed that the existence of decentralized political and economic institutions was the primary reason why America had managed to preserve its freedom"—to a modern view. The modern worldview was characterized by the realization that the modern economy was dominated by large-scale, market-dominant corporate enterprises. Lawyers and other social theorists worried about the need to reform legal and other institutions to respond to the new reality and to address the growing economic, social, and political inequality that threatened American freedom.[2]

As courts stepped up to defend property rights against the claims of workers, labor unions, reformers, and reform-minded legislatures and insisted upon the power of corporations to sweat their workers, they also became architects of the legal edifice of corporate intellectual property. While the anxiety about the social, economic, and political threats posed by the seemingly unchecked power of big business is well known when the combatants were steel magnates and labor unions, or banks and small farmers, less well known is the frustration experienced by inventors and creative people at the enforcement of newly minted rules dictating that innovations would henceforth be company property, and that hopes for advancement and wealth would be entirely dependent on the goodwill of their managers and the largesse of their firms.[3]

The legal and business changes in patent ownership in the last decades of the century represented a significant challenge to and demanded a redefinition of the free labor ideology as it existed after the Civil War.[4] Autonomy and entrepreneurship were essential to free labor, and both were founded, in part, on control over the fruits of one's ingenuity. Charles McCurdy identified two crucial tenets of the free-labor ideology that later manifested itself in the Lochnerist "liberty of contract" doctrine after 1886.[5] Corporate control of innovative employees undermined both. First, by divesting inventive employees of the rights over their ideas, the new intellectual property rules threatened the first tenet, which was that "[e]ach person determined how long he would work and on what terms. And not only were those decisions his to make but the fruits of such labor were his to keep." Second, it threatened the second tenet that free labor was "labor with economic choices, with the opportunity to quit the wage-earning class." Northerners, McCurdy asserted, "claimed that the North's dynamic, expanding economy, itself a product of the 'free labor' system, generated ample opportunities for the wage-earner's advancement." As the *New York Times* phrased it in 1857, "Our paupers today, thanks to free labor, are our yeomen and merchants of tomorrow." The "opportunity for upward mobility and eventual independence" were crucial, McCurdy says, because they distinguished free labor in the North from the "degraded condition" of southern labor. Loss of intellectual property rights diminished the prospects for entrepreneurship and demanded reexamination of the ideology of free labor that was central to nineteenth-century American law and politics. This change in legal doctrine and in company practice redefined the meaning of free labor and its relationship to middle-class status.

By the end of the *Lochner* era, the free-labor ideology, whose existence had been perpetuated in an oddly tortured form in the *Lochner*-era cases, began to take other forms. Judges no longer needed to construe employment agreements to maximize the possibility for upward mobility through intellectual property ownership because the ideological premises and social function of the liberty of contract and free labor ideologies were no longer a necessary bulwark against labor legislation and a reconciliation of free labor with the factory system. A middle class of educated men could exist securely but in a position of complete dependence in large corporations because of enlightened management policies. This new middle class did not need economic independence and upward mobility through entrepreneurship; it needed the status conferred by a good education, a stable job with a respected corporation, and the comfortable standard of living of the consumer society.

[175]

Patent law, copyright law, trade secret law, and the enforcement of non-compete agreements expanded the rights of employers dramatically between roughly 1895 and 1930. The rhetorical underpinnings of the doctrine changed perceptibly. In addition, whereas courts in the 1870s and 1880s found trade secrets or enforced patent and copyright assignments only on the basis of express contracts, after 1895 courts began to state that the duty to guard trade secrets and to assign patents was an implied term in *all* employment. Contract lost whatever character it had as a description of the actual understanding of the parties and instead became prescriptive of the proper content of every employment relationship. A New York appellate court stated the principle plainly in 1896 while upholding an injunction against a former factory superintendent and his assistant from using any knowledge they had acquired over the course of their entire working lives at a firm. There was no express agreement to guard company secrets, and the employees complained that the injunction would render them unemployable because all their working knowledge came from the one firm. The court nevertheless said, "[W]e do not see why the defendants . . . are not under just as strong an obligation to observe and keep sacred the trust reposed in them as they would be had they reduced the contract which the law implies to writing." Around 1900, a couple of courts recognized employers as the rightful owners of workplace-generated copyrights, and in 1909 Congress amended the Copyright Act to create the concept of an employer as the author of a work made for hire.[6]

The late nineteenth and the early twentieth centuries witnessed a radically new relationship between people and things. The proliferation of expositions and world's fairs in the United States portrayed modernity as a parade of new things. These ranged from new inventions, including new and improved locomotives and machines, to a vast array of consumer goods and commodities. The quantity and sophistication of advertising exploded, transforming American taste and creating enormous demand for all sorts of things. The huge array of companies that sprang up to serve the market for consumer goods became increasingly aware of the value of newness, the importance of brands, and the need for legal rules to protect the company's right to control them. Thus intellectual property rights of all kinds were inextricably tied to the expanding consumer culture.[7]

The expansion of the scope of copyright and patent to include ever more things mass-produced in a commercial setting did more than increase the incentives for corporations to hire creative workers to create ever more patented and copyrighted material. It gradually changed the popular understanding of patent, copyright, and innovation, and perhaps the self-understanding of idea workers. Innovation and creation were no longer the province of the artist, the intellectual, the scientist, or the tinkerer. It was the business plan and the marketing strategy of behemoth firms like General Electric, Kodak, Du Pont, and Ford.

A consumer culture focused on mass-produced novelty; on the pursuit of a middle-class standard of living measured by consumption and display of brand-name consumer goods of all kinds; on the endless proliferation of brand names and the thorough penetration of intellectual property of all kinds into daily life—all the hallmarks of the emerging American popular culture in the early twentieth century—has a very different relationship to idea creation and ownership than the culture of 1895. But the relationship is hardly unidirectional. Technological development had radically changed life by 1930—automobiles, telephones, electricity, cameras, and radios became features of middle- and upper-class daily life. Films and recorded music became staple entertainment. New magazines and new advertisements changed tastes. All these things brought home to Americans the impact of intellectual property and the value of innovation, even as they laid the groundwork for the demythologizing of the inventive process and desanctification of the creation of art, music, and literature.

Corporate Management of Science &
Scientific Management of Corporations

Many large corporations established research and development facilities in the first decade of the twentieth century to systematize invention. Innovations became more likely to be made in a research lab or in some other collective setting by someone working as an employee of a corporation. At the same time, large businesses adopted the methods of scientific management. They restructured jobs so that complex tasks were divided up and performed piecemeal by less-skilled workers, they rationalized production so that supervisors rather than skilled labor and foremen controlled the manufacturing process, and they improved record keeping so that the productivity (and therefore the wages) of each worker could be measured and calibrated. The pace and order of work and many aspects of working conditions were no longer left to the discretion of individual workers and foremen. The development of personnel management within a framework of managerial capitalism transformed working life. In the first few decades of the twentieth century, science was applied to management and management was applied to science. The scientific management of corporate science changed the ownership of ideas in the workplace.

The spread of bureaucratic employment practices and the growth of firms eventually narrowed differences in legal status ("master" and "servant") that previously had separated creative employees from machine operators and office clerks. After 1900, just as the social class line was becoming increasingly clear between the middle class and the working class and between office and manual workers, the legal class line between working- and middle-class employees was becoming increasingly faint. All were employees of large firms, not servants, but not masters. White male office workers still expected to rise in the business world and saw themselves as superior to factory workers, but in law the distinction between the legal rights of a middle-class employee and a working-class employee had largely disappeared.[1]

[178]

The newly defined employment contract assigned ownership and control of intellectual property rights, including patents and trade secrets, to the corporate employer. Lawyers and courts embraced the notion of collective invention in the newfangled corporate research facility as a basis for real-locating ownership rights to employee innovation. Some of the research employees no doubt relished the job security and the opportunity to work collaboratively on increasingly complex and sophisticated technology under the aegis of a well-respected corporation in the growing R & D facilities at large companies. They happily traded the rights to whatever intellectual property they generated for a secure career with a reputable firm. It may be that most R & D employees benefited more from the corporate manage-ment of science than they would have in the entrepreneurial world of the independent inventor of the nineteenth century. But many R & D employees thought they would have been better off with greater opportunities for indi-vidual entrepreneurship and resented the corporate control that modern law and modern management allowed. They did not think they benefited from the implicit trade of entrepreneurial opportunity for stability of corporate employment and had difficulty accommodating themselves to the new role of the corporate scientist as being dependent on corporate employment and subservient to corporate managers.

The New Employment Contract and the Emergence of Industrial Research

A phenomenon unknown before 1840—the large, multi-unit, professionally managed business corporation—was the dominant form of business by 1930. The American economy was controlled as much by managers as by markets, and people worked for others rather than for themselves.[2] Courts realized that combinations were rapidly replacing individuals in business relations and they began to transform their vision of the employment contract to fit the new reality. As Justice Oliver Wendell Holmes famously observed in *Vegelahn v. Guntner*, an 1896 case in which concerted action by a labor union challenged the liberal individualist conception of work relations, "It is plain from the slightest consideration of practical affairs, or the most su-perficial reading of industrial history, that free competition means combina-tion, and that the organization of the world, now going on so fast, means an ever-increasing might and scope of combination."[3] The management of the thousands of workers employed in the behemoth firms became ever more systematic and bureaucratic. Inventive employees were less likely than ever before to be entrepreneurs founding their own small firms, tending instead to be mid-level employees of a research division of a large corporation.

Factory manufacturing shifted control over the production process from workers to management and, in particular, shifted *knowledge* about the processes of production from skilled labor to middle management.[4] Workers and labor leaders had long known that their negotiating power vis-à-vis their employers came from their knowledge about work process; as Bill Haywood, the visionary leader of the radical Industrial Workers of the World union, succinctly stated, "The manager's brains are under the workman's cap."[5] Along with the better-known fights over wages, hours, and workplace safety, one of the most important workplace power struggles was over control of that knowledge. Frederick Winslow Taylor's scientific management was one weapon in that struggle; another was the redefinition of the employment contract that gave the corporation control over employee innovations and intellectual property. As Taylor explained, the key to modern ("scientific") factory management was to understand that workmen in each trade "have had their knowledge handed down to them by word of mouth. . . . The ingenuity and experience of each generation . . . have without doubt handed over better methods to the next. This mass of rule-of-thumb or traditional knowledge may be said to be the principal asset or possession of every tradesman." Taylor went on to explain that the "foremen and superintendents know, better than any one else, that their own knowledge and personal skill falls far short of the combined knowledge and dexterity of all the workmen under them."[6] Scientific management taught the corporation's managers to control all that knowledge. "Information formerly regarded as part of the foreman's 'secret' store of knowledge, such as wage rates and job content, was appropriated by the personnel manager much as the secrets of production had been appropriated by the engineer."[7]

The transformation of technology played a role in this process alongside the transformation of the business corporation. While many people with some inventive ability, education, skill, and access to a workshop might have been able to design and patent an improvement to the relatively simple steam engines of the early nineteenth century, by the end of the century only those with highly specialized knowledge of metals and mechanical engineering who had access to a locomotive and several miles of railroad track would be in a position to patent a major improvement. As technology grew exponentially more complex, the firms and factories that developed it grew larger. Opportunities for individual invention and entrepreneurship

Corporate Management of Science

based on individual patent ownership became less prevalent. Instead, it was far more likely in the early twentieth century that an inventor would be an employee of a large corporation and work with other employees using the tools and material of his employer to develop a patent. Invention became less democratic and entrepreneurial at the individual level. Both invention and entrepreneurship became corporate.[8]

[180]

Patent law requires the inventor(s)—natural persons—to be named in the patent application; a corporation could not be awarded a patent until 1952.[9] In 1885, only 12 percent of patents were assigned to corporations at the time of issuance; by 1950, at least three-quarters of them were.[10] Contracts between firms and employees requiring assignment of patents were rare before World War I, but that changed rapidly afterward. Naomi Lamoreaux and Kenneth Sokoloff have shown that between 1870 and 1910 patentees became more likely to assign away their rights to patents at the time the patent was issued. There was a particular increase in assignments to companies (from 24 percent of recorded assignments in 1870 to 64 percent of recorded assignments in 1910), and a significant increase in employees and corporate officers assigning patents to the firm.[11]

The explosive growth of corporate research and development dramatically changed both the environment in which workplace innovation occurred and how the lay and legal public imagined invention. In the popular and judicial imagination, perhaps more than in actual fact, the hero-inventor experimenting alone in his laboratory or workshop ceded his place to company men in laboratory coats working collaboratively on a corporate payroll to advance the progress of technology.[12] Legal doctrine changed accordingly, with twentieth-century courts becoming far more likely than their nineteenth-century predecessors to conclude either that employees were hired to invent and therefore the firm owned all employee patents, even in the absence of a specific agreement to transfer the patent from the inventor to the firm, or that the employee and the firm had validly contracted for assignment of employee patents.[13]

One of the characteristic features of twentieth-century research and development is the separation of the job functions of invention from those of supervision and management. The employees most likely to invent in large twentieth-century firms were likely to be professionally trained engineers and scientists in R & D divisions whose sole job was to invent, not to run the company. The professionalization of invention enhanced the status of some inventors from tinkerers and mechanics to scientists and professionals. But it also resulted in some employees of substantial education—who might in some measures be of an elevated class position—being treated and being forced to regard themselves as cogs in a corporate machine more than as men of stature and power within the firm. In Britain as in America, company practices in the management and compensation of inventive employees varied wildly: some rewarded employees handsomely, while others took employee ideas for company use without credit or reward.[14] As firms became more bureaucratic in their management of all aspects of business, the management of R & D was not immune. There are conspicuous exceptions, such as Charles P. Steinmetz, the quirky chief of research at General Electric, who also had a position in management. But chemists and engineers—like most skilled and unskilled white- and blue-collar labor throughout the newly reorganizing firms—were susceptible to being treated like all other inputs to production. All were commodities that must be managed.[15]

Companies found it difficult to elicit innovation, creativity, and loyalty from employees while maintaining control. Managers in the industrial research and development facilities established around the turn of the century at Du Pont, Eastman Kodak, General Electric, Westinghouse, Bell Telephone, and elsewhere struggled to maintain the respect for science necessary to recruit top scientists and an entrepreneurial spirit that would provide incentives to hard work and innovation. Some thought that the regimented managerial structure imposed to ensure that the R & D division was a productive and profitable segment of the firm was anathema to creative science and to entrepreneurial innovation. As law had consolidated corporate power over innovation, books such as the 1931 classic *The Psychology of the Inventor* began to appear, suggesting that innovation remained a personality trait that would thrive even as individual entrepreneurship disappeared from the world of large corporations and complex technology.[16] It took a generation or more for most firms to work out how to manage creative people, control the diffusion of economically valuable information, and capture the gains of their investment in R & D. Companies sometimes did, and sometimes did not, strike a balance that rationalized R & D while also offering a satisfactory degree of autonomy and a realistic hope of upward mobility for the best and brightest (or just the most successful) of the scientists and engineers in the corporate labs.[17]

A redefined employment contract was the legal device that played the most significant role in facilitating the application of scientific management to employee innovation. Courts redefined the terms of the employment contract to allocate innovations to the employer. As the author of an influential 1903 *Michigan Law Review* article on employee inventions baldly stated, ownership of inventions was solely a question of contract, "express or implied." The fact of employment did not alter the inventor's property in his inventions "outside the scope of employment," the author contended, but an implied contract could. The author did not attempt to explain how courts determined which inventions were within or outside the scope of employment. Nor did he suggest how the courts should decide whether an implied contract allocated intellectual property rights to employer or employee. Rather, he said only that the "essential considerations" included "what the employee was hired to do" and "what rights, expressed or implied," the employee had given to the employer. In case of doubt, as "where the employer and the employee both claim the invention the presumption is prima facie in favor of the employer."[18]

Every step of that author's analysis, especially the last one asserting a presumption of employer ownership, was prescriptive when it appeared to be only descriptive, and no step in the analysis was uniformly supported by the existing law. The cases that the author cited did not stand for the broad proposition claimed, and the article overlooked contrary authority. But in an area of law that had received little scholarly attention, the influence of the article was substantial. It combined ambition to strengthen employer rights with formalist confidence—typical of legal scholarship of the era—that the rigorous application of the "science" of contract law could dispel the apparent disorder in the case law and bring new organization, synthesis, and clarity to the problem of workplace inventions. Given that most law had been noteworthy for zealous protection of employee rights during a sixty-year period when courts were not otherwise terribly sympathetic to workers, the article was a novel effort to apply to employee-inventors the formalist, pro-employer version of contract law that courts had, up to that point, applied everywhere *but* to employee-inventors.

The new paradigm of corporate invention was incorporated into law through an assessment of the content of the implied (that is, judicially pre-scribed) contract of employment. Judges began to see that the stimulus to innovation was not individual employee ownership of patents but rather corporate ownership of the results of the research and development in which the corporation had invested. In 1911, a court held that the sole stockholders of a start-up company had a fiduciary duty to their corporation to assign patented improvements on the company's product that they had developed after the company terminated their employment. The opinion justified a broad duty to assign patents with a lengthy explanation of the collective nature of invention: "An invention is not something that, but for the particular inventor or inventors, would not have been. Inventions come along as the discovery of gas deposits come along—the contribution of some particular person to the world's knowledge—but if not by that person, then, in the course of time, and usually in a very short time, by someone else." The company should justly own the individual's patents because the employee, according to the court, had only an idea for a technological advance; the firm created the value in that idea: "[T]he exploration of the laws of nature and mechanics, for something that will aid a specific commercial or business end, practically and commercially is not different from explorations for mineral or gas deposits to a like commercial end. Neither has any value until it is obtained. Both create a value that did not exist before they were obtained."[19]

[183]

Reasoning that invention was a long and arduous endeavor of many contributors, not the product of an individual stroke of genius, courts concluded that agreements to assign future inventions ought to be treated no differently than agreements to assign any other property that someone might acquire in the future. The systematic advancement of technology, one judge said, would be best served by giving corporations control over employee patents because "[p]rotection for the future requires that inventions already controlled be not undermined and diverted by other inventions along the same line."[20] In *Wireless Specialty Apparatus Co. v. Mica Condenser Co.*, the Supreme Judicial Court of Massachusetts held that employees "wholly engaged in 'experimental work'" were obligated to treat all their inventions as belonging to their employer. Describing a firm that had converted from World War I production of radio condensers for the U.S. government into peacetime production of magneto condensers for manufacturers of electrical apparatus, the court noted that the inventions at issue were the joint work of several employees and that the employer should own them because the "work was substantially all performed in the plaintiff's shop, with its tools, at its expense, and under the general direction and supervision of . . . its chief engineer."[21]

The impact of corporate R & D on the transformation of contracts governing inventions can be seen most clearly in the Supreme Court's influential 1925 decision in *Standard Parts Co. v. Peck*, which cemented the rule of employer ownership of employee patents. William Peck had worked for Hess Spring and Axle Company in Carthage, Ohio, for five years, ending in 1912. Peck not only had developed the skills of a designer of machinery but also had become a patent lawyer. In 1915, Peck received a call from Mr. Hess, the principal stockholder of Hess Spring and Axle, to see if he was able to help solve a problem the company was having in the manufacture of front springs for Ford motor cars in its plant in Pontiac, Michigan. Initially, Peck declined Hess's offer to return to work for the company, but he was persuaded to tour several Hess manufacturing plants to see what machinery might be incorporated into the spring making plant. According to Peck, Hess promised that the company would establish a special R & D facility with Peck in charge, and in return, Peck promised to assign to the company any inventions he might develop in connection with such a job. The contract did not reflect any such promises, but simply specified that Peck was "to devote his time to the development of a process and machinery for the production of the front spring now used on the product of the Ford Motor Company."[22] The Hess-Pontiac company was to pay him $300 per month plus a bonus of $100 per month if the process and machinery were completed within four months of the commencement of employment and an additional bonus of $10 for each percent in reduction of labor costs achieved through use of the invention.[23] Peck returned to work for Hess-Pontiac for less than two years, and during that time he devised and built several machines for the company. He was paid for his work and a $660 bonus according to the contract. During his employment, Peck sought and received some patents for the machines.

Some years later, upon learning that a machine incorporating his patent was in use at the Standard Parts Company in Cleveland, Peck filed suit for patent infringement. Before the suit was filed, lawyers for Standard Parts had demanded that Peck provide all the drawings he had made while designing and building the machinery, and Peck had refused. Peck conceded that the drawings of the machines and the machines themselves were the work for which he had been paid and which his former employer owned, but insisted that the patents were his. Standard Parts, however, demanded the patent as well. When Peck sued, Standard Parts counterclaimed to get the patent, claiming that it had acquired all the assets of the Hess companies, including the Peck patent.

As he prepared his case, Peck focused considerable effort on showing that he was not hired to invent a specific thing but was hired generally to improve the spring manufacturing process, emphasizing that "the patent in suit was only one of at least eleven separate and distinct types of machines, and for as many separate and distinct purposes, that were built under the same contract."[24] Peck evidently hoped to fit himself within the cases, such as the Supreme Court's decision in *Hapgood v. Hewitt* (1886), which had held that an employee hired generally owned the patents for his inventions and that only when an employee was hired to invent a specific thing was the employer entitled to the patent. Peck's strategy was sensible because, at the time, it was not clear whether a specific oral or written agreement that the employee would assign inventions to the firm was necessary. Some insisted that a specific assignment contract was necessary, while others insisted that the assignment was implied by law.

The district court found that Peck "was not employed generally in a certain line of work" whose invention was simply incidental to his job; rather, "[h]e was employed and paid to develop a process or machinery or means of accomplishing a prescribed result." The court held that Pontiac owned the patent by virtue of the hiring to invent, and that Standard Parts Company, which acquired all of Pontiac's assets, had acquired the patents both to the manufacturing process and to the machinery. In the view of the district judge, Peck had "sold in advance whatever rights as an individual he may have had in and to his inventive powers, so far as they relate to the work he was to do or the results which he accomplished."[25]

[185]

The Sixth Circuit did not think "the settled law" allowed such a broad right of employer ownership of employee innovation. It read prior cases to establish that "an invention does not belong to the employer, merely by virtue of an employment contract, as well when that employment is to devise or improve a specific thing, as when the employment is to devise improvements generally in the line of the employer's business." In the Sixth Circuit's view, "If one is hired in a general supervising or advisory capacity . . . and it is expressly understood that he is to devote his talents and skill to making improvements . . . there would be strong ethical grounds for saying that the invention belonged to the employer, just as did the other fruits of the labor and skill which had been bought and paid for."[26] But the court could not bring itself to find a legal rule in that ethical obligation.

The Supreme Court reversed, and held Standard Parts entitled to the patent. The Court rejected the Sixth Circuit's narrow reading of the kinds of contract required to transfer patent rights from employee to employer. "It cannot be contended that the invention of a specific thing cannot be made the subject of a bargain and pass in execution of it."[27] The Court found such a bargain in Peck's contract. The opinion reads as if the Court were simply distinguishing the older cases on facts: Peck's contract was solely to invent and the earlier contracts were to improve a business generally, including by inventing. But since the allegations in earlier cases, such as *Hapgood v. Hewitt* (1886), included that the employees were to "improve and perfect" the employer's technology and that they had been hired because of experience in "devising and getting up the best plows" (in *Hapgood*) and in developing "valuable improvements" to the employer's technology, it is a bit difficult to say that employees like Peck, Hewitt, and others had not been hired to invent.[28] So it must be that an employee hired to invent *and to manage* was materially different than an employee hired only to invent.

The distinction leaves something to be desired as a matter of logic, but as a matter of a broad characterization of the different statuses of employees, the Supreme Court's view of the employer's rights in *Standard Parts* is quite revealing. An employee-inventor's product is the property "of him who engaged the services and paid for them" just as is the product of any other worker. It is "a provision for a business, a facility in it and an asset of it."[29]

The aspect of Peck's case that seemed to bother the Court the most was Standard Parts' averment in its counterclaim that Peck had licensed the patent to companies in competition with his former employer and had allowed the competitors to use his drawings of the machines, "notwithstanding the fact that said drawings were made by this plaintiff, or under his supervision, at the expense of defendant's predecessors."[30] Employee ownership of the invention would "subject the company to the rivalry of competitors" and would enable him to "give as great a right to any member of the mechanical world as to the one who engaged and paid him—a right to be used in competition with the one who engaged him and paid him."[31] In other words, Peck asked the Court to imagine him as an entrepreneur. The Court would not. In choosing between two visions of the inventive employee, the Court rejected the view that allowed the employee to compete, adopting instead the view that an employer who has bought the employee's service is entitled to absolute control of all the products of it.

The result and rule in *Standard Parts* facilitated the bureaucratization of invention by eliminating the need for employers expressly to contract with inventive employees regarding ownership of patents. Invention, like all other inputs to production, could be standardized and the firm would own all the products of the inventive employee, just as it owns the products of other forms of labor. As it happened, the invention at issue in the case was itself a product of Henry Ford's famous desire to reduce costs by standardizing parts and investing in mechanization (even though he was willing to pay much higher labor costs per hour/day than most manufacturers were then).[32] Perhaps not coincidentally, both the facts of the case and the Court's holding are manifestations of the same impulse toward modernization. Efficiency can be gained by substituting mechanization and standardization for handmade parts and idiosyncratic processes. The Court's new view of employee ingenuity as a service that can be standardized and commodified and should be assumed to be an asset of the business appears to flow seamlessly from the context of the case—mass producers sought technology that would standardize their operations, and the production of that technology could itself be standardized.

Standardization of invention, however, required legal rules that treated invention like any other input into production—including labor and materials—and made all of them the property of the firm without the necessity for individual contract negotiations. If ownership of intellectual property turned on individual negotiations, there would be the risk that individual employees could negotiate to own their intellectual property, or, even worse, a court might conclude that an inventor had done so when the company had been under the impression that it owned the patent. The standardization of innovation thus both required and enabled employee inventiveness to be treated like a commodity, which in turn depended upon a divorce of invention from entrepreneurship. To do all that, the Court collapsed what had been a large difference between the rights of the inventive employee and those of the laborer. Henceforward, both would be assumed to transfer, through a contract of employment, all the products of their time and effort. The new legal rules both built on and contributed to a new view of inventive employees as servants rather than as entrepreneurs, as parts of a corporate R & D hierarchy rather than as independent inventors. The Supreme Court eventually held in another case in 1933 that the employer's financial support of the employee, via payment of salary, was an investment in the technology and the basis for employer's contractual right to use the employee's patent. "Since the servant uses his master's time, facilities and materials to attain a concrete result, the latter is in equity entitled to use that which embodies his own property."[33]

Courts resorted to the legal fiction of implied contract to effect this change because fictitious consent was the only way to justify such a profound assault on the independence that was foundational to the postbellum free-labor ideology. The arguments for employer ownership in *Hapgood* seem quite compelling—he was, after all, hired to improve the company's plow business and designing a new plow would seem squarely within what he was hired to do. Yet the arguments for employee ownership seem equally compelling. The desire to create, and to control one's creations, is perhaps innate.[34] Prospects for upward mobility and entrepreneurship were at the core of the late nineteenth-century understanding of free labor and, indeed, of freedom itself. The fiction that the parties agreed that the employee in *Hapgood* or the employer in *Standard Parts* should own the invention allows the court to achieve an intuitively appealing result without stating a rule broader than necessary in a context in which an obviously broad rule favoring employer or employee would be troubling. The fiction of free consent had particular emotive force in the context of the free-labor ideology; and the rule and result were intellectually satisfying for, without involving the obvious creation of new doctrine of uncertain breadth, it achieved the intuitively appealing result.[35]

That the intuitively appealing result changed from one rule to its exact opposite over the course of a generation or two reflects the increasing acceptance of a middle class dependent on corporate employment as being consistent with rather than a threat to the notion of free labor. In the 1880s, the possibility of economic and social advancement through entrepreneurship was understood to be the hallmark of middle-class respectability. In the nineteenth century, young male office clerks and manual workers trained to become small business proprietors through their work experience, not primarily through education.[36] By 1925, formal education followed by stable employment at a growing corporation had increasingly supplanted entrepreneurship as the path to middle-class status. Translated into the contract terms favored by the courts, an implied term of the nineteenth-century employment agreement was the possibility of entrepreneurship as the reward for creativity and hard work. An implied term of the mid-twentieth-century employment agreement was stable employment and upward mobility through the firm as the reward for the same qualities.

The Use of Trade Secrets and Employment Contracts at Eastman Kodak

One of the important cases in the development of the law of corporate ownership of workplace knowledge was *Eastman Co. v. Reichenbach* (1892),[37] a dispute between the Eastman photography company and its first research chemist. The chemist had signed an express contract requiring him to assign inventions made in the course of his employment to the company. He and others started a competing business using secret processes they had been involved in developing while employed by Eastman. The company deemed this a misappropriation of its investment in research and product development, and the court agreed.

In this and other cases about trade secrets and restrictive covenants, Eastman (which later became Eastman Kodak, and finally just Kodak, because of the phenomenal success of the Kodak trademark) played a significant role in urging courts to adopt a view of workplace knowledge that equated a firm's investment in the development of technology with the firm's entitlement to own it. Early twentieth-century advances in corporate research and development enabled employers like Eastman Kodak to argue convincingly that enforcement of restrictive covenants was essential to protect their investment in a wide variety of secret knowledge. Eastman Kodak was a particularly zealous advocate of the view, new at the cusp of the twentieth century, that firms, rather than individuals, were pioneers of new technology and that firms hired employees for their knowledge rather than just their labor. The firm was a leader in industrial research and development and a vigorous advocate of company ownership of employee innovation. As a significant investor in research, the company aggressively protected company secrets while trying also to motivate research employees by allowing them to believe that their work for the company was genuine science. George Eastman's attention to patent matters, and to intellectual property rights generally, is legendary. "The ideal large corporation," he was quoted as saying, "is the [189] one that makes the best use of the brains within it." The aggressive use of emerging intellectual property law combined with the aggressive effort to develop new technologies makes the company an excellent case study of how a combined legal and R & D strategy transformed both the law and the practice of corporate control of workplace knowledge.

George Eastman patented the first usable photographic film, which consisted of a nitrocellulose solution on paper backing that was stripped off after the film was developed. After patenting the new film in March 1884, Eastman developed a roll holder to be used with spools of film, which was far more convenient than the heavy and fragile glass plates that photographers had previously used. Eastman energetically promoted his new invention, incorporating the Eastman Dry Plate and Film Company on October 1, 1884, and using letters, advertisements, and demonstrations to educate photographers about the new product. He designed machinery to manufacture the film and began production on March 26, 1885.[38]

In August 1886, Eastman hired Henry M. Reichenbach, an assistant to a respected chemist at the University of Rochester, to help him develop a better film while he advanced the business. Eastman was among the earliest American manufacturers to employ a full-time research chemist. Reichenbach was a skilled chemist but relied on Eastman for the necessary knowledge of photography. He worked full time testing ideas, often those suggested by Eastman. Many of Reichenbach's developments were in the area of emulsions, the chemical solutions coating the film. Emulsion formulae were crucial to success in the photographic trade, so Eastman guarded them fiercely as trade secrets, on one occasion sending his business partner a sample of one of Reichenbach's early emulsion experiments instead of a recipe.[39]

After two years of experimentation, Reichenbach invented a flexible film that did not require a paper backing. Eastman, meanwhile, had developed machinery for manufacturing Reichenbach's new film. Eastman instructed his patent attorneys to put the patent for the chemical process in Reichenbach's name and the mechanical processes in Eastman's own name, writing that "I should like very much to have Reichenbach's name connected with these applications and think it would please him." Patents were granted to both men. Eastman began selling the new film on August 27, 1889. Eastman reincorporated the business as the Eastman Company in late 1889. Reichenbach received fifty shares of company stock in exchange for agreeing that the company would own all the photographic inventions he produced during his employment with Eastman.[40]

On January 1, 1892, Eastman fired Reichenbach after discovering that Reichenbach and two other employees had formed a competing film company. One of these employees, S. Carl Passavant, was an analytical chemist whom Eastman had hired to assist Reichenbach when he became manager of Eastman's new film factory in Greece, New York. The other was Gus Milburn, a traveling salesman. Reichenbach had also attempted to recruit the manager of Eastman's film factory in Harrow, England. The dispute was evidently personal and bitter. Eastman's biographer said that Eastman had been quite fond of Reichenbach, considered him the "heir apparent" of the firm and "the future of photography." For his part, Reichenbach evidently was sufficiently angry at Eastman to sabotage some company supplies before leaving the firm.[41]

Eastman sought and received an injunction in the New York Supreme Court to stop Reichenbach, Passavant, and Milburn from using or disclosing any of the trade secrets they had taken from the company. Identifying two strands in the past decisions in the field, the trial judge deduced that "some are made to depend upon a breach of an express contract between the parties," while others rested on "the theory that, where a confidential relation exists between two or more parties engaged in a business venture, the law raises an implied contract between them" and that use or disclosure of such secrets "is a breach of trust and a violation of good morals, to prevent which a court of equity should intervene."

The court found that both lines of reasoning justified an injunction. Reichenbach and Passavant had been paid a salary to perform chemical research, and "under the terms of their employment, and by the strict letter of their contract," Eastman was entitled to the exclusive benefit of their discoveries. The defendants had clearly been aware of the value of these formulae and processes, since they had during their employment helped Eastman to keep them secret from the public and even from their coworkers. As the judge explained, Eastman had proved that "men employed in one department were not allowed to go into another department. Ingredients employed in compounding certain mixtures were guarded by lock and key, and various formulae were only given to those whose business it was to use them."[42]

Eastman hired other chemists to replace Reichenbach and Passavant. Meanwhile, Reichenbach and his associates sold their Eastman stock and raised money from investors to found the Photo Materials Company. Not to be outmaneuvered, Eastman worked to make sure its contracting partners remained loyal to Eastman rather than the new competitor. Eventually Reichenbach's venture failed, and Eastman bought what remained of the company cheap in order to get its land and machinery. Reichenbach meanwhile had left Photo Materials in 1897 to form Reichenbach, Morey & Will, which Eastman sued for patent infringement. Eventually, that business also failed. Reichenbach and Milburn at different times sought to return to the Eastman Company, but Eastman would not hire them back.[43]

Not content to rely solely on secrecy, the Eastman Company began including noncompetition clauses in employee contracts to prevent former employees from working in the photographic industry for up to twenty years.[44] In addition, regardless of the existence of noncompetition agreements, the company asserted in litigation that the existence of a trade secret should be a sufficient basis for prohibiting a former employee from working for competitors (not merely from revealing the secrets, as earlier cases had suggested).

Although Eastman Kodak was a jealous protector of its own secrets, the firm was an avid consumer of technological knowledge it could find elsewhere. Eastman himself took advantage of opportunities to gain access to competitors' information. He hired his former photography teacher George Monroe to supervise emulsion-making because Monroe had experience in certain St. Louis factories that produced better emulsions than the Eastman Company could make. However, he fired Monroe when he became dissatisfied with his performance and became concerned about Monroe's ability or willingness to keep secrets.[45]

A dispute between Eastman and a distributor-turned-competitor shows the challenge that Eastman faced in protecting what the firm considered its trade secrets. The Anthony Company, in business since 1841, dominated the trade in photographic supplies. The Anthony Company had been a distributor of Eastman products since 1880, but Eastman terminated the contract in March 1885 because Eastman had developed its own sales force. In July 1885, Eastman began machine-producing photographic paper, creating a higher-quality product while using substantially less labor and materials than the hand-coating method used in the Anthony factories. In January 1887, Eastman discovered that Anthony had hired away two valued employees, Franklin Millard Cossitt, the foreman in charge of papermaking, and David Cooper, a traveling salesman. Cossitt was helping Anthony to set up a papermaking machine just like Eastman's, while Cooper was laying the foundations for Anthony to sell the new paper.[46]

Eastman sent spies to speak with the employees and may even have sneaked into the plant himself to find evidence that Anthony was infringing the patent for his machinery. He brought suit in March 1887, but Anthony claimed that they had stopped using the machine as soon as they learned of Eastman's patent. Therefore, the judge denied Eastman a preliminary injunction but required Anthony to stipulate that they would not use the machine or allow it to leave their possession until a final hearing. No final hearing ever occurred, but Anthony fired Cooper and Cossitt and never used the machine.[47]

Eastman and a few other photographic companies controlled the secrets to emulsion technology, and Eastman recognized that technical superiority was crucial to its ability to stave off competition from other firms in the 1890s. "If we can get out improved goods every year," Eastman wrote, "nobody will be able to follow or compete with us."[48]

Eastman Kodak founded a research laboratory in 1913 to do basic scientific research shortly after Eastman visited the German research facility of Friedrich Bayer & Company, which had employed university-trained chemists to develop new dyes since the 1870s and which by the 1890s was a well-established industrial research laboratory that did not exist in American businesses until after the turn of the century.[49] Dr. C. E. Kenneth Mees, the first director of the Eastman research laboratory, told George Eastman from the beginning that no commercially valuable innovations were likely to be produced in the first ten years. The purpose of the laboratory was to establish the company's prestige as an innovator and to produce work that would protect the company's technological dominance over the long run.[50]

With the founding of a research lab and the desire to recruit and retain scientists, company officials realized that a balance had to be maintained between the corporate culture of secrecy and the scientific ethos of sharing and publication. Eastman Kodak managers and lawyers allowed research laboratory employees to publish results of their scientific work, both because the laboratory's work was not usually on products that were immediately profitable and as a way of motivating employees to stay current in their fields and to complete research projects in preparation for publication. As Mees explained in one of a pair of articles on industrial scientific research that he published in the journal *Nature* three years after the founding of the research lab:

> When the men come to the laboratory they are usually interested chiefly in the progress of pure science, but they rapidly become absorbed in the special problems presented to them, and, without definite effort on the part of those responsible for the direction of the laboratory, there is great danger that they will not keep up to date in what is being done by other workers in their own and allied fields.

CORPORATE INTELLECTUAL PROPERTY

Their interest can be stimulated by journal meetings and scientific conferences, but the greatest stimulation is afforded by the require-ment that they themselves should publish in the usual scientific journals the scientific results which they may obtain.[51]

[193]

Eastman Kodak's original agreement with Mees specified that the laboratory "will be allowed to publish the results of scientific investigations where they do not interfere commercially with the business" provided that before sub-mitting research for publication it was "always submitted to and approved by the Company."[52] The first published paper, a "purely mathematical con-sideration of photographic density," appeared in *Philosophical Magazine* in 1913; by 1925, over 240 papers and other items from the research laboratory had been published.[53]

In Mees's view, companies owed an obligation to science to publish the results of purely scientific work but owed no obligation to publish the results of their efforts to improve manufacturing technology. "Technology is the art of making things. It deals with the methods used for production," which a company could properly keep secret because technology "is of value only to other firms who use that particular technology." "Scientific advances," on the other hand, "must be published even when they are applicable to technol-ogy because science advances as a whole, and any attempt to withhold the publication of scientific work reacts to the disadvantage of the withholder. Moreover, scientific men will not continue to do satisfactory work unless they can publish that work and feel they are taking part in the advance-ment of science."[54] The challenge, of course, was to distinguish science from technology.

Although the company guarded secrets from outsiders, information within the laboratory was not restricted. Mees encouraged researchers to discuss their work with each other by developing a "conference" system in which researchers met informally each morning to discuss a particular area of research. Sometimes Eastman Kodak employees who were not research lab employees attended these conferences. Mees explained that the conference "procedure will enable a great saving in time to be made, since it will avoid the loss of time which continually occurs in laboratories from the wrong man doing a specific piece of work." Mees also insisted that the research division "building should be so arranged that all the laboratories are open to everybody in the scientific departments" so that researchers would have access to all the apparatus that they needed.[55]

Nevertheless, the company remained extremely secretive about technolo-gies it considered its competitive advantage. No employee could communicate an emulsion formula or other trade secret formula to another, regardless of who he was, without advance written permission by George Eastman.[56] Interestingly, Eastman sometimes even had to use such letters to force his employees to share information. William G. Stuber, Eastman's master emulsion maker, was said to guard his formulae so carefully that he was affronted even by a 1912 letter from Eastman stating: "You are hereby authorized and requested to impart to Dr. C. E. Kenneth Mees, as desired by him, any formulae in your possession."[57]

Eastman Kodak figured out that if emerging trade secret and noncompetition law prevented recruiting employees with the technical knowledge it wanted, it could simply purchase the competitor companies that employed the knowledgeable people and gain the information that way. In 1898, the Standard Dry Plate Company hired chemist Milton B. Punnett away from the M.A. Seed Company in order to obtain his knowledge of M.A. Seed's dry plate production methods and emulsion formulae. Standard's market performance greatly improved as a result, but strife within the company led Punnett to approach Eastman. In the spring of 1902, Eastman bought Standard Dry Plate and signed an employment agreement with Punnett. The emulsion formula Eastman thus obtained required much less silver nitrate than Eastman had previously been using, thereby saving double Eastman's purchase cost in just one year. Eastman then purchased M.A. Seed to get its emulsions formula as well, with additional agreements for certain key employees to come to Eastman. Finally, in 1904, Eastman bought the Stanley Dry Plate Company when he heard that it had obtained Standard's emulsion formula. Eastman also bought the Artura Paper Manufacturing Company after discovering that buying Artura's emulsion-making formula was not enough; Eastman needed access to Artura's secret manufacturing method. The practice of technology acquisition by corporate acquisition succeeded. In a letter of 1908, Eastman wrote: "In the last few years we have developed a scheme for making dry plates by combining all the improvements that we have found in the different factories we have bought, that is well nigh perfect."[58]

Although the company fought vigorously against Reichenbach's competitive employment in the 1890s, by the early 1900s Eastman showed little concern about an executive's threats to resign: "There are so many things required in order to make a success in this day in the photographic manufacturing business that the company is not greatly alarmed at what any man can do. All of our big competitors to-day can make good emulsions, some of them can make mighty good film; . . . some of them have been in business longer than the Kodak Company and people have left the Kodak Company to go into business, but with very few successes even when they started with conditions much more favorable than they are now."[59] Eastman Kodak may have held on to some of its emulsion secrets even after the 1921 antitrust decision against it, when no auction bids were placed for its dry plate businesses and Eastman Kodak manufactured the plates for the company who eventually bought the dry plate brands.[60] [195]

The legal regime governing employee innovation that had come into existence over the forty years of Eastman's aggressive business and litigation practices enabled Kodak and other firms in the 1920s to enjoy control over employees and their knowledge that would have been impossible in the past. In *Eastman Kodak Co. v. Powers Film Products, Inc.* (1919), for example, Eastman Kodak obtained enforcement of a two-year restrictive covenant against a former employee who had worked as a chemist. After describing the company's extensive research into film manufacturing and the defendant employee's long tenure with the company as a research chemist, the court justified the restriction on the ground that "the value of Warren's services to the defendant company arises from his experience while in the plaintiff's employ, growing out of the practical application of these trade secrets, and not otherwise." In the court's view, the employee acquired "special knowledge" through his exposure to the "secret processes" of the company. The court justified the extraordinary remedy of prohibiting the chemist from working in the film business on the ground that a narrower prohibition on simply using Kodak trade secrets "is more than likely to prove inefficient. The mere rendition of the service along the lines of his training would almost necessarily impart such knowledge to some degree. Warren cannot be loyal both to his promise to his former employer and to his new obligations to the defendant company."[61]

By the mid-1920s, the company had not only expanded its own control over employee knowledge through the careful use of contracts and careful guarding of information, but had played a crucial role in litigating the cases and articulating the legal theories that brought about legal change that enabled other employers to do the same. The expansion of the trade secret concept that Eastman Kodak urged in cases from *Reichenbach* in 1892 down to *Powers* in 1919 fueled a corresponding growth in the possible uses of restrictive covenants, which the company also was well positioned to benefit from, as it had for years been using restrictive covenants to prevent departing employees from working in the photographic supply business. The company was a beneficiary not only of its own business success but also of its own legal success, as its campaign of legal change created new ways that the company could control employee mobility and prevent the diffusion of knowledge it regarded as proprietary.

Discontented Entrepreneurs in Knowledge Factories

The shift to managerial capitalism and its impact on employees involved in innovation was as significant at E. I. du Pont de Nemours & Company as it had been at Eastman Kodak. Whereas with Eastman Kodak, we see the story from the top-down perspective of the company president and externally from the perspective of the courts, at Du Pont we see the story from the bottom-up perspective of a company chemist and from the inside perspective of company lawyers and senior managers. An episode from the Du Pont research lab that led to the U.S. Supreme Court deciding its first trade secrets case illustrates how a feared loss of status by a corporate scientist led him to hang onto the right to control his knowledge, and to litigate it zealously even when the litigation seemed to have benefited neither him nor Du Pont. The dispute became as much about power and status as it was about access to valuable knowledge.

Throughout the nineteenth century, Du Pont had been a family-controlled manufacturer of gunpowder and explosives. In 1902, three du Pont cousins gained control of the company and instituted a massive reorganization.[62] All three were trained as engineers and were familiar with the advanced administrative practices used by the railroads and in the steel, electrical, and machinery industries.[63] They decided to abandon the old structure of the firm, which had been a small family-controlled company that worked closely with a number of other small family firms to control the explosives industry through horizontal combination. Instead, Du Pont became a large, vertically integrated, and centrally administered firm.[64] As business historian Alfred Chandler explained, "Their aim was to dominate the industry by running the most efficient mills as fully and as steadily as possible and so to reduce their unit costs to levels that small competitors could not achieve."[65] By 1910 Du Pont employed "nearly all the basic methods that are currently used in managing big business."[66]

As part of the massive reorganization in 1902, Du Pont started two research and development laboratories to systematize and centralize the research and innovation that had occurred in diverse parts of the company's operations.[67] As Du Pont became more systematic and bureaucratic about inventive activity, it became more bureaucratic in its employment practices regarding inventive employees. For example, in 1904, when the company began holding monthly meetings of all the superintendents of its dynamite plants in the Wilmington area, the superintendents formulated common policies on a number of personnel issues, including searching employees for matches (an obvious threat in a dynamite factory), design and adoption of uniforms for all plant workers, installation of time clocks, and tabulation of labor costs and comparative yields. Although there was no discussion in those meetings of employee-generated intellectual property, in the same year Du Pont for the first time formally asserted ownership of its employees' patents. It began to require some employees working at the labs in an inventive capacity to sign employment agreements which acknowledged that "any inventions, improvements, or useful processes relating to explosives, their ingredients, manufacture or use, or to the appliances or machinery connected therewith, or to the treatment of by-products thereof" that the employee might make while in Du Pont's employ "shall be the sole and exclusive property" of the company. But the questions of which employees should be required to sign such a contract, which inventions the company ought to claim, how the company should assert its claims, and what to do if employees refused were not resolved then or for years to come.[68]

Personal relationships may have affected whether employees could successfully negotiate out of the patent assignment policy. Ernest du Pont, for example, signed a patent assignment contract when he took a job with the company in 1906. He left the firm in 1908, and two years after he returned in 1911 he insisted that the contract he previously signed was no longer in force because he was "re-employed by the company in an entirely different capacity, and at a lower rate of salary than I was getting when I signed the agreement."[69] The company readily agreed. The records do not reflect whether similar individual arrangements were ever made for employees who were not du Ponts.

Du Pont dealt with trade secrets by policy rather than by express contract. In 1908, the company sent a notice to all the employees in the smokeless powder plants and posted the same notice in the research laboratories and the dynamite plants. The notices advised employees that Du Pont "owns and possesses the right to use . . . secret processes . . . in connection with the manufacture of explosives and the appliances, packages, material, machinery, and other things relating to said business and used in connection therewith." It warned the employees sternly that it is "illegal for you during your employment or after its termination to reveal to any person, other than those in the employ of the company whose business it is to know . . . any information or matter whatsoever relating to the said secret processes, compositions, reagents, apparatus and machines." The warning went further: "It is also illegal during your employment, or after its termination, to use or employ any of the said processes, alone or in conjunction with others, except for the Company while in its employ." After the stern admonitions about the law, however, the notice concluded plaintively: "The company appreciates the high degree of loyalty and sense of right that has maintained with its employees during the many years it has been engaged in business and feels that calling attention in this way to the legal status of secret processes is all that is necessary."[70]

[198]

In 1911, Du Pont again reorganized its operations, moving chemical research from the development department into a department of its own, called the Chemical Department. In February of that year, perhaps as part of that reorganization, the Executive Committee appointed J. Amory Haskell and Arthur Moxham as a subcommittee to study and report on the question of whether employees should be made to sign a contract obligating them to assign to the company the rights to inventions they might develop.[71] The Executive Committee did not consider the 1904 contract to go far enough. So the subcommittee reconsidered what sorts of patents by which employees should be company property.

Moxham had proved his managerial ability to the du Ponts in his management of a Johnstown, Pennsylvania, streetcar rail manufacturing company. Pierre du Pont described him as "a master of cost sheets and orderly management." In 1895, Moxham had hired Frederick Winslow Taylor to reorganize the streetcar rail company's operations. Taylor's methods made a big impression on Moxham and the du Ponts, and when Moxham went to Du Pont after the 1902 reorganization, he brought with him Taylor's costing and control methods, which Moxham learned at Lorain Steel, a plant for which Taylor had consulted in that era.[72] Moxham came to Du Pont determined to rationalize its processes and saw revision of employee invention assignment policy as part of his mission.

The subcommittee of Moxham and Haskell concluded that, with respect to ownership of patents, Du Pont needed separate policies for two classes of employees. "Class 1" included "those employed in the original research laboratories," and they should be obligated to sign contracts assigning inventions. Class 2 encompassed unspecified other employees. The report went on: "[W]e do not believe it is wise to disturb the minds of our employees by adopting the cast iron rule that all salaried employees regardless of the nature of their employment should be expected to sign a contract." The committee evidently did not consider how nonsalaried employees would fit into the structure; they must have assumed that hourly employees were unlikely to innovate. Among Class 2 employees, the report suggested that only those "the nature of whose work makes it likely that they will be or might be contributors towards inventions or secret processes" should be expected to sign a contract assigning inventions. For Class 2 as well as Class 1, "all secret processes which are evolved out of the natural developments from the Company's business should be given without reservation to the Company." The subcommittee recommended that it be left to the heads of departments to decide which employees fell into Classes 1 or 2 and which employees should not be asked to sign either contract. "By this means a method is left to relieve the Company from embarrassment if called upon to decide between insisting upon the signing of a contract, or, as an alternative, upon the discharge of an employee refusing to sign."[73]

[199]

The two members of the subcommittee disagreed about how far the company should go in claiming employee inventions. One believed that the company should claim all rights to all employee inventions, regardless of the subject matter or the circumstances in which the employee created it. The other thought that, for inventions that could be applied to industries other than those in which Du Pont was engaged, or an industry "in which the Company represents a small or minority interest," Du Pont should obtain an exclusive license "for the purpose of making explosives only, and that everything else should belong to the inventor." Perhaps Moxham was the skeptic, as he himself had helped to invent a new steel rail before going to work for Du Pont. But both agreed that the company should demand by contract more rights to employee inventions than the default rule would allow. For example, although then as now companies were not entitled to any rights in employee inventions made without use of company time or resources, the subcommittee insisted that "in the case of inventions not made in the Company's time or developed by use of the Company's money, the company should be given a general shop right or ordinary license to manufacture."[74]

The Executive Committee debated the merits of the proposals but was unable to decide what to do and referred the matter to another subcommittee "for further consideration and report."[75] But the matter of what to do about employee contracts lingered on the Executive Committee's unfinished business agenda for at least the next three years. As late as 1914, Hamilton Barksdale, Du Pont's general manager, received a memo from the Executive Committee asking him to consider and report on what the company should do regarding employee contracts covering inventions. Barksdale's inattention was not due to his disinterest in details; indeed, some Du Pont senior management considered him too detail-oriented.[76]

After a few years, Du Pont did adopt a policy of requiring all employees working in the labs, not only chemists and engineers, but also clerks, stenographers, and other clerical employees, to sign contracts conveying to the company all rights in all patents and other inventions. And, as Du Pont diversified from explosives into other industries such as artificial leather and cellulose by-products, they revised their employment agreements to expand the range of intellectual property that the company claimed.[77]

Du Pont's reputation for enjoining secrecy upon its employees circulated to others in the industry. An official of U.S. Rubber, having heard that in Du Pont laboratories "even the stenographers and office boys" were "under confidential contract," asked for a copy of the Du Pont contract. As the U.S. Rubber official put it, "We have at present chiefly one form, which is rather extreme, excepting for technically trained men who can see a real future in the business, and we need a simpler form for others who should realize the importance of keeping information to themselves." Du Pont obligingly sent them a copy of the Du Pont contract used for "all salaried employees of the Chemical Department, including the research laboratories."[78]

As the company exerted greater control over the processes and results of innovation, it struggled to develop methods to motivate salaried employees to exert the utmost effort to invent, and to induce them not to take their valuable knowledge to jobs with competitors. Financial incentives were thought to be a solution, but it proved difficult to maintain the perfect system. Shortly after the 1902 reorganization, the Executive Committee began to consider ways to enlist the loyalty of managers now that they could no longer assume the personal and financial commitment that had come from family ownership and management of the firm. It was eventually as a part of this incentive system that the company began compensating employees for patents. In 1902, Coleman du Pont, the company president, asked the firm's local lawyer to draw up plans to permit "important employees" to purchase stock in the new firm. At that point, employee stock ownership was quite novel, although other firms began to adopt such programs at the same time. They set up one stock bonus plan in 1904 and another in 1906 to reward "merit." The stock bonus plan eventually was revised to include bonuses for patents. In the summer of 1912, Arthur Moxham, ever the imaginative one among Du Pont high-level managers, saw an article in *The Iron Age* describing a plan of the National Metal Trades Association for compensating employees for patents. Barksdale was quite interested and arranged to get a copy of the plan. Eventually, Du Pont adopted a system of compensating employees in Du Pont stock for patents, although employees complained that they were restricted from selling the stock and the dividends alone made the compensation plan unsatisfactory.[79]

Some Du Pont managers remained concerned about the fairness and desirability of allowing too little financial reward to inventive employees. For example, one Dr. Weedon, an employee of Du Pont's Chemical Department, invented a fluorescent screen. Shortly before Weedon died, he assigned the patent to Du Pont. The invention required further developmental work to make it commercially successful, and the work was done in the Du Pont lab. [201] Hamilton Barksdale recommended, and the Manufacturing and Sales Committee approved, that, after the Chemical Department determined whether the invention could be developed for commercial sale, "consideration shall be given as to whether or not any portion of the profits derived therefrom shall be turned over to Dr. Weedon's Estate."[80] It is unclear whether any profits were ever paid. Some companies, however, abandoned the practice of paying bonuses to employees for patents; after 1912, Bell Labs ceased its practice of paying $100 for each new patent because the research director thought the bonuses fostered destructive individual effort rather than the cooperative spirit that Bell Labs deemed most productive for maximal inventions by the corporation as a whole.[81]

The commodification of R & D, and of the people who did it, did not pass unnoticed in the labs. The managers' insistence that the scientists and engineers were working for a salary and that *all* their output—things, patents, processes, or ideas—were the company's property elicited some dissatisfaction among the employees in the Chemical Department. The story of Walter Masland, a Du Pont research chemist who left the firm to work in his family carpet manufacturing and textile business, illustrates how one highly educated employee who sought to be an entrepreneur chafed under the regime of corporate control. It may not be unique, but it is particularly well documented because his dispute with Du Pont over whether his knowledge of cellulose was a trade secret was litigated all the way to the Supreme Court. Rhetoric about a need for the law to protect the employer's investments in process or product development combined with the loose treatment of contractual obligations was particularly useful to Du Pont's efforts to prevent Masland from using alleged company trade secrets for manufacturing artificial leather.[82]

Masland went to work for Du Pont in 1904 after studying chemistry at the University of Pennsylvania. Masland obtained a number of patents during his ten-year employment at Du Pont, and he assigned all of them to the company pursuant to the form contract he signed in 1904. In 1914, Du Pont's work on artificial leather reached the point that the company was planning to build a plant to manufacture it for commercial sale. Du Pont acquired a monopoly (and a trademark brand) by acquiring a New York–based artificial leather company, Fabrikoid. Masland hoped to be promoted when Fabrikoid's assistant superintendent–chief chemist quit, but he was instead expected to pick up his work without a promotion or a raise. Feeling underpaid and unappreciated as others were promoted over him, Masland quit. Masland was not alone in feeling exploited; some of the younger chemists complained [202] that Charles Reese, the head of Du Pont's Chemical Department and chair of its Experimental Board, patented subordinates' work in his own name and displayed "intolerance and haughtiness in his manner." Masland complained to Reese that Du Pont often passed over for promotion men with talent in favor of men with family connections. As a consequence, he complained, men at the Experimental Station had few opportunities for promotion.[83]

Reese tried to persuade Masland that morality and loyalty to Du Pont should dissuade him from going into the artificial leather business with his family firm. According to Reese, Masland replied that "he had given the matter of his moral obligations a great deal of thought; that he did not believe he had a moral right to sell or give this confidential information to competitors, or to other parties." But, according to Reese, Masland did believe "that he had the right to use personally any information, confidential or otherwise, which he had obtained either through his own effort or efforts of others during his employment with the company."[84] This characterization of Masland's belief—that he had a right to use knowledge that he had participated in developing—reflected an issue that had vexed trade secret law for thirty years. Masland's own work and intelligence had produced the advances in the chemistry of artificial leather, and in his view he sought merely to use the knowledge he had developed over the course of his career. In Du Pont's view, however, because he had been paid to develop that knowledge and Du Pont wanted to keep the results of the research for itself, he was both morally and legally obligated to give Du Pont the exclusive use of his knowledge of artificial leather. In the ensuing litigation, Masland never claimed that he had the right to use secret knowledge so long as he had participated in developing it; his theory was that the chemistry of artificial leather that he planned to use was common knowledge among chemists familiar with cellulose and artificial leather.

The company's aggressive position regarding employee intellectual property prompted a series of discussions between its chemists and lawyers about the threat that employee mobility posed to company intellectual property. After Masland announced his intentions but before he left the firm, the lawyers and company officials met and, according to notes taken by company patent lawyer Edwin Prindle, they agreed among themselves that "the moral questions involved group themselves under two heads." First, there was "an *implied contract* between the Company and Mr. Masland that he would not make use in any way of any confidential matters concerning the Company and its work." Second, according to Prindle, Masland's "proposed line of conduct places the Company under an unfair handicap in competing with him. The Company has spent large sums of money in perfecting the process under consideration. When its goods are placed on the market, therefore, it will have to charge enough for its product to cover the cost of its investigations. As Mr. Masland has borne none of this cost, he can sell at a lower price than the company, and destroy its market. If he thinks this is fair, his moral judgment is either very much atrophied or greatly warped."[85]

Du Pont sued him seeking an injunction against his using processes that Du Pont claimed to be trade secrets. Masland claimed they were, rather, common knowledge among chemists and insisted that he had developed his knowledge both before going to Du Pont and while working there and ought not be enjoined from using his accumulated chemical knowledge.[86] The litigation never resolved that question. Rather, the litigation focused primarily on whether Masland could obtain expert testimony to establish that the process that Du Pont claimed as trade secret was in fact common knowledge among chemists of cellulose and artificial leather. Du Pont wanted to prevent Masland from drawing his experts from the ranks of their competitors, preferring that he serve as his own expert or that he use experts drawn from government or academia. Masland contended that all the experts whom Du Pont suggested either consulted for Du Pont or relied on Du Pont for business. The district court enjoined Masland from revealing Du Pont's processes to expert witnesses, and it was that order that was appealed eventually all the way to the Supreme Court and left standing in a short opinion by Justice Holmes. The opinion stated essentially that the trial judge had discretion to determine whether disclosure of trade secrets to experts was necessary to the defense or whether it would suffice for him to disclose "whatever public facts were nearest to the alleged secrets."[87]

Prindle persuaded Du Pont officials to see their employment practices regarding patent assignment agreements as part of a deliberate competitive strategy. Prindle explained his ideas in a series of articles published in *Engineering Magazine* in 1906 and in a 1908 book, *Patents as a Factor in Manufacturing*. The avowed purpose of the book was to suggest to "manufacturers" the benefit of obtaining legal advice about patents to aid their business; no doubt the unstated purpose was to enhance his reputation (and presumably expand his business) as a lawyer. "There are many manufacturers who could and would strengthen their position commercially through patents, if they but saw the neglected material at hand, or understood the fuller possibilities of material." The book contained a chapter on "the patent relations of employer and employee," which formed the basis of Prindle's advice to Du Pont about the necessity of getting experimental employees to sign invention assignment agreements.[88]

As Prindle saw it, because patents may be issued only in the name of the [204] inventor, for a corporation to gain an effective monopoly on a technology, "it is desirable to have a contract with every employee who is at all likely to make inventions which relate to the business of the employer."[89] Recognizing that some employees would be reluctant to sign such contracts, particularly since they did not require additional consideration beyond the employee's regular salary, Prindle recommended that corporate leaders use "psychology" by signing the same contracts requested of employees. Contracts by officers, Prindle recognized, were "a mere matter of form, as [the corporate officer] is frequently a man who is either not inventive or one who is glad to take his returns in the form of dividends from the stock."[90] Thus, Prindle recognized that patent assignment agreements would be perceived as rendering employees part of the dependent middle class, and proposed that the status effects be masked by corporate leaders signing the same agreement.

There was a reasonable basis for Prindle's concern that inventive employees might refuse to assign patents. Recent histories of company research in the 1880s and 1890s have uncovered examples of employees (one at Westinghouse and one at the Edison Machine Works) refusing to assign patents for inventions they had been hired to invent, and although there is no reason for these specific instances to have been familiar to Prindle, such stories no doubt circulated among company managers and lawyers. The recalcitrant inventors may have felt that hanging onto their patents was the only way to ensure that their creativity and hard work were credited and rewarded. Company lawyers recognized that the reluctance of the inventive employees may have been about status and self-respect as much as about money. The lawyers for Edison Machine Works, for example, explained that an invention "belongs wholly to the person who first receives the idea and reduces it to a practical form. It makes no difference that at the time he may be in the employ of another man who is paying him for devoting his time to the very subject in connection with which the invention is made." The lawyer suggested that the firm "enter into a contract with each of their employees to the effect that all inventions made in matters connected with the work which they are engaged to perform during their connection with the company shall belong to the company." "This," the lawyer advised, "while it would doubtless cause considerable trouble for the company, seems to be the best way in which the difficulty can be avoided. Whether it is practicable for you to make such contracts is of course a question for you to decide. We fear our suggestion is somewhat impracticable."[91]

Building on the established patent law division of the act of inventing into distinct and separable parts, the "mental conception of the invention" and its reduction to practice, Prindle justified employer ownership of patents by imagining that the employer was generally responsible for the mental conception. To capture the attention of the "manufacturers" who were his intended audience, Prindle posited the scenario (highly stylized but drawn from a case) of a shoe manufacturer who "had trouble with his operatives" and wished to mechanize the part of his operation requiring skilled labor (the troublesome operatives) so that he could use "a class of labor that could easily be trained so that a strike of the trained operatives could be broken by training new hands." In Prindle's telling, the manufacturer "went to machinists and outlined a machine to accomplish his purpose. The manufacturer described the principal elements of the machine, and how they would work with relation to each other." When "the machinists" filed a patent application for the resulting machine and litigation ensued, Prindle explained, the court held that the machinists failed to rebut the presumption that the employer was the inventor. Prindle's narrative about invention was drawn from an antebellum workshop in which a master craftsman supervises a few apprentices and in which inventions can be traced to the idea of a single person. The story ignored the reality of invention in corporate R & D facilities but set up the metaphor that the corporation was the master craftsman and all the R & D employees were the "operatives" who simply reduced his ideas to practice. Elsewhere Prindle cautioned that special care was needed by one who "employs clever men and has them instructed in the details of his business" lest he "lay himself peculiarly open to the possibility that his employees may make inventions which would seriously hurt his business if he had to compete with them."[92]

Prindle concluded the chapter with the advice that firms "have a contract with every employee who is at all likely to make inventions which relate to the business of the employer" and asserted that the contracts would be enforceable even if supported by "no further provision for return for the inventions than the payment of the ordinary salary." Prindle asserted the existence of "manufacturing concerns where every man in the drafting room and in the sales department, and every skilled employee, is under such a contract."[93] Clearly, DuPont had found in Prindle a lawyer who shared its perspective on the necessity of protecting the firm from the challenges of its inventive employees.

After Du Pont sued Masland, company officials began to examine more closely their practices with respect to employee ideas. They realized, to their chagrin, that the form contract Masland and other Experimental Station

[205]

employees had signed in 1905 covered only patents and inventions related to explosives, not their newer lines of business such as artificial leather. The contract also did not explicitly protect trade secrets. Du Pont's in-house counsel became anxious that the litigation might publicize these deficiencies in the contract, and might also alert employees to the fact that the company had insisted that its chemists assign patents that plainly were not covered by the contract: "This, of course, would be very suggestive to certain other employees in the laboratory," he worried, adding that widespread knowledge of it "is apt to be demoralizing" to "certain classes of employees of the company."[94] While the Masland suit was pending between 1914 and 1917, the company tried to get all employees working in its labs to sign contracts not to disclose company secrets.[95]

Du Pont officials remained anxious that Masland's firm was producing artificial leather. Prindle employed a private detective agency for all sorts of cloak-and-dagger snooping around the Masland factory to confirm his client's suspicions. One snuck through a fence, one obtained a meeting with Masland by posing as a businessman interested in purchasing artificial leather for export, one applied for a job at the Masland firm, and one even tried to pose as a Philadelphia Electric Company employee for purposes of gaining access to the Masland factory.[96] When a detective finally reported in 1918 that the Masland factory was not manufacturing artificial leather, the company settled its accounts with its lawyers. All told, they paid Prindle's firm nearly $12,000 for their work on the case.[97] Meanwhile, between 1911 and 1919, Du Pont's artificial leather business produced average profits of 15 percent, although the shoes made from Fabrikoid, which Du Pont had tested by forty mail carriers and a local shoe store in Wilmington, Delaware, were of only middling quality.[98]

EASTMAN KODAK AND DU PONT exhibit the kind of multipronged strategy about innovation that mid-twentieth-century business students studied and business boosters cheered. In the labs, and in the offices of company managers, lawyers, and marketers, Eastman Kodak and Du Pont sought ways to innovate. They envisioned and sometimes created new and improved products; new and improved advertising campaigns based on new and improved trademarks; and new and improved legal relations with their new and improved employees, who enjoyed a new and improved middle-class life in the suburbs surrounding the companies' headquarters in Rochester and Wilmington.

A number of the firms that were the most zealous advocates of employer intellectual property rights were also at the forefront of the development of consumer culture and the vigorous use of advertising brand-name products to generate customer demand for constantly new and improved products. The Eastman Kodak Company linked aggressive intellectual property protec- [207] tion, particularly with respect to employees, with aggressive marketing of its devices. Its cameras and film were protected through patent, trade secret, and trademark law, and its advertising campaigns were protected, as soon as the law said they could be protected, by copyright. Its vigilance in protecting intellectual property rights went hand in hand with its pioneering use of advertising to create a mass market for cameras and amateur photography.[99] The exponential growth in amateur snapshot photography was driven by Eastman Kodak's continual creation of new, more reliable, easier to use, and more affordable cameras in the years between 1895 and 1930. The company's business strategy, which proved wildly successful for several decades, linked constant innovation with unceasing efforts to create demand for new products through advertising. Eventually the company concluded that it was easier to create a demand for the company's products by brand name than to prevent competitors from learning about Kodak technology by recruiting Kodak employees.

The expansion of the types of information subject to intellectual property rights that accompanied the development of consumer culture in the early twentieth century transformed the legal conception of employees' rights to capitalize on their skills and training in subsequent employment. If the popular attitudes about creativity and innovation were buffeted from many directions by the conflicting visions of the role of intellectual property in American life, the winds of change that firms described in courts blew all in one direction. The trend in the case law by the 1920s was toward ever broader and ever more robust intellectual property rights. Between 1895 and 1930 courts expanded the types of information that could be claimed as trade secrets and that could be patented or copyrighted, and employers claimed as proprietary increasingly broad categories of knowledge. Courts had understood throughout the nineteenth century that craft knowledge was economically valuable. They realized, for example, that the precise recipe for gunpowder was valuable and so were the techniques for mixing, handling, and storing it. They also recognized that firms would want the exact dimensions of a machine as well as rule-of-thumb knowledge about how to cast its metal components and keep it in working order. What changed so quickly after 1900 was not the judicial ability to imagine the economic value of all the knowledge and experience of a skilled workman or the value of a new design for a poster or handbill or the value of a new compilation of information, but the judicial ability to imagine such knowledge as the exclusive property of a firm.

Once the judicial imagination caught fire about the benefits of corporate ownership of knowledge, the doctrinal consequences were significant. The focus of trade secret law shifted from tangible things (e.g., the drawings of a machine) to ideas (the design innovations contained in them);[100] from the list of customers to the knowledge of their identities, locations, needs, and goodwill;[101] and from the precise written formula for a substance to the general knowledge of the process and techniques for making it.[102] Negative knowledge (i.e., what does not work to achieve a particular purpose) came to be recognized for the first time as a trade secret so that an employee could be restrained not only from using knowledge about what works to make a product, but also from using knowledge of what does not work. Compilations of publicly available facts gained protection as trade secrets or through copyright.[103] As the scope of copyright, trademark, and trade secrets expanded, the scope of an employee's freely usable general knowledge, or even specialized skill and experience, diminished, and the public domain began to shrink.

As more and more types of information became intellectual property, in theory fewer and fewer forms of employee knowledge could permissibly be used in subsequent employment. Courts struggled to find an easily administrable "bright line" rule that would allow a desirable element of competition while allocating intellectual property rights to the corporation. One such "bright line" rule was the notion that employees leaving for subsequent employment could take information in their heads with them but nothing in writing, the so-called "memory rule."[104] Critics of the memory rule were fond of pointing out that tort liability ought not turn on whether former employees have bad memories or excellent recall.[105] The persistence of the memory rule lay in the appeal of property concepts to define the scope of the employer's rights. It also had the appeal of loosely corresponding to the judges' intuitive sense of the difference between trade secrets and general knowledge. Yet even the memory rule lacked both specificity and the capacity to balance freedom to work with protection for corporate intellectual property when courts began to see that trade secrets could encompass ideas (the idea, for example, of using a particular chemical compound as an emulsion on photographic film) as well as things (a specific emulsion formula). The difficult task of assigning ownership of knowledge inevitably turned upon distinguishing protectable trade secrets from nonprotectable general knowledge, which always depended on understanding complicated technology through the testimony of self-interested witnesses. Beyond that, it has been and remains a core normative judgment about the freedom and attributes of creative employees. Then, as now, courts tended to hide, perhaps from themselves, their normative judgments in their findings of fact.[106]

The litigation brought by Eastman Kodak and Du Pont against Reichenbach, Masland, and others had significant consequences for the nature and culture of corporate R & D. Corporate control of intellectual property enabled collective invention of a spectacular array of electrical, chemical, and mechanical technologies that fueled the rapid growth of the American economy. It financed vast accumulations of wealth for some, and a degree of comfort and security for inventive employees of which their early nineteenth-century forebears could only have dreamed. It may or may not have produced a more equitable distribution of compensation among all of a company's inventors than would have occurred in a legal regime that allocated intellectual property rights to the individual rather than to the firm. But it fundamentally changed the entrepreneurial prospects of inventive employees in many industries.

The scientists and engineers employed in corporate R & D were prevented by law from using the strategy for upward mobility that had been common in the nineteenth century. Unlike their predecessors, they could not easily take their economically valuable knowledge and go into business for themselves. The legal rules that restricted their mobility had the overtones of the old actions for enticement, treating their effort to depart their service for their corporate employers just as early nineteenth-century law treated a servant who was enticed from his master's service. The diminished legal status of the inventive employee was obscured because the class divide between university-trained engineers and office clerks was thought far more germane than their dwindling prospects for entrepreneurship and independent control of the products of their labor. In other words, the significant erosion of the entrepreneurial prospects and social status of inventive employees was camouflaged by the education and other markers of upper-middle-class status of research employees in a large corporation.

While some inventors and authors remained entrepreneurial about controlling the intellectual property they produced by remaining outside the context of corporate employment, by the third decade of the twentieth century a large number of creators had accepted corporate jobs and forsaken the risks and rewards of controlling their own intellectual property. Within firms, what began to loom larger for many employees than intellectual property ownership was credit for the work they did and acknowledgment of the importance of their creative effort in creating the company's products. Most chemists at Du Pont seemed to accept quite readily the legal obligation to

[209]

assign their patents to the firm. What they could not accept so easily was failing to be listed as an inventor, even if it had no legal consequence for ownership of a patent, and failing to be acknowledged within the firm as the originator of an idea, a patent, or a copyrighted work. Increasingly, employees sought recognition as much as financial reward from their employers. Attribution, and the respect accorded to inventors and authors, began to substitute for intellectual property (and the legal status of being *the* inventor or author) as the currency that would enable employees to advance their careers.

The Corporation's Money Paid
for the Painting; Its Artist Colored It;
Its President Designed It

Inventors and authors have long been imagined to be individual humans because originality and creativity are imagined to be uniquely human attributes. As patent and copyright law came to recognize the validity of corporate intellectual property in the twentieth century, courts and legislators had to reconsider the relation between the creative employee and the corporate employer. In the burgeoning twentieth-century market for intellectual property as consumer goods, firms used the names of individual creators as markers of quality or authenticity to brand their products even as the commercialization of the production of art and books demanded corporate control of intellectual property. As businesses sought intellectual property protection for an increasingly broad and commercialized array of products, particularly in the area of copyright, the legal justifications proffered by their lawyers and accepted by judges for granting copyrights changed from protection of individual artistic expression to protection of corporate investment in producing innovative artifacts of popular culture. Firms insisted upon control of employee talent while demanding intellectual property protection for commercial products that were not "art" or "literature" as defined by the romantic celebrations of individual creativity. Their lawyers reconciled competing imperatives of corporate control and individual artistic expression by developing informal systems for attributing works to employees while insisting that legal rules of express or implied contract gave their clients ever greater control of both the process and products of employee creativity. Authorship became a brand and a legal fiction, and the contract of employment emerged as a technology of authorship.

Courts and firms deployed romantic images of individual authorship to ex-
pand intellectual property rights in works that were created in a bureaucratic business environment anathema to the romanticized notion of authorship that had previously justified copyright monopolies. Courts first analogized the corporation to the studio or *atelier* of the great artist where the corporation's president did the creative work and the corporate employees, like a great painter's assistants, filled in the background and unimportant details. Walt Disney was to his animated films as Titian was to his paintings. Eventually it was no longer necessary to imagine the corporate president as the artist; as the legal fiction of corporate personhood gained traction in popular culture, law imagined the corporations as the artist. The Disney Corporation became the author.

While corporate personality was transforming the notion of collective authorship of commercial works, the implied contract of employment acquired new meaning that consolidated corporate control of employee creativity. Courts began to see commercial creation of books, lithographs, and other popular copyrighted works as a form of corporate R & D which firms should own by virtue of the corporate investment in the creative process. Courts used contract concepts to justify a shift from the old rule of presumptive employee ownership to a new rule of corporate ownership. Contract was fictionalized as an exercise of individual will and intention just as authorship ceased to be imagined as an exercise of individual will and intention.

Rand McNally, the map publisher, accommodated the realities of bureaucratic production of copyrights with the persistent need to attribute works to individual creators by devising internal corporate processes for attribution that substituted for copyright ownership. At Rand McNally, authorship became simultaneously a process of collective production and a brand advertising certain attributes of a commercial product. In the market for commercial art and texts, corporate "authors" deployed norms of attribution in the place of the law of copyright as the cultural capital of authorship. A nonlegal custom of attribution as a creator was all that was left to artists, authors, and inventors. A claim to attribution became the intellectual capital—but never the property—of the employee-creator. It also became the way in which corporate merchants of commercial products of "art" and "literature" built consumer loyalty to the corporate brand. Attribution of corporate products to individual employees guaranteed the artistic authenticity of the fabricated cultural commodities.

The Corporate Author and the Expansion of Intellectual Property

As intellectual property became more likely to be created in collaborative work settings, no single individual could plausibly claim to be the inventor or author, and no one person could have a compelling moral claim to control the idea or knowledge. As a consequence, when the employer was a corporation, its claim to be the "author" of the works created by its employees required that the corporation as a fictional person be analogized to *the* inventor or *the* author, and thus fit the individualist nineteenth-century paradigm of invention and originality. The turn-of-the-century conceptualization of the corporation as a rights-holding "person" played exactly this crucial rhetorical role. In a legal regime that preferred, both as a matter of rhetoric and as a matter of legal analysis, that some "person" be identified as *the* inventor of every patent or as *the* author of every copyrighted work, the creation of the corporate "person" occurred at exactly the right time. The legal fiction of the corporate person bridged the conceptual gap between collective and individual creation just when a bridge was needed.

Legal scholarship on the law of corporate personality in the 1890s and thereafter struggled to assimilate the behavior of groups into the legal concepts that had been built upon the behavior of individuals, like creativity, will, and intention.[1] Ultimately, corporations were recognized as being "an aggregation of capital" rather than an "association of persons."[2] Once that occurred, it became possible for courts to conceive of innovation as being the product of wise management of corporate assets rather than the achievement of individual employees. But that process was not complete until the controversy over corporate personality abated in the third decade of the twentieth century.

As corporations grew in size and influence, they had to be assimilated as rights-holders within the traditional, individualist frameworks that dominated legal doctrines across the spectrum of American law. Reconciling individualism with the newly dominant business corporation presented a fundamental challenge to the legal theory of intellectual property. Before 1910, courts imagined workplace invention in largely individualist terms, assuming that the workplace was a congregation of individuals working in loose association and that rights to creative products could be attributed to individuals in the way that the law of partnership treated the rights and obligations of the firm as being rights and obligations of the individual partners. Even as corporations replaced partnerships as the dominant form of business organization, corporate law until the turn of the century tended to treat

The Corporation's Money Paid for the Painting .

corporations not very differently from partnerships.[3] The re-imagining of a corporation as a single person made a big difference for copyright ownership. The ultimate legal fiction underlying modern copyright law is the fiction of corporate authorship. If the fiction were merely a shorthand way of saying that the corporation is the assignee of the works of an author, it would be one thing. But not every case that recognized employer ownership did so simply by assuming that the employee had expressly or implicitly agreed to assign a copyright. Some courts persisted in analyzing the matter as if the employer itself had to be the creator. In this context, the rise of the corporation played an ambiguous role. On the one hand, if judges saw authorship as a collaborative process, the fact that a business entity was a corporate body helped the employer's case. The claim of a corporate "author," composed of many different people working toward a common end, had greater rhetorical appeal than the claim of one individual partner to the work of another. On the other hand, the rise of corporate power threatened the very individualist premises and values of much nineteenth-century law. Inasmuch as courts regarded authorship as uniquely individual, corporate authorship was simultaneously oxymoronic and repugnant. Courts did not immediately capitulate to the empire-building tendencies of the growing corporations in this area any more than they did in any other area of law. One way to understand the schizophrenic state of the law of ownership of ideas is that judges were working out the tension between individualism and corporatism in American law and society.[4]

The first case in which a court explicitly held that a corporation owned a copyright in an employee's creation did not require significant departure from past rhetoric because the president of the corporation, "himself an artist of respectable attainments," had been personally involved in the design of the advertising woodcut at issue. The employee, a painter named Stecher, allegedly painted the print under the supervision of the corporation's president, one Schumacher. The corporation's "money paid for the painting; its artist colored it; its president designed it, his was the 'originating, inventive, and master mind.'" Analogizing the corporation to the artist's studio, the court said: "The fact that the artist Stecher executed Schumacher's design cannot defeat the copyright. The sculptor seldom touches the marble from which his statues are carved. The fact that the brush which embodied Schumacher's idea was held by another artist rather than by himself cannot be important in considering a question of this character."[5] The personal involvement of the corporation's president made the step to the fiction of corporate creation seem to be nothing more than an easy step of agency law attributing to the corporation the acts of its chief officer.

Eventually courts accepted corporate authorship even without evidence of corporate officers' involvement in the acts of creation. In 1908, an author employed to write a book on the law of corporations challenged enforcement of a contract assigning the entire interest in the manuscript to the employer. [215] The court endorsed the idea of corporations as authors when it rejected the employee-author's contention that the defendant had breached the contract by causing the book to be copyrighted in the name of a corporation that was not a party to the contract.[6]

Similarly, corporate authorship was normalized into the copyright paradigm in a 1911 case concerning a catalog of designs for the newly popular phenomenon of ready-to-wear clothing. The basis for the corporation's claim to authorship and therefore copyright was that the corporation's managers "exercised the most careful supervision and discrimination and made large outlays and expenditures." The court did not find the corporate manager's artistic or literary creativity wholly irrelevant—there was "the most careful supervision and discrimination"—but the case made it possible to attribute the intellectual creativity of the employees to the corporate employer for purposes of determining the "author" of a copyrighted work. The corporation employed "artists and authors of peculiar skill and ability," and the pictures and text "embodied the personal reaction of artists of recognized skill in their calling, and were pictures of artistic merit." These qualities were necessary, in the court's view, to justify a copyright at all.

To justify corporate ownership of the copyright (given that the court had just characterized the pictures as being "the personal reaction" of the employee-artists), the court then emphasized the "peculiar value" of the pictures "as portraying original conceptions and creations relating to wearing apparel, of great interest to a large proportion of the public on account of the originality and exercise of trained aesthetic faculties displayed in said illustrations."[7] Citing a mid-nineteenth-century case that had rejected the notion of employer authorship of employee works, along with two recent cases in which courts had accepted that employers might own the rights to texts prepared in collective workplace settings, the opinion fused earlier notions of employee authorship with the still-new idea of corporate authors of copyrighted advertisements and other purely commercial works.[8]

At the same time that courts were first contemplating corporate authorship, they also were grappling with growth in the types of materials subject to copyright. Courts alternately invoked and ignored eighteenth- and nineteenth-century notions of authorship to justify the existence of copyrights in new media such as advertising. By analogizing these commercial and corporate creations to the great artistic works of the past, judges and lawyers

The Corporation's Money Paid for the Painting

legitimated new property rights in new media. Schumacher was "an artist of respectable attainments," and his involvement as corporate president was akin to the master sculptor in his studio who "seldom touches the marble."[9]

[216] In *Burrow-Giles Lithographic Company v. Sarony*, an 1884 U.S. Supreme Court case involving the copyright to a photograph of Oscar Wilde, the Court held that a portrait photographer used sufficient creativity in the composition and lighting of a publicity shot of Wilde to make a photograph a proper subject of copyright.[10] The case is known primarily for its holding that photographs can be copyrighted. A significant but little-noticed feature of the opinion, however, is the Court's approach to the hiring contract of the photographer. Parsing the contract in assessing the authorship of the photographs, the Court articulated a new view of the way that creativity could be hired. Although *Burrow-Giles Lithographic Co.* did not address an ownership dispute between employer and employee, its approach to the nature of creativity makes it an important point in the development of legal concepts of the creativity for hire.

That a dispute over the image of Oscar Wilde should have been part of the construction of the law of creativity for hire is revealing, and not entirely serendipitous, even though Wilde himself seems to have had no involvement in the litigation. Wilde (1854–1900) was a celebrated writer, lecturer, and aesthete who carefully protected his literary property rights but also freely allowed others to borrow his work and freely transgressed any number of social norms, including plagiarism.[11] He was an early modern celebrity, the person who creates and markets his personality as a form of entertainment for others. He presented himself as a great talker and a larger-than-life personality; indeed, some of his contemporaries thought that Wilde's "personality and conversation were far more wonderful than anything he wrote."[12] As Wilde himself said, "all Art [is] to a certain degree a mode of action, an attempt to realize one's own personality on some imaginative plane out of reach of the trammeling accidents and limitations of real life."[13]

Wilde's self-constructed persona, which merged the late Romantic celebration of the artiste-aesthete with the burgeoning fin-de-siècle commercial and consumer culture, allowed him to explore "the corrosive impact of market exchange on cultural meaning."[14] One place the market most changed cultural meaning was in how corporations became purveyors of art, and celebrity became the way that commercialized art was valued. The commercialization of creativity facilitated the development of a market for celebrity in a consumer culture. At the time, mass-produced photographs of actors and other celebrities were popular consumer goods, as were mass-produced lithographs of paintings and other copies of works of fine art.[15]

Wilde was an irresistible subject for an enterprising portraitist who fancied himself an artist and wanted to make a buck. An artistic photograph of Wilde the aesthete would appeal to the "art"-loving consumer public that imagined that possessing such an image would connect them to the world of aesthetics. It would also connect the entrepreneur-photographer to the world of art while making money too. What made the Wilde photograph worth litigating over was a commercial culture supporting the mass-marketing of images of literary celebrities. And what makes the case interesting is the way the Court portrayed the nature of creative authorship to accommodate the new reality that someone who saw a market for a new item of intellectual property would often hire someone else to generate a creative product.

Oscar Wilde arrived in New York in 1882 to do a series of poetry readings and lectures on aesthetics. Wilde's tour was promoted by his manager, Richard D'Oyley Carte, to publicize Gilbert and Sullivan's new production, *Patience*. Carte, who also had a business relationship with Gilbert and Sullivan, realized that *Patience*, which satirized English aestheticism, was so contemporary that American audiences would not get it. As Wilde was a leading figure in aestheticism, it made perfect sense to have him lecture in a city just before or during the opera's run in order to alert audiences to the subject of the work, although the connection between the two was never specifically advertised.[16] With a little help, audiences might recognize Wilde in a character in the opera:

A most intense young man,
A soulful-eyed young man,
An ultra-poetical, super aesthetical,
Out-of-the-way young man![17]

As part of the publicity for the tour, Carte arranged for Wilde to be photographed dressed in a velvet jacket and vest, silk knee-breeches, and slippers adorned with bows—"the costume, in short, that made him the hit of the New York social whirl that season."[18] The photographer was Napoleon Sarony, a leading portrait photographer of entertainers in that era. Multiple images were taken in various poses.[19] Sarony himself neither took the photographs nor printed them. His studio employees put the plates into the camera, removed and replaced the lens cap, handled the props and costumes, and printed the photographs. It was, indeed, Sarony's own lack of technical involvement that the Court latched onto in its opinion as defining his artistic contribution to the photograph. As the Supreme Court said, quoting the trial court's findings, which in turn quoted Sarony's complaint, the photograph

The Corporation's Money Paid for the Painting

represented Sarony's "own original mental conception, to which he gave visible form by posing the said Oscar Wilde in front of the camera, selecting and arranging the costume, draperies, and other various accessories in said photograph, arranging the subject so as to present graceful outlines, arranging and disposing the light and shade, suggesting and evoking the desired expression."[20]

[218]

The case was litigated without a jury on a thin record consisting mainly of an agreed statement of facts and copies of the photographs in dispute. The trial court's findings about the nature of the Wilde photograph and Sarony's involvement in making it are drawn verbatim from the allegations in Sarony's complaint.[21] Sarony's lawyer chose that characterization of his involvement in making photographs in order to refute a view of photographs, common at that time, as being unmediated representations of nature produced by light and machine rather than constructed images created by human creativity.[22] But the description of Sarony's work also suited Sarony's own self-conception and marketing strategy; Sarony played up his ability to compose a scene and to make the sitter look a certain way and played down any involvement in the nitty-gritty of producing photographs: "About the chemistry of photography, he told an interviewer, he knew nothing and cared less. He limited his role in the operation to setting up the camera and posing the sitter. He did not even take the pictures himself. 'If I make a position and his camera is right,' Sarony once said, 'my long-time assistant Benjamin Richardson, is able to catch my ideas as deftly and quickly as necessary.'"[23]

Sarony's job was to hustle up business, which he did by relentless socializing and self-promotion, and to coax, cajole, flatter, and bully the subject into posing as Sarony thought best. What the Court had to decide, in a litigation that arose because the Wilde tour created such a sensation that a lithography studio copied the photo, was whether Sarony's contribution to the photograph involved enough creativity to render the photograph a proper subject of copyright.

In teasing out whether the fact that the photographer created for hire somehow vitiated the degree of creativity necessary to sustain a copyright, Justice Miller's opinion for the Court sought guidance from an English case involving a photograph of an Australian cricket team.[24] The dispute in the English case was whether a London firm, which had arranged for the photo to be taken and "sent one of the artists in their employ from London to some country town to do it," was the author of the photo because it "owned the establishment in London, where the photographs were made from the negative, and were sold, and . . . had the negative taken by one of their men."[25] The English court held that the author was the man who "superintended the arrangement, who . . . actually formed the picture by putting the persons in position and arranging the place where the people are to be."[26] Justice Miller noted approvingly that the English court held that the photographer, not his employer, was entitled to the copyright, and then translated the relevance of that fact into the Wilde photo case by discerning a principle that "the author is the man who really represents, creates, or gives effect to the idea, fancy, or imagination."[27] The English firm that had hired the photographer had not been present when the photo was composed and taken, and thus it could not be the author. Sarony, by contrast, was described as the person who created the image of Wilde by composing the scene.

Of course, *Burrow-Giles* was a dispute over the scope of copyright (is a photograph copyrightable?) and not over ownership of the photo. As between the lithography firm that indisputably copied the Wilde photograph and Sarony, it is clear that Sarony deserved to win. The case did not address the degree of creativity that Sarony, as opposed to his assistants, would have to exercise in order to justify him in claiming the photograph as his work. What is significant in the discussion of hiring is that the Court found nothing inconsistent between hiring creativity, on the one hand, and the nature of authorship and original intellectual creation, on the other. Creativity could be hired, and the products of creativity could be sold in an employment contract. The photo was therefore an appropriate subject for copyright, notwithstanding its commercial for-hire character.

Burrow-Giles sits firmly in the nineteenth century in its presumption that the employee is the author of a work made for hire when it is the employee's creativity that is reflected in the work. Until the first decade of the twentieth century, employee authorship, and therefore employee copyright ownership, would remain the presumptive rule. What had begun changing in the 1870s and 1880s, however, was that courts chose to analyze ownership and control of workplace knowledge in contractual terms rather than according to the older notion that the products of any person's creativity were necessarily the creator's property. Initially, courts interpreted these putative contracts favorably to employees. Nevertheless, the establishment of contract as the dominant framework was the foundation upon which radical change occurred at the end of the century. The newly dominant notion that all work relationships are entirely contractual was the legal conduit for a rapid shift at the turn of the twentieth century from employee ownership to employer ownership of innovation. By the early twentieth century, courts presumed that firms owned the products of employee creativity and abandoned the approach to contract interpretation that had given employees control over their creativity and its products.

The Corporation's Money Paid for the Painting

[220] The concept of corporate personality transformed how courts understood the relationship of employment by enabling judges and lawyers to see these cases not as a dispute between two individuals, in which the employer as a person was claiming an idea that was not his, but rather as a dispute between a corporate entity, of which the employee had been a part, and an employee who was trying to appropriate for himself one of the corporation's valuable assets. Courts began to see the importance to firms of freely using the knowledge of their employees. The production of commercial texts was seen as a form of corporate research and development. For example, a court found valid the copyright to an encyclopedia of law without the traditional need to identify the actual authors. To identify a human author was "unnecessary, as it might be impracticable," because the "publication is the result of the intellectual labor of the editors and compilers employed by the complainant."[28] At the same time, courts became more inclined to characterize the rules regarding copyright ownership in contract terms rather than in the terms of immutable rules and moral right that had predominated in earlier cases. The judicial endorsement of a contractarian view of copyright ownership paved the way for corporations to gain control of copyrights by contracting around employee rights that previously had been all but irrevocable.

Contract concepts were useful in reconciling corporate copyright ownership with earlier nineteenth-century commitments to free labor and entrepreneurship. And firms managed to substitute non–legally binding norms of internal attribution of creativity to individuals for the old practice of employee copyright ownership. The result was that firms owned the copyrights to employee works, and employees received only that degree of authorship credit that firms deemed necessary to maintain employee loyalty and to facilitate consumer identification of particular products with the newly valuable corporate brands.

At the turn of the twentieth century, courts began to find that employing a worker or commissioning a work sufficed to entitle the employer to the copyright. The courts in these cases typically did not acknowledge the difference between the precedents, all of which involved an express contractual allocation of copyright, and the instant situations in which no such contract existed. In the widely cited case of *Colliery Engineer Co. v. United Correspondence School Co.* (1899), a salaried employee had the job of preparing and revising instructional materials for a correspondence school. In subsequent employment, the employee-author sought to write similar materials, and the former employer sued to prevent the employee from taking the job. The court denied the request for a preliminary injunction against competitive employment, finding it unclear from the evidence whether the proposed new materials would infringe the copyright because both the allegedly infringing materials and the materials prepared for the first employer were compilations drawn from other sources. The court nevertheless stated without elaboration that the former employer was entitled to the copyright on the original materials, which of course raised the possibility of future copyright infringement litigation against the employee. The court acknowledged the possibility that the employee would be unduly constrained from using the knowledge he had acquired about teaching and so attempted to find a middle ground:

> [A]lthough Ewald was not at liberty to reproduce so much of his work as had been copyrighted by the employers for whom it was prepared, even by availing of his recollection of the contents of the copyrighted pamphlets, he was not debarred, after his contract terminated, from making a new compilation, nor from using the same original sources of information, nor from availing of such information as to the needs of students and the best methods of getting in mental touch with them as he may have acquired while superintending complainant's school.[29]

A similar phenomenon could be seen in a case in which the author was not hired to produce works on an ongoing basis but was instead hired to produce just one thing. In *Press Publishing Co. v. Monroe* (1896), which involved a poem commissioned by the World's Fair organizing committee, the court found that an ambiguous contract that allocated the copyright to the poet granted the committee a license to publish and reproduce it.[30] The irony of the case was that the World's Fair organizing committee—which was nominally dedicated to sharing knowledge and innovation throughout the world—was the driving force behind greater control of intellectual property.

The popularity with lawyers and judges of contract as the totalizing view of commercial relations was the motive force behind the transformation of employee ownership of copyrights. In the influential 1888 opinion in *Callaghan v. Myers*, an action alleging infringement of the reported decisions of the Illinois Supreme Court, the U.S. Supreme Court insisted for the first time that employer-employee disputes over copyright ownership should be resolved by reference to the "agreement" between the parties, even though in *Callaghan* there was no express contract.[31] The power of the Court's rhetoric was its emphasis on freedom of contract. The power of the Court's result was to enable courts to drastically revise the law while appearing to do nothing except honor the will of the parties, even though the parties had not clearly expressed their views about copyright ownership. In the case, Myers, a seller of law books in Chicago, had purchased the copyrights to several years' worth of reported decisions of the Illinois Supreme Court from Norman Freeman, the reporter of decisions. Myers had arranged to have the decisions printed and bound, along with supplemental material written by Freeman (such as short descriptions of each case, headnotes with the principal points of law established in the opinion, statements of the facts of the case where they were not stated in the court's opinion, statements of the issues presented, and a table of cases in each volume). Myers then planned to sell the books in his shop in Chicago or through traveling salesmen who visited lawyers throughout the state.

The Callaghan firm, a competing seller of law books, sought to sell its own complete series of decisions of the Illinois courts and had already purchased the copyrights to the first thirty volumes of the state supreme court's decisions. Callaghan wanted to purchase the copyrights to Myers's volumes. They could not agree on a price. Callaghan tried and failed to get Freeman to grant the right to publish the reports and also was involved in the introduction of a bill to the Illinois legislature that would make the Callaghan firm the official publishers of the reports. None of these strategies worked. Freeman was involved in selling some of his books for himself; he and Myers considered it in their mutual interest to keep Callaghan from getting the rights to a complete set, and so wanted to be sure that Myers maintained control of volumes 32 to 46. As Freeman wrote to Myers, "[L]et us pull together in this matter and beat the d——d Irishman. He has told enough lies about you and me to pave hell over ten feet deep."[32] Believing that only a complete set of all the decisions, beginning with volume 1, would sell, particularly as many Chicago lawyers had lost their libraries in the great fire of 1871, Callaghan eventually went ahead and copied the decisions published in Myers's published volumes and proceeded to sell its own complete series of the court's decisions. Myers sued.

The defendants argued that because Freeman, the reporter, could acquire no valid copyright in decisions (because the judges were the authors) or in the supplemental materials (because Freeman wrote them while in the employ of the Illinois Supreme Court), Myers had no valid copyright. The lower court found the contention would have "great force" "if an adequate compensation was paid by the state to the reporter for the work done by him in preparing volumes of reports." But the court believed that the reporter's compensation was so low that it must have been the state's intention that the profits from the sales of the reports "constituted part of the perquisites of his office."[33] On appeal, the Supreme Court reached the same result for different reasons. Whereas the lower court had relied on an express agreement between the parties, the Supreme Court relied on an implied agreement: "Even though a reporter may be a sworn public officer, appointed by the authority of the government which creates the court of which he is made the reporter, and even though he may be paid a fixed salary for his labors, yet, in the absence of any inhibition forbidding him to take a copyright for that which is the lawful subject of copyright in him, or reserving a copyright to the government as the assignee of his work, he is not deprived of the privilege of taking out a copyright, which would otherwise exist." Later, the Court added that whether the reporter was compensated by salary (he was not), or even by the state's purchase of a certain number of volumes, was irrelevant: "[I]n the view we take of the case, the question of a salary or no salary has no bearing upon the subject." Rather, the Court said, there was "*a tacit assent by the government* to his exercising such privilege."[34]

[223]

The concept of "tacit assent" or "implied contract" opened the door to a later reallocation of patent and copyright ownership simply by judicial reinterpretation of the implied contract between employer and employee to include a principle of employer ownership. In other words, once the courts began to think of copyright ownership as a matter of "tacit assent"—rather than as a virtually inalienable right associated with ownership of real property or in terms of the strong tie connoted by the ideology of the hero-inventor or the romantic author—courts felt a different default rule was appropriate.[35]

Early cases following *Callaghan* concluded that employees owned copyrights because their compensation was too paltry to justify a sale of the copyright to a valuable work. As the New York high court explained in awarding the copyright to a star catalog to the director of a college observatory instead of the college: "Since the college was financially unable to pay him anything approaching a reasonable salary, it may easily be inferred that the director would be allowed and expected to do for himself much work of his own for which he would not be accountable to the college, and which he could use or dispose of as he pleased."[36] As in *Callaghan*, the trial court had found that there was no agreement between the observatory and the director as to who should own the copyright to the catalog. Also as in *Callaghan*, the trial court thought that in the absence of any explicit agreement, "it can hardly be claimed the observatory or college would become the owners of the work [the employees] might, as authors, produce and publish to the world." The institution could look only to the more intangible benefits that flow from having in their employ "men who might become eminent and distinguished by reason of the mental labor and results they achieved."[37]

The Corporation's Money Paid for the Painting

In both *Callaghan* and the college observatory case, the employee-authors enjoyed a substantial degree of independence in the manner, means, and timing of their work, which combined with the measly salary suggests that these men were what today would be deemed independent contractors rather than employees. But the distinction between employees and independent contractors did not exist as clearly in American law then as it does today, and, in any event, the courts never mentioned whether the author was a "servant" or a "contractor." Nor did courts observe the distinction when they applied the rule to cases involving workers who today would be deemed employees. It may very well have been the independence of the creative employee that influenced the court to adopt a default rule of employee ownership, and thus the intuition of early courts was similar to the intuition underlying the modern law that independent contractors should presumptively own the copyrights to their works. But none of that was made explicit in the cases. Rather, the courts contended simply that one must examine the "contract express or implied" between the parties, without articulating the basis for interpreting implied understandings.[38]

The notion that employer ownership of copyrights was implicit in the contract of hiring a creative worker was finally established firmly by statute, not by judicial decision. In 1909, when Congress thoroughly revised the copyright law, advocates of a strong rule of employer ownership of copyrights to employee-generated works gained a significant victory in persuading Congress to add to the statute, for the first time, a provision addressing ownership of copyrighted works created in an employment context.[39] The legislative history of the revision process is the one place where we have an archival record of the debates among advocates for employers and for writers over the policy of corporate control of employee-generated copyrights. The debate occurred in the context of a pair of conferences convened by the Librarian of Congress in 1905 and 1906. The Library of Congress played a significant institutional role in copyright law as the repository of all registered copyrighted works, so it was the logical entity for the task of overhauling copyright law as delegated by Congress. Herbert Putnam, the Librarian of Congress, invited representatives from a number of industries and from the American Authors' League, which represented writers, to discuss the need for and the desirable terms of a revised copyright law.

The draft bill presented at the first conference stated that only "authors" could obtain copyrights.[40] In a series of discussions on that provision, representatives of various publishing and lithographic firms advocated recognition of the right of employers to obtain copyrights. Samuel J. Elder of Boston urged that publishers of encyclopedias and other works requiring the assistance of a large number of people needed some method other than individual assignments to obtain effective ownership of the copyright to the complete project. The problem, he explained, was that only the "author" of a work, and not the "proprietor" who owned the copyright based on assignment from the author, could obtain the renewal of the copyright. To renew the copyright to an encyclopedia, the publisher would "have to go searching all over the world for widows and legitimate children, and the search is so great that the renewal term can hardly be obtained." Elder noted, however, that any revision to enable publishers to obtain renewals would have to define the employer as an "author" because Congress's power to grant copyrights is "confined by the language of the Constitution to authors." The simple expedient, therefore, was simply to adopt the expansive definition of "author" to include "the assignees of authors."[41]

[225]

Robert Underwood Johnson, secretary of the American Authors' Copyright League, objected to the notion that an employer should be deemed the "author" of works created by employees. He proposed that the statute create two categories of copyright owners: "authors" and "proprietors." He insisted that "a man who gets up a cyclopedia and contracts with other people to write for him" was only "the proprietor and ought to be considered the proprietor, and not the author."[42] The notion of "author" was to be reserved only for the actual creator, and was not to be treated as simply a term of art.

The Copyright Office of the Library of Congress drafted a revised bill that did not have a general work-for-hire provision, but which did list in separate sections the various persons who would be entitled to claim a copyright. Among them was the "publisher of a composite or collective work (a 'series,' a 'library,' or an encyclopedia) which has been produced at his instance and expense." In a separate section, the draft bill stated that the person who commissions a portrait would be entitled to the copyright "as if he were the author, in the absence of any agreement in writing to the contrary."[43]

Discussion on the revised draft revealed that representatives of publishers and employers remained dissatisfied. One complained: "We have people who work for us who make engravings or etchings for us under salary. Under the new law—if it becomes a law as drafted—they would have the right to copyright, and I think it would be well to express in such a law that where no agreement exists to the contrary the payment of a salary to an employee shall entitle an employer to all rights to obtain a copyright in any work performed during the hours for which such salary is paid. It seems to me these things should not be left to the courts to decide."[44]

The principle of employer ownership in the case of truly jointly authored works was uncontroversial, even to the representatives of authors. For ex-

The Corporation's Money Paid for the Painting

ample, the American Authors' Copyright League proposed alternative language for the definition of author to include not only writers, composers, and painters, but also "the conductors of a periodical, the joint authors of a collaborative work, a corporate body with respect to the publications of such corporation, and a person or persons at whose instance and expense a composite work is produced."[45] Some insisted that any such rule should give employers only so much of a right in the works as the employer's investment in salary or materials justified. The representative of the Lithographers' Association and the Reproductive Arts Copyright League argued that "the case of manufactures" should be distinguished from the case of other artists and writers: "Now it seems to me that . . . the right belonging to that artist who is employed for the purpose of making a work of art so many hours a day, or that literary producer who is employed for so many hours, should be very different from the right that is held by the independent artist or man who makes a painting for art's sake."[46]

After the second conference, the Librarian of Congress and the Copyright Office circulated a new draft bill. This version contained a new provision that an author entitled to a copyright could include "[a]n employer, in the case of a work produced by an employee during the hours for which salary is paid, subject to any agreement to the contrary."[47] The final version of the work-for-hire provision, which appeared in 1906 in bills introduced at joint hearings held before the House and Senate committees, stated that "the word 'author' shall include an employer in the case of works made for hire"—the language that has been in the statute ever since.[48]

The 1909 Copyright Act enshrined in statute a particular vision of the nature and role of implied and express agreements regarding the circumstances in which an employer would own the rights to employee creativity. The statute made it unnecessary for employers to contract with employee authors to acquire the copyrights to their work by adopting a presumption that employee works are always made for hire. Corporations became not merely the owners of the copyright but their legally defined authors. Authorship became a legal fiction just as corporations became, at least in the public mind, ever more real.

Mapping a New Approach to Innovation

The story of corporate authorship told in the 1909 copyright revision hearings by advocates for publishers was reflected in the evolution of the Rand McNally firm, publishers of maps and globes. It was a move from employee ownership of copyrights to an organized corporate strategy to control copyrights through the development of bureaucratic employment practices and insistence on the contractual designations of the firm as the author of all employee works. What also appears in the Rand McNally story, however, is the development of the modern norm of crediting employee-authors within the firm's internal culture while insisting on corporate authorship as a form of brand identity to the external world. When employees were credited as authors to the external world it was to leaven the dry and anonymous corporate brand with the authenticity of a reference to an actual human creator.

In 1856, William H. Rand established a printing office above a bookstore on Lake Street in Chicago. It was a job shop, printing mainly tickets and railroad timetables. In 1858 Rand hired Andrew McNally and in 1864 they formed a partnership. Rand McNally & Company moved aggressively in the map publishing business, aiming to reduce costs and increase the quality and the number of publications. To that end, the company acquired patents from anyone—including both employees and outsiders to the firm—who seemed to have a better method of designing, engraving, or printing maps. Company employees from the beginning routinely assigned their patents to the firm, as Andrew McNally did in 1871 on a patent for an improvement in map mounting.[49]

Rand McNally's aggressive protection of intellectual property may be attributable to the fact that the company early on understood itself to be a firm that produced and sold knowledge. Unlike other businesses of the 1880s and 1890s (such as railroads) that allowed employees greater control over the intellectual property they generated because the intellectual property rights were a means to an end (e.g., more efficient transportation), at Rand McNally intellectual property rights were the company's business. The firm could also build on the long tradition in publishing of obtaining copyright assignments from all authors. But Rand McNally, unlike traditional publishers, employed a large number of authors as employees on a long-term basis. Many firms that produced technology thought about contracting with outsiders to acquire intellectual property rights (usually patents), but lacked an industry tradition of contracting with employees because, for the most part, employees were not seen primarily as generators of intellectual property. Rand McNally, however, regarded itself as a company in a constant process of gathering information to improve its existing products and encouraging its employees to develop new products. Organized and even bureaucratized research and innovation were part of the firm culture, and Rand McNally's claim to own all employee copyrights and patents rested on that. To do this, the company sought out associations with talented geographers, cartographers, and draftspersons. When the reputation of the employee would enhance the firm's reputation as a producer of quality products, it marketed its products with its employees' names attached.

Circumstances seemed to dictate the Rand McNally policy toward intellectual property rights as much as company policy. The company routinely incorporated material from government sources into its maps. Beginning in the 1870s, it contracted with various people to produce material to be published by the firm, and the ownership of copyright and credit for the creation seemed to have been negotiated on a case-by-case basis. In some cases, the copyright page or copyright registrations indicate that Rand McNally was only the publisher and the author was the copyright owner; in others Rand McNally claimed the copyright as the author but gave credit to an author or editor.[50] And in some, such as Rand McNally's *Banker's Monthly*, which it began publishing in 1884, no credit was given to any employee except occasionally a byline in an article published in it.[51]

Some early Rand McNally works credited individual authors. A guidebook published by William Rand in 1859, *The Complete Guide to the Gold Districts of Kansas and Nebraska*, credited Pease and Cole as authors. In 1869 and 1871, Rand McNally & Company published their first *Western Railway Guide—The Traveler's Handbook to All Western Railway and Steamboat Lines*, which said it was arranged and compiled by Robert A. Bower, who was the editor of the *Railway Guide*. The guide carried a "General Railway Map" that credited Gaylord Watson of New York as engraver.[52] Typically, however, Rand McNally did not publicly identify the compilers, cartographers, or draftsmen who helped create its maps, but only at most the supervising engraver. An 1876 map, for example, stated that it was "engraved under the direction of C. H. Waite." Immediately below that line, however, the map's title cartouche read, "Drawn, Engraved and Printed in Colors (under Letters Patent) by Rand McNally & Co., Chicago."[53]

In the early days, the company was willing to produce maps for others without claiming copyright or credit. In 1877, for example, the Chicago & Northwestern Railroad published a timetable with a Rand McNally map of part of the United States showing the railroad. The only attribution on the map was a covert one that would be intelligible only to insiders and that was for the purpose of deterring unauthorized copying rather than publicizing the company or honoring the employees who made it: the map deliberately and erroneously labeled an Oregon mountain "Mt. R. A. Bower" (Bower was the editor of Rand McNally's railway guide). Yet even this form of clandestine author credit leaves doubt about whether Bower was an author of the map or simply the head of the office that produced it.

At the beginning, employees with special talents or who brought valu-able compilations of information to the company were permitted to operate almost as inside contractors who could profit from the sale of directories or other books produced by employees they supervised. Thus, even though the company claimed ownership of all copyrights, it made arrangements with some employees to share the profits from them. In 1876, for example, the company began publishing a bankers' directory which in the early years was described as being "compiled by" Charles R. Williams. The original agree-ment between Williams and Rand McNally was a matter of dispute: Williams claimed he compiled the directory in 1875 and arranged with Rand McNally to publish it in 1876 and that the two agreed to split the profits. Rand McNally claimed Williams was an employee and that the firm owned the rights to the directory. In 1880, Williams and Rand McNally entered into an agreement by which Williams was to receive one-third of the profits. The parties also agreed that Williams would run the publishing of the directory, including paying the bills, and that Rand McNally would charge the bills against the profits of the directory. By 1892, the directory was producing $100,000 in profit annually. Williams grew dissatisfied and threatened to leave Rand Mc-Nally. Rand McNally filed criminal charges against him, asserting that he had forged the endorsement on a number of company checks in connection with the operation of the directory business. When confronted by the company's attorney, he signed a document stating that he owed the company $16,000 and agreed to cancel his employment agreement with the firm. Williams later testified that he had signed the document under duress. After a bitterly fought criminal trial, Williams was acquitted, evidently based on testimony that he had believed he was authorized to endorse the checks. Williams moved to New York and announced his intention to publish a bankers' direc-tory there.[54] In later years, as we will see, although the company continued to have some high-level employees who were responsible for certain proj-ects and supervised Rand McNally employees to produce them, there were no similar profit-sharing arrangements. Individual entrepreneurs no longer existed within the firm, and instead they profited only from working for a respected company.

[229]

Opportunities for entrepreneurship for employees were limited to the possibility of leaving the firm to start a new company. And, while the firm aggressively claimed all intellectual property rights to employee work, it was largely powerless to restrict former employees from starting competing firms. Company officials sometimes tried to stop such defections but had little success. In 1900, a Rand McNally employee named Caleb S. Hammond left the firm to found the New York map publishing firm that still bears his name and was run by Hammond family members for much of the twentieth century. Louis Andrews, another Rand McNally employee, left to found another competitor, the American Map Company.[55] The most acrimonious dispute with a former employee who left to found a competing firm was that with Harry M. Gousha, who left Rand McNally's successful road map division in 1926 to start a competing road map business, the H. M. Gousha Company, which became a significant competitor to Rand McNally. Rand McNally filed a civil suit against Gousha in Illinois state court, but no records of the suit survive.

As Rand McNally's list of maps, atlases, guides, globes, educational texts, and trade books grew, it became increasingly organized about developing strong intellectual property rights. By the mid-1890s, the company had an established process for applying for patents and copyrights to globes, maps, map display cases, atlases, and other materials produced by the staff of full-time employees and contract workers who participated in all phases of the production process. Both current employees and outside authors assigned the copyright or patent to the firm.[56]

Rand McNally's production of maps, globes, atlases, and other guides resembled the evolution of corporate research laboratories occurring in other industries in that era. First, the company made organized efforts to develop new material and to improve on existing company products through collaborative innovation. From its earliest maps through the twentieth century, the company's managers and employees designed and maintained an active research program aimed at gathering geographic and other information from every possible source. They devised a system of using postcards mailed to businesses and government officials all over the country to gather information that was then incorporated into the various road maps, atlases, indexes, and business directories that the company published.[57] Second, the company also sought out associations with talented geographers, cartographers, draftspersons, and artists whose knowledge and reputation would enhance the firm's store of knowledge and its reputation both with other firms and with customers. Third, the company insisted upon ownership of all intellectual property rights to company products. Fourth, the company created an internal economy of credit and reputation that in some ways substituted for the old system whereby employees owned the intellectual property. Rand McNally, for example, often credited the employees as the authors (both in communications within the firm and in the products sold outside the firm). It was the informal, noncontractual, and extralegal process of author attribution that was the crucial mechanism by which the company reconciled its creative and high-status employees to the new regime of bureaucratic work

[230]

and the loss of entrepreneurial opportunity and economic dependence that came with total employer control of intellectual property rights. Attribution and honoring employee creativity is an important psychic reward to most people, and firms like Rand McNally realized that credit could substitute for intellectual property ownership as a reward to encourage employee innovation.

This corporate practice of attracting top talent to enhance the firm's reputation and then informally and implicitly exchanging author attribution for corporate copyright ownership may be seen in Rand McNally's longtime affiliation with University of Chicago professor of geography J. Paul Goode. Goode first began working with Rand McNally in 1900 while he was finishing a Ph.D., three years before he joined the faculty at the University of Chicago. In the following years, Rand McNally published a number of works designated as "his," including *Goode's School Atlas*, *Goode's Wall Maps*, and eventually *Goode's Political Globe*. While Goode, like other authors, assigned his copyrights in these works and their multiple revised editions to Rand McNally, the company relentlessly promoted the products as being his work: "Originally conceived by Dr. J. Paul Goode, eminent cartographer, professor of geography at the University of Chicago, and editor of the *Goode Series of Wall Maps* and *Goode School Atlas*, every line and letter was placed on the globe under his personal supervision; each color was applied under his direction."[58] The company produced a catalog featuring his photograph devoted exclusively to "his" works.[59] Although the original contracts between Goode and the company are lost, the extracts of them in the company files note only his agreements with the firm about copyright assignments and his share of the profits; there is nothing about whether credit to him for his work was a term of their agreement.

The precise allocation of intellectual property rights between Goode, the University of Chicago, and Rand McNally remain unclear. While Rand McNally owned the copyright to the books and maps they published under his name, the University of Chicago owned the copyright to one of his most famous innovations in cartography, the homolosine equal-area projection, a method of portraying the entire globe on a flat map with minimal distortion in the size of the continents. The 1932 edition of his *School Atlas* lists Rand McNally as the copyright owner of the book, and also separately of every map included in it. Yet, in the preface, Goode thanked the University of Chicago as owner of the copyright "for permission to use Goode's homolosine equal-area projection for the world maps in this edition."[60] Even in the acknowledgment of copyright ownership, Goode still insisted on attaching his name to the homolosine equal-area projection. Both Goode and Rand

The Corporation's Money Paid for the Painting

McNally believed it was in their interest for Goode's name to be attached to his work wherever possible, regardless of copyright ownership. Goode was an eminent cartographer and published influential academic papers on map projections. On account of his university affiliation and academic reputation, Rand McNally's use of his name was a sort of trademark attesting to the quality and reliability of Rand McNally maps.[61]

Rand McNally's approach to granting credit for creation, even as it owned all intellectual property rights, may have stemmed in part from the number of important innovators who were not technically company employees. In addition to Goode, another map innovator at the firm, John G. Brink, worked for the company on a contract basis for many years, at one point in 1923 running a twenty-employee drafting room on the tenth floor of the company's Chicago headquarters. Brink was widely credited in company literature and trade publications as being the "Father of Road Maps" and the person who first conceived the company's ambitious efforts to dominate the road map business. He had his own art studio in Waukegan in 1916 when he was suggested to Rand McNally as someone who could draft county maps on the side. The county map business was declining, and the company announced a competition to its employees for ideas for new products. The employee who submitted the winning idea would receive a $100 prize. Brink won with a suggestion that the company produce maps on which each road was identified by a distinguishing symbol to make them easier to read.

At the time, roads were not numbered and most did not have consistently used names, which made drawing legible road maps quite challenging. The company adopted Brink's idea, and his Illinois "Auto Trails" map, published by Rand McNally in 1917, became the first road map to show numbered highways. The company quickly realized that for the system to be really helpful, roads would need signs with numbers that corresponded to the route numbers on the map. So the company began an ambitious effort, which Brink oversaw for several years, of working with cities, counties, local automobile associations, and local utilities to number roads and then to install numbers on the telephone and power poles along the road side. The road sign and road map project, and the vigorous marketing of road maps to businesses that would sell them to consumers, became a huge business for Rand McNally in the 1920s until the oil companies began to distribute free road maps to promote their new gasoline filling stations and to build customer loyalty to their brand. In 1925, when creation of a national highway system was first discussed in a committee under the secretary of agriculture, John Brink and other Rand McNally employees collaborated with government officials on the numbering system. As Brink said in his diary, "I have marked up several sets of maps and submitted them to Mr. James [of the U.S. Bureau of Public Roads] for a numbering scheme. It would be of great benefit to us, for it will lessen the ever-confusing problems of showing trails on our maps."[62]

As Rand McNally's road map business was growing, Brink was persuaded [233] to move his operations from his own office in Waukegan to the company headquarters in Chicago. Upon taking over the Auto Trails road map project, he became involved not only in drafting maps but in the physical numbering of highways upon which the map symbols were based. He personally supervised the installation of road signs all over the United States; one 1921 contract between Rand McNally and the manager of the engineering division of the Jacksonville, Florida, auto club stipulated that the quality of the road signs that would be installed pursuant to the contract would be the same as the work completed "and inspected in the presence of Mr. John G. Brink on September 12, 1921."[63]

Notwithstanding his full-time work for Rand McNally and his responsibility for the Auto Trails project, Brink remained technically an independent contractor. The road map project did not formally become part of Rand McNally until 1926, and until it did Brink operated it as a firm within the firm. When the young Helmuth Bay, who later became one of the lead cartographers for Rand McNally, first applied to the company for a job in 1923, he was told to go see John Brink. "Brink told me he made road maps for Rand McNally on a contract basis, that he had a full crew, and therefore suggested that I go down and try the Map Drafting Department which was operated by the Company. So I went down to the main offices on the second floor and was shown to the office of James McNally, better known as 'Uncle Jim.'"[64] (Uncle Jim, after chatting with him long enough to decide he had potential, sent Bay to apply for a job with the head of the map drafting department, who agreed to hire him only if he could prove by drawing a "practice map" that he had the necessary skills.)[65] Although Brink worked as an independent contractor, his maps were copyrighted by Rand McNally. Indeed, his 1917 road map of Illinois, the first road map showing numbered highways, was the basis for what the company described as the first successful copyright infringement suit involving a road map.[66]

As Rand McNally's map, atlas, and globe business grew, and as the number of employees working on research, compilation, drafting, and printing grew, the company became more systematic in procuring patents and copyrights and obtaining assignments of all patents and copyrights from their employees and independent contractors. In many cases, Rand McNally credited authors or editors of books, but not in every case.[67] The multiplicity of contributors as its products built on the work of more and more people may have explained

The Corporation's Money Paid for the Painting

why individual attributions were not made. The description of the cartographer who supervised the development of Rand McNally's new system of air route maps in the early days of aviation shows how, in a collaborative and multilayered product development process, individual attributions could and could not be made.

In 1928, just as Rand McNally's first series of automobile road maps was declining as a source of revenue because gasoline companies were distributing them for free, the company began to market "Air Trails Maps" for the navigation of airplanes. The first step in the development of the map was to compile a file of all U.S. airports, which numbered about 1,500 in the mid-1920s. Rand McNally employees mailed questionnaires to every airport, requesting full information as to facilities. Then the information was added onto the company's "Standard Indexed Pocket Maps," which were an established and familiar product to many, and which also had the advantage of being constructed on a projection that was ideal for solving air navigation problems. The Air Trails Map had the standard state map on one side and the same map overprinted with aeronautical data on the verso. The index booklet that accompanied each map was enlarged to include the airport directory that had been compiled from the survey along with a discussion of the existing aids to navigation such as beacons, radio stations, elevations, and airways. Authorship was credited only to a small part of the overall project: an eight-page treatise on the "Elements of Practical Air Navigation" attached to the map which stated that it had been compiled by Thoburn C. Lyon, a Rand McNally employee who supervised production of the maps. It is unclear whether Lyon was credited because he actually researched and wrote the text or because he supervised others who did and had the status within the firm to demand attribution.[68]

Within the company's internal culture of recognition, there seems to have been a hierarchy, and the hierarchy was at least in part quite gendered. In the early to mid-1920s, the head of the company's editorial department was a "Miss Hammit," the heads of the map coloring department and the map indexing department were also women, and many if not most of the employees in the map indexing and map coloring departments were women. Male cartographers were identified by name within and outside the firm; women remained more anonymous. Contributions of the many women employed at Rand McNally were rarely acknowledged in the copyright applications or elsewhere, except in the reminiscences of individual employees. It may be that their contributions were less significant, and that women were employed more in the role of office managers and draftspersons rather than as cartographers, but it may be that the men who devised the marketing materials and internal company documents simply could not imagine the contributions of the women to have been significant. Thus, even as credit began to replace intellectual property ownership as one of the chief markers and rewards of innovation in the twentieth-century corporation, it also appears that who was credited remained a function of social status. [235]

Employment and Authentic Creativity in a Consumer Culture

As innovative firms were reorganizing into increasingly large corporations and as legal doctrine was changing, the kinds of works that were subject to intellectual property protection changed too. Increasingly firms created products for the rapidly expanding consumer culture. And the employees who made the products were consumers too. As consuming replaced producing as the principal marker of social status, both lawyers and society at large shifted their views about the nature, causes, and use of innovation and technological development. Innovation could produce new consumer goods (like cameras and small household appliances), not just new technologies to improve manufacturing or transport (like heavy machinery and locomotives). Innovation came to be seen as something firms marketed to consumers ("Get the new and improved ——!"). Companies advertised how their scientific research would improve the quality of their consumer products and, therefore, their consumers' lives. As Du Pont said, "Better living through chemistry." Intellectual property rights expanded to include more material produced by employees for consumers, and employment law changed to accommodate the expansion of intellectual property. Meanwhile, firms began to market their innovative products with brand names that they hoped consumers would take to be the gold standard for whatever general sort of item the company was selling ("Kodak is photography") and to use selective attribution of their products to particularly innovative employees whenever the company's advertising directors deemed it necessary to convince consumers of the quality, creativity, and authenticity of their products (hence photos of Thomas Edison with "his" lightbulb or phonograph, or Alexander Graham Bell with "his" telephone, or Paul Goode with "his" maps).

Deciding what kinds of materials could be treated as intellectual property became ever more difficult as the subjects of copyright protection expanded from books into new media. Questions naturally arose: Is it the idea or the expression that is protected? What is it about a particular work that makes it appropriate to grant a monopoly over its use? If rewarding and encouraging creativity were crucial in justifying the existence of copyrights at all, it became all the more important to identify and lionize the originator. To the extent that property rights are justified by the moral superiority of the individual artist, corporate authorship is troubling. But to the extent that intellectual property rights exist to encourage investment in intellectual endeavor, corporate authorship is essential.

This difficulty of reconciling corporate ownership and individual artistic expression is evident in Justice Holmes's opinion for the Supreme Court in *Bleistein v. Donaldson Lithographing Co.*[69] *Bleistein* was a major event in copyright history, not only for its well-known ruling on the scope of copyright but also as the first case in which the Supreme Court recognized the employer as the author of a work made for hire. The Court held that three chromolithographs prepared by employees of a corporation for use as advertisements were proper subjects for copyright protection.

Bleistein was an action brought by six partners of an unincorporated lithographic and printing firm, Courier Company, in Buffalo, New York. Courier employed a few men on a $100 weekly salary to design commercial artwork for use as advertisements. The particular works in question were designs used as posters to advertise a circus. Courier had no written contracts with the designers; as Bleistein testified: "He is an employee. . . . [W]e engage his talent and his services and pay for them. What he does produce belongs to us, because we pay for it to him." When asked whether the designers had written employment contracts or any other written agreement transferring the rights to their designs to the firm, Bleistein said they did not; "We simply pay for his talent . . . and what he produces belongs to us."[70] Courier copyrighted its employees' designs and then entered into agreements with clients promising to produce a certain number of posters using Courier's copyrighted designs. Under the agreement, the client would get the exclusive use of the design for a specified period, but thereafter the Courier firm would be entitled to use the design for other clients. When Donaldson, a Kentucky lithography firm, produced posters using a similar design, the Courier partners brought suit alleging copyright infringement.

On appeal, the principal issue was whether commercial artworks of the sort in issue were a proper subject of copyright. Justice Holmes justified copyright protection on the basis of the artistic genius and the uniqueness or singularity of the "personality" expressed in the works by the artist. In determining that a lithograph for use as an advertisement was the sort of creative work that should be accorded copyright protection, Holmes wrote a paean to the individuality of artistic genius. If commercial art were not copyrightable simply because it was intended to be more realistic than high art, it "would mean that a portrait by Velasquez or Whistler was common property because others might try their hand on the same face."[71] Holmes insisted that even realistic pictures intended to portray actual persons for commercial purposes were "the personal reaction of an individual upon nature. Personality always contains something unique. It expresses its singularity even in handwriting, and a very modest grade of art has in it something irreducible, which is one man's alone. That something he may copyright unless there is a restriction in the words of the act."[72]

Given the importance Holmes ascribed to the role of the artist, it is interesting that he found employer ownership of copyright to be entirely unremarkable. The fiction that the employer was the author, without even the necessity of the assignment of the copyright from the artist to the firm, allowed Holmes to elide the question of how a corporation or partnership could be entitled to copyright an advertisement if the justification for the copyright is "the personal reaction of the individual upon nature."[73] The legal fiction of employer authorship had a greater impact on lived experience than many legal fictions, however, for it reoriented the relationship between creative employees and the firms for which they worked.

Holmes's opinion in *Bleistein* is more commonly read as a case about the expanding scope of copyright to include popular and commercial media than it is as a case about corporate authorship. But it is necessarily a case about both. Holmes made it clear that the question of corporate (or employer) authorship of creative works was part of the case by citing both *Carte v. Evans* (the case involving the arrangement to the *Mikado*) and the *Colliery Engineer* decision about the ownership of materials for a correspondence course. He invoked the traditional notion of authorship as artistic creation—"the personal reaction of an individual upon nature"—while giving it an entirely new significance: corporate authorship of advertisements. To expand copyright protection into new media, he equated the art of Goya, Velasquez, Whistler, and Manet with commercial advertising.[74] He did so precisely because giving new content to the old form of authorship was an effective rhetorical strategy to expand copyright protection. By eliding the distinction between the legal fiction of corporate authorship and the fact of collaborative creation in a corporate setting, and by effacing the (ever-shrinking) difference between advertising and art, Holmes made a significant change in doctrine while seeming to do nothing more revolutionary than drawing a simple analogy.

The notion of copyrighted advertisements was not without detractors. Justice Harlan's dissenting opinion asserted that an advertisement could not be copyrighted because it was not "art" and lacked sufficient "connection with the fine arts to give it intrinsic value."[75] Harlan's opinion, which was largely a long quotation of the opinion of the court below, reflected a view that copyright and other intellectual property rights ought to be limited to important and genuinely distinctive creations. The mass of goods produced for consumers and the growing advertising machinery for selling them simply did not fit this understanding of the lofty nature of *intellectual* property. Harlan was not so much a defender of the public domain as a snob about

what kinds of things are sufficiently worthwhile so as to deserve the label of property.

Harlan was on the losing side of modernity's battle over the popularization and commercialization of art. Art had aesthetic value if people liked it; aesthetic value was reflected in what people would buy. Intellectual property law did not exist to demarcate the line between the worthy and the unworthy, or to reward genius, but, rather, to provide a return on investment in generating ever more goods for consumers. Holmes rejected Harlan's view of the proper scope of copyright law as leading to unacceptable censorship by a judiciary ill-equipped to distinguish art from commerce:

> It would be a dangerous undertaking for persons trained only to the law to constitute themselves final judges of the worth of pictorial illustrations, outside of the narrowest and most obvious limits. At the one extreme, some works of genius would be sure to miss appreciation. Their very novelty would make them repulsive until the public had learned the new language in which their author spoke. It may be more than doubted, for instance, whether the etchings of Goya or the paintings of Manet would have been sure of protection when seen for the first time. At the other end, copyright would be denied to pictures which appealed to a public less educated than the judge. Yet if they command the interest of any public, they have a commercial value,—it would be bold to say that they have not an aesthetic and educational value,—and the taste of any public is not to be treated with contempt. It is an ultimate fact for the moment, whatever may be our hopes for a change.[76]

Of course Holmes oversimplified to make his point: copyright eligibility depended on more than the taste of the public. As James Joyce discovered in the fracas over the American publication of *Ulysses*, a work must be published in the United States to be copyrighted, and as his book was censored for a time it did not initially receive an American copyright.[77]

The expanding realm of copyright became a subject of art, not merely the legal regime that reacted to it. As Paul Saint-Amour has shown, a number of prominent writers and critics in the late nineteenth and early twentieth centuries made the scope of copyright and the question of originality part of their literary subject.[78] And they did not just advocate for greater copyright protection. Certainly many celebrity authors did, then and now. But some were quite concerned about the impact of extensive copyright protection on the public domain from which many drew their inspiration.

What did it mean to creative workers whose employers increasingly claimed copyrights on their work? Their voices are not preserved in the [239] cases or company archives. It is possible that the anonymous draftspersons and lithographers whose work was the subject of the *Bleistein* litigation felt valorized that their work became intellectual property, and thus occupied the same legal category as a book, a painting, or a symphony. On the other hand, they may, like the Du Pont experimental employees described in the last chapter, have felt that their ideas and expression had been taken from them unfairly with too little credit to them.

The consolidation of the regime of corporate intellectual property fundamentally changed the way corporate managers and employees, as well as lawyers and judges, regarded workplace knowledge. Ideas became property and employee knowledge became a corporate asset. Creativity, or even the capacity for creativity, was commodified as another form of wealth; it became human capital. And once it was thus commodified, judges easily added it to other corporate assets. Yet neither firms nor courts were willing to sever the connection between real people and corporate intellectual property. The authenticity, and therefore the desirability, of fabricated cultural commodities necessitated that a real person be associated with a creative work.[79] Firms maintained the connection by attributing products to their workers. Courts did it by rejecting the most aggressive efforts to declare workplace knowledge to be a trade secret, or by preventing an unconsenting employee's name from use as a company trademark, and sometimes by refusing to enforce expansive copyright and patent assignments. But, for the most part, the search for authenticity in the mass of expanding corporate intellectual property was conducted outside the realm of law.

The Corporation's Money Paid for the Painting

CONCLUSION

Attribution, Authenticity, & the Corporate Production of Technology and Culture

The growth of corporations and the rapid spread of office and factory work significantly changed the application of legal rules regarding intellectual property ownership. As is always the case with law, the changing applications ultimately changed the rules themselves. As the settings in which ideas were manufactured became more "corporate"—more bureaucratic, more collective, and, quite literally, under the aegis of corporations—and as the claimants to idea ownership increasingly were corporations, what judges thought of idea ownership and how firms managed creative employees changed too. Judges came to believe that people learned workplace skills in large offices and factories rather than as apprentices in small workshops or as clerks in small offices. At the same time, judges developed a view of contract law generally, and the employment contract specifically, that operated both as a conceptual technology and as a mechanism of social control to enable a shift in idea ownership. The old legal conception of individual invention (and, therefore, individual ownership) seemed anachronistic. The acceptance of corporations as legal "persons" with all the rights and privileges of personhood provided a new legal framework to reconcile the traditionally individualist presuppositions of patent and copyright law, which focus on *the* author or *the* inventor, with the new social reality of collective innovation. The cultural change and the legal change coincided and reinforced one another in ways that naturalized the radical developments and made a revolution seem normal, inevitable, and uncontroversial.

The Dependent Corporate Engineer and the Modern Middle Class

By the third decade of the twentieth century, creative and educated people of scientific or technical skill who worked in business rather than academia had become employees of a big corporation in the middle layers of a large bureau-cracy. For the most part, they no longer had either the option or the obliga-tion to parlay their scientific knowledge and business acumen (if they had any) into a successful business venture; they could count on their positions as [241] respected researchers at prestigious corporations and their stable corporate salaries for their social status. They enjoyed some measure of security, but not the kind of power or the opportunity for tremendous financial gain that the lucky and enterprising inventor had enjoyed fifty years before.

The triumph of the mid-twentieth-century employment contract was to elevate inventive workers to a position of safe dependence amid the prosper-ity and job security that characterized white-collar male employment at the major American manufacturing firms. What had been risky became safe. The erratic but brilliant hero-inventor yielded his place to the competent, dili-gent, slightly dull, consumer-oriented 1950s company man. Companies like Kodak and Du Pont became exemplars of midcentury corporate technology giants: large, risk-averse, and generally not the place for an entrepreneur-ial young scientist or engineer to make a major breakthrough. There were dramatic inventions—vinyl, nylon—but they were corporate feats, not the achievements that created an individual legend like Bell's or Edison's.

Decades later, looking back over the course of the twentieth-century transformation of invention from a world of entrepreneurship to a world of stable corporate employment, judges expressed both anxiety about whether corporate research sufficiently promoted individual ingenuity and nostalgia for an imagined past in which great inventors could become great leaders. As the New Jersey Supreme Court noted in one of the leading cases on pre-invention assignment agreements, *Ingersoll-Rand v. Ciavatta* (1989), there is a "dichotomy of our views on the rights of an inventor and rights of an em-ployer." The court expressed concern that employer control over inventions was fueling an alleged decline in patenting by Americans. Justice Garibaldi's opinion for a unanimous court contrasted a stagnant America with the then-ascendant Japan, noting that Japan had "witnessed a dramatic increase in the number of inventions generated by employed inventors" after the adoption of a 1959 law that tied employed inventors' compensation to the market value of their inventions. The story behind the case justifies the court's wistful view about the loss of the entrepreneurial spirit at major American manufacturing firms and the dependence of inventors on corporate employment.[1]

A New Jersey company founded in 1871 by a number of inventor-entre-preneurs who parlayed their inventions and business acumen into a suc-cessful firm based on new technology using compressed air, Ingersoll-Rand eventually became a large, diversified manufacturer of heavy equipment,

Conclusion

power tools, locks, and a wide array of machinery and parts for the auto, construction, and industrial equipment industries. In the early twentieth century, Ingersoll-Rand drills were used on the construction of the New York subway, the Panama Canal, the Hoover Dam, the Cascade Tunnel (then the longest mountain railroad tunnel on the North American continent), and Mt. Rushmore. Just as notably, Ingersoll-Rand patented the original jackhammer. An 1887 *Scientific American* article on the construction of the New York aqueduct reads like an advertisement for Ingersoll drills.[2] As the *New York Times* obituary of one company founder breathlessly explained in 1907, "It was his development of the drill which made possible many of the great engineering feats of the last century and those now in progress."[3]

The early history of the companies that eventually united to form Ingersoll-Rand was characterized by a combination of the mechanical ingenuity of the founders with the business acumen necessary to make the patented inventions a success in the marketplace. Simon Ingersoll invented and patented a rock drill that became the foundation of the company's business. He sold the patents to the firm he founded in 1871. He himself never enjoyed a large share of the wealth generated by the company that bore his name because he had sold his patents to the firm. Henry Clark Sergeant received over sixty patents for various inventions and is credited with the innovation that made the rock drill successful. He formed his own company to market his inventions, and that company eventually merged with the Ingersoll Drill Company in 1888; the Ingersoll-Sergeant Company specialized in tunnel driving and quarrying. Meanwhile, brothers Albert, Jasper, and Addison Rand founded a firm specializing in mining work based on their own, independent drill technology. When Ingersoll-Sergeant merged with Rand in 1905, the announcement of the merger focused on the uniting of the patents as much as anything else.[4]

If the early success of the firm exemplified the happy marriage between invention and entrepreneurship that characterized many nineteenth-century technology businesses, the history of the firm in the first several decades of the twentieth century exemplified the life story of the large, vertically integrated, and massively diversified manufacturing corporation whose fate was linked with capital spending in American manufacturing, construction, and mining. By the mid-twentieth century, although it was still possible for a talented man to rise in the ranks from a low-level technical position to the top of the corporate hierarchy, entrepreneurial possibilities for R & D people were very limited and were systematically discouraged by the company's practice of demanding assignments of all employee patents while failing to develop some product ideas that many employees believed to be promis-

[242]

ing. In the 1990s, Ingersoll-Rand's chairman quipped to *Forbes* magazine, the firm was "not a glamorous company."[5] The corporate R & D experience turned the mechanical engineer from the hero of midcentury gee-whiz feats of construction marvel into the man in the gray flannel suit. By the 1970s, [243] promising young engineers shunned that sort of boring job security in favor of the high-risk, high-reward start-up mania in the field of computer engineering in Silicon Valley.[6]

Those at Ingersoll-Rand who sought to strike out on their own as entrepreneurs encountered legal obstacles in their path. Armand Ciavatta was among them. The son of a working-class Italian American family from New England, Ciavatta worked for Ingersoll-Rand from 1972 until he was fired in 1978 in a dispute about the quality of devices for stabilizing mine roofs, a product for which Ciavatta was the manufacturing manager. Several years before, while Ciavatta was employed in the research division of Ingersoll-Rand, he had signed an agreement promising to assign to the company any inventions he might make during his employment or for a year thereafter that "relates to . . . the business of [Ingersoll-Rand] or any of its affiliates." Ciavatta had bubbled with ideas during his early years at Ingersoll-Rand and had submitted thirteen ideas for inventions to his superiors. The company declined to pursue any of his concepts, so Ciavatta lost the motivation to invent and did not submit any further ideas. As others described the anemic research culture at Ingersoll-Rand and similar companies, the problem was that cautious managers found it easier to nix innovative product development ideas than to pursue them and risk the embarrassment and career setback of a flop. The corporate R & D culture became focused on weeding out poor ideas that would fail when they hit the market after years of expensive development. As one engineer described it, the marketing department might dream up a product and "toss the idea over the wall" separating marketing and engineering. Engineering would work up a design and toss it over another wall to the manufacturing department that would make the product and then heave it over yet another wall to sales. Too often, engineering would toss the idea back to marketing because the engineers considered the idea unworkable, or manufacturing would return an idea to engineering for reworking when they thought the design or the prototype was flawed. By the 1980s, Ingersoll-Rand executives had become so concerned about product development that they initiated a major overhaul to try to reunite the innovative and the entrepreneurial.[7]

While unemployed after his termination from Ingersoll-Rand, Ciavatta went back to tinkering. Standing on a ladder installing a light fixture in his home, he came up with an idea for a new mine roof stabilizer. He developed a prototype with kitchen utensils borrowed from his wife and the assistance of a neighborhood boy. Investing his life savings, along with money borrowed from a bank and from his brother, Ciavatta patented his stabilizer and started his own small business to market his invention. When Ciavatta's stabilizer proved a success in the marketplace, Ingersoll-Rand sued to force him to relinquish the patent. Although Ciavatta eventually won the litigation in a unanimous decision of the New Jersey Supreme Court, the long legal fight and Ingersoll-Rand's massive power in the marketplace eventually drove Ciavatta's product out of the market and his company into ruin.

Armand Ciavatta's fight against Ingersoll-Rand occurred in the early 1980s as American corporate employment and innovation were undergoing seismic shifts. The stability of corporate jobs was disappearing as firms faced new global competition and unprecedented pressure from Wall Street to boost share prices by reducing labor costs. Corporate R & D departments were often targeted because they were perceived by cost-cutting management consultants as being too bureaucratic, too expensive, and insufficiently creative and entrepreneurial. Firms that had once offered stable jobs in exchange for long-term loyalty of their employees began laying off employees by the thousands and insisting that workers be much more entrepreneurial. As the vice president of human resources at AT&T said in 1996 when the firm announced a plan to eliminate 40,000 jobs, "People need to look at themselves as self-employed, as vendors who come to this company to sell their skills. . . . [W]e have to promote the whole concept of the work force being contingent." Yet the contracts that these companies' lawyers had drafted for employees to sign made it quite difficult, as Armand Ciavatta found, to be entrepreneurial. Ciavatta was the company man without a company at a time when secure corporate jobs for middle-aged engineers were becoming harder to find. He never did find another stable job.

WHEN THE LEGAL AND BUSINESS regulation of workplace knowledge was being cemented in the late 1920s, there was little awareness of how precarious workers were in their dependence on corporate employment, given the legal regime that made it difficult for employees to use their knowledge entrepreneurially. Such awareness was at least fifty years in the future. The expansion of the American economy in this period, outside of the seismic dislocations of the Great Depression and the recessions of the 1970s and 1980s, could have led lawyers, judges, and employees to the conclusion that the implicit exchange of stable employment for employer control of workplace knowledge was a good deal for inventors and authors. Although modern

Conclusion

management of intellectual property reduced the independence and upward mobility of inventive employees, even the architect of modern management, Frederick Winslow Taylor, astutely recognized the importance of employee attitudes in enabling firms to control their employees' work to an extent that [245] might otherwise have been fiercely resisted. In describing his own experiences reworking the management of employees and production at Midvale Steel, he recognized that one's ascribed class position based on education or family background can cloud everyone's perception of the worker's actual position within the hierarchy. Writing about himself in the third person, Taylor confessed, "[O]wing to the fact that he happened not to be of working parents, the owners of the company believed that he had the interest of the works more at heart than the other workmen, and they therefore had more confidence in his word than they did in that of the machinists who were under him."[8] Taylor saw this, but nowhere in his *Principles of Scientific Management* did he suggest the enormous impact scientific management might have on the prospects of the sons and daughters of "nonworking" parents like his.

As workplace knowledge became corporate intellectual property, the combination of new legal and business practices transformed not only work relations but also class relations for creative people. Yet, as befits a not strictly material form of property, the relation between the new intellectual property ownership and class is symbolic as well as material.[9] The creation of social class is like gazing into a distorted looking glass: as Pierre Bourdieu said, when each of us sees a description of our social position as a representation of ourselves, we create a class.[10] Neither the working class nor the middle class exists ready-made in reality; they are historically variable creations of "material and symbolic struggles waged simultaneously over class and between classes."[11] Such a material and symbolic struggle over ownership of ideas occurred among lawyers and judges, employees and managers. In material terms, the reallocation of intellectual property rights from employees to firms reduced the opportunities for entrepreneurship and the economic wealth it might bring. When creative employees acceded to corporate ownership of intellectual property, they became a new middle class. In symbolic terms, the dependence on corporate employment, the characterization of oneself as part of the company research team rather than as the inventor, transformed the class identity of the inventive employee. When judges described them so, and when inventive employees saw themselves so, they became a new middle class.

Changes in legal doctrine, along with many more significant changes in corporate practice, contributed to a fundamental change in the nature of the middle class. Many have argued—most famously, C. Wright Mills—that the early twentieth century witnessed the creation of a new middle class, distinct from an old middle class of independent entrepreneurs.[12] Among the many facets of this change was an "occupational transformation" associated with "the systematization of knowledge in universities and the ensuing certification process."[13] This new middle class was "a mental rather than an occupational category" in the sense that the employees in question were, as before, technically trained engineers who worked for firms to develop new technologies.[14] The difference was in the diminished independence and entrepreneurial prospects of the twentieth-century employee-inventor.

[246]

Class is a function of many things; education and wealth are part of it, but economic power, social stature, and self-conception are too. Both Walter Masland and Edwin Prindle saw quite clearly how company ownership of employee intellectual property diminished the class position of well-paid and highly educated men whose education and compensation might otherwise have put them relatively high in the ranks of the middle class. Du Pont's insistence that it owned every new idea, every patent, and every secret process its employees might develop may have been desirable to encourage technological development, but it limited employees' prospects as entrepreneurs. To some, it was also an affront to their dignity. They were parts of the Du Pont team, but they were not independent. Although they were chemists with Ph.D.s, they were going to remain all their lives as wage earners. They were in the same position as the working class—dependent on wages or salary without prospects for upward mobility and eventual independence.[15] They were the elite of the middle class, but corporate ownership of their intellectual property was the difference between independence and dependence, and that was a crucial difference. They traded the status of the small-time independent entrepreneur for the economic and social security of a company man at a leading corporation. They were the new middle class, and their relationship to their companies' intellectual property was part of what made them who they were.[16]

It is perhaps not too much an oversimplification to treat the independent inventor-manager and the small-scale entrepreneur as the archetypes of the nineteenth-century inventive man and "old" middle class, and Walter Masland and Armand Ciavatta as the archetypes of the twentieth century's new innovator and "new" middle class. The courts' use of the rhetoric of contract and the legal fiction of consent effected a legal change that both facilitated and reflected the changing corporate practice and thereby brought about the social change. Of course, companies' strategies toward innovation mattered as well. Railroads, for example, innovated within a limited range;

Conclusion

they did not, particularly at the end of the nineteenth century, aim to develop radically new technology or significant innovations on existing practice.[17] Du Pont, by contrast, did, especially after 1902. Thus, a firm's attitude toward employee intellectual property and entrepreneurship is in part a function of the economic strategy it and its competitors choose. A company such as the Reading Railroad might discourage employees from innovating in ways that would threaten the push toward uniformity and toward maximally efficient use of the existing structure. This strategic choice might lead a firm, as it did the Reading, to adopt a rather casual attitude toward controlling employee intellectual property. Du Pont, by contrast, proved willing to diversify away from its core business (explosives) in radically new directions (chemicals, then textiles, paints, plastics, etc.). The pursuit and control of new technology as a corporate strategy led Du Pont into a different relationship with its employees, and it used law in different ways than railroads did to facilitate that strategy. The steady growth of Du Pont and the steady decline of the railroads seemed an implicit argument about the superiority of the one regime over the other, until the globalization and the Silicon Valley phenomenon made people wonder about the future of large corporate innovation.

Yet even different strategies regarding innovation ultimately seem to have mattered less than the development of bureaucratic employment practices and an effort to standardize intellectual property policies. During the first two decades of the twentieth century, railroads seem to have changed their policies and contracts vis-à-vis employee inventions in a manner similar to the changes at Du Pont. As Naomi Lamoreaux and Kenneth Sokoloff have documented, the Pullman Company began to revise its practices for evaluating employee inventions in 1912 by establishing a Committee of Standards to evaluate both employees' and outsiders' inventions, and it adopted a policy to require employees to "give the Company preference in disposing of the title to such invention and the patent therefor, in addition to the shop-right which the law implies." As Lamoreaux and Sokoloff explain, the company offered to pay a bonus of $250 for any employee invention the company patented, which was "a radical and unilateral change in the nature of the employment contract." Though the bonus offer was articulated as an effort to encourage innovations by employees, "the purpose of the policy was to impose restrictions on employees' behavior."[18] Firms encountered significant difficulty in persuading employees that new policies such as that adopted by Pullman were in their interest. Under this thinking, employees stood to benefit from trading their entrepreneurial potential, as expressed by retaining one's patents, for a job within a single firm that would be assigned those very same patents.

Conclusion

But Du Pont, Kodak, and Ingersoll-Rand employees, and others like them, were in a distinctly different position. The separation of management from innovation enabled courts to say that their employment agreements accorded their employer many more rights to the products of their labor and ingenuity than employers previously had enjoyed. Courts began to see that invention, like any other form of labor, could be commodified; therefore, an employee hired to "improve" a business necessarily was hired to invent.

Ultimately, corporate control over intellectual property changed inventive employees' perceptions of their own status. Masland left Du Pont because he despaired about rising in the firm. He was acutely aware of the dependence of inventive employees and he did not want to be a cog in the Du Pont machine. Complaints about the lack of prospects for advancement and about Charles Reese's condescending attitudes reveal their anxiety of status. The dependence that troubled Masland and many others of the era was not merely economic dependence but also the loss of his identity and being submerged into the corporation.[19] What could be a more acute experience of the loss of self than being told that your ideas, your inventions, and even your knowledge were your employer's, not yours?

Entrepreneurial prospects were not the only difference between the class positions of creative employees in the nineteenth century and in the twentieth; supervisory responsibility was also important. The supervisory position of an inventor-manager gave him control over the use and development of his ideas; Masland had much less. That fact may have affected an inventor-manager's ability to exploit his own invention, even if his employer might otherwise have been inclined to claim the patent for itself. So, too, it may have affected what the employee and the firm understood the employment agreement to encompass, by giving him greater bargaining power and by making him seem to be a man of greater stature within the organization. Stature within an organization is one thing that distinguishes the upper and upper-middle classes from those solidly in the middle class.

The existence of supervisory responsibility affected more than the inventor's perception of his status, and more even than his ability to exert leverage in his negotiations with his employer. It also affected how judges saw employees. The specialization of invention in the large corporate R & D facility constrained the negotiations between employer and employee, shaped the perceptions of each when no explicit negotiations occurred, and ultimately changed the perceptions of courts in allocating rights when negotiations had not occurred. Rare would be the person like Thomas Edison, who after founding his "laboratory" at Menlo Park in 1876 remained active as a researcher and inventor while managing the enterprise and keeping a substantial ownership stake in the firm.[20]

In the nineteenth century, judges often emphasized the independence and ingenuity of the creative employee. Judges did not see inventive employees as part of the dependent working class, and middle-class status connoted independence. Independence required the possibility of being an entrepreneur based on inventive ideas. Consequently, judges concluded—sometimes in the teeth of the facts—that employment contracts contained implied terms allocating intellectual property rights to employees. Judges' perception of the perquisites of the employees' middle-class status vastly increased the employees' chances of becoming entrepreneurs if they were not already. Mid-nineteenth-century judges seized upon the employee's having allowed the employer to use the invention as a basis for employer ownership. Later judges emphasized that the employer's time or materials had been invested in the project, that the employee had allowed or encouraged the employer to use the invention, and that the employee had implicitly contracted for employer control of the intellectual property.[21] As the Wisconsin Supreme Court said in 1887, the origin of the *idea* is less important than "[t]he mere fact that, in making the invention, an employee uses the materials of his employer, and is aided by the services and suggestions of his co-employees and employer in perfecting and bringing the same into successful use."[22] Yet many judges clung to the view that an employee's ideas were inalienably his. The Wisconsin Supreme Court dismissed the claim that the employer's contribution of material and labor entitled the firm to own the product: it "confound[s] the machine with the invention that it embodies. Of course, there must be a machine which will operate before it can be patented. That implies material, workmanship, and skill combined. But such combination itself is not enough to secure a patent."[23] Because the employee supplied the idea, the employee should own the patent. It was in the twentieth century, when judges imagined firms as originators, or at least essential incubators, of the *idea*, that the position of the inventive employee changed. That change in thinking required a significant re-imagining of the status and nature of inventors.

The creative employees represented in this narrative by the nineteenth-century inventor-managers represent the best case of free labor. They were autonomous and upwardly mobile because they owned the fruits of their creativity. As firms increasingly were able to control ownership of intellectual property, they limited the entrepreneurial prospects of their employees. Innovative employees became, at most, middle managers; they did not become business owners themselves. And even as middle managers, they enjoyed fewer entrepreneurial opportunities and less autonomy than the middle managers of the nineteenth century. Legal rules thus facilitated the redefinition of the middle class in the early years of the twentieth century, helping to transform America from an economy of small entrepreneurs to an economy of corporations. Legal rules were one of the social and economic factors that shaped the middle class—that "ambiguous and shifting middle zone of social and political space" that today seems to encompass the identity of 90 percent of the American public.[24]

[250]

At the turn of the twentieth century, technology firms presented themselves as the embodiment of the ambitions and sagacity of their founders and investors. Technology employees felt ill-used by firms that built their name on the talent of their employees but sought to claim ownership of that talent exclusively for the firm, even if the corporate claims were consistent with what the law would allow. It was the failure to give credit that led some engineers derisively to claim that corporate research and development did not reflect a spirit of cooperative investigation, as claimed by the R & D managers, but rather, as a later critic described it, a regime "of collective subservience."[25] No one doubted that the growing complexity of science and technology had rendered invention increasingly a collective rather than a solitary activity, and that the efforts of many contributed to the developments of patentable technology. Nor did scientists and technicians working in research facilities underestimate the risk of opportunistic behavior as one person sought to claim more credit for inventions than his contribution might merit (whether the credit was being named on a patent, recognized in a company bulletin, or collecting a financial bonus). It was the power relations within the hierarchically organized corporation that seemed to irk employees the most—the fact that the director of the research lab could get away with claiming significant responsibility for an invention that in fact was developed by others. Moreover, the bureaucratic direction of creativity—you must work on this line of research or you must abandon that one—seemed a denial of autonomy. People whose graduate education inculcated in them the belief that they were men of status and independence found themselves cogs in the corporate scientific wheel. They realized that they had traded freedom and the possibility of entrepreneurship for the stability of a corporate job and the comforts of a well-equipped lab. The legal rule that facilitated corporate ownership of patents, combined with the social changes that brought corporate control of the decision when, whether, and on what to seek a patent, played crucial roles in this fundamental change in the status of a scientist or inventor.[26] Law and corporate culture together created a new segment of the middle class.

Work relations vis-à-vis intellectual property changed just as intellectual property gained salience in the consumer culture that developed so rapidly [251] after the turn of the twentieth century. The organs of popular culture—advertising, magazines, radio, and mass communication—increasingly emphasized consumption rather than production or "industry" (in the sense of diligent work) as a most desirable form of human activity. The plethora of consumer goods and the new media that sold them led to an explosion in the kinds of ideas for which intellectual property status was claimed. Copyright was no longer just for books and maps, as it had been in the early nineteenth century, but was claimed for advertisements, recorded music, photographs, and film. Simultaneously, the technology that could be patented grew in scope and complexity. In both areas, the knowledge that employees possessed—and that employers sought to protect as intellectual property—became ever more likely to be collectively created in a commercial setting. At the same time, consumer culture diminished the moral and social value of labor as opposed to the moral and social value of consumption. This in turn changed how judges and lawyers defined and justified intellectual property rights. As the boundaries of intellectual property grew, and as the creation of intellectual property simultaneously became ever more collective, courts, firms, and the people who populated both sets of institutions came to think differently about how to draw the line between corporate intellectual property and employee knowledge.

Attribution as the New Intellectual Property and the Search for Authenticity

People throughout history have valued the reputations they gain by associating their names with their work; great artists of all kinds have destroyed work that they thought did not measure up to their standards, even when they might have profited more (at least in the short term) from selling their lesser works rather than destroying them. Nineteenth-century courts were aware that equating intellectual property ownership with attribution had both intrinsic and instrumental motivations above and beyond the economic value of property rights themselves. Intrinsically, it acknowledged the moral value of creativity. Instrumentally, it encouraged creativity by linking the honor to the actual creator rather than to the firm. Scholars and judges of the early twentieth century feared that corporate intellectual property ownership would undermine the reward function of attribution. This was part of a more general concern that large firms threatened entrepreneurship because creative and potentially entrepreneurial people might believe their own work and risk-taking could go unnoticed or unrewarded. The influential economic theorist Joseph Schumpeter believed that "[i]n the modern corporation, entrepreneurial gains are as a rule merged with many other elements into the profit item, and the individuals who fill the entrepreneurial function are separated from them—accepting the salaries and other prerequisites of executives in lieu of them."[27] He worried that bureaucratization of the entrepreneurial process would undermine the will to overcome resistance to change and lead to a decline in entrepreneurship. As Schumpeter correctly predicted, the challenge of the twentieth century was to preserve the entrepreneurial spirit within the harness of bureaucratic work.[28]

[252]

By the end of the twentieth century, corporate intellectual property ownership became the norm and individual invention and authorship the exception. The late twentieth-century erasure of the natural person's name from the responsibility for innovation has dehumanized intellectual property and the ideas and work embodied in it. Yet the moral claims of corporations as intellectual property rights holders still are not as persuasive as the claims of individuals. So when the Disney Corporation seeks yet another extension of the term of copyright, they bring out creative individuals—Arnold Schoenberg's grandchildren, Bob Dylan—as their advocates.[29] And when the Motion Picture Association of America launched a major public relations initiative in 2003 to discourage unauthorized copying of DVDs, they used the working man to state their case that piracy is bad. Clearly the MPAA knows that it cannot rely solely on the dire FBI warnings that precede every DVD because viewers regard them as just so much noise. So the MPAA, through an organization called Respect Copyrights, ran a series of short "public service" films before the previews in movie theaters featuring a worker who contributes to the making of a film (a set designer, a stuntman). The workers describe how they feel about their contributions to the movie, how important their hard work and talent is to the success of the movie, and how piracy in effect steals "their" property.

Consider the spot featuring the set builder David Goldstein. Goldstein, a nice-looking guy wearing a well-worn shirt, was filmed talking about his work in front of a row of shelves holding paints and set construction materials. Piracy, he says, is bad because it doesn't really hurt the producers, or, he corrects himself, it "does affect the producers, but it's minuscule to the way it affects me, the guy working on construction, the lighting guy, the sound guy." There follows a montage of the great movies he's worked on, with his voiceover saying he met his wife making *The Big Chill*. Then he looks quite

Conclusion

heartfelt and says, "I'm not a million dollar employee. . . . I'm lucky if I can put together twelve months of work in a year. All I want to do is do the best product I can." The honest labor of a guy in work boots and a flannel shirt, a man who is paid by the hour or the day and will never see a penny of royal- [253] ties produced by the film's copyright, is the movie studio's best moral claim to own the work he generates.[30]

Goldstein's reminiscences about meeting his wife while working on the set of *The Big Chill* invites viewers to form an emotional bond linking their sentimental feelings, evoked by the wildly popular movie soundtrack of Motown songs, with his sentimental feelings about the community of set builders, electricians, costume designers, and actors who worked together to create the movie. Thus, Goldstein enables us to see *The Big Chill* as something we all share, and to see how pirating it becomes hurtful in a personal way. It is the movie studio's investment, true, but that investment is made to represent the creation of community that in turn creates a thing that somehow we all share, and that we all have a duty to protect.

The late nineteenth- and early twentieth-century debate over corporate intellectual property rights seemed to have been settled by 1930 in favor of broad corporate rights. But the debate never really ended. Once intellectual property rights were cut loose from individual effort and creativity, their *moral* claims as property lost some of their force. An investment theory of intellectual property never had the same emotional resonance as a labor theory. When technological developments made it easier than ever before to copy copyrighted or patented materials and for employees with little job security to take customer lists, software, and other valuable know-how with them to new jobs, companies had no convincing argument as to why their investment entitles them to broad intellectual property rights. So when public opinion must be marshaled, they go back to the same images of the working man and the creative genius that have been floating around for two centuries or more.

The regime of corporate intellectual property that was established by 1930 remained stable throughout most of the twentieth century. Some economic sectors, notably Hollywood, adapted to a regime of corporate ownership of intellectual property by devising non-property regimes like screen credit to acknowledge and reward employee innovation. Virtually every business attributes credit in collaborative projects to identify, motivate, and reward productive, creative, and diligent employees. Credit for good work is valued for its own sake, but also as a marker of the existence of human capital among a highly mobile workforce, and sometimes as a status symbol. Informal norms of attribution played some of the roles (rewarding good work, punishing

Conclusion

shoddy work, deterring shirking, and signaling the existence of human capital) that were previously played by legal rules that made employee intellectual property and workplace knowledge almost inalienable.[31]

[254] But norms of attribution can never be a perfect substitute for ownership of the underlying intellectual property or workplace knowledge. That is, while it is valuable to be credited as the person who designed a particularly nifty invention, it is not enough if a broad law of trade secrets or an ironclad noncompete agreement prevents the employee from building on past work. Early in the twenty-first century, some believe that excessively broad intellectual property rights stifle innovation because, as illustrated by Silicon Valley, innovation is spurred by information spillovers linked to employee mobility.[32] A certain segment of talented computer engineers in the 1970s and afterward desperately wanted to avoid being the company men in a corporate R & D facility and chose the risks, independence, and opportunity to make a name for themselves in the start-up culture of Silicon Valley. The middle-class R & D employee, born and bred in the early twentieth century by a regime of bureaucratic and restrictive employment practices and strong corporate intellectual property rights, now seems like a stock character from the past. He does not represent a segment of society in which the young generation of would-be entrepreneurs in Silicon Valley can see themselves.

Legal rights to knowledge may be moving away from the nineteenth-century regime in which ownership of intellectual property was inextricably tied to the person who created it. It may also be moving away from the corporate intellectual property regime that developed at the turn of the twentieth century, in which both ownership of the intellectual property and credit for its creation were firmly located in the corporation. The new model is a fragmented regime in which the corporation owns the intellectual property but the creative employees may obtain other economically valuable ways to capitalize on their creativity. The divorce of intellectual property rights from credit for innovation can be seen as an effort to return to the entrepreneurial approach to knowledge that characterized nineteenth-century American law.

While the participants, terms, and results of employer-employee disputes over control, ownership, and attribution of innovation changed over the course of the nineteenth century and again over the course of the twentieth, the conflicts and accommodations of the past shed light on the nature of creative work of the present. The line between individual and collective contributions to the production of ideas cannot be drawn as a matter of logic or nature. It changes with changes in the nature of the human personality and the social setting of work. As people worked together to create ideas and things, they used and ignored legal rules and, in the process, created new law while creating new inventions, texts, and ways of working. Knowledge about how knowledge was produced in the past reminds us of the contingency of the particular mix of individual and corporate entrepreneurship that characterizes early twenty-first-century arrangements over the control and attribution of innovations and intellectual property. It may also remind us to think skeptically about reductionist just-so stories and economic claims about the efficiency of the current regime of legal rules. Finally it asks us to think about how a more just regime may be brought into being—not only by judges and lawyers, but also by the daily activity of each of us as workers, creators, consumers, and citizens.

[255]

NOTES

ABBREVIATIONS

DPA
Du Pont Archive, Longwood Manuscripts,
Hagley Museum and Library, Wilmington, Del.

EDPC
Eleuthera (Bradford) du Pont Collection,
Hagley Museum and Library, Wilmington, Del.

JBDP
James Buchanan Duke Papers, Rare Book, Manuscript,
and Special Collections Library, Duke University, Durham, N.C.

RHWP
Richard Harvey Wright Papers, Rare Book, Manuscript,
and Special Collections Library, Duke University, Durham, N.C.

RMR
Rand McNally and Company Records,
Newberry Library, Chicago, Ill.

INTRODUCTION

1. Frederick W. Taylor, *The Principles of Scientific Management* (New York: Norton, 1967), 31–32.

2. Although no one has attempted a history of employer-employee disputes over intellectual property, labor histories have considered the importance of skill and knowledge, and business and technology histories have noted the importance of labor. See, e.g., Daniel Nelson, *Managers and Workers: Origins of the Twentieth-Century Factory System in the United States, 1880–1920*, 2d ed. (Madison: University of Wisconsin Press, 1995); David Montgomery, *Workers' Control in America: Studies in the History of Work, Technology, and Labor Struggles* (New York: Cambridge University Press, 1979); Paul Israel, *From Machine Shop to Industrial Laboratory: Telegraphy and the Changing Context of American*

Invention, 1830–1920 (Baltimore: Johns Hopkins University Press, 1992); Philip Scranton, *Figured Tapestry: Production, Markets, and Power in Philadelphia Textiles, 1885–1941* (New York: Cambridge University Press, 1989).

3. Economic histories of innovation include B. Zorina Khan, *The Democratization of Invention: Patents and Copyrights in American Economic Development, 1790–1920* (New York: Cambridge University Press, 2005); B. Zorina Khan and Kenneth L. Sokoloff, "The Early Development of Intellectual Property Institutions in the United States," 15 *Journal of Economic Perspectives* 233 (2001); Naomi R. Lamoreaux and Kenneth L. Sokoloff, "The Geography of Invention in the American Glass Industry, 1870–1925," 60 *Journal of Economic History* 700 (2000); Naomi R. Lamoreaux and Kenneth L. Sokoloff, "Inventors, Firms, and the Market for Technology in the Late Nineteenth and Early Twentieth Centuries," in *Learning by Doing in Markets, Firms, and Countries*, ed. Naomi R. Lamoreaux, Daniel M. G. Raff, and Peter Temin (Chicago: University of Chicago Press, 1999). Two influential articles arguing for the efficiency of corporate ownership of employee intellectual property are Dan Burk, "Intellectual Property and the Firm," 71 *University of Chicago Law Review* 3 (2004); and Robert P. Merges, "The Law and Economics of Employee Inventions," 13 *Harvard Journal of Law & Technology* 1 (1999). Some of the scholars cited above paid attention to employed inventors in the works cited and elsewhere, such as in Kenneth L. Sokoloff and David Dollar, "Agricultural Seasonality and the Organization of Manufacturing in Early Industrial Economies: The Contrast Between England and the United States," 57 *Journal of Economic History* 288 (1997). Others who have explicitly studied employment relationships in the history of invention include Christine MacLeod, "Negotiating the Rewards of Invention: The Shop-Floor Inventor in Victorian Britain," 41 *Business History* 17 (1999).

4. E. P. Thompson, *The Making of the English Working Class* (London: Penguin, 1963), 12.

5. Aspinwall Manufacturing Co. v. Gill, 32 F. 697, 700 (C.C.D.N.J. 1887).

6. H. B. Wiggins Sons' Co. v. Cott-A-Lap Co., 169 F. 150, 152 (C.C.D. Conn. 1909).

7. Thomas Jefferson to Isaac McPherson, August 13, 1813, reprinted in *The Writings of Thomas Jefferson* (1903), vols. 13–14: 333–34.

8. John S. Mill, "On Liberty," in *Utilitarianism; On Liberty; Considerations on Representative Government*, ed. Geraint Williams (London: J. M. Dent, 1993), 171–72. On penal and specific enforcement of labor contracts in the nineteenth century, see Robert J. Steinfeld, *Coercion, Contract, and Free Labor in the Nineteenth Century* (New York: Cambridge University Press, 2001), 253–314.

9. Christopher G. Tiedeman, *A Treatise on State and Federal Control of Persons and Property in the United States, Considered from Both a Civil and Criminal Standpoint*, 2d ed. (St. Louis: F. H. Thomas Law Book Company, 1900), 315. Amy Dru Stanley identified this aspect of Tiedeman's work and the importance of the wage contract in postbellum jurisprudence of freedom. Amy Dru Stanley, *From Bondage to Contract: Wage Labor, Marriage, and the Market in the Age of Slave Emancipation* (New York: Cambridge University Press, 1998), 74.

10. Almost none, however, seem to have been union members. Unions had a great deal to say about the control of skill and workplace, but almost nothing to say—until the

guilds in Hollywood—about the control of patents, copyrights, trade secrets, or noncompete agreements, or about court-ordered performance of personal services contracts. An analysis of what unions had to say about law and the control of workplace knowledge would examine a very different set of workers than this book examines.

11. Sir Henry Maine, *Ancient Law* (1866; New Brunswick, N.J.: Transaction Books, 2002), 170 ("we may say that a movement of progressive societies has hitherto been a movement from Status to Contract").

12. Gregory S. Alexander, *Commodity and Propriety: Competing Visions of Property in American Legal Thought, 1776–1970* (Chicago: University of Chicago Press, 1997), 145.

13. John R. Commons, *Legal Foundations of Capitalism* (New York: Macmillan, 1924), 14.

14. Paul K. Saint-Amour, *The Copywrights: Intellectual Property and the Literary Imagination* (Ithaca, N.Y.: Cornell University Press, 2003).

15. Thorstein Veblen, *The Theory of the Leisure Class: An Economic Study of Institutions* (New York: Vanguard Press, 1932).

16. Yochai Benkler, *The Wealth of Networks: How Social Production Transforms Markets and Freedom* (New Haven, Conn.: Yale University Press, 2006); Eric Von Hippel, *Democratizing Innovation* (Cambridge: MIT Press, 2005).

PART I

1. Daniel Nelson, *Managers and Workers: Origins of the Twentieth-Century Factory System in the United States, 1880–1920*, 2d ed. (Madison: University of Wisconsin Press, 1995), 3; Christopher Clark, "Social Structure and Manufacturing before the Factory: Rural New England, 1750–1830," in *The Workplace Before the Factory: Artisans and Proletarian, 1500–1800*, ed. Thomas Max Safley and Leonard N. Rosenband (Ithaca, N.Y.: Cornell University Press, 1993); Sean Wilentz, *Chants Democratic: New York and the Rise of the American Working Class, 1788–1850* (New York: Oxford University Press, 1984), 27–28; Alfred D. Chandler Jr., *The Visible Hand: The Managerial Revolution in American Business* (Cambridge, Mass.: Harvard University Press, 1977), 17–19, 50–52, 75; Bruce Laurie, *Artisans into Workers: Labor in Nineteenth-Century America* (New York: Noonday Press, 1989), 15–46; David A. Hounshell, *From the American System to Mass Production, 1800–1932: The Development of Manufacturing Technology in the United States* (Baltimore: Johns Hopkins University Press, 1984), chap. 1.

2. Alexander Hamilton, "Report on Manufactures," in vol. 1, *Reports of the Secretary of the Treasury* (Washington, D.C.: Blair & Rives, 1837), 132.

3. Richard B. Morris, *Government and Labor in Early America* (New York: Columbia University Press, 1946), 26–27; Doron S. Ben-Atar, *Trade Secrets: Intellectual Piracy and the Origins of American Industrial Power* (New Haven, Conn.: Yale University Press, 2004), 78–141; David J. Jeremy, *Artisans, Entrepreneurs and Machines: Essays on the Early Anglo-American Textile Industries, 1770–1840s* (Brookfield, Vt.: Ashgate, 1998); David J. Jeremy, *Transatlantic Industrial Revolution: The Diffusion of Textile Technologies between Britain and America, 1790–1830s* (Cambridge, Mass.: MIT Press, 1981).

4. Hamilton, "Report on Manufactures," 87, 88.

5. Leonard S. Reich, *The Making of American Industrial Research: Science and Business at GE and Bell, 1876–1926* (Cambridge: Cambridge University Press, 1985), 15; Bruce Sinclair, *Philadelphia's Philosopher Mechanics: A History of the Franklin Institute, 1824–1865* (Baltimore: Johns Hopkins University Press, 1974).

6. Alexis de Tocqueville, *Democracy in America*, 2 vols. (New York: Knopf, 1945), 1:297, 2:42. On early American patent law and policy, see B. Zorina Khan, *The Democratization of Invention: Patents and Copyrights in American Economic Development, 1790–1920* (New York: Cambridge University Press, 2005), 8–9; Ben-Atar, *Trade Secrets*, 78–103; Neil L. York, *Mechanical Metamorphosis: Technological Change in Revolutionary America* (Westport, Conn.: Greenwood Press, 1985).

7. David R. Meyer, *Networked Machinists: High-Technology Industries in Antebellum America* (Baltimore: Johns Hopkins University Press, 2006); Paul Israel, *From Machine Shop to Industrial Laboratory: Telegraphy and the Changing Context of American Invention, 1830–1920* (Baltimore: Johns Hopkins University Press, 1992), 14. See also Brooke Hindle, *Emulation and Invention* (New York: New York University Press, 1981); Brooke Hindle and Steven Lubar, *Engines of Change: The American Industrial Revolution, 1790–1860* (Washington, D.C.: Smithsonian Institution Press, 1986).

8. On conditions of production in business enterprises at the turn of the nineteenth century, see Chandler, *Visible Hand*, 50–64. On craft production, see Jonathan Prude, *The Coming of Industrial Order: Town and Factory Life in Rural Massachusetts, 1810–1860* (New York: Cambridge University Press, 1983); Laurie, *Artisans into Workers*; Carl Bridenbaugh, *The Colonial Craftsman* (New York: New York University Press, 1950); Jeremy, *Artisans, Entrepreneurs and Machines*; John F. Kasson, *Civilizing the Machine: Technology and Republican Values in America, 1776–1900* (New York: Penguin Books, 1977); York, *Mechanical Metamorphosis*. On the rarity of corporations, see Morris, *Government and Labor in Early America*, 38; Lawrence M. Friedman, *A History of American Law* (New York: Simon & Schuster, 1973), 166.

9. Charles G. Sellers, *The Market Revolution: Jacksonian America, 1815–1846* (New York: Oxford University Press, 1991); Ben-Atar, *Trade Secrets*; Khan, *Democratization of Invention*.

CHAPTER 1

1. On early American law publishing, see Erwin C. Surrency, *A History of American Law Publishing* (New York: Oceana Publications, 1990). On the law reports and law reporters of particular courts and states, see Ann Fidler, "'Till You Understand Them in Their Principal Features': Observations on Form and Function in Nineteenth-Century American Law Books," 92 *Papers of the Bibliographical Society of America* 427 (1998); Joel Fishman, "The Digests of Pennsylvania," 90 *Law Library Journal* 481 (1998); Joel Fishman, "The Reports of the Supreme Court of Pennsylvania," 87 *Law Library Journal* 643 (1995); Craig Joyce, "The Rise of the Supreme Court Reporter: An Institutional Perspective on Marshall Court Ascendancy," 83 *Michigan Law Review* 1291 (1985); John H. Langbein, "Chancellor Kent and the History of Legal Literature," 93 *Columbia Law Review* 547

[260]

(1993); Kurt X. Metzmeier, "Blazing Trails in a New Kentucky Wilderness: Early Kentucky Case Law Digests," 93 *Law Library Journal* 93 (2001); and Erwin C. Surrency, "Law Reports in the United States," 25 *American Journal of Legal History* 48 (1981).

2. Daniel J. Boorstin, *The Mysterious Science of the Law: An Essay on Blackstone's Commentaries, Showing How Blackstone, Employing Eighteenth-Century Ideas of Science, Religion, History, Aesthetics, and Philosophy, Made of the Law at Once a Conservative and a Mysterious Science* (Boston: Beacon Press, 1958), iii–v. [261]

3. Bruce Bugbee, *The Genesis of American Patent and Copyright Law* (Washington, D.C.: Public Affairs Press, 1967).

4. Sir William Blackstone, vol. 2 of *Blackstone's Commentaries: With Notes of Reference to the Constitution and Laws of the Federal Government of the United States and of the Commonwealth of Virginia*, ed. St. George Tucker (Philadelphia: W. Y. Birch and A. Small, 1803); James Kent, vol. 2 of *Commentaries on American Law*, 14th ed. (Boston: Little, Brown, 1896), 247–66.

5. John Gother, *Instructions for Masters, Traders, Labourers, &c.* (London: n.p., 1699); David Gibbons, *Rudimentary Treatise on the Law of Contracts for Works and Services* (London: John Weale, 1857), 54, 109, contrasts the obligations owed by contractors with those owed by servants.

6. Gibbons, *Rudimentary Treatise on the Law of Contracts*.

7. Christopher L. Tomlins, "Law and Power in the Employment Relationship," in *Labor Law in America*, ed. Christopher L. Tomlins and Andrew J. King (Baltimore: Johns Hopkins University Press, 1992), 71–98; Christopher L. Tomlins, *Law, Labor, and Ideology in the Early American Republic* (New York: Cambridge University Press, 1993), 268. The multiple forms of employment relationships and the possibility that the terms "master" and "servant" had multiple meanings is discussed, with citations to numerous treatises, in Robert J. Steinfeld, *The Invention of Free Labor: The Employment Relation in English and American Law and Culture, 1350–1870* (Chapel Hill: University of North Carolina Press, 1991), 17–22. Wood's 1877 and 1886 treatises indeed tried to create a unitary category of master-servant out of what he recognized were multiple and different relations. Horace Gay Wood, *A Treatise on the Law of Master and Servant: Covering the Relation, Duties and Liabilities of Employers and Employees* (Albany, N.Y.: J. D. Parsons, Jr., 1877).

8. Lawrence M. Friedman, *Contract Law in America* (Madison: University of Wisconsin Press, 1965), 17–18; P. S. Atiyah, *The Rise and Fall of Freedom of Contract* (New York: Oxford University Press, 1979).

9. Steinfeld, *Invention of Free Labor*, 55; Richard B. Morris, *Government and Labor in Early America* (New York: Columbia University Press, 1946), 401–14.

10. Robert J. Steinfeld, *Coercion, Contract, and Free Labor in the Nineteenth Century*, ed. Christopher L. Tomlins (New York: Cambridge University Press, 2001); Morris, *Government and Labor*, 167–82, 187–88.

11. See, e.g., Boston Glass Manufactory v. Binney, 21 Mass. (4 Pick.) 425, 428 (1827); John Nockleby, Note, "Tortious Interference with Contractual Relations in the Nineteenth Century: The Transformation of Property, Contract, and Tort," 93 *Harvard Law Review* 1510, 1514–15 (1980); Tapping Reeve, *The Law of Baron and Femme, of Parent and*

Child, Guardian and Ward, Master and Servant and of the Powers of the Courts of Chancery: With an Essay on the Terms Heir, Heirs, Heirs of the Body, 3d ed. (Albany, N.Y.: W. Gould, 1862), 536; Morris, *Government and Labor*, 21, 414–34, 510–12.

12. 1829 Apprenticeship Agreement between William Whittaker & Sons of Philadelphia and Henry Barber, Hagley Museum and Library, Acc. 1471, Box 198; Indenture of Apprenticeship (1459), reprinted in A. E. Bland et al., *English Economic History: Select Documents*, 2d ed. (London: G. Bell and Sons, Ltd., 1915), 147; W. J. Rorabaugh, *The Craft Apprentice: From Franklin to the Machine Age in America* (New York: Oxford University Press, 1986), 32–33. On the role of apprenticeship contracts and the duty to guard the master's secrets in fostering technological innovation in pre-industrial Europe, see S. R. Epstein, "Craft Guilds, Apprenticeship, and Technological Change in Preindustrial Europe," 58 *Journal of Economic History* 684, 703–4 (1998).

13. See, e.g., Edward P. Cheyney, *An Introduction to the Industrial and Social History of England*, rev. ed. (n.p., 1920), 1338; William Holdsworth, vol. 8 of *A History of English Law*, 2d ed. (London: Methuen & Company, 1926), 58; Morris, *Government and Labor*, 378–80.

14. Kent, vol. 2 of *Commentaries on American Law*, 263 (quoting N.Y. Rev. Stat., ii. 160, §§39, 40).

15. Blackstone, *Blackstone's Commentaries*, 427–28.

16. See John R. Commons, David J. Saposs, Helen L. Sumner, E. B. Mittelman, H. E. Hoagland, John B. Andrews, and Selig Perlman, vol 1. of *History of Labour in the United States* (New York: Macmillan, 1918), 43–47, 340.

17. Makepeace v. Jackson, 128 Eng. Rep. 534, 534 (1813).

18. George T. Curtis, *A Treatise on the Law of Patents for Useful Inventions in the United States of America* (Boston: C. C. Little and J. Brown, 1849), 43, n. 1.

19. See Cheyney, *Introduction to the Industrial and Social History of England*, 133–38; Milton Handler and Daniel E. Lazaroff, "Restraint of Trade and the Restatement (Second) of Contracts," 57 *New York University Law Review* 669, 721–24 (1982); Ephraim Lipson, *The Economic History of England*, 7th ed. (London: A. and C. Black, 1937), vol. 1, chap. 8, and vol. 8, 279–94, 347–51; Michael J. Trebilcock, *The Common Law of Restraint of Trade: A Legal and Economic Analysis* (Toronto: Carswell, 1986), chap. 1; Harlan M. Blake, "Employee Agreements Not to Compete," 73 *Harvard Law Review* 625, 632–38 (1960); Charles E. Carpenter, "Validity of Contracts Not to Compete," 76 *University of Pennsylvania Law Review* 244, 246 (1928); William L. Letwin, "The English Common Law Concerning Monopolies," 21 *University of Chicago Law Review* 355, 379–80 (1954). The original case disapproving of noncompete agreements against craftsmen was the Dyer's Case, Y.B. 2 Hen. 5, fol. 5, Michaelmas, pl. 26 (Eng. 1414). William Holdsworth's influential *History of English Law* cited some cases from the fifteenth and sixteenth centuries upholding covenants in limited circumstances, typically in connection with the sale of a business and with the efforts of guilds to control the trade in a particular town. Holdsworth, *History of English Law*, 58–59.

20. Alger v. Thacher, 36 Mass. (19 Pick.) 51, 52 (1837).

21. In 1711, the landmark English decision Mitchel v. Reynolds stated a rule that has been followed (with variations) more or less ever since, allowing noncompetition agreements to be enforced against employees only when reasonable. Mitchel v. Reynolds,

24 Eng. Rep. 347 (Q.B.) (1711). In *Mitchel*, the defendant was a baker who apparently violated a restrictive covenant he had signed when he leased his bakery to the plaintiff. The defendant argued that the covenant was void because he was a baker, had served an apprenticeship in it, and could not be restrained from practicing his trade. The court upheld the covenant and gave an elaborate opinion defending the legal rule in terms of policy and establishing a multifactored analysis of reasonableness that still dominates the law's approach to contractual restraints on the practice of a trade and thus to the dissemination of workplace knowledge. The court devised a rule presuming restrictive covenants invalid, but allowing the party seeking enforcement to prove that, in the particular circumstances, it is "a just and honest contract." A "just and honest contract" must, first of all, be supported by adequate consideration. In addition, the restriction should be only such as necessary to benefit the person seeking enforcement (i.e., limited in time, in geographic scope, and in the occupations that are prohibited). Finally, the public must not be unduly injured by the restriction.

22. Caroline F. Ware, *The Early New England Cotton Manufacture: A Study in Industrial Beginnings* (Boston: Houghton Mifflin, 1931), 262.

23. George Sweet Gibb, *The Saco-Lowell Shops: Textile Machinery Building in New England, 1813–1949* (Cambridge, Mass.: Harvard University Press, 1950), 43.

24. George Rogers Taylor, "Introduction," in Nathan Appleton and Samuel Batchelder, *The Early Development of the American Cotton Textile Industry* (New York: Harper & Row, 1969), xiii (citing Perry Walton, *The Story of Textiles, A Bird's Eye View of the History of the Beginning and the Growth of the Industry by Which Mankind Is Clothed* [Boston, 1912], 178).

25. See, e.g., Alan Dawley, *Class and Community: The Industrial Revolution in Lynn* (Cambridge, Mass.: Harvard University Press, 1976); Rorabaugh, *Craft Apprentice*, 32–33; Charles G. Steffen, "Changes in the Organization of Artisan Production in Baltimore, 1790–1820," 36 *William & Mary Quarterly* 101 (1979); Christopher L. Tomlins, "The Ties That Bind: Master and Servant in Massachusetts, 1800–1850," 30 *Labor History* 193 (1989).

26. See Dawley, *Class and Community*; Rorabaugh, *Craft Apprentice*, 32–33; Steffen, "Changes in the Organization of Artisan Production," 101; Tomlins, "The Ties That Bind," 193; Morris, *Government and Labor*, 139–55; Bruce Laurie, *Artisans into Workers: Labor, in Nineteenth-Century America* (New York: Noonday Press, 1989); Tomlins, *Law, Labor, and Idealogy*; Sean Wilentz, *Chants Democratic: New York and the Rise of the American Working Class, 1788–1850* (New York: Oxford University Press, 1984).

27. Doron S. Ben-Atar, *Trade Secrets: Intellectual Piracy and the Origins of American Industrial Power* (New Haven, Conn.: Yale University Press, 2004), 135–39.

28. On the origins and early history of what is today known as the intellectual property clause, see Oren Bracha, "The Commodification of Patents, 1600–1836: How Patents Became Rights and Why We Should Care," 38 *Loyola of Los Angeles Law Review* 177 (2004); Bugbee, *Genesis of American Patent and Copyright Law*; Steven Lubar, "The Transformation of Antebellum Patent Law," 32 *Technology & Culture* 932 (1991); Edward C. Walterscheid, *To Promote the Progress of Useful Arts: American Patent Law and Administration, 1798–1836* (Littleton, Colo.: F. B. Rothman, 1998), 23–80.

29. Lewis Hyde, "Frames from the Framers: How America's Revolutionaries Imagined Intellectual Property," *Research Publication* 2005, ⟨http://cyber.law.harvard.edu/publications⟩ (quoting Thomas Jefferson, *The Complete Jefferson*, ed. Saul K. Padover [New York: Buell, Sloan and Pearce, 1943], 1016), 15; Thomas Jefferson, *Jefferson Cyclopedia*, ed. John Foley (New York: Funk & Wagnalls, 1900), 432; Thomas Jefferson, *The Writings of Thomas Jefferson: Correspondence*, ed. Andrew A. Lipscomb (Washington, D.C.: Thomas Jefferson Memorial Association, 1903).

30. *Federalist* no. 43 (James Madison).

31. B. Zorina Khan, *The Democratization of Invention: Patents and Copyrights in American Economic Development, 1790–1920* (New York: Cambridge University Press, 2005), 54–59. On early American patent administration, see also Walterscheid, *To Promote the Progress of Useful Arts*.

32. See, e.g., Naomi R. Lamoreaux and Kenneth L. Sokoloff, "Inventors, Firms and the Market for Technology in the Late Nineteenth and Early Twentieth Centuries," in *Learning by Doing in Markets, Firms, and Countries*, ed. Naomi R. Lamoreaux, Daniel M. G. Raff, and Peter Temin (Chicago: University of Chicago Press, 1999); B. Zorina Khan and Kenneth L. Sokoloff, "'Schemes of Practical Utility': Entrepreneurship and Innovation among 'Great Inventors' in the United States, 1790–1865," 53 *Journal of Economic History* 289 (1993).

33. 27 U.S. 1, 6 (1829).

34. Jennifer Nedelsky, *Private Property and the Limits of American Constitutionalism: The Madisonian Framework and Its Legacy* (Chicago: University of Chicago Press, 1990); Gregory S. Alexander, *Commodity and Propriety: Competing Visions of Property in American Legal Thought, 1776–1970* (Chicago: University of Chicago Press, 1997), 69–70; Morton J. Horwitz, *The Transformation of American Law, 1870–1960: The Crisis of Legal Orthodoxy* (New York: Oxford University Press, 1992); J. G. A. Pocock, *The Machiavellian Moment: Florentine Political Thought and the Atlantic Republican Tradition* (Princeton, N.J.: Princeton University Press, 1975); Friedman, *History of American Law*, 202–27.

35. See Trebilcock, *Common Law of Restraint of Trade*, 82. For example, a reference in a nonlegal publication (a book publishing secret recipes for various medical and household purposes that the author claimed to have obtained while working for several technical journals) referred to "all those recipes and so-called 'trade secrets' which have been so extensively advertised and offered for sale." John Phin, *Trade "Secrets" and Private Recipes: A Collection of Recipes, Processes and Formulae That Have Been Offered for Sale by Various Persons at Prices Ranging From Twenty-Five Cents to Five Hundred Dollars* (New York: Industrial Publication Company, 1887), iii.

36. 12 Pa. 56 (1849).

37. Clare Pettitt, *Patent Inventions—Intellectual Property and the Victorian Novel* (New York: Oxford University Press, 2004), 75 (quoting "The Literary Profession," *Chambers's Edinburgh Journal* 226 [August 6, 1842]); "Proposed New Copyright Law," *Chambers's Edinburgh Journal* 104 (April 21, 1838).

38. Kent, vol. 2 of *Commentaries on American Law*, 356, 361, 365.

39. By the mid-1870s, "intellectual property" was occasionally used to refer to patent and copyright collectively, and even patent, copyright, and trademark. Into the twentieth

century, treatise writers debated whether trademark really belonged. An 1875 treatise insisted that trademarks were "analogous" but still distinct; a 1906 treatise insisted that "trademarks have no analogy to patents or copyrights." According to Terry Fisher, it was rare to see the term "intellectual property" used to refer to patent, copyright, and trademark until after World War II. See William W. Fisher III, "Geistiges Eigentum—ein ausfernder Rechtsbereich: Die Geschichte des Ideenschutzes in den Vereinigten Staaten," in *Eigentum im internationalen Vergleich*, ed. Hannes Siegrist and Davis Sugarman (1999), 265, translated in William W. Fisher III, "The Growth of Intellectual Property: A History of the Ownership of Ideas in the United States," 22 and n. 105 (1999), ⟨http://cyber.law.harvard.edu/people/tfisher/iphistory.pdf⟩.

[265]

40. Davoll v. Brown, 7 F. Cas. 197 (C.C.D. Mass. 1845); Peter K. Yu, "Intellectual Property and the Information Ecosystem," 2005 *Michigan State Law Review* 1, 3, n. 12 (2005).

41. Henderson v. Vaulx, 18 Tenn. 30, 37–38 (1836).

42. Bracha, "Commodification of Patents."

43. On the ideology of political economy of America in the founding era, see Stanley Elkins and Eric McKitrick, *The Age of Federalism: The Early American Republic, 1788–1800* (New York: Oxford University Press, 1993), 19–20; Gordon S. Wood, *The Creation of the American Republic, 1776–1787* (Chapel Hill: University of North Carolina Press, 1969); Joyce Appleby, *Capitalism and a New Social Order: The Republican Vision of the 1790s* (New York: New York University Press, 1984); Wilentz, *Chants Democratic*; Pocock, *Machiavellian Moment*; J. G. A. Pocock, "Virtue and Commerce in the Eighteenth Century," 3 *Journal of Interdisciplinary History* 119 (1972).

44. Richard Godson, *A Practical Treatise on the Law of Patents for Inventions and of Copyright*, 2d ed. (London: W. Benning, 1844).

45. Willard Phillips, *The Law of Patents for Inventions: Including the Remedies and Legal Proceedings in Relation to Patent Rights* (Boston: American Stationers' Company, 1837), 418–19. It seems implausible that there were no such cases before 1843, but they evidently did not capture the interest of the limited number of people who reported court decisions.

46. W. M. Hindmarch, *A Treatise on the Law Relative to Patent Privileges for the Sole Use of Inventions and the Practice of Obtaining Letters Patents for Inventions* (Harrisburg, Pa.: I. G. M'Kinley and J. M. G. Lescure, 1847), 16.

47. Curtis, *Treatise on the Law of Patents*, 42–43. In support of this, Curtis cited a number of English cases, including Minter v. Wells, 149 Eng. Rep. 1130 (N.P.) (1834) (holding that person originating idea is inventor, not treating employment as determinative of ownership. The fact of employment is not mentioned in the opinion, which deals mainly with whether specification was valid because it described a novel application of a principle); Rex v. Arkwright, Webs. Pat. Cas. 64 (1785) (which held that the employer was the inventor because he communicated the idea to the workmen); Hill v. Thompson, 8 Taunt. 375, 395 (1818) (same); Barker and Harris v. Shaw, 1 Webs. Pat. Cases 126 (n.d.) ("But if a person be employed to perfect the details of or carry into execution the original idea of the patentee, that which he suggests or invents while so employed, and subsidiary to such idea, is in law the invention of the patentee"); and Makepeace v. Jackson, 128

Eng. Rep. 534 (1813) (employer owns calico dyer's recipe book, which includes recipes devised by the employee). In none of these cases except Makepeace v. Jackson did the court analyze the rights of the employer in the employee's inventions.

48. Ware, *Early New England Cotton Manufacture*, 262.

49. Gibb, *Saco-Lowell Shops*, 34–35; Taylor, "Introduction," in Appleton and Batchelder, *Early Development of the American Cotton Textile Industry*, xxviii.

50. Nathan Appleton, *Introduction of the Power Loom and Origin of Lowell* (1858), reprinted in Appleton and Batchelder, *Early Development of the American Cotton Textile Industry*, 22–24; Kirk Boot to Patrick Tracy Jackson, June 20, 1823, in Andrew J. King, ed., *The Papers of Daniel Webster, Legal Papers*, vol. 3, *The Federal Practice* (Hanover, N.H.: University Press of New England, 1989), 858.

51. Samuel Batchelder, *Introduction and Early Progress of the Cotton Manufacture in the United States*, reprinted in Appleton and Batchelder, *Early Development of the American Textile Industry*, 41–46, 71; David J. Jeremy, *Transatlantic Industrial Revolution: The Diffusion of Textile Technologies between Britain and America, 1790–1830s* (Cambridge, Mass.: MIT Press, 1981), 87–89, 95–103, 106–10, 130, 136.

52. The litigation was handled for the Boston Manufacturing Company by Daniel Webster, and the litigation documents are reprinted in King, *Papers of Daniel Webster, Legal Papers*, vol. 3, *The Federal Practice*, 824–58. Boston Manufacturing Company's litigation against Moody is also discussed in Jeremy, *Transatlantic Industrial Revolution*, 185–86, 193.

53. Dixon v. Moyer, 7 F. Cas. 758 (C.C.D. Pa. 1821) (No. 3931); Sparkman v. Higgins, 22 F. Cas. 878 (C.C.S.D.N.Y. 1846) (No. 13,208); Goodyear v. Day, 10 F. Cas. 677 (C.C.D.N.J. 1852) (No. 5566); Dental Vulcanite Co. v. Wetherbee, 7 F. Cas. 498 (C.C.D. Mass. 1866) (No. 3810). Some later cases also reached the same result. See, e.g., Matthews & Willard Manufacturing Co. v. Trenton Lamp Co., 73 F. 212, 215–16 (C.C.D.N.J. 1896). Not every case rejected the defense, however. In an 1888 infringement action, the court determined the patent invalid because the employer's idea—to imitate in print fabric the crinkly texture of the seersucker weave—was not novel; the court suggested that the novelty lay in the employee's print design. Streat v. White, 35 F. 426, 427–28 (C.C.S.D.N.Y. 1888).

54. Act of July 4, 1836, ch. 357, §6. See also Curtis, *Treatise on the Law of Patents*, 208. The right of the "true inventor" to the patent comes from the English Statute of Monopolies, which prohibited the monarch from granting monopolies except, inter alia, "to the true and first inventor and inventors" of "any new manner of manufactures within this realm. . . ." 21 James I, c. 3 §5.

55. George T. Curtis, *A Treatise on the Law of Patents for Useful Inventions: As Enacted and Administered in the United States of America*, 3d ed. (Boston: Little, Brown, 1867), 40–54, 62–88; Curtis, *Treatise on the Law of Patents* (1849 ed.). Cases involving ownership of patented inventions arose in both state and federal courts. Congress had placed exclusive jurisdiction over the validity of patents in the patent office and the federal courts; some of the litigation about ownership of inventions occurred in appeals from patent office decisions awarding patents or in infringement suits. In some cases, however, the validity or infringement of a patent was not in issue; the issue was ownership of the patent and the idea it protected. Such cases were regarded as matters of contract law or master and

servant law and were litigated in state court unless the parties resided in different states and therefore could invoke the diversity of citizenship jurisdiction of the federal courts. There was a certain amount of confusion in the early cases about whether state courts had jurisdiction over suits alleging, for example, breach of promise to assign patents because of the exclusive jurisdiction in federal courts over the validity of patents, but mainly state courts understood that they could enforce the contracts without inquiry into the validity of the patents. E.g., Middlebrook v. Broadbent, 47 N.Y. 443 (1872); Binney v. Annan, 107 Mass. 94 (1871).

56. Allen v. Rawson, 1 C.B. 551, 573, 575, 135 Eng. Rep. 656, 665, 666 (1845).

57. Teese v. Phelps, 23 F. Cas. 832, 834 (C.C.N.D. Cal. 1855); see also Alden v. Dewey, 1 F. Cas. 329, 330 (C.C.D. Mass. 1840).

58. 42 U.S. (1 How.) 202 (1843).

59. 42 U.S. at 204.

60. Deposition of Philip Kingsland, Supreme Court Record of McClurg v. Kingsland, 8.

61. See the bibliography for a discussion of the sources I relied on in constructing the story of Du Pont.

62. Jonathan Prude, *The Coming of Industrial Order: Town and Factory Life in Rural Massachusetts, 1810–1860* (New York: Cambridge University Press, 1983), 47 (quoting letters written by Samuel Slater).

63. This early history is told in the first several chapters of William S. Dutton, *Du Pont: One Hundred and Forty Years* (New York: Charles Scribner's Sons, 1942). I have also drawn some of the background material on the family and the business from John B. Riggs, *A Guide to the Manuscripts in the Eleutherian Mills Historical Library* (Greenville, Del.: Eleutherian Mills Historical Library, 1970), 21–25, 576–80.

64. B. G. du Pont, *E. I. du Pont de Nemours and Company* (New York: Houghton Mifflin, 1920), 37 (observing that du Pont's "unusual experience as both chemist and machinist" was essential to his success).

65. See Prude, *Coming of Industrial Order*, xv.

66. Raphael Duplanty, E. I. du Pont de Nemours & Co., to James Rogers, February 7, 1809, Group 5, Series C, Box 48; Peter Bauduy to Daniel Call, 1809, Group 5, Series C, Box 48; Charge to the Jury in Munns v. Du Pont, 17 F. Cas. 993 (D. PA 1811) (No. 9926), Group 5, Series C, Box 48; all in DPA.

67. Raphael Duplanty to James Rogers.

68. Charge to the Jury in Munns v. Du Pont.

69. Brown, Page & Co. to Charles Munns, December 18, 1808, Group 5, Series C, Box 48, DPA; Charge to the Jury in Munns v. Du Pont.

70. Peter Bauduy to Daniel Call, supra note 66; Peter Bauduy to James Hudson (1809), Group 5, Series C, Box 48, DPA.

71. Charge to the Jury in Munns v. Du Pont.

72. Charles Munns to Brown Page & Co., December 23, 1808, Group 5, Series C, Box 48, DPA.

73. Raphael Duplanty, E. I. du Pont de Nemours & Co., to Daniel Call (1809), Group 5, Series C, Box 48, DPA; Brown, Page & Co. to Charles Munns, December 18, 1808.

74. Brown, Page & Co. to E. I. du Pont de Nemours & Co., January 7, 1809, Group 5, Series C, Box 48, DPA.

75. Brown, Page & Co. to Charles Munns, December 18, 1808 (emphasis in original).

76. Du Pont to Brown, Page & Co., January 21, 1809, Group 5, Series C, Box 48, DPA.

77. Raphael Duplanty to James Rogers, February 7, 1809.

78. Daniel Call to E. I. du Pont de Nemours & Co., January 21, 1809, Group 5, Series C, Box 48, DPA.

79. C. J. Ingersoll to E. I. Du Pont de Nemours & Co., December 18, 1810, Group 5, Series C, Box 48, DPA.

80. Charles Munns to William Clarke Frazer, December 14, 1810, Group 5, Series C, Box 48, DPA.

81. Case of Malicious Prosecution, Munns v. Du Pont, 17 F. Cas. 993 (D. Pa. 1811), Group 5, Series C, Box 48, File: Special, Munns Lawsuit (documents), DPA.

82. Jury in Munns v. Du Pont, 17 F. Cas. 993 (D. Pa. 1811), Group 5, Series C, Box 48, DPA.

83. Factory Rules, EDPC, Accession 146, Box 3, Folder 30.

84. Raphael Duplanty to Daniel Call, 1809.

85. E. I. du Pont, E. I. du Pont de Nemours & Co., to Thomas Ewell, December 14, 1811, EDPC, Accession 146, Box 2, Folder 13.

86. Thomas Ewell to E. I. du Pont de Nemours & Co., December 8, 1811, EDPC, Accession 146, Box 2, Folder 13.

87. E. I. du Pont to Thomas Ewell, December 14, 1811.

88. Thomas Ewell to E. I. du Pont de Nemours & Co., December 22, 1811, EDPC, Accession 146, Box 2, Folder 13.

89. Thomas Ewell to Charles Munns, November 24, 1811, EDPC, Accession 146, Box 2, Folder 13.

90. E. I. du Pont, E. I. du Pont de Nemours & Co., to Thomas Ewell, April 8, 1812, Group 5, Series C, Box 48, DPA.

91. The letter that du Pont threatened to publish read, "Mr. Mitchel your friend tells me you are an excellent hand at the manufacture of Gunpowder, and that you had expressed a willingness to engage with the powder makers at New York with Mr. Quigg." Thomas Ewell to Hugh Flannighan, E. I. du Pont de Nemours & Co., March 27, 1812, Group 5, Series C, Box 48, DPA. Ewell offered $800 per year and a wage increase after six months "if you manage well." *Id.*

92. Du Pont, *E. I. du Pont de Nemours & Company*, 38 n. 2.

93. Thomas Ewell to E. I. du Pont, E. I. du Pont de Nemours & Co., April 12, 1812, Group 5, Series C, Box 48, File: Special, Ewell Corres. (out), DPA.

94. *Id.*

95. Du Pont Advertisement, To Powder Makers, in *The Watchman* (Wilmington, Delaware), April 14, 1812, Group 5, Series C, Box 48, DPA.

96. *Id.* The clipping has with it a handwritten note stating: "the following singular advertisement has been published in the Watchman of Wilmington Delaware, posted

up at the workers home in Wilmington and distributed in hand bills to all the workmen of E. I. Du Pont & Co. Manufactory."

97. Thomas Ewell to Hugh Flannigan, E. I. du Pont de Nemours & Co., May 3, 1812, Group 5, Series C, Box 48, DPA.

98. E. I. du Pont, *Villainy Detected* (1812) (pamphlet), Hagley Museum and Library.

99. E. I. du Pont de Nemours to Johanno (believed May 1817) (quoted and translated in du Pont, *E. I. du Pont de Nemours & Company*, 51–52).

100. John Nockleby, Note, "Tortious Interference with Contractual Relations," 93 *Harvard Law Review* 1510, 1514–15 (1980); Kent, vol. 2 of *Commentaries on American Law*; Charles Smith, *A Treatise on the Law of Master and Servant Including Therein Masters and Workmen in Every Description of Trade and Occupation* (Philadelphia: T. & J. W. Johnson, 1852); Karen Orren, *Belated Feudalism: Labor, the Law, and Liberal Development in the United States* (New York: Cambridge University Press, 1991), 98–100; John F. Witt, "Rethinking the Nineteenth Century Employment Contract, Again," 18 *Law & History Review* 627, 633 (2000).

101. 21 Mass. (4 Pick.) 425, 427–28 (1827).

102. William E. Nelson, *Americanization of the Common Law: The Impact of Legal Change on Massachusetts Society, 1760–1830* (Cambridge, Mass.: Harvard University Press, 1975), 161.

103. Joseph Story, vol. 1 of *Commentaries on Equity Jurisprudence*, 1st English ed., ed. W. E. Grigsby (London: Stevens and Haynes, 1884), 184.

104. Yovatt v. Winyard, 37 Eng. Rep. 425 (Ex. Ch.) (1820); Bryson v. Whitehead, 57 Eng. Rep. 29 (V.C.) (1822).

105. Vickery v. Welch, 36 Mass. (19 Pick.) 523 (1837).

106. Story, vol. 2 of *Commentaries on Equity Jurisprudence*, 621.

107. 37 Eng. Rep. 425.

108. *Id.* at 426.

109. Morison v. Moat, 68 Eng. Rep. 492, 501 (V.C.) (1851) (enjoining defendant from using secret recipe for patent medicine because he had learned the recipe illicitly).

110. Merryweather v. Moore, 2 Ch. 518 (1892).

111. 34 Eng. Rep. 515 (1815).

112. 57 Eng. Rep. 659 (Ch.) (1827).

113. James A. Brundage, *The Medieval Origins of the Legal Profession: Canonists, Civilians, and Courts* (Chicago: University of Chicago Press, 2008).

114. Cf. generally Deborah A. Ballam, "The Development of the Employment at Will Rule Revisited: A Challenge to Its Origins as Based in the Development of Advanced Capitalism," 13 *Hofstra Labor & Employment Law Journal* 75 (1995); Jay M. Feinman, "The Development of the Employment at Will Rule," 20 *American Journal of Legal History* 118 (1976).

115. Kent, vol. 2 of *Commentaries on American Law*, 614–15.

116. Reeve, *The Law of Baron and Femme*. This work does not mention trade secrets in the sections on the law of master and servant, on the law of apprentices, or even in the section on the powers of chancery courts.

117. See generally Sir Edward Fry, *A Treatise on the Specific Performance of Contracts: Including Those of Public Companies* (Philadelphia: T & J. W. Johnson, 1858); Theophilus Parsons, *The Law of Contracts*, 6th ed. (Boston: Little, Brown, 1873); James Schouler, *Law of the Domestic Relations Embracing Husband and Wife, Parent and Child, Guardian and Ward, Infancy, and Master and Servant* (Boston: Little, Brown, 1905).

118. 57 Eng. Rep. at 31; Vickery v. Welch, 36 Mass. (19 Pick.) 523, 523 (1837).

119. 24 Eng. Rep. 347 (Q.B.) (1711).

120. Vickery, 36 Mass. (19 Pick.) at 527. Six years later, New York adopted the concept of a trade secret as being the saleable property of a business. Jarvis & Lobdell v. Peck, 10 Paige Ch. 118 (N.Y. Ch. 1843); accord Hard v. Seeley, 47 Barb. 428 (N.Y. Sup. Ct. 1865) (enforcing covenant ancillary to the sale of a business by which seller promised not to reveal "the art and mystery of compounding and manufacturing" a medicine known as "Dermador").

121. A New York decision, Deming v. Chapman, 11 Pow. Pr. 382, 388 (N.Y. Sup. Ct. 1854), is illustrative. In *Deming*, an employer had obtained a preliminary injunction based on an express written contract that the employee would not divulge the employer's technique for marbleizing iron or slate. The New York Supreme Court dissolved the injunction, suggesting that the federal patent law was the sole source of protection for such economically valuable and novel information. The court's view that it lacked the ability to grant equitable enforcement even of a signed contract promising to keep a particular named secret suggests the novelty of the employer's claim.

CHAPTER 2

1. Copyright Act, 1st Cong., 2d Sess., ch. 15, May 31, 1790 (emphasis added). On the early copyright law, see L. R. Patterson and Craig Joyce, "Copyright in 1791: An Essay Concerning the Founders' View of the Copyright Power Granted to Congress in Article I, Section 8, Clause 8 of the U.S. Constitution," 52 *Emory Law Journal* 909 (2003).

2. The comparison between book production in the pre-Renaissance period and wage labor in the nineteenth century has been noted: "With the so-called 'book revolution' of the twelfth century and university supervision of copying, there came a 'putting out' system. Copyists were no longer assembled in a single room, but worked on different portions of a given text, receiving payment from the stationer for each piece. . . . Through a sort of guilt by association, we can see how wage labor might metonymically become associated with the capacity to possess the knowledge which is the source and aim of the labor. We can also envision how the 'employer' of copyists might become a metonym for the owner of the knowledge and thus of the authority supposedly contained within the text." Marlon B. Ross, "Authority and Authenticity: Scribbling Authors and the Genius of Print in Eighteenth-Century England," in *The Construction of Authorship: Textual Appropriation in Law and Literature*, ed. Martha Woodmansee and Peter Jaszi (Durham, N.C.: Duke University Press, 1994), 236 (quoting Elizabeth Eisenstein, *The Printing Press as an Agent of Change*, vol. 1, 12–13 [New York: Cambridge University Press, 1979]). On patronage and freelance work relationships in artistic creation, see Timothy King, "Patronage and the Market in the Creation of Opera before the Institution of Intellectual

Property," 25 *Journal of Cultural Economics* 21 (2001), and F. M. Scherer, "The Evolution of Free-Lance Music Composition, 1650–1900," 25 *Journal of Cultural Economics* 307 (2001).

3. See generally Martha Woodmansee and Peter Jaszi, eds., *The Construction of Authorship: Textual Appropriation in Law and Literature* (Durham, N.C.: Duke University Press, 1994); Mark Rose, *Authors and Owners: The Invention of Copyright* (Cambridge, Mass.: Harvard University Press, 1993).

4. Sir William Blackstone, vol. 3 of *Blackstone's Commentaries: With Notes of Reference to the Constitution and Laws of the Federal Government of the United States and of the Commonwealth of Virginia*, ed. St. George Tucker (Philadelphia: W. Y. Birch and A. Small, 1803), 405–6; Rose, *Authors and Owners*, 75.

5. Rose, *Authors and Owners*, 6, 25, 114.

6. The celebrity author copyright advocates include Daniel Defoe, Alexander Pope, and William Wordsworth. See Rose, *Authors and Owners*, 34–37, 60–65, 110–12. A modern example of the successful melding of celebrity with copyright advocacy is the Sonny Bono Copyright Extension Act, Pub. L. no. 105–298, 11 Stat 2827 (codified in scattered sections of 17 U.S.C.), named for the late entertainer, even though Hollywood cared far more about Mickey Mouse never entering the public domain than the music and lyrics to "I Got You, Babe."

7. B. Zorina Khan, *The Democratization of Invention: Patents and Copyrights in American Economic Development, 1790–1920* (New York: Cambridge University Press, 2005), 236.

8. In the period from 1790 to 1800, for example, 17 percent of the registrations were for dictionaries, directories, atlases, maps, and works of "commerce." Among books that likely had individual authors, 14 percent were for what Khan calls "social and political" books and another 17 percent were for textbooks. Eleven percent were for music, poetry, and plays, and 5.7 percent were for law books. *Id.*

9. *Id.*

10. Binns v. Woodruff, 3 F. Cas. 421 (C.C.D. Pa. 1821) (No. 1424).

11. Copyright Act, 1st Cong., 2d Sess., ch. 15, Stat. 124, May 31, 1790.

12. On early American law publishing, see Erwin C. Surrency, *A History of American Law Publishing* (New York: Oceana Publications, 1990). On the law reports and law reporters of particular courts and states, see Ann Fidler, "'Till You Understand Them in Their Principal Features': Observations on Form and Function in Nineteenth-Century American Law Books," 92 *Papers of the Bibliographical Society of America* 427 (1998); Joel Fishman, "The Digests of Pennsylvania," 90 *Law Library Journal* 481 (1998); Joel Fishman, "The Reports of the Supreme Court of Pennsylvania," 87 *Law Library Journal* 643 (1995); Craig Joyce, "The Rise of the Supreme Court Reporter: An Institutional Perspective on Marshall Court Ascendancy," 83 *Michigan Law Review* 1291 (1985); John H. Langbein, "Chancellor Kent and the History of Legal Literature," 93 *Columbia Law Review* 547 (1993); Kurt X. Metzmeier, "Blazing Trails in a New Kentucky Wilderness: Early Kentucky Case Law Digests," 93 *Law Library Journal* 93 (2001); and Erwin C. Surrency, "Law Reports in the United States," 25 *American Journal of Legal History* 48 (1981).

13. Wheaton v. Peters, 33 U.S. 591 (1834).

14. My account of Wheaton v. Peters draws heavily on G. Edward White, *The Marshall Court and Cultural Change, 1815–1835* (New York: Macmillan, 1988), 384–426; Joyce, "Rise of the Supreme Court Reporter"; and Craig Joyce, "The Story of Wheaton v. Peters: A Curious Chapter in the History of Judicature," in *Intellectual Property Stories*, ed. Jane Ginsburg and Rochelle C. Dreyfuss (New York: Foundation Press, 2006).

15. See White, *Marshall Court and Cultural Change*, 389–90; Joyce, "Rise of the Supreme Court Reporter," 1343, 1347; Joyce, "Story of Wheaton v. Peters," 44.

16. 33 U.S. at 634–35, 667–68; The Reporters' Act of March 3, 1817, ch. 63, 3 Stat. 376.

17. Joyce, "Rise of the Supreme Court Reporter," 1326–27, 1336–37; White, *Marshall Court and Cultural Change*, 390–91, 393, 402; The Reporters' Act of March 3, 1817, ch. 63, 3 Stat. 376; 33 U.S. at 614.

18. 33 U.S. at 668.

19. See Joyce, "Rise of the Supreme Court Reporter," 1313, 1322. On the effect of the boardinghouse residence on Marshall Court practice, see White, *Marshall Court and Cultural Change*, 160–61, 190–91.

20. Today, there can be no copyright at all in works produced by U.S. government employees. 17 U.S.C. §§101, 105. Section 105 provides that copyright protection "is not available for any work of the United States Government," and §101 defines such works to include "a work prepared by an officer or employee of the United States Government as part of that person's official duties." The legislative history of the 1976 revision of §105 states that the concept should be construed "in the same way" as works made for hire. H.R. Rep. no. 94–1476, 59 (1976). The purpose of §105, according to the legislative history of the 1976 Act, was "to place all work of the United States Government, published or unpublished, in the public domain." *Id.* The predecessor to §105 first appeared in the Printing Act of 1895, ch. 23, 28 Stat. 601 (1895), and was recodified and retained unchanged in the 1909 Copyright Act. Act of March 4, 1909, ch. 320, 35 Stat. 1075. See H.R. Rep. no. 60–1 (to accompany H.R. 28192, February 1909). Even prior to 1895, there was some recognition that copyrighting federal government materials was problematic. See Robert M. Gellman, "Twin Evils: Government Copyright and Copyright-Like Controls Over Government Information," 45 *Syracuse Law Review* 999 (1995).

21. Little v. Gould, 15 F. Cas. 612, 613 (C.C.N.D.N.Y. 1852) (No. 8395). Other phases of the litigation over the copyright to the reports were published as well. Little v. Hall, 59 U.S. 165 (1855); Little v. Gould, 15 F. Cas. 604 (C.C.N.D.N.Y. 1851) (No. 8394).

22. 19 F. Cas. 652, 14 Copyright Decisions 2075, 2087–89 (C.C.D.Mass. 1846).

23. Atwill v. Ferrett, 2 F. Cas. 195, 197–98 (C.C.S.D.N.Y 1846) (No. 640).

24. *Id.* at 198.

25. 2 F. Cas. 195, 198 (C.C.S.D.N.Y. 1846) (No. 640). The 1909 Copyright Act, repeating the prior rule established in the Printing Act of 1895, prohibited copyright in "any publication of the United States Government." Act of March 4, 1909, ch. 320, 35 Stat. 1075. 17 U.S.C. §§101, 105. However, if a cartographer copyrighted the map before publication by the government, he might have retained the copyright, as §8 also provided that "the publication or republication by the Government, either separately or in a public

document, of any material in which copyright is subsisting shall not be taken to cause any abridgement of the copyright." *Id.*

26. Robert Hogan, *Dion Boucicault* (New York: Twayne Publishers, 1969), 30 (quoting George Rowell, *The Victorian Theatre, A Survey* [London, 1956], 1). On the evolving nature of melodrama in the mid-nineteenth century, see Bruce A. McConachie, *Melodramatic Formations: American Theatre and Society, 1820–1870* (Iowa City: University of Iowa Press, 1992). [273]

27. See 4 Stat. 436 (1831) (music); 11 Stat. 138 (1856) (dramas); 13 Stat. 540 (1865) (photographs); 16 Stat. 212 (1870) (painting, drawing, and sculpture); 37 Stat. 488 (1912) (motion pictures).

28. J. B. Harley, *The New Nature of Maps: Essays in the History of Cartography*, ed. Paul Laxton (Baltimore: Johns Hopkins University Press, 2001), 35–36, 199, noted a debate among cartographers about the ethics of copyright but insisted that a more pressing ethical issue for cartographers should be the political and social judgments they make when they draw maps, such as when cartographers of South Africa made the white urban areas the center of city maps and the black townships all but invisible. John Rennie Short, *Representing the Republic: Mapping the United States, 1600–1900* (London: Reaktion Books, 2001), 34, argued that "the illusion of single authorship" and that "maps resulted solely from the gaze of the Western observer" are two misconceptions about early American maps, but that maps were often composites building on earlier maps, the notes and sketches of travelers, and the reports of indigenous peoples.

29. See Walter W. Ristow, *American Maps and Mapmakers: Commercial Cartography in the Nineteenth Century*, 20–23 (Detroit: Wayne State University Press, 1985); Short, *Representing the Republic.*

30. See, for example, the discussion of Henry Francis Walling and his "Map Establishment" in New York City. Ristow, *American Maps and Mapmakers*, 332. Some of his maps stated that the surveys had been made "under the direction of H. F. Walling"; some have the imprint "Engraved, Printed, Colored Mounted at H. F. Walling's Map Establishment"; and some have the imprint "Walling & Rice, Publishers." *Id.*, 335. See also Judith A. Tyner, "Images of the Southwest in Nineteenth-Century American Atlases," in *The Mapping of the American Southwest*, ed. Dennis Reinhartz and Charles C. Colley (College Station: Texas A&M University Press, 1987), 60–77 (discussing various atlases from 1817 to the 1880s).

31. Henry Francis Walling used this method, for example. See Ristow, *American Maps and Mapmakers*, 327.

32. *Id.*, 339–53.

33. The editors' note following one case stated that "[t]he publication of a map made from materials collected while in the service of the government as draughtsman belongs to the government." Chapman v. Ferry, 12 F. 693, 696 (C.C.D. Ore. 1882). However, the report of the case indicates it concerned available remedies for copyright infringement rather than ownership of the copyright as between employer and employee. *Id.* at 695.

34. This 1796 map was obviously the product of work by postal employees. My account draws primarily on Ristow, *American Maps and Mapmakers*, 20, 70.

35. See Robert S. Martin, "United States Army Mapping in Texas, 1848–50," in *The Mapping of the American Southwest*, ed. Dennis Reinhartz and Charles C. Colley (College Station: Texas A&M University Press, 1987), 42–43, n. 16. This article reveals nothing about the copyright on the map or about the nature of the employment relation (if any) between Ford, Neighbors, and the U.S. Army. I infer it was privately published because the citation is to a New York publisher and to Creuzbaur for the Texas publication. However, the maps prepared by Neighbors and Ford probably were incorporated, along with maps and surveys conducted by other Army personnel in 1848–1850, into a larger map that was presented to the Senate and printed by the War Department in 1850. *Id.* at 55–56 and n. 50. Thus, the private publication and perhaps sale of the earlier version might not have been objectionable, since the U.S. Army obtained what it wanted in the process.

36. Pennsylvania v. Desilver, 3 Phila. 31, 14 Copyright Decisions 2039 (C.P. 1858).

37. 7 Op. Att'y Gen. 656, 656–57 (1856), 15 Copyright Decisions 3049.

38. 11 F. Cas. 1031 (C.C.S.D.N.Y. 1857) (No. 6324).

39. *Id.* at 1032.

40. *Id.* at 1033.

41. David Gibbons, *Rudimentary Treatise on the Law of Contracts for Works and Services*, 2d ed. (London: John Weale, 1857), 110.

PART II

1. David A. Hounshell, *From the American System to Mass Production, 1800–1932: The Development of Manufacturing Technology in the United States* (Baltimore: Johns Hopkins University Press, 1984); Walter Licht, *Industrializing America: The Nineteenth Century* (Baltimore: Johns Hopkins University Press, 1995).

2. See B. Zorina Khan, *The Democratization of Invention: Patents and Copyrights in American Economic Development, 1790–1920* (New York: Cambridge University Press, 2005), 3.

3. Abraham Lincoln, First Lecture on Discoveries and Inventions, April 1858, in Roy P. Basler, ed., *The Collected Works of Abraham Lincoln*, 3d ed. (New Brunswick, N.J.: Rutgers University Press, 1953).

4. Abraham Lincoln, Second Lecture on Discoveries and Inventions, February 11, 1859, in ibid., 356, 363.

5. Lawrence M. Friedman, *Contract Law in America* (Madison: University of Wisconsin Press, 1965), 17–18. See also Grant Gilmore, *The Death of Contract* (Columbus: Ohio State University Press, 1974); P. S. Atiyah, *The Rise and Fall of Freedom of Contract* (New York: Oxford University Press, 1979), 402.

6. See Amy Dru Stanley, *From Bondage to Contract: Wage Labor, Marriage, and the Market in the Age of Slave Emancipation* (New York: Cambridge University Press, 1998).

7. 49 Mass. 49, 56, 58 (1842). On the significance of contract and *Farwell* as foundational developments in nineteenth-century labor law, see Alfred S. Konefsky, "As Best to Subserve Their Own Interests: Lemuel Shaw, Labor Conspiracy, and Fellow Servants," 7 *Law & History Review* 219 (1989).

8. As Morton Horwitz explained, "one of the primary functions of the classical legal

treatise" was "not simply to report on the state of the law but to advance a highly abstract and integrated version that was grounded in a picture of a decentralized, individualistic economic and political order." And nowhere was that project more influential, and more zealously pursued by treatise authors, than in the area of contract. Morton J. Horwitz, *The Transformation of American Law, 1870–1960: The Crisis of Legal Orthodoxy* (New York: Oxford University Press, 1992), 45. See also Atiyah, *Rise and Fall of Freedom of Contract*; James W. Hurst, *Law and the Conditions of Freedom: In the Nineteenth-Century United States* (Madison: University of Wisconsin Press, 1956), 14. [275]

9. John C. Gray, *Restraints on the Alienation of Property*, 2d ed. (Boston: Boston Book Company, 1895), 66. On Gray, see Stephen A. Siegel, "John Chipman Gray and the Moral Basis of Classical Legal Thought," 86 *Iowa Law Review* 1513 (2001).

10. Gray, *Restraints on the Alienation*, 66.

11. Elisha Greenhood, *The Doctrine of Public Policy in the Law of Contracts, Reduced to Rules* (Chicago: Callaghan & Company, 1886).

12. See Horwitz, *Transformation of American Law*, 35.

13. O. W. Holmes, "The Path of the Law," 10 *Harvard Law Review* 457, 466 (1897).

14. On the enormous popularity and widespread influence of Taylor's scientific management, see generally Robert Kanigel, *The One Best Way: Frederick Winslow Taylor and the Enigma of Efficiency* (New York: Viking, 1997).

15. Pressed Steel Car Co. v. Standard Steel Car Co., 60 A. 4, 8 (Pa. 1904).

16. Dempsey v. Dobson, 184 Pa. 588, 593 (1898) (quoting Dempsey v. Dobson, 174 Pa. 122, 130 [1896]).

17. Charles W. McCurdy, "The Roots of 'Liberty of Contract' Reconsidered: Major Premises in the Law of Employment, 1867–1937," *Supreme Court Historical Society Yearbook* 20 (1984).

18. Roscoe Pound, "Liberty of Contract," 18 *Yale Law Journal* 454, 454 (1909).

19. See Robert J. Steinfeld, *Coercion, Contract, and Free Labor in the Nineteenth Century* (New York: Cambridge University Press, 2001); Robert Hale, "Coercion and Distribution in a Supposedly Non-Coercive State," 38 *Political Science Quarterly* 478 (1923).

20. The shop-right doctrine, which gave an employer a right to use employees' workplace inventions, was not mentioned in master-servant law treatises for forty years after the right was created in 1843. Even the second edition of Wood's influential *Treatise on the Law of Master and Servant* in 1886 dealt with the ownership of employee inventions only in a couple of sentences, putting inventions in the category of the master's entitlement to the servant's earnings but stating that "the master is not entitled to the patent as against the servant, unless the servant was hired for th[e] purpose [of inventing]." Horace Gay Wood, *A Treatise on the Law of Master and Servant: Covering the Relation, Duties and Liabilities of Employers and Employees* (San Francisco: Bancroft-Whitney, 1886), 200; see also *id.* at 76 ("an apprentice or servant who invents a machine during the period of his apprenticeship or service is entitled to the patent thereon, but, in the case of a servant, the rule is different, if he was employed for the express purpose of inventing"). Wood cited Hill v. Thompson, 8 Taunt. 375 (1818), and Bloxam v. Elsee, 1 C & P 568 (1827), but in neither did the employment relationship play into the court's analysis. Wood also cited Green v. Willard Barrel Co., 1 Mo. App. 202 (1876), which was a wrongful discharge

proceeding, and Joliet Mfg. Co. v. Dice, 105 Ill. 649 (1883), which involved an express contract.

21. See Atiyah, *Rise and Fall of Freedom of Contract*, 398–412; Friedman, *Contract Law in America*, 20; Gilmore, *Death of Contract*.

22. Wood, *Treatise on the Law of Master and Servant*, 265.

23. *Id.*

24. James L. High, *A Treatise on the Law of Injunctions*, vol. 2, 4th ed. (Chicago: Callaghan, 1905), 15.

25. *Id.* at 236 (quoting Shepherd v. Conquest, 17 C.B. 427, 445).

26. Eaton S. Drone, *A Treatise on the Law of Property in Intellectual Productions in Great Britain and the United States* (Boston: Little, Brown, 1879), 236–61.

CHAPTER 3

1. Charles River Bridge v. Warren Bridge, 36 U.S. (11 Pet.) 420 (1837). Herbert Hovenkamp, *Enterprise and American Law, 1836–1937* (Cambridge, Mass.: Harvard University Press 1991), 110–14.

2. Gregory S. Alexander, *Commodity and Propriety: Competing Visions of Property in American Legal Thought, 1776–1970* (Chicago: University of Chicago Press, 1997), 130.

3. Barnes v. Ingalls, 39 Ala. 193 (1863).

4. See David J. Jeremy, *Artisans, Entrepreneurs and Machines: Essays on the Early Anglo-American Textile Industries, 1770–1840s* (Brookfield, Vt.: Ashgate, 1998), esp. chapter 7.

5. Leonard S. Reich, *The Making of American Industrial Research: Science and Business at GE and Bell, 1876–1926* (Cambridge: Cambridge University Press, 1985), 17. On the professionalization of engineering, see Monte Calvert, *Mechanical Engineer in America, 1830–1910: Professional Cultures in Conflict* (Baltimore: Johns Hopkins University Press, 1967); Edwin Layton, *The Revolt of the Engineers: Social Responsibility and the American Engineering Profession* (Baltimore: Johns Hopkins University Press, 1986); A. Michal McMahon, *The Making of a Profession: A Century of Electrical Engineering in America* (New York: IEEE Press, 1984); Bruce Sinclair, *A Centennial History of the American Society of Mechanical Engineers, 1880–1980* (Toronto: University of Toronto Press, 1980).

6. See generally Phillip Scranton, *Endless Novelty: Specialty Production and American Industrialization, 1865–1925* (Princeton, N.J.: Princeton University Press, 1997); Philip Scranton, *Figured Tapestry: Production, Markets, and Power in Philadelphia Textiles, 1885–1941* (New York: Cambridge University Press, 1989).

7. *Practical Machinist*, October 19, 1859, 11; *Practical Machinist*, November 2, 1859, 30; *Practical Machinist*, January 4, 1860, 98. All these are at the Hagley Museum and Library, Wilmington, Delaware. Not once from 1859 through 1860 did an article mention trade secrets or the enforceability of restrictive covenants.

8. John K. Brown, "When Machines Became Gray and Drawings Black and White: William Sellers and the Rationalization of Mechanical Engineering," 25 *Industrial Archaeology* 29, 40 (1999).

9. *Id.*

10. *Id.* at 42.

11. Vol. 2 of *Engineering*, December 1866, 448.

12. Vol. 3 of *Engineering: An Illustrated Weekly Journal*, January–June 1867, 543.

13. 53 Pa. 467 (1866).

14. 103 Mass. 73, 77 (1869).

15. 98 Mass. 452 (1868).

16. Peabody v. Norfolk, 98 Mass. 452, 460 (1868). Bill of Complaint, Peabody v. Norfolk, 98 Mass. 452 (1868). The pleadings in Peabody are in the Hagley Museum and Library, Wilmington, Delaware, Accession 1305, Box 771. A lawyer for the Du Pont company made copies of the Peabody pleadings when Du Pont was litigating a trade secret case against a former employee in the early twentieth century. I discuss the Du Pont litigation in chapter 6.

17. Demurrer, Peabody v. Norfolk, 98 Mass. 452 (1868), Hagley Museum and Library, Wilmington, Del., Accession 1305, Box 771. Points for James P. Cook, Peabody v. Norfolk, 98 Mass. 452 (1868).

18. 98 Mass. at 458.

19. *Id.* at 453.

20. James L. High, *A Treatise on the Law of Injunctions as Administered in the Courts of the United States and England* (Chicago: Callaghan, 1873), 408.

21. A. V. du Pont to Frederick Wright, November 2, 1847 (rejecting application for employment and describing company's policy against hiring outsiders); unknown to Charles McKinney, December 1843 (declining application for employment and describing company's policy not to hire those who have worked at other powder factories). These letters and other Du Pont materials discussed in this chapter are at the Hagley Museum and Library, Wilmington, Delaware, Longwood Manuscripts, Group 5, Series A, Boxes 1 and 2.

22. David A. Hounshell and John K. Smith Jr., *Science and Corporate Strategy: R & D at Du Pont, 1902–1980* (New York: Cambridge University Press, 1988), 38. On the prevalence of the acquisition of patents from independent inventors rather than from persons employed by the firm, see Naomi R. Lamoreaux and Kenneth L. Sokoloff, "Inventors, Firms, and the Market for Technology in the Late Nineteenth and Early Twentieth Centuries," in *Learning by Doing in Markets, Firms, and Countries*, ed. Naomi R. Lamoreaux, Daniel M. G. Raff, and Peter Temin (Chicago: University of Chicago Press, 1999); Naomi R. Lamoreaux and Kenneth L. Sokoloff, "Long-Term Change in the Organization of Inventive Activity," 93 *Proceedings of the National Academy of the Sciences of the United States of America* 12686, 12687–90 (1996).

23. Lammot du Pont made an extensive tour of European powder mills in 1858 for the sole purpose of learning the latest methods. Journal entry of Lammot du Pont (1858); Lammot du Pont to Mother, April 4, 1858, Group 5, Series A, Box 2. On American efforts to learn European technological innovations, and European efforts to resist that in the early nineteenth century, see "Transatlantic Industrial Espionage in the Early Nineteenth Century: Barriers and Penetrations," in Jeremy, *Artisans, Entrepreneurs and Machines*, chapter 7.

24. B. G. du Pont, *E. I. du Pont de Nemours and Company: A History, 1802–1902* (New York: Houghton Mifflin, 1920), 80.

25. Dutton, *Du Pont*.

26. See, e.g., Stone v. Goss, 55 A. 736 (N.J. 1903) (affirming an injunction against a chemist and his new employer against using plaintiff's secret formula for a depilatory, against using a process for making the depilatory that the chemist had developed while in the employ of the plaintiff, and against using any information derived from the employee with reference to the secret process).

27. See generally Scranton, *Endless Novelty*; Robert C. Allen, "Collective Invention," *Journal of Economic Behavior & Organization* 1, 1–10 (March 1983). The archives of the railroads (Accession 1520), Lukens Steel (Accession 50), and the mid-Atlantic machine and textile shops (Accessions 736 and 1178) are at the Hagley Museum and Library.

28. [1892] 2 Ch. 518, 523–24. Three years later, in Robb v. Green, [1895] 2 Q.B. 315, 317 (C.A.), Lord Esher applied the new concept of trade secret to customer list and stated that "in a contract of service the Court must imply such a stipulation as I have mentioned, because it is a thing which must necessarily have been in view of both parties when they entered into the contract."

29. 10 Ohio Decisions Reprint 84 (Super. Ct. 1887).

30. Alpheus T. Mason, *William Howard Taft, Chief Justice* (reprint, Lanham, Md.: University Press of America, 1983), 13.

31. "The Right of Private Property," 3 *Michigan Law Review* 215 (1894).

32. Cincinnati Bell, 10 Ohio Decisions Reprint 154, 157–58 (Super. Ct. 1887).

33. For example, in New Method Laundry Co. v. MacCann, 161 P. 990, 992 (Cal. 1916), the court refused to enjoin employee from collecting laundry for a company that competed with his former employer because an injunction would interfere with employee's liberty; the court insisted: "The laborer has the same right to sell his labor, and to contract with reference thereto, as any other property owner. . . ." Freedom of contract was invoked as a basis for upholding a covenant in Kellogg v. Larkin, 3 Pin. 123, 139 (Wis. 1851). The court explained that "while the avenues to enterprise are so multiplied, so tempting and so remunerative, giving to labor the greatest freedom for competition with capital, perhaps, that it has yet enjoyed, I question if we have much to fear from attempts to secure exclusive advantages in trade, or to reduce it to few hands."

34. 85 F. 271, 282 (6th Cir. 1898), modified, 175 U.S. 211 (1899).

35. Herbert Hovenkamp, *Enterprise and American Law, 1836–1937* (Cambridge, Mass.: Harvard University Press, 1991), 287.

36. John E. Hannigan, "The Implied Obligation of an Employee," 77 *University of Pennsylvania Law Review* 970, 978 (1929), lamented that the courts' emphasis on whether the knowledge constituted a trade secret "mislead[s] courts to adopt an inadequate test. . . . The essential question is: Has there been an abuse of confidence? If there has been, it is not necessary that the secret be a business secret."

37. Gilmore, *Death of Contract*, 98.

38. Ernst Homburg, "The Emergence of Research Laboratories in the Dyestuffs Industry, 1870–1900," 25 *British Journal for History of Science* 91, 110 (1992).

39. Scranton, *Figured Tapestry*, 24 n. 6.

40. Y.B. 2 Hen. 5, fol. 5, Michaelmas, pl. 26 (Eng. 1414).

41. Makepeace v. Jackson, 128 Eng. Rep. 534 (1813).

42. George T. Curtis, *A Treatise on the Law of Patents for Useful Inventions in the United States of America* (Boston: C. C. Little and J. Brown, 1849), 43 n. 1.

43. Scranton, *Figured Tapestry*, 200.

44. Dempsey v. Dobson, 174 Pa. 122, 130, 34 A. 459 (1896).

45. Dempsey v. Dobson, 184 Pa. 588, 593, 39 A. 493 (1898).

46. *Id.* at 593, citing Curtis, *Treatise on the Law of Patents* (1849 ed.), 43 n. 1.

47. William Blackstone, *Commentaries on the Law of England, (Blackstone's Commentaries)*, vol. 1; Andrea C. Loux, Note, "The Persistence of the Ancient Regime: Custom, Utility, and the Common Law in the Nineteenth Century," 79 *Cornell Law Review* 183 (1993).

48. Scranton, *Figured Tapestry*, 203.

49. Herold v. Herold China & Pottery Co., 257 F. 911, 917 (6th Cir. 1919) (dissolving injunction against former employee using or disclosing alleged trade secret methods of making, glazing, and firing pottery).

50. Cameron Mach. Co. v. Samuel M. Langston Co., 115 A. 212, 214 (N.J. Ch. 1921).

51. Salomon v. Hertz, 40 N.J. Eq. 400, 403 (1885).

52. Wood, *Treatise on the Law of Master and Servant*, 225.

53. National Tube Co. v. Eastern Tube Co., 3 Ohio C.C. (n.s.) 459, 460–61, 465 (Cir. Ct. 1902).

54. Pressed Steel Car Co. v. Standard Steel Car Co., 60 A. 4, 8–10 (Pa. 1904).

[279]

CHAPTER 4

1. Christian Schussle, *Men of Progress* (1863); Samuel Smiles, *Lives of the Engineers* (1863).

2. James Brooke-Smith, "Mediating Invention at the End of the Nineteenth Century," unpublished paper delivered at Con/Texts of Invention Conference, Case Western Reserve University, April 2006. See also Clare Pettitt, *Patent Inventions—Intellectual Property and the Victorian Novel* (New York: Oxford University Press, 2004).

3. Thomas P. Hughes, *American Genesis: A Century of Innovation and Technological Enthusiasm, 1870–1970* (New York: Viking, 1989), 19. John Rae, "The Application of Science to Industry," in *The Organization of Knowledge in Modern America, 1860–1920*, ed. Alexandra Oleson and John Voss (Baltimore: Johns Hopkins University Press, 1979), 250, observed: "The ingenious tinkerer enjoyed an astonishing longevity as an American folkhero, reaching an apex in fact in the twentieth century with Thomas A. Edison and Henry Ford—though Edison depended far more on a well-equipped laboratory and a scientifically trained staff than his popular image suggested."

4. R. S. Woodward, review of *Invention, the Master-key to Progress*, by Bradley A. Fiske, 27 *American Historical Review* 541, 542 (1922).

5. Roger Burlingame, *March of the Iron Men, a Social History of Union through Invention* (New York: C. Scribner's Sons, 1938). Examples of the hero-inventor genre include Holland Thompson, *The Age of Invention: A Chronicle of Mechanical Conquest* (New Haven, Conn.: Yale University Press, 1921). The nineteenth-century "heroic inventor" writing in England is described in Harold Irvin Dutton, *The Patent System and Inventive Activity*

during the Industrial Revolution, 1750–1852 (Manchester: Manchester University Press, 1984), 1–2 (citing Samuel Smiles, *Industrial Biography* [1863] and *Lives of the Engineers: Early Engineering* [1904]). More recent books in the same vein include Mitchell Wilson, *American Science and Invention, a Pictorial History: The Fabulous Story of How American Dreamers, Wizards, and Inspired Tinkerers Converted a Wilderness into the Wonder of the World* (New York: Simon & Schuster, 1954); Edmund Fuller, *Tinkerers and Genius: The Story of the Yankee Inventors* (New York: Hastings House, 1955). On the demise of the hero-inventor, see Roger Burlingame, *Inventors behind the Inventor* (New York: Harcourt, Brace, 1947), 3–4.

[280]

6. Frederick C. Dietz, review of *A History of Mechanical Inventions*, by Abbott Payton Usher, 35 *American Historical Review* 399, 399 (1930).

7. See, e.g., Bruce Catton, *The Civil War* (New York: Houghton Mifflin, 1987), 3; Kenneth C. Davis, *Don't Know Much about the Civil War: Everything You Need to Know about America's Greatest Conflict but Never Learned* (New York: William Morrow, 1996), 92. Even some of the contemporary revisionist accounts adhere to the individual genius paradigm; they just emphasize that the geniuses weren't all white men. See Anne L. Macdonald, *Feminine Ingenuity: Women and Invention in America* (New York: Ballantine Books, 1992), xx–xxiv (attributing a crucial idea for the cotton gin to Whitney's hostess, Catherine Greene); Portia P. James, *The Real McCoy: African-American Invention and Innovation, 1619–1930* (Washington, D.C.: Smithsonian Institution Press, 1989) (describing the many inventions of African Americans).

8. See S. C. Gilfillan, *The Sociology of Invention: An Essay on the Social Causes of Technic Invention and Some of Its Social Results; Especially as Demonstrated by the History of the Ship* (Chicago: Follett Publishing, 1935), 77–78. Indeed, the reaction against the hero-inventor thesis in favor of the view that technological change is entirely incremental has recently produced a counterreaction. Scholars have called for at least some attention to be paid to the contributions of particular persons. Joel Mokyr, *The Lever of Riches: Technological Creativity and Economic Progress* (New York: Oxford University Press, 1990), 12.

9. Useful historiographic essays on American technology include Thomas P. Hughes, "Emerging Themes in the History of Technology," 20 *Technology and Culture* 697 (1979); "The Historiography of American Technology," 11 *Technology and Culture* 1 (1969). A history that mixes the modern and the traditional ways of thinking about invention using the examples of the steamboat and the telegraph to explore the social and psychological nature of the inventive process is Brooke Hindle, *Emulation and Invention* (New York: New York University Press, 1981).

10. 74 U.S. 583, 585, 588 (1868).

11. Deposition of John Goulding, Supreme Court Record of Agawam v. Jordan, 342–43.

12. *Id.* at 354.

13. Deposition of Edward Winslow, Supreme Court Record of Agawam v. Jordan, 49; Second Deposition of Edward Winslow, *Id.*, 838.

14. Act of 1800, ch. 25, §4, cited in 16 U.S. (3 Wheat.) App. n. ii at 24 (1818) (a note on patent law written by Justice Story; see Craig Joyce, "The Rise of the Supreme Court

Reporter," 83 *Michigan Law Review* 1291, n. 267 [1985]). The Supreme Court held in Kinsman v. Parkhurst, 59 U.S. (18 How.) 289 (1855), that a patentee's agreement to assign an existing patent to another and then to manufacture the patented invention on behalf of the other and to share the profits from it was a valid contract not in restraint of trade. Contracts to assign future inventions were held enforceable, at least in connection with an assignment of an existing patent, in Littlefield v. Perry, 88 U.S. (21 Wall.) 205 (1874); see also Kinsman v. Parkhurst, 59 U.S. (18 How.) 289 (1855). [281]

15. Assignments were supposed to be in writing and to be recorded with the Patent Office within a specified time after the alleged assignment. There were limits on the types of interests that could be assigned. See Blanchard v. Eldridge, 1 Wall. Jr. C.C. 337, 3 F. Cas. 624 (C.C.E.D. Pa. 1849); Brooks v. Byam, 2 Story 525, 4 F. Cas. 261 (C.C.D. Mass. 1843); Gayler v. Wilder, 51 U.S. (10 How.) 477, 495 (1850); Potter v. Holland, 19 F. Cas. 1154 (C.C.D. Conn. 1858).

16. See, e.g., Burr v. De La Vergne, 102 N.Y. 415, 7 N.E. 366 (1886); Blakeney v. Goode, 30 Ohio St. 350 (1876).

17. Slemmer's Appeal, 58 Pa. 155, 166–67 (1868).

18. An earlier case, Joliet Mfg. Co. v. Dice, 105 Ill. 649, 651–52 (1883), had held that a contract requiring an employee to "work for the best interest of the company in every way that he can, and in whatever way such aid can be given shall belong to the company,—that is, improvements (previous to this date not included) that he may make or cause to be made" did not require assignment of a patent. The court discerned a "general rule" that "where a mechanic, in laboring for an employer in the construction of a machine, invents a valuable improvement, the invention is the property of the inventor and not that of his employer." Pointing out that the contract hired the employee in manufacturing "shellers and mowers," the court concluded that the employee's invention—a "check rower"—was not within the scope of the contract. On the growth of deliberate innovation in agricultural implements, see John Nader, "The Rise of an Inventive Profession: Learning Effects in the Midwestern Harvester Industry, 1850–90," 54 *Journal of Economic History* 397 (1994).

19. Bill of Complaint, Hapgood v. Hewitt, 119 U.S. 226 (1886), microformed on U.S. Supreme Court Records and Briefs, Part IV, number 261 (Info. Handling Serv.).

20. Hapgood v. Hewitt, 119 U.S. 226, 228, 229 (1886).

21. 11 F. 422, 424 (C.C.D. Ind. 1882).

22. 119 U.S. at 233.

23. Aspinwall Mfg. Co. v. Gill, 32 F. 697, 700 (C.C.D.N.J. 1887).

24. See, e.g., James L. High, *A Treatise on the Law of Injunctions: As Administered in the Courts of the United States and England* (Chicago: Callaghan, 1873), 1091–92, 1095; John N. Pomeroy, *Specific Performance of Contracts: As It Is Enforced by Courts of Equitable Jurisdiction in the United States of America*, 3d ed. (Albany, N.Y.: Banks & Company, 1926), §145; Roscoe Pound, "The Progress of the Law, 1918–1919, Equity," 33 *Harvard Law Review* 420, 433 (1920); Ham v. Johnson, 55 Minn. 115, 118, 56 N.W. 584, 585 (1893) (declining to specifically enforce an executory contract to convey land because the lots to be conveyed were not specifically described).

25. Hayes v. O'Brien, 149 Ill. 403, 37 N.E. 73, 76 (1894) (grants specific performance of contract to convey land); Work v. Welsh, 160 Ill. 468, 43 N.E. 719, 721 (1896) (same); Mudgett v. Clay, 5 Wash. 103, 31 P. 424, 426 (1892) (same).

[282]

26. Lester Agricultural Chemical Works v. Selby, 68 N.J. Eq. 271, 278, 59 A. 247, 250 (1904) (grants specific performance of contract to sell land; supplies missing price term by appraisal of market value); Lawson v. Mullinix, 104 Md. 156, 64 A. 938, 943 (1906) (grants specific performance of contract to convey land; supplies missing time for performance by saying reasonable time).

27. Slemmer's Appeal, 58 Pa. 155, 166 (1868); Eustis Manufacturing Co. v. Eustis, 27 A. 439, 441 (N.J. Ch. 1893).

28. Triumph Electric Co. v. Thullen, 225 F. 293, 297 (D.C.E.D. Pa. 1915) (refusing to order employee to assign patent to former employer); Joliet Manufacturing Co. v. Dice, 105 Ill. 649 (1883).

29. See Continental Windmill Co. v. Empire Windmill Co., 6 F. Cas. 366, 367 (C.C. D.N.Y. 1871); Wilkens v. Spafford, 29 F. Cas. 1242 (1878). In both cases, the court awarded the employer a license to use machines built by former employees; in neither case did the court order the former employee to assign the patent. The rulings would allow the employee to use and sell their inventions, but not to prevent their former employer from doing so.

30. See, e.g., Niagara Radiator Co. v. Meyers, 16 Misc. Rp. 593, 40 N.Y. Supp. 572, 574–75 (1896) (employee entitled to presumption of ownership of invention and employer ownership must be "clearly established" to rebut presumption).

31. Withington-Cooley Manufacturing Co. v. Kinney, 68 F. 500, 501–2 (6th Cir. 1895). Similarly, an Eighth Circuit decision from 1910 found that the director and business manager of a firm organized for the manufacture and sale of furnace grates who invented a furnace grate on the job was employed only generally and had not contracted to give his employer "the fruit of his inventive genius" and thus did not have to assign his patent to his employer. Johnson Furnace & Engineering Co. v. Western Furnace Co., 178 F. 819, 823 (8th Cir. 1910).

32. Jencks v. Langdon Mills, 27 F. 622, 624 (C.C.D.N.H. 1886). Another case from the same year also rejected the fairness notion of the shop right in favor of an implied obligation to allow the employer to use an invention that was developed on the job. American Tube-Works v. Bridgewater Iron Co., 26 F. 334, 335 (C.C.D. Mass. 1886).

33. Alfred D. Chandler Jr., *The Visible Hand: The Managerial Revolution in American Business* (Cambridge, Mass.: Harvard University Press, 1977), 120.

34. Steven W. Usselman, *Regulating Railroad Innovation: Business, Technology, and Politics in America, 1840–1920* (New York: Cambridge University Press, 2002), 63.

35. Chandler, *Visible Hand*, 187.

36. The Reading Railroad Archives are in the Hagley Museum and Library, Wilmington, Del., Accession 1520, boxes 14, 15, 55, 57, 64, 209, 246, 253, and 311. The biographical information on Wootten is drawn from James L. Holton, "John Wootten: Locomotive Pioneer," 44 *Historical Review of Berks County* 97, 98–99 (Summer 1979), and from the history of the Reading written by the archivists at the Hagley. On railroads' use of general managers and master mechanics, see Usselman, *Regulating Railroad Innovation*, 71.

37. Quoted in Holton, "John Wootten: Locomotive Pioneer," at 99. Wootten's work in developing the new firebox is described in Usselman, *Regulating Railroad Innovation*, 196–97.

38. A lawyer applied for a patent for C. G. Steffe, who was an employee of the office of the Engineer of Machinery. Steffe had been involved in measuring water use of Reading engines. See L. B. Paxson to J. E. Wooten, January 19, 1884.

39. E. A. Quintard to J. E. Wootten, July 14, 1878; C. Lindt, Frankfurt, Germany, to Wootten, March 4, 1879, said he read in the January 24 issue of *Engineering* an article on the Wootten locomotive displayed at the Paris exposition, seeking some photographs of the locomotive.

40. Usselman, *Regulating Railroad Innovation*, 197.

41. George R. Kaercher, general counsel, to Archibald A. McLeod, vice president and general manager, July 30, 1889 (Kaercher was the general counsel of the Reading from 1887 to 1890); J. E. Wootten to A. A. McLeod, August 10, 1889; A. A. McLeod to J. E. Wootten, December 6, 1889; J. E. Wootten to A. A. McLeod, December 7, 1889; Holton, "John Wootten: Locomotive Pioneer," 103.

42. An index of agreements and reports contained in two files covering the period 1878–97 contains no contracts with employees, though it contains references to things having to do with employees (e.g., "Examination of Conductors and Trainmen of the Phila. & Reading R.R.—Written Examination," or "Engineers and Architects—Schedule of Charges," or "Employes—Conference of Committee with Gen. Supt. Sweigard—December 27th 1886"). The bulk of the index was probably prepared at one time, as the handwriting and pen is uniform, but there were obviously additions over time. Probably some clerk went through the files and made the index so they would know what they had in the files and where it was filed, because there are numbers next to each entry. Among three surviving files of correspondence labeled as being from the company lawyers, J. D. Campbell, solicitor (1890–94), George R. Kaercher, general counsel (1887–90), and S. P. Wolverton, Sunbury, Pa., company lawyer (1888–89), there was nothing regarding employee intellectual property. One file contains draft employment contracts from 1893 for telegraph operators and train dispatchers, one for conductors and trainmen, and one for engineers and firemen. All appear to be proposed by the employees in negotiations. (They contained provisions requiring just cause for discharge.) But there were no contracts for the white-collar or technical employees.

Evidence of Reading lawyers advising on patents includes F. S. Stevens to A. A. McLeod, October 28, 1890; C. Heebner to A. A. McLeod, October 23, 1890; J. C. Fraley to C. Heebner, October 22, 1890.

43. Leonard S. Reich, *The Making of American Industrial Research: Science and Business at GE and Bell, 1876–1926* (Cambridge: Cambridge University Press, 1985), 28–29; Usselman, *Regulating Railroad Innovation*, 98.

44. Usselman, *Regulating Railroad Innovation*, 72–73.

45. *Id.* at 103 (quoting Minutes of the Pennsylvania Railroad Board of Directors from several dates in 1866 and 1867, all of which are available on microfilm at the Hagley).

46. Reich, *Making of American Industrial Research*, 28–29.

47. *Id.* at 189.

48. *Id.* at 208.

49. Chandler, *Visible Hand*, 188.

50. Holton, "John Wootten: Locomotive Pioneer," 103.

51. Usselman, *Regulating Railroad Innovation*, 104–5.

52. On engineers and the changing middle class in the late twentieth century, see Robert Zussman, *Mechanics of the Middle Class: Work and Politics among American Engineers* (Berkeley: University of California Press, 1985), 205–7. On the social status of engineers in the early nineteenth century, see David F. Noble, *America by Design: Science, Technology, and the Rise of Corporate Capitalism* (New York: Knopf, 1977), 35. On the evolving relationship between labor, management, and technical training and the effect of that relationship on the pace and direction of technical change in Western Europe, see David S. Landes, *The Unbound Prometheus: Technological Change and Industrial Development in Western Europe from 1750 to the Present* (New York: Cambridge University Press, 1969), 313–48.

53. The archives related to the Bonsack Company are in the Duke companies' archives in the Perkins Library, Duke University, Durham, North Carolina. Background on the Bonsack company is from Nannie M. Tilley, *The Bright Tobacco Industry, 1860–1929* (Chapel Hill: University of North Carolina Press, 1948), 570–72.

54. Hulse v. Bonsack, 65 F. 864, 866 (4th Cir. 1895).

55. Robert F. Durden, *The Dukes of Durham, 1860–1929* (Durham, N.C.: Duke University Press, 1975), 27–28; *Tobacco*, November 17, 1893, 4; Tilley, *Bright Tobacco Industry*, 573; J. B. Duke Testimony, February 25, 1908, United States v. American Tobacco Co., 3285, JBDP; J. B. Duke to D. B. Strouse, March 16, 1888; Patrick G. Porter, "Origins of the American Tobacco Company," 43 *Business History Review* 59, 68 (1969).

56. Samuel A. Ashe, "William Thomas O'Brien," in *A Biographical History of North Carolina*, ed. Samuel A. Ashe, (Greensboro, N.C.: Charles L. Van Noppen, 1906), 304–5; Tilley, *Bright Tobacco Industry*, 574; William K. Boyd, *The Story of Durham, City of the New South* (Durham, N.C.: Duke University Press, 1927), 89; Durden, *Dukes of Durham*, 27; See B. N. Duke to D. B. Strouse, June 6, 1886, JBDP; D. B. Strouse to W. Duke Sons & Co., August 11, 1887, JBDP; D. B. Strouse to W. Duke, Sons & Co., July 24, 1886, JBDP.

57. James B. Duke Testimony, February 27, 1908, United States v. American Tobacco Co., 3487–88, JBDP.

58. J. B. Duke to Strouse, May 21, 1885, JBDP; J. B. Duke to Strouse, April 20, 1889, JBDP; G. W. Watts to Strouse, April 10, 1889, JBDP (exclaiming that "we do not propose to educate hands for Mr. Kinney or Mr. Hulze [*sic*] or anybody else"); Hulse to Wright, January 22, 1894, RHWP (referring to Hulse's former days working for Bonsack at Kinney).

59. Wright v. Duke, 36 N.Y.S. 853, 854–55 (N.Y. Gen. Term 1895), cited in Tilley, *Bright Tobacco Industry*, 574–75. See also Durden, *Dukes of Durham*, 32; Porter, "Origins of the American Tobacco Company," 68 (citing Bonsack Machine Co. v. S. F. Hess, 68 F. 119, 125 [4th Cir. 1895]). The royalties were to be reduced to 20 cents per thousand once Duke started using machines on all of its cigarettes. Durden, *Dukes of Durham*, 45; J. B. Duke to Strouse, March 27, 1889, JBDP; Bonsack Machine Co. v. S. F. Hess, 68 F. 119, 130 (4th Cir. 1895).

60. Durden, *Dukes of Durham*, 37; J. B. Duke to Strouse, October 13, 1885, JBDP; J. B.

Duke to D. B. Strouse, January 21, 1888, JBDP; J. B. Duke to Strouse, March 20, 1889, JBDP; Porter, "Origins of the American Tobacco Company," 71–72; Theo E. Allen to Wright, July 15, 1891, RHWP. See also Hulse to Wright, October 3, 1892, RHWP; Strouse to J. B. Duke, November 22, 1889, JBDP; Strouse to J. B. Duke, November 25, 1889, JBDP.

61. J. B. Duke to D. B. Strouse, July 16, 1886, JBDP; Durden, *Dukes of Durham*, 37.

62. "Blow at Cigarette Trust," *Evening World*, March 12, 1895, RHWP. See also Bonsack Machine Co. v. Smith, 70 F. 383, 385 (C.C.W.D.N.C. 1895) (describing other companies' accusations that Bonsack and the American Tobacco Company brought frivolous patent infringement suits to unfairly squelch competition); Porter, "Origins of the American Tobacco Company"; Strouse to J. B. Duke, July 8, 1887; J. B. Duke to D. B. Strouse, July 19, 1887; D. B. Strouse to W. Duke, Sons & Co. and Allen & Ginter, February 8, 1888, JBDP; Durden, *Dukes of Durham*, 45; Strouse to J. B. Duke, May 4, 1888, JBDP; J. B. Duke to Strouse, December 12, 1889, JBDP.

63. Jim Wise, "A Man with Big Ideas: Visionary Richard Harvey Wright Invented a Company That Sent Products to the Moon," *Durham* (N.C.) *Herald-Sun*, January 18, 2004, E1; Durden, *Dukes of Durham*, 19, 28, 50–54; Wright v. Duke, 36 N.Y.S. 853, 854–55 (N.Y. Gen. Term 1895); Wright-Guerrant contract, February 9, 1889; A. & G. Cameron to Wright, February 6, 1889, RHWP; H. H. Benedict to Wright, February 8, 1889; Smith Premier Typewriter Co. to F. B. Lewis, January 19, 1892; Yale & Towne Mfg. Co. to Wright, December 7, 1894, RHWP.

64. See Wright-Bonsack contract, December 12, 1888, §§1–2, RHWP; Durden, *Dukes of Durham*, 41; J. B. Duke to Strouse, March 20, 1889, JBDP, quoted in Durden, *Dukes of Durham*, 41. See W. C. Seddon & Co. to Wright, December 18, 1888, RHWP; Theo E. Allen to Wright, September 20, 1890, RHWP; Duncan to Wright, August 5, 1892, RHWP; W. G. Mathews to Wright, January 3, 1895, RHWP.

65. Wright to Strouse, April 29, 1889, RHWP; Wright to Strouse, September 20, 1892, RHWP; G. W. Argabrite to Wright, September 19, 1889, RHWP; Strouse to Wright, September 21, 1889, RHWP; Strouse to Morgan, July 8, 1890, RHWP; Hulse to Wright, July 20, 1890, RHWP; Hulse to Wright, July 20, 1890, RHWP; Hulse to Wright, July 27, 1890, RHWP; Hulse to Wright, August 5, 1890, RHWP; Hulse to Wright, August 9, 1890, RHWP.

66. Mustard & Co. to Wright, July 8, 1890. Wright wanted Mustard & Co. to agree not to reproduce any of the machines that were sent to them, but one of their managers expressed concern about this, due to the possibility that the American Tobacco Company would convince Bonsack to revoke Wright's exclusive agency. Mustard & Co. to R. H. Wright, June 26, 1890, RHWP. There were also continuing annoyances in the United States from possible competing machines. Joseph A. Bonsack to R. H. Wright, July 18, 1890, RHWP (calling the Hardee-Elliotte and Ludington machines "*undoubtedly* infringements on patents" of the Bonsack Company, but advising Wright that "you want to get your matters in the East consummated at the earliest possible day"). Hulse to Wright, August 18, 1890, RHWP; Hulse to Wright, November 2, 1890, RHWP.

67. Hulse to Wright, November 20, 1890, RHWP; Hulse to Wright, 1891, RHWP; Hulse to Wright, June 19, 1891, RHWP; Hulse to Wright, February 27, 1891, RHWP.

68. Hulse to Wright, July 30, 1891, RHWP; Hulse to Wright, February 4, 1892, RHWP.

69. Hulse to Wright, August 14, 1891, RHWP; Wright-Hulse contract, August 20, 1891, RHWP; Hulse to Wright, August 27, 1891, RHWP.

70. Hulse to Wright, August 27, 1891, RHWP.

71. Hulse v. Bonsack, 65 F. at 865–66.

72. J. B. Duke to Josephus Plenty, January 3, 1900, RHWP.

73. See Duncan to Wright, September 22, 1894; Hulse to Wright, September 25, 1894; Hulse to Wright, November 20, 1890, RHWP; Bonsack v. Hulse, 57 F. 519, 522 (C.C.W.D. Va. 1893); Hulse v. Bonsack, 65 F. at 865.

74. Hulse to Wright, August 27, 1891, RHWP; Hulse to Wright, September 30, 1891, RHWP; Hulse to Wright, October 2, 1891, RHWP; Hulse to Wright, November 14, 1891, RHWP; Hulse to Wright, November 21, 1891, RHWP; Hulse to Wright, January 14, 1892, RHWP; Strouse to Wright, June 27, 1891, RHWP; Krise to Wright, November 12, 1891, RHWP; Duncan to Wright, March 16, 1892, RHWP; Duncan to Wright, November 12, 1891, RHWP; Duncan to Hulse, January 30, 1892, RHWP.

75. Hulse to Wright, November 29, 1891, RHWP; Duncan to Wright, February 2, 1892, RHWP; Hulse to Wright, January 14, 1892, RHWP; Hulse to Wright, January 29, 1892, RHWP; Duncan to Wright, February 2, 1892, RHWP; P. S. Bowles to Wright, January 30, 1892, RHWP; Hulse to Wright, February 4, 1892, RHWP.

76. Hulse to Wright, February 4, 1892, RHWP; Duncan to Wright, March 16, 1892, RHWP; Hulse to Wright, March 23, 1892, RHWP; Hulse to Wright, March 30, 1892, RHWP; Hulse to Wright, March 23, 1892, RHWP; Goff to Busbee, January 10, 1893, RHWP.

77. Hulse to Wright, March 30, 1892, RHWP.

78. See Duncan to Wright, April 11, 1892, RHWP; Duncan to Wright, August 5, 1892, RHWP.

79. Hulse to Wright, April 5, 1892, RHWP; Hulse to Wright, April 7, 1892, RHWP; Hulse to Wright, May 6, 1892, RHWP; Allen to Wright, April 26, 1892, RHWP; Busbee to Wright, July 16, 1892, RHWP; Hulse v. Bonsack, 65 F. at 865.

80. Busbee to Wright, July 11, 1892, RHWP; Duncan to Wright, July 12, 1892, RHWP; Busbee to Wright, July 15, 1892, RHWP.

81. Busbee to Wright, August 1, 1892, RHWP; Wright to Strouse, September 20, 1892, RHWP; Hulse to Wright, September 21, 1892, RHWP; Strouse to Wright, February 7, 1893, RHWP.

82. Duncan to Wright, September 22, 1894, RHWP; Duncan to Wright, October 14, 1892, RHWP; Hulse to Wright, September 21, 1892, RHWP; Duncan to Wright, October 20, 1892, RHWP; Busbee to Goff, July 11, 1893, RHWP; Duncan to Wright, July 17, 1893, RHWP; Busbee to Wright, September 9, 1893, RHWP; Busbee to Wright, December 10, 1893, RHWP.

83. See Strouse to Wright, February 7, 1893, RHWP; Busbee to Wright, February 9, 1893, RHWP; Busbee to Wright, February 13, 1893, RHWP; Busbee to Wright, February 20, 1893, RHWP; Busbee to Wright, February 25, 1893, RHWP.

84. Busbee to Wright, February 9, 1893, RHWP; Busbee to Wright, February 13, 1893,

RHWP; Busbee to Wright, February 20, 1893, RHWP; Busbee to Wright, March 4, 1893, RHWP; Busbee to Wright, July 7, 1893, RHWP; Bonsack v. Hulse, 57 F. at 522.

85. Bonsack v. Hulse, 57 F. at 522; Allen to Wright, August 8, 1893, RHWP.

86. See Busbee to Wright, August 16, 1893, RHWP; Hulse to Wright, December 7, 1893, RHWP; Busbee to Wright, December 3, 1893, RHWP; Hulse to Wright, December 7, 1893, RHWP; Hulse to Wright, December 10, 1893, RHWP; settlement contract, February 4, 1895, RHWP. See Hulse v. Bonsack, 65 F. at 865.

87. Hulse to Wright, August 7, 1893, RHWP; Busbee to Wright, December 8, 1893, RHWP; Burroughs to Busbee, December 11, 1893, RHWP; Hulse power of attorney declaration, April 24, 1894, RHWP.

88. See Hulse to Busbee, March 8, 1895, RHWP; Allen to Wright, September 18, 1894, RHWP; Busbee to Wright, October 8, 1894, RHWP; Wills to Wright, May 2, 1894, RHWP; Bonsack-Wills contract, May 5, 1894, RHWP; Bonsack-Wills contract, May 15, 1894, RHWP; Wills to Wright, May 2, 1894, RHWP; Bonsack-Wills contract, May 5, 1894, RHWP; Bonsack-Wills contract, May 15, 1894, RHWP. A Transvaal patent was issued for Butler's crimper. W. D. & H. O. Wills, Ltd. accepted this, but made sure to assert their right to Hulse's device as well. W. D. & H. O. Wills, Ltd. to Wright, February 28, 1895, RHWP; Serrell to Wright, July 24, 1894, RHWP; Serrell to Wright, October 24, 1894, RHWP.

89. Settlement contract, February 4, 1895, RHWP; Bonsack-Wright-Allen contract, February 4, 1895, RHWP.

90. Hulse v. Bonsack, 65 F. at 870; Busbee to Wright, February 6, 1895, RHWP ("I do not know why the court decided to file their opinion after my telegram. It may be that Gen. Duncan wired them to deliver the opinion if it was in favor of the Company, in order to have a good effect upon subsequent cases; and if your settlement with the Company was complete, I do not object to this").

91. Hulse v. Bonsack, 65 F. at 868.

92. Id.

93. Walker to Wright, February 12, 1895, RHWP; Strouse to Wright, September 30, 1895, RHWP; Wright to American Trading Co., March 16, 1896, RHWP; Strouse to Wright, September 30, 1895, RHWP; Strouse to Wright, October 11, 1895, RHWP; Strouse to Wright, October 28, 1895, RHWP; Strouse to Wright, October 28, 1895, RHWP; Wright to American Trading Co., March 16, 1896, RHWP.

94. Hulse to Wright, May 9, 1893, RHWP; Hulse to Wright, May 25, 1893, RHWP; Hulse to Wright, December 10, 1893, RHWP; Hulse to Wright, August 2, 1894, RHWP; Hulse to Wright, August 16, 1894, RHWP; Hulse to Wright, December 5, 1894, RHWP; Hulse to Wright, January 28, 1895, RHWP; Hulse to Wright, June 2, 1893, RHWP; Hulse to Wright, January 15, 1894, RHWP; Hulse to Wright, September 17, 1894, RHWP (reporting that he has acquired machines at two Richmond factories in "good running order, and the boys verry [sic] well trained to handle them"); E. O. Shelby Tobacco Co. to G. W. Moore, RHWP; Otto C. Schneider to G. W. Moore, April 19, 1894, RHWP; Wellman & Dwire Tobacco Co. to Wright, August 1, 1894, RHWP; S. W. Venable Tobacco Co. to Wright, October 3, 1894, RHWP; S. W. Venable to W. C. Seddon, January 18, 1895, RHWP; Schneider to Wright, February 18, 1895, RHWP.

95. Hulse to Wright, January 17, 1894, RHWP.

96. Hulse to Wright, January 22, 1894, RHWP.

CHAPTER 5

1. See generally Richard Fawkes, *Dion Boucicault* (New York: Quartet Books, 1979); Robert G. Hogan, *Dion Boucicault* (New York: Twayne Publishers, 1969).

2. The numbers were Shakespeare, 2,314; Boucicault, 1,587; Tom Taylor, 934; J. B. Buckstone, 839; John Brougham, 829; and J. M. Morton, 652. Bruce A. McConachie, *Melodramatic Formations: American Theatre and Society, 1820–1870* (Iowa City: University of Iowa Press, 1992), 241.

3. 11 Stat. 138 (1856).

4. Hogan, *Dion Boucicault*, 33 (quoting Dion Boucicault, "The Decline of the Drama," 125 *North American Review* 243 [September 1877]).

5. Among them was Laura Keene, who was said by others to prefer European plays because she could get them for free. Tice L. Miller, "The Image of Fashionable Society in American Comedy, 1840–1870," in *When They Weren't Doing Shakespeare: Essays on Nineteenth-Century British and American Theatre*, ed. Judith L. Fisher and Stephen Watt (Athens: University of Georgia Press, 1989), 244.

6. Dion Boucicault, "The Octoroon," in *Selected Plays by Dion Boucicault*, ed. Andrew Parkin (Washington, D.C.: Catholic University of America Press, 1987), 135–90. On Boucicault's effort to appeal to a wide American audience in the play, see James Hurt, "Dion Boucicault's Comic Myths," in *When They Weren't Doing Shakespeare*, 255.

7. Hogan, *Dion Boucicault*, 40; Mary C. Crawford, *The Romance of the American Theatre* (Boston: Little, Brown, 1913), 369.

8. Roberts v. Myers, 20 F. Cas. 898, 899 (C.C.D. Mass. 1860); Boucicault v. Fox, 3 F. Cas. 977 (C.C.S.D.N.Y. 1862) (No. 1691).

9. Roberts v. Myers, 20 F. Cas. at 899.

10. Boucicault v. Fox, 3 F. Cas. at 980.

11. On the many uses of parental rights metaphors to justify copyrights, see Mark Rose, *Authors and Owners: The Invention of Copyright* (Cambridge, Mass.: Harvard University Press, 1993).

12. De Witt v. Brooks, 7 F. Cas. 575 (C.C.S.D.N.Y. 1861). The report in Federal Cases contains only the headnotes. The report of the decision in Copyright Decisions contains the declarations of the plaintiff and the defendants filed in the case and a note indicating that the opinion of the court has been lost. De Witt v. Brooks, 13 Copyright Decisions 756.

13. 14 F. Cas. 180 (C.C.E.D. Pa. 1861); Tom Taylor, *Our American Cousin: The Play That Changed History*, ed. Welford D. Taylor (Washington, D.C.: Beacham Publishing, 1990).

14. 14 F. Cas. at 182–83.

15. Vernanne Bryan, *Laura Keene: A British Actress on the American Stage, 1826–1873* (Jefferson, N.C.: McFarland & Company, 1993), 136–42. An interesting coincidence is that Lincoln saw the play on the closing night at Ford's Theater; the play scheduled to

open the next night was *The Octoroon*. See Taylor, *Our American Cousin*, 30 (showing a photograph of Ford's Theater draped in black following the assassination, and in the foreground a billboard announcing *The Octoroon*, which was scheduled to open). The enormous popularity of both plays makes the coincidence not improbable. Boucicault and Keene had also collaborated on other projects. He wrote the famous play *The Colleen Bawn* for her, which premiered in March 1860. Crawford, *Romance of the American Theatre*, 370–71.

16. Joseph Jefferson, *The Autobiography of Joseph Jefferson* (New York: Century Company, 1889), 193–94. On Keene's contribution, see Bryan, *Laura Keene*, 83.

17. Bryan, *Laura Keene*, 83, 115–16.

18. *Id.* at 81.

19. *Id.* at 83–84 (quoting *Frank Leslie's Illustrated Newspaper*, March 5, 1859).

20. See Crawford, *Romance of the American Theatre*, 334.

21. *Id.* at 327–33.

22. Bryan, *Laura Keene*, 84 (quoting Jefferson, *Autobiography*, 194).

23. 14 F. Cas. at 185, 187.

24. Under today's copyright law, the copyright in the original play might prevent Keene from obtaining any legal right in her adaptation because the original copyright would encompass adaptations as "derivative works." At the time, there was no concept of a copyright extending to a derivative work. Copyright protection was extended to derivative works in 1870 after a notorious case in which Harriet Beecher Stowe discovered she had no rights in a German translation of *Uncle Tom's Cabin*.

25. Keene v. Clark, 2 Abb. Pr. (n.s.) 341 (N.Y. Sup. Ct. 1867). In Keene v. Clark, Keene sought to prove that her entitlement to *Our American Cousin* had been conclusively determined by the prior judgment in Keene v. Wheatley. The trial court refused to consider the decree in the prior case, but on appeal the Superior Court held that the trial court should have examined the effect of the prior judgment. The Superior Court thus remanded for a trial at which Keene would prevail if she could prove the following: that she had not printed or otherwise dedicated to the public the manuscript to her version of *Our American Cousin*, and that Clark had obtained a copy of it from a "surreptitious source" and intended to produce it in New York. *Id.* at 341. Neither the published opinion nor Keene's biography indicates what happened after the Superior Court sent the case back for trial. Presumably it settled, though on what terms remains unknown.

26. On Edwin Booth's life and relationship to John Wilkes Booth, see Crawford, *Romance of the American Theatre*, chap. 13.

27. Bryan, *Laura Keene*, 144–45 (quoting Ben G. Henneke, *Laura Keene, A Biography* [1990], 222–23).

28. *Id.* at 145.

29. 14 F. Cas. at 188.

30. See 14 F. Cas. at 186–87 (citing Makepeace v. Jackson, 4 Taunt. 770, and Lumley v. Wagner, 42 Eng. Rep. 687 [Ch. 1852]).

31. 15 F. Cas. 26 (C.C.D. Mass. 1869).

32. Charles F. Adams, vol. 2 of *Richard Henry Dana: A Biography* (New York: Houghton Mifflin, 1891), 283–84. See also "Note to Article V: Mr. Dana's Notes on Wheaton's

Elements of International Law," *North American Review* 626 (October 1866); "Affairs in Massachusetts," *New York Times*, September 30, 1867, 8.

33. Adams, *Richard Henry Dana*, 285–88. The memorandum said that "Mr. Lawrence will write to Mr. Brockhaus, in terms to bring to Mrs. Wheaton the right to draw on Mr. Brockhaus at once for 6,000 francs. He will also endeavor to get from Mr. Brockhaus as much as he can towards the actual expense of having the French translation made here. . . . On the payment of her draft on B., Mrs. Wheaton will agree formally to make no use of Mr. Lawrence's notes in a new edition without his written consent, and Mrs. Wheaton will give to Mr. Lawrence the right to make any use he wishes of his notes." *Id.* at 287. For a review of the French edition, see "Commentaire sur les Elements du Droit International et sur l'Histoire des Progres du Droit des Gens de Henry Wheaton," *American Law Review* 409 (June 1881), 288. On November 2, 1863, Lawrence closed the correspondence on the matter in a letter stating that he declined to accept "any paper whatever from Mrs. Wheaton."

34. Adams, *Richard Henry Dana*, 284; "Breach of Copyright: The Important Case of Lawrence v. Dana," *New York Times*, September 22, 1869, 5; "Note to Article V," 626–27.

35. Adams, *Richard Henry Dana*, 289. See also "Breach of Copyright," 5 (stating that Dana undertook the project "for the express purpose of superseding the labors of his predecessor, which were stated to have been seriously unsatisfactory, to have injured the original work, and to be, in many matters concerning the rebellion in our own country, disloyal and obnoxious to Northern sentiment").

36. Adams, *Richard Henry Dana*, 292, 310–12, 417; "Elements of International Law," *American Law Review* 185 (October 1866) (book review).

37. See "Note to Article V," 627. See also *id.* at 628 (quoting a large excerpt from Lawrence's letter to *New York Evening Post*, August 22, 1866).

38. "Breach of Copyright."

39. See "A Literary Controversy: An Interesting Case of Alleged Plagiarism," *New York Times*, November 2, 1866, 8; "Affairs in Massachusetts," *New York Times*, September 30, 1867, 8; "Affairs in Massachusetts," *New York Times*, October 23, 1867, 2; "Affairs in Massachusetts," *New York Times*, November 13, 1867, 2; Adams, *Richard Henry Dana*, 325–26, 394–95; 15 F. Cas. at 46–51, 63.

40. See Rochelle C. Dreyfuss, "Collaborative Research: Conflicts on Authorship, Ownership, and Accountability," 53 *Vanderbilt Law Review* 1162, 1172–79 (2000). John F. Witt has argued that uncertain default rules enhance the ability of employers to use express contracts to their preferred results. See John F. Witt, "Rethinking the Nineteenth-Century Employment Contract, Again," 18 *Law & History Review* 627, 654–56 (2000).

41. The issue arose recently in Thompson v. Larson, 147 F.3d 195 (2d Cir. 1998), a dispute between a dramaturg and the heirs of the playwright of *Rent*, the successful Broadway musical of the 1990s. There was no clear agreement about allocation of the copyright and compensation. The case and the issue are discussed extensively in Paulette S. Fox, Note, "Preserving the Collaborative Spirit of American Theater: The Need for a 'Joint Authorship Default Rule' in Light of the *Rent* Decision's Unanswered Question,"

19 *Cardozo Arts & Entertainment Law Journal* 497 (2001); see also Seth F. Gorman, "Who Owns the Movies? Joint Authorship under the Copyright Act of 1976 after *Childress v. Taylor* and *Thompson v. Larson*," 7 *UCLA Entertainment Law Review* 1 (1999); Jane C. Lee, Comment, "Upstaging the Playwright: The Joint Authorship Entanglement between Dramaturgs and Playwrights," 19 *Loyola of Los Angeles Entertainment Law Review* 75 (1998).

42. 14 F. Cas. at 186–87 (citing Makepeace v. Jackson, 4 Taunt. 770 and Lumley v. Wagner, 42 Eng. Rep. 687 [Ch. 1852]).

43. Percy MacKaye, vol. 1 of *Epoch: The Life of Steele MacKaye, Genius of the Theatre, in Relation to His Times and Contemporaries* (New York: Boni & Liveright, 1927), 200, 228, 232–33, 277, 282, 297–99, 301, 303, 307–8, and 377 (quoting a letter from MacKaye to W. R. Alger regarding his plans, an article in the *Daily Graphic* to describe MacKaye's innovations in theater, and an interview with MacKaye in the *New York Tribune*, January 12, 1881, regarding MacKaye's views on Mallory). The author is Steele MacKaye's son, and the biography clearly favors his father's side of the dispute. For a very brief summary of Steele MacKaye's career, see Wayne S. Turney, "James Steele MacKaye (1842–94)," ⟨http://www.wayneturney.20m.com/mackayesteele.htm⟩. See also Rev. G. S. Mallory's *Death, New York Times*, March 3, 1897, 12.

44. MacKaye, *Epoch*, 367.

45. *Id.* at 313–16, 369–72.

46. *Id.* at 316, 323–24, 347, 396, app. at xl. See also "The Madison-Square Theatre: Mr. MacKaye's Improvements in the Stage Mechanism," *New York Times*, February 1, 1880, 5; Mallory v. MacKaye, 86 F. 122, 123 (C.C.S.D.N.Y. 1898).

47. MacKaye, *Epoch*, 340 (quoting *Spirit of the Times*, February 4, 1880: "Not to have seen the Madison Square Theatre is to be behind the age in theatrical intelligence and artistic knowledge"); *id.* at 342–43 (quoting a "New York despatch" to the *New Orleans Picayune*, February 5, 1880: "The double elevator-stage, invented by Steele MacKaye, is one of the wonders of the century, and perhaps marks the beginning of a new stage era"). "Movable Theatre Stages," *Scientific American*, April 5, 1884, 207–8. However, MacKaye's obituary in *New York Times* called the double stage "preposterous" and the "bane of stage managers." "Founder of Two Theatres," *New York Times*, February 26, 1894, 1. See also "The Success of Hazel Kirke," *New York Times*, October 11, 1881, 4.

48. MacKaye, *Epoch*, 346–47, 359, 362–65. See also *id.* at 376 (quoting MacKaye's interview in *New York Tribune*, January 12, 1981: "Thousands and thousands of dollars were made for the Mallorys, and the enterprise was firmly established. But no profit and little credit were given to me by the owners"). See also "Joseph Hatton's Reading," *New York Times*, October 17, 1880, 2; "Amusements," *New York Times*, May 11, 1880, 5; "General Mention," *New York Times*, March 30, 1881, 5; "Plans for the Poe Entertainment," *New York Times*, January 27, 1881, 8 ("A message was received from the Messrs. Mallory, of the Madison-Square Theatre, asking that credit for anything that theatre might do be not given to Mr. Steele MacKaye, but to the theatre"); "Plays and Actors," *New York Times*, March 20, 1881, 7 ("Mr. Steele MacKaye announces that his connection with the Madison-Square Theatre has permanently ceased. The result of his lawsuit against the Messrs. Mallory will not affect his determination to labor hereafter entirely

for himself"); Mallory v. MacKaye, 86 F. at 123; "Hazel Kirke in the Courts," *New York Times*, September 18, 1881, 9.

49. MacKaye, *Epoch*, 385 (quoting from an article May 7, 1881 in an unspecified publication).

50. *Id.* at 418–20; MacKaye v. Mallory, 6 F. at 746; MacKaye v. Mallory, 12 F. 328 (C.C.S.D.N.Y. 1882). See also "Hazel Kirke in the Courts," *New York Times*, September 18, 1881, 9; "Hazel Kirke in the Court," *New York Times*, April 15, 1882, 8.

51. See *The Critic*, January 15, 1881, 8 ("Mr. MacKaye unquestionably has the sympathy of the public and of 'the profession' in his quarrel with the Messrs. Mallory. . . ."); MacKaye, *Epoch*, 375–79 ("'Profits for Parsons' and 'Fraternal Speculators' soon became by-words in the press with reference to 'the religio-dramatic firm of Mallory Bros.'"); MacKaye, *Epoch*, 377 (quoting *Springfield Republican*, January 16, 1881: "The whole business is saddening—that two churchmen should have repeated the oft-told story, ground down a struggling mortal to the dust, and grown rich out of his brains").

52. MacKaye, *Epoch*, 378–79 (quoting *New York Dramatic News*, January 15, 1881, and *Chicago Tribune*).

53. *Id.* at 379 (quoting *The Continent*).

54. MacKaye v. Mallory, 12 F. at 330. See also MacKaye, *Epoch*, 418–20.

55. 12 F. at 330.

56. MacKaye, *Epoch*, 458–60, 470–76; Stephen Fiske, "Dramatic Feuilleton," *Art Amateur*, April 1885, 99. MacKaye's first folding theater chairs were installed at the Union Square theater, but received mixed reviews. See Stephen Fiske, "Dramatic Feuilleton," *Art Amateur*, January 1884, 27; "The Religious Editor: He Tries Steele MacKaye's New Patent Theatre Chair, and Don't Like It," *National Police Gazette*, December 22, 1883, 6. On the competition, see Stephen Fiske, "Dramatic Feuilleton," *Art Amateur*, October 1884, 94 ("No matter which of them makes the more money, both are sure to benefit the profession and the public"); MacKaye, *Epoch*, 468 (quoting the *Morning Journal*, August 28, 1884: "The Mallorys, who are two pretty sharp and cunning little Christians, are growing panicky at the growing importance of the new Lyceum Theatre, as a rival of the Madison Square, of which the original genius was Steele MacKaye. The result appears to be a war of the Red and the White Roses").

57. MacKaye v. Mallory, 79 F. 1, 1 (2d Cir. 1897); MacKaye v. Mallory, 80 F. 256 (C.C.S.D.N.Y. 1897); Mallory v. MacKaye, 86 F. at 123; MacKaye, *Epoch*, 375, 386.

58. The Berne Convention, a treaty obligating signatory nations to extend protection through their domestic copyright law to copyrighted foreign works, came into force in 1886, but the United States did not become a signatory to it until 1989.

59. 27 F. 861, 863 (C.C.D. Mass. 1886); Andrew Goodman, *Gilbert and Sullivan at Law* (Rutherford, N.J.: Fairleigh Dickinson University Press, 1983), 203–7; Arthur Lawrence, *Sir Arthur Sullivan: Life-Story, Letters, and Reminiscences* (London: James Bowden, 1899), 127–30, 136.

60. 27 F. at 862, 864–65; "'The Mikado' Again in Court," *New York Times*, January 31, 1886, 1; "D'Oyly Carte and Mr. Evans," *New York Times*, February 17, 1886, 1.

61. Goodman, *Gilbert and Sullivan at Law*, 206, 211–13; Lawrence, *Sir Arthur Sullivan*, 140.

62. Lumley v. Wagner, 42 Eng. Rep. 687, 693 (Ch.) (1852).

63. Lumley v. Gye, 118 Eng. Rep. 749, 755 (Q.B.) (1853). [293]

64. See generally Marc Linder, *The Employment Relationship in Anglo-American Law: A Historical Perspective* (Westport, Conn.: Greenwood Press, 1989), 70–74; John Nockleby, Note, "Tortious Interference with Contractual Relations in the Nineteenth Century: The Transformation of Property, Contract, and Tort," 93 *Harvard Law Review* 1510 (1980); C. B. Labatt, "Enticement and Harboring of Servants," in vol. 7 of *Commentaries on the Law of Master and Servant, Including the Modern Laws on Workmen's Compensation, Arbitration, Employer's Liability, etc.*, 2d ed. (Rochester, N.Y.: Lawyers Co-operative Publishing Company, 1913), 8015–94; Horace Gay Wood, *A Treatise on the Law of Master and Servant: Covering the Relation, Duties and Liabilities of Employers and Employees* (San Francisco: Bancroft-Whitney, 1886), 452–65.

65. See Lea S. VanderVelde, "The Gendered Origins of the *Lumley* Doctrine: Binding Men's Consciences and Women's Fidelity," 101 *Yale Law Journal* 775, 793 (1992); Linder, *Employment Relationship in Anglo-American Law*. See generally Robert J. Steinfeld, *The Invention of Free Labor: The Employment Relation in English and American Law and Culture, 1350–1870* (Chapel Hill: University of North Carolina Press, 1991), chapter 6 (on indentured servitude in the antebellum United States).

66. Butler v. Galletti, 21 How. Pr. 465, 465 (N.Y. Sup. Ct. 1861).

67. Ford v. Jermon, Phila. Reports 6 (Phila. Ch. 1865).

68. Some courts determined that the existence of a liquidated damages clause in the contract was a sufficient remedy. Hahn v. The Concordia Society of Baltimore, 42 Md. 460, 466 (1875); Mapleson v. Del Puente, 13 Abb. N. Cas. 144 (N.Y. Sup. Ct. 1883).

69. Cholmondeley v. Clinton, 34 Eng. Rep. 515 (1815); Yovatt v. Winyard, 37 Eng. Rep. 425 (Ex. Ch.) (1820).

70. Joseph Story, *Commentaries on Equity Jurisprudence*, vol. 1 (1836), 121.

71. See Steinfeld, *Invention of Free Labor*; Amy Dru Stanley, *From Bondage to Contract: Wage Labor, Marriage, and the Market in the Age of Slave Emancipation* (New York: Cambridge University Press, 1998).

72. Salter v. Howard, 43 Ga. 601 (1871); Bryan v. State, 44 Ga. 328 (1871); Hudson v. State, 46 Ga. 624 (1872); Lee v. West, 47 Ga. 311 (1872); Barron v. Collins, 49 Ga. 580 (1873); Tucker v. State, 86 Ark. 436, 111 S.W. 275 (1908); Haskins v. Royster, 70 N.C. 601 (1874); Langham v. State, 55 Ala. 114 (1876); Jones v. Stanly, 76 N.C. 355 (1877); Morgan v. Smith, 77 N.C. 37 (1877); Huff v. Watkins, 15 S.C. 82 (1881); Dickson v. Dickson, 33 La. Ann. 1261 (Louisiana 1881); Chambers & Marshall v. Baldwin, 91 Ky. 121, 15 S.W. 57 (1891); Duckett v. Pool, 34 S.C. 311, 13 S.E. 542 (1891); Armistead v. Chatters, 71 Miss. 509, 15 So. 39 (1893); State v. Aye, 63 S.C. 458, 41 S.E. 519 (1902); Hudgens v. State, 126 Ga. 639, 55 S.E. 492 (1906); Bright v. State, 4 Ga. App. 333, 61 S.E. 289 (Ga. App. 1908); Johns v. Patterson, 138 Ark. 420, 211 S.W. 387 (1919); Rhoden v. State, 161 Ga. 73, 129 S.E. 640 (1925); Schilling v. State, 143 Miss. 709, 109 So. 737 (1926); Hill v. Duckworth, 155 Miss. 484, 124 So. 641 (1929).

73. See VanderVelde, "Gendered Origins." McCaull v. Braham, 16 F. 37 (C.C.S.D.N.Y. 1883) (Lillian Russell enjoined from performing in any theater other than the plaintiff's); Hammerstein v. Sylva, 66 Misc. 550, 124 N.Y.S. 535 (1910) (singer enjoined from singing for any other manager).

74. Hayes v. Willio, 11 Abb. Pr. (N.S.) 167, 176 (N.Y. Common Pl. 1871).

75. Cort v. Lassard, 18 Ore. 221, 225, 22 P. 1054, 1056 (1889).

76. Carter v. Ferguson, 12 N.Y.S. 580, 581 (N.Y. Sup. Ct. 1890).

77. Schubert v. Angeles, 80 N.Y.S. 146, 147 (App. Div. 1903).

78. Winter Garden Co. v. Smith, 282 F. 166, 170 (2d Cir. 1922). The New York Supreme Court found a comedian's talents unique and granted an injunction based largely on a string of quotations from reviews of his shows from newspapers. Harry Hastings Attractions v. Howard, 196 N.Y.S. 228 (Sup. Ct. 1922).

79. Hammerstein v. Mann, 122 N.Y.S. 276, 278 (N.Y. App. 1910); see also Ziegfeld v. Norworth, 118 N.Y.S. 1151 (1909) ("the defendant was the real star around whom the whole production of the plaintiff's play centered, and that she had been heavily featured in announcements and advertisements, so as to give her chief prominence").

80. 202 Pa. 210, 215, 217, 51 A. 973, 974 (1902).

81. "'Twere all one That I should love a bright particular star, And think to wed it." Shakespeare, *All's Well That Ends Well*, 1.1.98.

82. Hammerstein v. Sylva, 66 Misc. 550, 557, 124 N.Y.S. 535 (1910) (quoting Edwards v. Fitzgerald [no cite]).

83. Bourlier Bros. v. Macauley, 91 Ky. 135, 140–41, 15 S.W. 60, 61 (1891).

84. *Id.* at 141–42, 15 S.W. at 61.

85. *Id.* at 140, 15 S.W. at 61.

86. *Id.*

87. *Id.* at 141, 15 S.W. at 61.

88. Although courts characterized talent as a valuable commodity, they did not always recognize the need for actors to control their contracts in order to protect their reputation, voice, or health, and would deny performers the right to buy their way out of their contracts if they disagreed with the performers' assessments of their own needs. See McCaull v. Braham, 16 F. 37 (C.C.S.D.N.Y. 1883); Comstock v. Lopokowa, 190 F. 599, 601 (C.C.S.D.N.Y. 1911).

89. Metropolitan Exhibition Co. v. Ward, 9 N.Y.S. 779, 783 (Sup. Ct. 1890); Philadelphia Ball Club v. Hallman, 8 Pa. C.C. 57 (Com. Pl. 1890).

90. 20 Ill. App. 50, 51 (1886).

91. *Id.* at 59.

92. The William Rogers Manufacturing. Co. v. Rogers, 20 A. 467, 468, 469 (Conn. 1890). In the same year, a New York trial court refused to treat the abilities of a lithographer as unique talent. In Strobridge Lithographic Co. v. Crane, which was later cited by many courts in cases of this sort, the court explained that "even with regard to the higher branches of the art [of lithography and design], there was nothing uncommon in the defendant's qualifications. He is simply a talented and rising young member of the guild of lithographic sketchers. His name adds no special value to the good work he

does." 12 N.Y.S. 898, 899 (Sup. Ct. 1890). Other cases finding white-collar work to be not unique include Burney v. Ryle, 91 Ga. 701, 17 S.E. 986 (Ga. 1893) (insurance agent); Geo. A. Kessler & Co. v. Chappelle, 77 N.Y.S. 285 (App. Div. 1902) (champagne salesman); E. Jaccard Jewelry Co. v. O'Brien, 70 Mo. App. 432 (1897) (jewelry salesman). Cases citing Strobridge as authority to deny an injunction include W. J. Johnston Co. v. Hunt, 66 Hun. 504 (Gen. Term 1892).

93. H. W. Gossard Co. v. Crosby, 132 Iowa 155, 109 N.W. 483 (1906); Rosenstein v. Zentz, 118 Md. 564, 85 A. 675 (1912).

94. Sternberg v. O'Brien, 22 A. 348, 350–51 (N.J. Eq. 1891).

95. 165 U.S. 578 (1897).

96. Rabinovich v. Reith, 120 Ill. App. 409, 417 (1905).

97. Crosby, 109 N.W. at 488–89, 491.

98. 72 N.W. 140, 144 (Mich. 1897).

99. 165 N.Y.S. 367 (Sup. Ct. 1917).

100. Taylor Iron & Steel Co. v. Nichols, 65 A. 695, 702 (N.J. Ch. 1907), rev'd, 69 A. 186, 188 (N.J. 1908).

101. H. B. Wiggins Sons' Co. v. Cott-A-Lap Co., 169 F. 150, 151–52 (D. Conn. 1909).

102. 147 N.Y.S. 579 (App. Div. 1914).

103. 69 N.Y.S. 813 (Sup. Ct. 1901).

PART III

1. M. Owen Fiss, *Troubled Beginnings of the Modern State, 1888–1910* (New York: Macmillan, 1993). The cases are Lochner v. New York, 198 U.S. 45 (1905); Plessy v. Ferguson, 163 U.S. 537 (1896); In re Debs, 158 U.S. 564 (1895); Loewe v. Lawlor, 208 U.S. 274 (1908); Adair v. United States, 208 U.S. 161 (1908). The Insular Cases are Downes v. Bidwell, 182 U.S. 244 (1901); Hawaii v. Mankichi, 190 U.S. 197 (1903); Dorr v. United States, 195 U.S. 138 (1904); Balzac v. Porto Rico, 258 U.S. 298 (1922). The Chinese Exclusion Cases are Chae Chan Ping v. United States, 130 U.S. 581 (1889); Chew Heong v. United States, 112 U.S. 536 (1884); United States v. Jung Ah Lung, 124 U.S. 621 (1888); Fong Yue Ting v. United States, 149 U.S. 698 (1893).

2. Morton J. Horwitz, *The Transformation of American Law, 1870–1960: The Crisis of Legal Orthodoxy* (New York: Oxford University Press, 1992), 4, 77–79. I am indebted to Stephen Siegel for pointing this out to me.

3. Arnold M. Paul, *Conservative Crisis and the Rule of Law: Attitudes of Bar and Bench, 1887–1895* (Gloucester, Mass.: Peter Smith, 1976), 1–2, notes the anxiety of "small businessmen," "professional and white-collar people" that the "traditional fluidity of American society" and "individual opportunity" were fast disappearing in the face of corporate consolidation, the accumulation of great wealth among the few, and the growing disparity between rich and poor.

4. Daniel J. Walkowitz, *Working with Class: Social Workers and the Politics of Middle-Class Identity* (Chapel Hill: University of North Carolina Press, 1999).

5. Charles W. McCurdy, "The Roots of 'Liberty of Contract' Reconsidered: Major Prem-

ises in the Law of Employment, 1867–1937," *Supreme Court Historical Society Yearbook* (1984), 27, 33.

6. Little v. Gallus, 38 N.Y.S. 487, 489–90 (N.Y. App. Div. 1896). See also Empire Steam Laundry v. Lozier, 130 P. 1180, 1182 (Cal. 1913) ("equity always protects against the unwarranted disclosure and unconscionable use of trade secrets"); Westervelt v. Nat'l Paper & Supply Co., 57 N.E. 552, 554 (Ind. 1900) (the employer's "machine was a secret, and, under the facts alleged, even if no agreement was made, one would be implied, that [the employee] was not to disclose the secret of the construction of the machine"); Aronson v. Orlov, 116 N.E. 951, 952–53 (Mass. 1917) (equity requires implied contract); O. & W. Thum Co. v. Tloczynski, 72 N.W. 140, 144 (Mich. 1897); MacBeth-Evans Glass Co. v. Schnelbach, 86 A. 688, 693 (Pa. 1913) (implied duty not to disclose); Stevens & Co. v. Stiles, 71 A. 802, 806 (R.I. 1909) (not necessary that there be an express contract).

7. On the development of consumer culture, see generally Richard W. Fox and T. J. Jackson Lears, *The Culture of Consumption: Critical Essays in American History, 1880–1980* (New York: Pantheon, 1983); Simon J. Bronner, *Consuming Visions: Accumulation and Display of Goods in America, 1880–1920* (New York: Norton, 1989); Thomas Richards, *The Commodity Culture of Victorian England: Advertising and Spectacle, 1851–1914* (Stanford, Calif.: Stanford University Press, 1990); T. J. Jackson Lears, *Fables of Abundance: A Cultural History of Advertising in America* (New York: Basic Books, 1994); William Leach, *Land of Desire: Merchants, Power, and the Rise of A New American Culture* (New York: Pantheon, 1993); John Frow, *Time and Commodity Culture: Essays on Cultural Theory and Postmodernity* (New York: Oxford University Press, 1997); Don Slater, *Consumer Culture and Modernity* (Malden, Mass.: Blackwell, 1997).

CHAPTER 6

1. Stuart M. Blumin, *The Emergence of the Middle Class: Social Experience in the American City, 1760–1900* (New York: Cambridge University Press, 1989), 258–97; Sanford M. Jacoby, *Employing Bureaucracy: Managers, Unions, and the Transformation of Work in American Industry, 1900–1945* (New York: Columbia University Press, 1985), 279.

2. Alfred D. Chandler Jr., *The Visible Hand: The Managerial Revolution in American Business* (Cambridge, Mass.: Harvard University Press, 1977); James W. Hurst, *The Legitimacy of the Business Corporation in the Law of the United States, 1780–1970* (Charlottesville: University of Virginia Press, 1970).

3. Vegelahn v. Guntner, 167 Mass. 92, 108, 44 N.E. 1077, 1081 (1896) (Holmes, J., dissenting).

4. Christopher L. Tomlins, *The State and the Unions: Labor Relations, Law, and the Organized Labor Movement in America, 1880–1960* (New York: Cambridge University Press, 1985).

5. William D. Haywood and Frank Bohn, *Industrial Socialism* (Chicago: Charles H. Kerr, n.d.), 25. This quote is found in David Montgomery, *Workers' Control in America: Studies in the History of Work, Technology, and Labor Struggles* (New York: Cambridge University Press, 1979), 9. On Haywood, his involvement in radical unionism of the

early twentieth century, and the Wobblies, see Joseph R. Conlin, *Big Bill Haywood and the Radical Union Movement* (Syracuse: Syracuse University Press, 1969); Melvin Dubofsky, *"Big Bill" Haywood* (Manchester 1987).

6. Frederick W. Taylor, *The Principles of Scientific Management* (New York: Norton, 1967), 31–32 (emphasis removed).

7. Jacoby, *Employing Bureaucracy*, 48. On scientific management, see Robert Kanigel, *The One Best Way: Frederick Taylor and the Enigma of Efficiency* (New York: Viking, 1997); Samuel Haber, *Efficiency and Uplift: Scientific Management in the Progressive Era, 1890–1920* (Chicago: University of Chicago Press, 1964).

8. See David Hounshell, *From the American System to Mass Production, 1800–1932: The Development of Manufacturing Technology in the United States* (Baltimore: Johns Hopkins University Press, 1984); Joseph Schumpeter, *The Theory of Economic Development: An Inquiry into Profits, Capital, Credit, Interest, and the Business Cycle*, translated by Redvers Opie (Cambridge, Mass.: Harvard University Press, 1934); Joseph A. Schumpeter, *Capitalism, Socialism, and Democracy*, 3d ed. (New York: Harper & Row, 1950); Philip Scranton, *Endless Novelty: Specialty Production and American Industrialization, 1865–1925* (1997); Steven W. Usselman, *Regulating Railroad Innovation: Business, Technology, and Politics in America, 1840–1920* (New York: Cambridge University Press, 2002); Catherine L. Fisk, "Removing the 'Fuel of Interest' from the 'Fire of Genius': Law and the Employee-Inventor, 1830–1930," 65 *University of Chicago Law Review* 1127 (1998); Catherine L. Fisk, "Working Knowledge: Trade Secrets, Restrictive Covenants in Employment, and the Rise of Corporate Intellectual Property, 1800–1920," 52 *Hastings Law Journal* 441 (2001).

9. 35 U.S.C. §118, enacted in 1952 as P.L. 593, 66 Stat. 800, allows a corporation to whom the inventor has assigned his patent rights to apply for a patent if the inventor himself declines to do so. See American Cyanamid Co. v. Ladd, 225 F. Supp. 709 (D.D.C. 1964).

10. David Noble, *America by Design: Science, Technology, and the Rise of Corporate Capitalism* (New York: Knopf, 1977), 87.

11. Naomi R. Lamoreaux and Kenneth L. Sokoloff, "Inventors, Firms and the Market for Technology in the Late Nineteenth and Early Twentieth Centuries," in *Learning by Doing in Markets, Firms, and Countries*, ed. Naomi R. Lamoreaux, Daniel M. G. Raff, and Peter Temin (Chicago: University of Chicago Press, 1999).

12. See John Rae, "The Application of Science to Industry," in *The Organization of Knowledge in Modern America, 1860–1920*, ed. Alexandra Oleson and John Voss (Baltimore: Johns Hopkins University Press, 1979), 258–65. See generally Elizabeth Brayer, *George Eastman: A Biography* (Baltimore: Johns Hopkins University Press, 1996) (on the founder of the Eastman Kodak Company and the firm); Ronald P. Kline, *Steinmetz: Engineer and Socialist* (Baltimore: Johns Hopkins University Press, 1992).

13. See Louis Galambos, "The American Economy and the Reorganization of the Sources of Knowledge," in *The Organization of Knowledge in Modern America, 1860–1920*, ed. Alexandra Oleson and John Voss, 269–82 (Baltimore: Johns Hopkins University Press, 1979); David A. Hounshell and John K. Smith Jr., *Science and Corporate Strategy: Du Pont R & D, 1902–1980* (New York: Cambridge University Press, 1988); Lamoreaux and

Sokoloff, "Inventors, Firms, and the Market for Technology"; Noble, *America by Design*; Leonard S. Reich, *The Making of American Industrial Research: Science and Business at GE and Bell, 1876–1926* (Cambridge: Cambridge University Press, 1985).

14. Christine MacLeod, "Negotiating the Rewards of Invention: The Shop-Floor Inventor in Victorian Britain," 41 *Business History* 17 (1999).

15. See Kline, *Steinmetz: Engineer and Socialist*; Charles P. Steinmetz, *America and the New Epoch* (New York: Harper & Bros., 1916).

16. Joseph Rossman, *The Psychology of the Inventor: A Study of the Patentee* (Washington, D.C.: Inventors Publishing Company, 1931).

17. See, e.g., George Wise, *Willis R. Whitney, General Electric, and the Origins of U.S. Industrial Research* (New York: Columbia University Press, 1985); Margaret B. W. Graham and Bettye H. Pruitt, *R&D for Industry: A Century of Technical Innovation at Alcoa* (New York: Cambridge University Press, 1990); Reich, *Making of American Industrial Research*; Hounshell and Smith, *Science and Corporate Strategy*; David A. Hounshell, "Interpreting the History of Industrial Research and Development: The Case of E. I. du Pont de Nemours & Co.," 134 *Proceedings of the American Philosophical Society* 387 (1990); Lamoreaux, Raff, and Temin, *Learning by Doing in Markets, Firms, and Countries*; Lamoreaux and Sokoloff, "Inventors, Firms, and the Market," 21; David C. Mowery and Nathan Rosenberg, *Technology and the Pursuit of Economic Growth* (New York: Cambridge University Press 1989); David C. Mowery and Nathan Rosenberg, *Paths of Innovation: Technological Change in Twentieth-Century America* (New York: Cambridge University Press, 1998).

18. Dwight B. Cheever, "The Rights of Employer and Employee to Inventions Made by Either during the Relationship," 1 *Michigan Law Review* 384, 384–85 (1903).

19. National Wire Bound Box Co. v. Healy, 189 F. 49, 55, 56 (7th Cir. 1911).

20. *Id.* at 55.

21. 239 Mass. 158, 131 N.E. 307, 308 (1921). Courts still occasionally insisted upon the rights of the inventive employee as entrepreneur. For example, in a 1911 decision involving an improved light bulb invented by employees of General Electric's research labs, although the opinion paid great attention to the size and sophistication of the GE lab, the judge nevertheless held that the former employee was entitled to the patent because GE's chemists initially dismissed the employee's idea as impractical and refused to apply for a patent on it. Ladoff v. Dempster, 36 App. D.C. 520, 531 (1911).

22. The contract between the parties and Peck's affidavit describing their relationship are in the Supreme Court record of the case, Standard Parts Co. v. Peck, 264 U.S. 52 (1924), which is available on microfilm.

23. Peck v. Standard Parts Co., 282 F. at 444–45.

24. Motion by Plaintiff for Rehearing, January 4, 1921, Supreme Court Record at 20.

25. Peck v. Standard Parts Co., 295 F. 740, 745 (N.D. Ohio 1920).

26. Peck v. Standard Parts Co., 282 F. at 453, 446.

27. Standard Parts Co. v. Peck, 264 U.S. 52, 60 (1924).

28. Hapgood v. Hewitt, 119 U.S. 226, 229 (1886).

29. 264 U.S. at 60.

30. Answer, Record in Supreme Court at 6.

31. 264 U.S. at 60.

32. On Ford, see Hounshell, *From the American System to Mass Production*, chapter 6, and Douglas Brinkley, *Wheels for the World: Henry Ford, His Company, and Century of Progress, 1903–2003* (New York: Viking, 2003).

33. United States v. Dubilier Condenser Co., 289 U.S. 178, 187–89 (1933); Direct Examination of John Dellinger, Record of United States v. Dubilier Condenser Co., 50. The rule articulated in *Dubilier* remains the law regarding employee inventions. See Henry C. Workman, "Rights of Employers and Employees in Inventions Made by the Latter," 20 *American Bar Association Journal* 538, 538–40 (1934); New Jersey: Crowe v. M&M/Mars, 577 A.2d 1278, 1280 (N.J. 1990); Kinkade v. New York Shipbuilding Corp., 21 N.J. 362, 122 A.2d 360, 365 (1956); New York: Eenkhoorn v. New York Telephone Co., 130 Mis.2d 744, 497 N.Y.Supp.2d 303, 304 (N.Y. City Ct. 1986); California: Banner Metals, Inc. v. Lockwood, 178 Cal. App.2d 643, 3 Cal. Rptr. 421, 432 (1960); Colorado: Hewett v. Samsonite Corp., 32 Colo. App. 150, 507 P.2d 1119, 1122 (1973); Illinois: Velsicol Corp. v. Hyman, 338 Ill. App. 52, 87 N.E.2d 35, 42 (1949); Pennsylvania: Aetna-Standard Engineering Co. v. Rowland, 343 Pa.Super. 64, 493 A.2d 1375, 1382 (1985); Ohio: Gemco Engineering & Mfg. Co. v. Henderson, 151 Ohio St. 95, 84 N.E.2d 596, 600 (1949).

34. See David Lange, "At Play in the Fields of the Word: Copyright and the Construction of Authorship in the Post-Literate Millennium," 55 *Law & Contemporary Problems* 139, 149 (1992) ("the requirements of human existence will not suffer the author to die").

35. See Lon L. Fuller, *Legal Fictions* (Stanford, Calif.: Stanford University Press, 1967), 67–68.

36. Blumin, *Emergence of the Middle Class*.

37. 20 N.Y.S. 110 (Sup. Ct. 1892).

38. Carl W. Ackerman, *George Eastman* (New York: Houghton Mifflin Company, 1930), 46–55; Brayer, *George Eastman*, 43–44.

39. Brayer, *George Eastman*, 49; Reese V. Jenkins, *Images and Enterprise: Technology and the American Photographic Industry, 1839 to 1925* (Baltimore: Johns Hopkins University Press, 1975), 221; Walter Clark, "Charles Edward Kenneth Mees, 1882–1960," 7 *Biographical Memoirs of Fellows of the Royal Society* 173, 186 (1961); "Eastman Kodak Says Ex-Employee Leaked Trade Secrets to 3M," *Wall Street Journal*, November 21, 1997, 1.

40. Ackerman, *George Eastman*, 55–62; Brayer, *George Eastman*, 69–76. The company history is also recounted on the Kodak website at ⟨http://www.kodak.com/global/en/corp/historyofkodak/1878.jhtml⟩.

41. Brayer, *George Eastman*, 82, 89; Ackerman, *George Eastman*, 89–90.

42. Eastman Co. v. Reichenbach, 20 N.Y.S. at 112, 113.

43. Brayer *George Eastman*, 89–91, 188; Ackerman, *George Eastman*, 90–94 and n. 2 (quoting a 1909 letter from Eastman to Reichenbach declining to hire him).

44. Brayer, *George Eastman*, 103.

45. *Id.*, 94.

46. *Id.*, 45, 50–51; Ackerman, *George Eastman*, 69–72.

47. Ackerman, *George Eastman*, 73 (quoting a letter from George Eastman to J. B. Church in which Eastman said, "The truth is they beat us by superior generalship"); Brayer, *George Eastman*, 51–52.

48. Jenkins, *Images and Enterprise*, 162, 229; Ackerman, *George Eastman*, 199; Brayer, *George Eastman*, 162.

49. John J. Beer, "Coal Tar Dye Manufacture and the Origins of the Modern Industrial Research Laboratory," 49 *Isis* 123, 124–25, 129 (1958).

50. Jenkins, *Images and Enterprise*, 305–7; Brayer, *George Eastman*, 221–22; C. E. Kenneth Mees, "The Organization of Industrial Scientific Research," 97 *Nature* 411, 431 (1916).

51. Mees, "Organization of Industrial Scientific Research," 432.

52. T. H. James, *A Biography-Autobiography of C. E. Kenneth Mees: Pioneer of Industrial Research* (1990), 51 (quoting George Eastman to Mees, February 5, 1912).

53. *Id.* at 73–74; Jenkins, *Images and Enterprise*, 312.

54. C. E. Kenneth Mees, "Secrecy and Industrial Research," 170 *Nature* 972 (1952).

55. C. E. Kenneth Mees, "A Photographic Research Laboratory," 5 *Scientific Monthly* 481, 484–85 (1917); Mees, "Organization of Industrial Scientific Research," 431; Clark, "Charles Edward Kenneth Mees," 181.

56. Jenkins, *Images and Enterprise*, 186 (quoting Eastman to Senier, October 5, 1901, and Eastman to H. L. Quigley, October 20, 1905).

57. James, *Biography-Autobiography of Mees*, 72–73.

58. Jenkins, *Images and Enterprise*, 226–33; James, *Biography-Autobiography of Mees*, 72–73; Brayer, *George Eastman*, 395.

59. Ackerman, *George Eastman*, 199–200.

60. Jenkins, *Images and Enterprise*, 322; Blake McKelvey, *Rochester: The Quest for Quality, 1890–1925* (Cambridge, Mass.: Harvard University Press, 1956), 344.

61. Eastman Kodak Co. v. Powers Film Products, Inc., 179 N.Y.S. 325, 330 (App. Div. 1919).

62. Chandler, *Visible Hand*, 417; Alfred D. Chandler Jr. and Stephen Salsbury, *Pierre S. du Pont and the Making of the Modern Corporation* (New York: Harper & Row, 1971), 47–120.

63. Chandler, *Visible Hand*, 438.

64. Chandler and Salsbury, *Pierre S. du Pont*, 56, 74–78.

65. Chandler, *Visible Hand*, 439.

66. *Id.* at 417.

67. On the development of organized R & D at Du Pont, see Hounshell and Smith, *Science and Corporate Strategy*, and Hounshell, "Interpreting the History of Industrial Research and Development," 387.

68. W. B. Lewis to T. W. Bacchus, October 15, 1904; Lewis to Bacchus, November 1, 1904, Acc 518, Box 1004, File 15; Minutes of Meeting no. 6 of Superintendents, April 6, 1905; Minutes of Meeting no. 11 of Superintendents, September 7, 1905. These and all other twentieth-century materials are from the DPA: Du Pont Records; Vice Presidential Files; Hamilton Barksdale Papers, Accession 518, Box 1004, File 15; or in Accession 1305, Boxes 679, 680, 772, or 773, or in Irenee du Pont Papers, Accession 228, Series H, Box 40, Files F-ID-42.

69. Ernest du Pont to H. M. Barksdale, June 18, 1913; Agreement of October 22, 1906, between Ernest du Pont and E. I. du Pont Company. Other copies of the contract

and correspondence relating to it include R. Mudge to E. Prindle, June 24, 1914, and Affidavit of Charles Reese, E. I. du Pont de Nemours Powder Co. v. Masland, Exhibits A & D; H. M. Barksdale to Ernest du Pont, June 19, 1913; Alexis I. du Pont to Ernest du Pont, June 20, 1913.

70. Exhibit B to Affidavit of Charles Reese, E. I. du Pont de Nemours Powder Co. v. Masland, 216 F. 271 (E.D. Pa. 1914).

71. A. J. Moxham and J. A. Haskell to Executive Committee, February 9, 1911. On the role of the Executive Committee in running the Du Pont Company during this era, see Chandler, *Visible Hand*, 443–45, and Chandler and Salsbury, *Pierre S. du Pont*, 125–37.

72. Kanigel, *One Best Way*, 298–301.

73. A. J. Moxham and J. A. Haskell to Executive Committee, February 9, 1911.

74. *Id.*; Chandler and Salsbury, *Pierre S. du Pont*, 129.

75. L. R. Beardslee, Secretary to Du Pont Executive Committee, to J. A. Haskell, A. J. Moxham, and H. M. Barksdale, April 14, 1911 (reporting on actions of Executive Committee of April 12, 1911).

76. Executive Committee Matters Awaiting Attention. The Executive Committee periodically sent Barksdale reminders that the Executive Committee awaited his report. L. R. Beardslee to H. M. Barksdale, February 16, 1912. L. R. Beardslee to H. M. Barksdale, June 12, 1912. An Extract from Minutes of Executive Committee, February 13, 1912, was received in Barksdale's office on February 6, 1914. February 16, 1912. Chandler and Salsbury, *Pierre S. du Pont*, 308.

77. Chemical Dept. to I. du Pont, March 2, 1915, Chemical Dept. to I. du Pont, January 14, 1915. C. Reese to Legal Department, April 7, 1915.

78. R. B. Price to I. du Pont, December 16, 1913; C. Reese to R. B. Price, December 19, 1913.

79. A. J. Moxham to H. M. Barksdale, July 19, 1912; H. M Barksdale to A. J. Moxham, July 22, 1912; Affidavit of Walter Masland, E. I du Pont de Nemours Powder Co. v. Masland, 216 F. 271 (E.D. Pa. 1914). Chandler and Salsbury, *Pierre S. du Pont*, 135–37; Chandler, *Visible Hand*, 444; Jacoby, *Employing Bureaucracy*, 52 (U.S. Steel adopted a stock bonus plan in 1903 to reward employees who were loyal to the company).

80. H. M. Barksdale to Manufacturing and Sales Committee, July 17, 1912; L. R. Beardslee to C. L. Reese, July 31, 1912.

81. Noble, *America by Design*, 119.

82. E. I. du Pont de Nemours Powder Co. v. Masland, 244 U.S. 100 (1917). The record of the litigation is available on Supreme Court Records microfilm, as well as in the Hagley Museum and Library in Wilmington, Delaware; citations here are to the archives at the Hagley.

83. (Second) Affidavit of Walter Masland, E. I. du Pont de Nemours Powder Co. v. Masland; Charles Reese to William Whitten. Du Pont's acquisition of Fabrikoid and its work on artificial leather is described in Hounshell and Smith, *Science and Corporate Strategy*, 68–71. The description of Reese is from Hounshell and Smith, *Science and Corporate Strategy*, 26 (quoting an article on Reese written by one of Du Pont's dye chemists and published in the *Dictionary of American Biography*).

84. Charles Reese to William Whitten.

85. Edwin Prindle to E. I. du Pont de Nemours Powder Co. Chemical Department, June 4, 1914.

86. E. I. du Pont de Nemours Powder Co. v. Masland, 216 F. 271 (E.D. Pa. 1914), 222 F. 340 (E.D. Pa. 1915); E. I. du Pont de Nemours Powder Co. v. Masland, 244 U.S. 100 (1917).

87. 244 U.S. at 103.

88. Edwin J. Prindle, *Patents as a Factor in Manufacturing* (published as part of the Works Management Library of *Engineering Magazine*, printed by the Waverly Press, Baltimore, 1908).

89. Edwin J. Prindle, "Patents as a Factor in a Manufacturing Business," 32 *Engineering Magazine* 407, 415 (October 1906).

90. *Id.* at 415–16.

91. Wise, *Willis R. Whitney*, 71.

92. Prindle, *Patents as a Factor in Manufacturing*.

93. *Id.*

94. R. Mudge to Edwin Prindle, June 22, 1914.

95. Irenee du Pont Papers.

96. Irving Klein to Edwin Prindle; E. R. Hughes to Edwin Hammer.

97. J. Laffey to Prindle, Wright, & Small.

98. Hounshell and Smith, *Science and Corporate Strategy*, 69–70.

99. Nancy M. West, *Kodak and the Lens of Nostalgia* (Charlottesville: University Press of Virginia, 2000). A history of the Eastman Kodak company contains the following "publisher's note" that identifies the company's ambiguous position with regard to intellectual property rights:

"Before modern trademark laws developed, many companies, including the Eastman Kodak Company, used trademarks and names creatively but not necessarily wisely. At the time, usage such as 'Take a Kodak with you' or 'Kodak as you go' was permitted in advertisements and marketing releases. Some examples of this usage are mentioned in this book for historical reference only.

"As correct usage legally became clearer, the Eastman Kodak Company moved to protect its trademarks vigorously and without loss of rights. All Kodak trademarks are now managed with great care and guarded with the appropriate attention."

Douglas Collins, *The Story of Kodak* (New York: Harry N. Abrams, 1990), 8 (publisher's note).

100. See, e.g., Westervelt v. National Paper & Supply Co., 57 N.E. 552, 553 (Ind. 1900) (issuing an injunction against defendant's use of plaintiff's trade secret paper-bag machine where defendant hired plaintiff's former employee to design a paper-bag folding machine similar to the one the employee had designed for the plaintiff); Pressed Steel Car Co. v. Standard Steel Car Co., 60 A. 4, 10 (Pa. 1904).

101. See, e.g., Hackett, 62 N.Y.S. at 1078; Witkop & Holmes Co. v. Boyce, 112 N.Y.S. 874, 878 (Sup. Ct. 1908).

102. See, e.g., Stone v. Goss, 55 A. 736, 737 (N.J. 1903) ("The secret consisted in a knowledge of the proper method of mixing the ingredients").

103. Board of Trade v. Christie Grain & Stock Co., 198 U.S. 236, 250 (1905); F. W. Dodge Co. v. Construction Information Co., 66 N.E. 204, 205 (Mass. 1903).

104. The Restatement (Second) of Agency §396 (1958) articulated the memory rule for trade secret protection, with an ambiguous qualifier at the end. The agent cannot, after the termination of agency, use "trade secrets, written lists of names, or other similar confidential matters. . . . The agent is entitled to use general information concerning the method of business of his principal and the names of the customers retained in his memory, if not acquired in violation of his duty as agent." Cases holding that employees should be free to use information committed to memory, so long as it was not copied and memorized surreptitiously, include Hamilton Manufacturing Co. v. Tubbs Manufacturing Co., 216 F. 401, 408 (C.C.W.D. Mich. 1908); Fulton Grand Laundry Co. v. Johnson, 117 A. 753 (Md. 1922); Grand Union Tea Co. v. Dodds, 128 N.W. 1090, 1091 (Mich. 1910); Boosing v. Dorman, 103 N.E. 1121 (N.Y. 1913); S. W. Scott & Co. v. Scott, 174 N.Y.S. 583, 586–87 (App. Div. 1919); Peerless Pattern Co. v. Pictorial Review Co., 132 N.Y.S. 37, 39 (App. Div. 1911); Stevens & Co. v. Stiles, 71 A. 802, 802 (R.I. 1909).

105. Some courts protected employer customer lists and other information regardless of whether the information had been surreptitiously copied. Empire Steam Laundry v. Lozier, 130 P. 1180, 1183 (Cal. 1913); Wireless Specialty Apparatus Co. v. Mica Condenser Co., 131 N.E. 307, 310 (Mass. 1921); Hackett v. A. L. & J. J. Reynolds Co., 62 N.Y.S. 1076, 1078 (App. Term. 1900).

106. Recent examples of using findings of fact to make significant choices about the extent to which firms should be able to control employee mobility include Hoskins Manufacturing Co. v. PMC Corp., 47 F. Supp. 2d 852 (E.D. Mich. 1999) (cable manufacturer failed to prove that former employees who worked for competing firm would inevitably disclose or use trade secrets rather than general knowledge); Utah Medical Products, Inc. v. Clinical Innovations Associates, Inc., 79 F. Supp. 2d 1290 (D. Utah 1999) (medical device manufacturer failed to prove that former executives who started competing firm used trade secrets rather than general knowledge in designing and marketing a competing product); Microbiological Research Corporation v. Muna, 625 P.2d 690, 699 (Utah 1981).

[303]

CHAPTER 7

1. See Ernst Freund, *The Legal Nature of Corporations* (Chicago: University of Chicago Press, 1897); Seymour Thompson, *Commentaries on the Law of Private Corporations* (San Francisco: Bancroft-Whitney 1895); Harold J. Laski, "The Personality of Associations," 29 *Harvard Law Review* 404 (1916).

2. Freund, *Legal Nature of Corporations*, 59–60.

3. See Morton J. Horwitz, *The Transformation of American Law, 1870–1960: The Crisis of Legal Orthodoxy* (New York: Oxford University Press, 1992), 71–73.

4. Even today there are differences in copyright protection depending on whether the author is an individual or a corporation; for example, when the "author" is a corporation, the term of copyright is different than when the author is a natural person.

5. Schumacher v. Schwencke, 25 F. 466, 466, 468 (C.C.S.D.N.Y. 1885).

6. Clark v. West, 86 N.E. 1 (N.Y. 1908).

7. National Cloak & Suit Co. v. Kaufman, 189 F. 215, 216 (C.C.M.D. Pa. 1911).

[304] 8. The court cited Atwill v. Ferrett (1846), discussed above in chapter 2, Colliery Engineer Co. v. United Correspondence Schools (1899), discussed below, and Schumacher v. Schwencke.

9. Schumacher v. Schwencke, 25 F. at 466, 468.

10. 111 U.S. 53, 61 (1884).

11. Paul K. Saint-Amour, *The Copywrights: Intellectual Property and the Literary Imagination* (Ithaca, N.Y.: Cornell University Press, 2003), 92–96.

12. *Id.*, 94 (quoting Robert Ross in *The Letters of Oscar Wilde*, 862 [Rupert Hart-Davis ed., 1962]).

13. Oscar Wilde, "The Portrait of Mr. W. H.," in *Blackwood's Edinburgh Magazine* 146 (1889), quoted in Saint-Amour, *Copywrights*, 106.

14. T. J. Jackson Lears, *Fables of Abundance: A Cultural History of Advertising in America* (New York: Basic Books, 1994), 270.

15. Peter C. Marzio, *The Democratic Art: Pictures for a 19th Century America, Chromo-lithography, 1840–1900* (Boston: David R. Godine and Amon Carter Museum of Western Art, 1979).

16. Andrew Goodman, *Gilbert and Sullivan at Law* (Rutherford, N.J.: Fairleigh Dickinson University Press, 1983), 175. The history of the *Burrow-Giles* case, Sarony, the relationship between Sarony and Wilde, and the social context that led to the litigation over the photograph will be told by Mark Rose in his forthcoming book, *Authors in Court: Scenes in the History of Literary Property*. I am grateful to him for sharing a draft of his chapter and some of his thoughts with me.

17. W. S. Gilbert and Arthur Sullivan, *Patience* (London, 1881).

18. Ben L. Bassham, *The Theatrical Photographs of Napoleon Sarony* (Kent, Ohio: Kent State University Press, 1978), 74.

19. *Id.* (quoting Lloyd Lewis and Henry Justin Smith, *Oscar Wilde Discovers America* [STGT ed., 1967], 418–19).

20. Sarony, 111 U.S. at 60.

21. The record of Burrow-Giles Lithographic Co. v. Sarony, 111 U.S. 53 (1884), in the Supreme Court is available on microfilm. The complaint and trial court findings are in the record at pp. 4 and 14.

22. On the nineteenth-century view of photographs as being the work of machines rather than authors, see Christine H. Farley, "The Lingering Effects of Copyright's Response to the Invention of Photography," 65 *University of Pittsburgh Law Review* 385 (2004).

23. Bassham, *Theatrical Photographs*, 14.

24. Sarony, 111 U.S. at 60–61 (citing Nottage v. Jackson, 11 Q.B. 627 [1883]).

25. *Id.* at 60.

26. *Id.* at 61 (quoting 11 Q.B. Div. 627 [1883] [Brett, M.R.]).

27. *Id.* at 60.

28. Edward Thompson Co. v. American Law Book Co., 119 F. 217, 219 (C.C.S.D.N.Y. 1902).

29. 94 F. 152, 153 (C.C.S.D.N.Y. 1899).

30. 73 F. 196, 198–99 (2d Cir. 1896).

31. 128 U.S. 617 (1888).

32. Freeman to Myers, February 15, 1877 (reprinted in Supreme Court Record of Callaghan v. Myers at 366).

33. Myers v. Callaghan, 5 F. 726, 727 (C.C.N.D. Ill. 1881).

34. 128 U.S. at 647, 650 (emphasis added).

35. The implied contract concept was used in patent cases of this era as well. See Salomon v. Hertz, 2 A. 379 (N.J. 1890).

36. Peters v. Borst, 36 N.E. 814, 815 (N.Y. 1894).

37. Root v. Borst, 9 N.Y.S. 789, 789, 790 (Sup. Ct. 1889).

38. At that time, the distinction between servants and contractors functioned to determine the liability of the employer to third parties for torts committed by the servant or contractor. See Horace Gay Wood, *A Treatise on the Law of Master and Servant*, 601 (1877) (defining a servant as "a person who, by contract or operation of law, is for a limited period subject to the authority or control of another person in a particular trade, business or occupation," and explaining that an employer is not liable for the acts of contractors "except when he retains control over the manner or instrumentalities of the work"). Mechem's treatise on the law of agency confessed that "[t]he line of demarcation between the relation of principal and agent, and that of master and servant is exceedingly difficult to define. This difficulty arises largely from the fact that the two relations are essentially similar. Indeed, there is much reason for saying that the difference between them is one of degree only, and not of kind." Floyd R. Mechem, *A Treatise on the Law of Agency* (Chicago: Callaghan, 1889), 2. Mechem ultimately concluded that agency properly relates to transactions of business with third persons, and implies more or less of discretion in the agent as to the time and manner of his performance. Service, on the other hand, has reference to actions upon or about things. It deals chiefly with matters of mere manual or mechanical execution, in which the servant acts under the direction and control of the master. *Id.*, 3. The distinction between "things" and "business" obviously no longer holds, although the different degrees of supervision are today the essential distinction between employees and independent contractors. But Mechem went on to note all the exceptions to the notion of supervision as being determinative, and added that the agent typically works by the project rather than for a fixed period. He then cautioned, however, that an agent's period of employment might be fixed. *Id.*, 4. See generally William Evans, *A Treatise upon the Law of Principal and Agent in Contract and Tort* (Chicago: Chicago Legal News, 1879) (containing a chapter on the liability of employers for injuries caused by the negligence of fellow servants but little discussion otherwise of employment, and no discussion of the distinction between agents and servants); Francis Wharton, *A Commentary on the Law of Agency and Agents* (Philadelphia: Kay & Bro., 1876), §§321, 227 (explaining that an agent is paid by commission, whereas a servant is paid by wages).

39. Act of March 4, 1909, ch. 320, 35 Stat. 1075.

40. B. Fulton Brylawski and Abe Goldman, eds., *Legislative History of the 1909 Copyright Act* (South Hackensack, N.J.: F. B. Rothman, 1976), 2:xxiv.

41. 1 *id.*, 56.

42. *Id.*

43. 2 *id.*, xxiv.

44. *Id.*, 65.

45. *Id.*, 143–44.

46. *Id.*, 188.

47. 3 *id.*, xxx.

48. 4 *id.* at pt. J.

49. Except as otherwise noted, all the history on the Rand McNally Company and citations to archival materials are to the Rand McNally Company Records, John M. Wing Foundation on the History of Printing, Newberry Library, Chicago.

50. Series 3, Box 8, Folder 89, RMR.

51. Series 3, Box 13, Folder 193, RMR.

52. Series 3, Box 8, Folder 89, RMR. This is drawn from an unpublished history of the company written by Bruce Grant and draws on a short history of the company prepared by James McNally.

53. Walter R. Ristow, *American Maps and Mapmakers: Commercial Cartography in the Nineteenth Century* (Detroit: Wayne State University Press, 1985), 471–72. The patents were presumably for the color printing process. A similar phenomenon regarding authorship—usually, but not always, the publisher claimed it—may be seen in the maps of the American Southwest discussed in Judith A. Tyner, "Images of the Southwest in Nineteenth-Century American Atlases," in *The Mapping of the American Southwest*, ed. Dennis Reinhartz and Charles C. Colley (College Station: Texas A&M University Press, 1987), 60–77 (discussing various atlases from 1817 to the 1880s).

54. Bruce Grant, unpublished manuscript on the history of the company, quoting Inland Printer, February 1894, 410–11, Series 1, Box 6, Folder 160, RMR.

55. Harland Manchester, "The World of Rand McNally," *Saturday Review of Literature*, January 21, 1950, 35.

56. L. M. Hopkins, Attorney at Law, to Rand McNally, January 4, 18, 1906, Series 2, Box 1, Folder 6 (transmitting patent and patent assignments); copyright registrations received by Rand McNally from the Register of Copyrights at the Library of Congress for various maps and books in the 1890s and 1900s, Series 2, Box 7, Folder 124; both in RMR.

57. Series 3, Box 3, Folder 5, RMR.

58. Series 3, Box 7, Folder 75, RMR.

59. Series 3, Box 7, Folder 69, RMR.

60. Folio Rand McNally Atlas, G6, 1932 (see p. xvi for the preface and pp. 4–5 for the Rand McNally copyright claim on the map for which the University of Chicago owned the projection).

61. On Goode's homolosine equal-area projection and the challenge and controversy associated with different methods of portraying the relative size of continents on a flat

map, see Mark Monmonier, *Drawing the Line: Tales of Maps and Cartocontroversy* (New York: Henry Holt and Company, 1995), 9–44, and Mark Monmonier, *Rhumb Lines and Map Wars: A Social History of the Mercator Projection* (Chicago: University of Chicago Press, 2004), 130–37.

62. Series 3, Box 6, Folder 47, RMR.

63. Series 2, Box 7, Folder 113, RMR.

64. Helmuth Bay, "My Thirty-Eight Years with Rand McNally & Co.," pamphlet (Washington, D.C., 1964), Series 2, Box 14, Folder 211, RMR.

65. *Id.*

66. Helmuth Bay, "The Beginning of Modern Road Maps in the United States," paper, Series 2, Box 14, Folder 211, RMR.

67. For example, William E. Johnson, who was chief cartographer at the firm in the 1920s and 1930s, assigned several patents to his inventions to the firm and was rarely credited for his work. One example of a Rand-McNally book that credited no author was an 1897 atlas, *The World's Peoples and the Countries They Live In*, Series 3, Box 17, Folder 252, RMR.

68. Helmuth Bay, "Air Trails Maps: A Chapter in the Early History of Aeronautical Charts," 15 *Surveying and Mapping* 322 (1955), reprint in Series 2, Box 14, Folder 211, RMR.

69. 188 U.S. 239 (1903).

70. Testimony of George Bleistein, Supreme Court Record of Bleistein v. Donaldson Lithographing Co. at 34–35.

71. 188 U.S. at 249.

72. *Id.* at 248.

73. Another court did not bother to justify it, simply relying on Schumacher as controlling authority. See Mutual Advertising Co. v. Refo, 76 F. 961, 963 (C.C.D.S.C. 1896).

74. 188 U.S. at 249–50.

75. 188 U.S. at 252 (Harlan, J., dissenting).

76. *Id.*, 251–52.

77. See Saint-Amour, *Copywrights*, 160–63.

78. *Id.*

79. Matthew Wheelock Stahl, "Reinventing Certainties: American Popular Music and Social Reproduction," Ph.D. dissertation, University of California, San Diego, 2006; Matthew Stahl, "Authentic Boy Bands on TV? Performers and Impresarios in *The Monkees* and *Making the Band*," 21 *Popular Music* 307 (2002).

CONCLUSION

1. Ingersoll-Rand Co. v. Ciavatta, 542 A.2d 879 (N.J. 1988).

2. Ingersoll-Rand Company, *The Story of the Hoover Dam* (New York: Ingersoll-Rand, 1932–36); Charles W. Hobart, "The Cascade Tunnel and the Man That Made It," 13 *Magazine of Western History* 534 (1991); Johannes H. Wisby, "Compressed Air," *Los Angeles Times*, November 19, 1899, A10; "New York Water Supply," *Scientific American*, June 4, 1887, 351 (describing the use of Ingersoll drills in the construction of the New York aqueduct).

3. Obituary, Henry C. Sergeant, *New York Times*, February 1, 1907, 9.

4. George Koether, *The Building of Men, Machines, and a Company* (n.p., 1971); Obituary, Henry C. Sergeant; Wisby, "Compressed Air."

5. Paul Klebnikov, "A Traumatic Experience," *Forbes*, January 18, 1993, 83.

6. The story of Armand Ciavatta is drawn from oral history I conducted with him in August 2005. On the Ingersoll-Rand story and the role of law in striking a balance between corporate management of science and opportunities for entrepreneurship among inventive employees, see Catherine L. Fisk, "The Story of *Ingersoll-Rand v. Ciavatta*: Employee Inventors in Corporate Research and Development—Reconciling Innovation with Entrepreneurship," in *Employment Law Stories*, ed. Samuel Estreicher and Gillian Lester (New York: Foundation Press, 2007), 143–74.

7. John Seely Brown, "Foreword," in Henry W. Chesbrough, *Open Innovation: The New Imperative for Creating and Profiting from Technology* (Cambridge, Mass.: Harvard Business School Press, 2003); N. R. Kleinfeld, "How 'Strykeforce' Beat the Clock," *New York Times*, March 25, 1990.

8. Frederick W. Taylor, *Principles of Scientific Management* (New York: Norton, 1967), 50–51.

9. See William G. Roy, "The Organization of the Corporate Class Segment of the U.S. Capitalist Class at the Turn of This Century," in *Bringing Class Back In: Contemporary and Historical Perspectives*, ed. Scott G. McNall, Rhonda F. Levine, and Rick Fantasia (Boulder, Colo.: Westview Press, 1991), 139, 141.

10. Bourdieu said that a class exists "when there are agents capable of imposing themselves, as authorized to speak . . . upon those who, by recognizing them as endowed with full power to speak and act in their name, recognize themselves as members of the class, and in doing so, confer upon it the only form of existence a group can possess." Pierre Bourdieu, "What Makes a Class? On the Theoretical and Practical Existence of Groups," 32 *Berkeley Journal of Sociology* 1, 15 (1987).

11. Loïc J. D. Wacquant, "Making Class: The Middle Class(es) in Social Theory and Social Structure," in *Bringing Class Back In: Contemporary and Historical Perspectives*, ed. Scott G. McNall, Rhonda F. Levine, and Rick Fantasia (Boulder, Colo.: Westview Press, 1991), 57.

12. C. Wright Mills, *White Collar: The American Middle Classes* (New York: Oxford University Press, 1953).

13. Olivier Zunz, *Making America Corporate, 1870–1920* (Chicago: University of Chicago Press, 1990), 8.

14. *Id.* On engineers and the transformation of the middle class in the twentieth century, see Robert Zussman, *Mechanics of the Middle Class: Work and Politics among American Engineers* (Berkeley: University of California Press, 1985), chaps. 1, 11.

15. Charles W. McCurdy, "The Roots of 'Liberty of Contract' Reconsidered: Major Premises in the Law of Employment, 1867–1937," *Supreme Court Historical Society Yearbook* 20, 27 (1984).

16. The vast expansion of relatively low-paid nonmanual office work without opportunity for upward mobility was one of the most significant social and economic changes in the emergence of the modern middle class: it weakened the distinction between manual

and nonmanual work as it also eliminated office work as a form of business apprentice-ship leading to eventual independence. See Stuart M. Blumin, *The Emergence of the Middle Class: Social Experience in the American City, 1760–1900* (New York: Cambridge University Press, 1989), 290–91.

17. The expert on railroad innovation on whose work I have relied extremely heavily is Steven W. Usselman. See Usselman, "Patents, Engineering Professionals, and Pipelines of Innovation," chapter 2 in *Learning by Doing in Markets, Firms, and Countries*, edited by Naomi R. Lamoreaux, Daniel M. Raff, and Peter Temin (Chicago: University of Chicago Press, 1998); and Usselman, *Regulating Railroad Innovation*.

18. Naomi R. Lamoreaux and Kenneth L. Sokoloff, "Inventors, Firms, and the Market for Technology in the Late Nineteenth and Early Twentieth Centuries," in *Learning by Doing in Markets, Firms, and Countries*, 48 and n. 47. The quotation of the Pullman Company document is "Policy and Procedure in Patent Matters," November 21, 1913, Secretary and Treasurer, Office of the Secretary and Treasurer, Box 1, Folder 2, Pullman Company Archives.

19. Christopher P. Wilson, *White Collar Fictions: Class and Social Representation in American Literature, 1885–1925* (Athens: University of Georgia Press, 1992), 29 (discuss-ing the portrayal of white-collar employees in the work of O. Henry: "[T]he problem of white collar dependence was more subtle, and the alterations in middle-class ideolo-gies less cataclysmic than may be supposed. For 'dependence' could mean not simply a loss of entrepreneurial energy or a putative freedom to act, but something that went to the core of cultural justifications for character, loyalty, even self-hood itself. It could mean disappearing into a corporation's identity at the expense of one's own; it could mean a threat to the borders between what was legitimately inside work and outside of it; it could signify identification with the corporation, loyalty to the commodity, at the expense of other loyalties to family or community").

20. Paul Israel, *Edison: A Life of Invention* (New York: John Wiley & Sons, 1998); Ernst Homburg, "The Emergence of Research Laboratories in the Dyestuffs Industry, 1870–1900," 25 *British Journal for the History of Science* 91, 95 (1992).

21. Hapgood v. Hewitt, 119 U.S. 226, 230–31 (1886).

22. Fuller & Johnson Mfg. Co. v. Bartlett, 68 Wis. 73, 31 N.W. 747, 752 (1887).

23. *Id.*, 753.

24. Daniel J. Walkowitz, *Working with Class: Social Workers and the Politics of Middle-Class Identity*, xv, 6 (Chapel Hill: University of North Carolina Press, 1999).

25. David F. Noble, *America by Design: Science, Technology, and the Rise of Corporate Capitalism* (New York: Knopf, 1977), 120.

26. *Id.*, 120. E. B. Craft of Bell Labs described the corporate control over all phases of the patent process as follows: all of the research leading up to a possible patent "is very carefully recorded in our laboratory notebooks, a complete record of all the work that is done, and these are turned over to the patent organization and they determine who the inventors are" (quoting E. B. Craft, Bell Educational Conference, 1925 47 [New York: Bell System, 1925]).

27. Joseph A. Schumpeter, *The Economics and Sociology of Capitalism*, edited by Richard Swedberg (Princeton, N.J.: Princeton University Press, 1991), 40.

28. Joseph A. Schumpeter, *The Theory of Economic Development* (Cambridge, Mass.: Harvard University Press, 1951), 93.

29. See "*Eldred v. Ashcroft*: How Artists and Creators Finally Got Their Due," 2003 *Duke Journal of Law & Technology* 14 (May 2003).

30. See Patrick Goldstein, "The Big Picture: Hollywood Deals with Piracy, A Wary Eye on CDs," *Los Angeles Times*, September 9, 2003, E1.

31. Catherine L. Fisk, "Credit Where It's Due: The Law and Norms of Attribution," 95 *Georgetown Law Journal* 49 (2006).

32. Annalee Saxenian, *Regional Advantage: Culture and Competition in Silicon Valley and Route 128* (Cambridge, Mass.: Harvard University Press, 1994); Alan Hyde, *Working in Silicon Valley: Economic and Legal Analysis of a High-Velocity Labor Market* (Armonk, N.Y.: M.E. Sharpe, 2003).

BIBLIOGRAPHY

MANUSCRIPT COLLECTIONS

Du Pont

My account of Du Pont is based on the company archives at the Hagley Museum and Library, Wilmington, Delaware, and the secondary literature discussed below. I am grateful for the assistance of the Hagley archivists and for permission to quote and refer to letters and other documents archived there. Anyone who studies Du Pont benefits from the wealth of scholarly writing on the company. The history of Du Pont research and development in the twentieth century is told in David A. Hounshell and John K. Smith Jr., *Science and Corporate Strategy: Du Pont R & D, 1902–1980* (New York: Cambridge University Press, 1988). David A. Hounshell, "Interpreting the History of Industrial Research and Development: The Case of E. I. du Pont de Nemours & Co.," 134 *Proceedings of the American Philosophical Society* 387 (1990), is a fascinating essay on the writing of this leading work. A leading work of business history is Alfred D. Chandler Jr. and Stephen Salsbury, *Pierre S. du Pont and the Making of the Modern Corporation* (New York: Harper & Row, 1971). A very sympathetic, even romantic, telling of the nineteenth-century history of the Du Pont Company for a popular audience is William S. Dutton, *Du Pont: One Hundred and Forty Years* (New York: C. Scribner's Sons, 1942). The family is the subject of William H. A. Carr, *The du Ponts of Delaware* (New York: Dodd, Mead, 1964). Many of the histories of the family and the company in the nineteenth century rely on an understandably sympathetic book by B. G. du Pont, *E. I. du Pont de Nemours and Company: A History, 1802–1902* (New York: Houghton Mifflin, 1920), as well as on the vast quantity of notes and documents she assembled in preparing the history; her notes are preserved intact at the Hagley Museum and Library. A far less sympathetic discussion of Du Pont in the twentieth century is Gerard Colby, *Du Pont: Behind the Nylon Curtain* (Englewood Cliffs, N.J.: Prentice-Hall, 1974).

The company manuscript collections on the nineteenth century that were of particular relevance to this project include Accession 1471; Accession 146 (the Eleuthera [Bradford] du Pont Collection), Boxes 2, 3; and the Longwood Manuscripts, Group 5, Series A and C. The collections on the early twentieth century include Accession 1305, Boxes 679, 680, 771, 772, 773; Accession 518, Box 1004; and Accession 228, Series H, Box 40.

Hulse and Bonsack

The story of William A. Hulse and his fight with the Bonsack Company over the patent to improved mechanized cigarette manufacturing technology is drawn from the Duke family and business manuscript collections in Perkins Library, Duke University, Durham, North Carolina. I owe an enormous debt of gratitude to Katherine Scott, Duke Law School Class of 2007, for her Herculean efforts in combing through the voluminous archive and piecing together the story of Hulse and his crimper. We both owe a debt of gratitude to the librarians at Perkins for their assistance. The letters that form the basis of the story told in this book are in two collections of correspondence: the James Buchanan Duke Papers and the Richard Harvey Wright Papers.

Ingersoll-Rand and Armand Ciavatta

As indicated in the notes, my account of Ingersoll-Rand is drawn largely from publicly available books, cases, news reports, and other secondary sources. The one exception is the oral history of Armand Ciavatta's dispute with the company, which is based on a series of conversations I had with Mr. Ciavatta in August 2005 and on documents he provided to me from his files. I am enormously grateful for his willingness to share his time, ideas, and recollections with me.

Rand McNally

My history of the Rand McNally Company is based on the company records at the Newberry Library in Chicago. The Newberry does not have the complete corporate archive. I reviewed every file that seemed relevant to the company's dealings with its employees over intellectual property issues; I suspect that if there were a complete archive of the company's activities, I would have found more. Nevertheless, of particular relevance are Series 1, Box 6, Folder 160; Series 2, Boxes 1, 7, 10, 15; and Series 3, Boxes 3, 6, 7, 8, 13, 17.

In addition, the Newberry has the manuscript of a history of the company written by Bruce Grant, which was a helpful source. I am grateful to the Newberry Library and its staff for assistance in working in the collection and for permission to quote and refer to the manuscripts.

Reading Railroad

The complete surviving archive of the Reading Railroad company is Accession 1520 in the Hagley Museum and Library, Wilmington, Delaware. Boxes 14, 15, 55, 57, 64, 209, 253, and 311 were particularly relevant. I am grateful to the Hagley archivists for their assistance in helping me find my way through the vast archive to the material I needed and to the museum for permission to use and quote the manuscripts.

BOOKS

Ackerman, Carl W. *George Eastman*. New York: Houghton Mifflin, 1930.

Adams, Charles F. *Richard Henry Dana: A Biography*. New York: Houghton Mifflin, 1891.

Adams, Stephen B., and Orville R. Butler. *Manufacturing the Future: A History of Western Electric*. New York: Cambridge University Press, 1999.

Alexander, Gregory S. *Commodity and Propriety: Competing Visions of Property in American Legal Thought, 1776–1970*. Chicago: University of Chicago Press, 1997.

Appleby, Joyce. *Capitalism and a New Social Order: The Republican Vision of the 1790s*. New York: New York University Press, 1984.

Appleton, Nathan, and Samuel Batchelder. *The Early Development of the American Cotton Textile Industry*. New York: Harper & Row, 1969.

Arnold, Thurman W. *The Folklore of Capitalism*. New Haven, Conn.: Yale University Press, 1937.

Ashe, Samuel A. "William Thomas O'Brien." In *A Biographical History of North Carolina from the Colonial Times to the Present*, edited by Samuel A. Ashe, Stephen B. Weeks, and Charles L. Van Noppen, 303–7. Greensboro, N.C.: C. L. Van Noppen, 1906.

Atiyah, P. S. *The Rise and Fall of Freedom of Contract*. New York: Oxford University Press, 1979.

Basler, Roy P., ed. *The Collected Works of Abraham Lincoln*. 3d ed. New Brunswick, N.J.: Rutgers University Press, 1953.

Bassham, Ben L. *The Theatrical Photographs of Napoleon Sarony*. Kent, Ohio: Kent State University Press, 1978.

Ben-Atar, Doron S. *Trade Secrets: Intellectual Piracy and the Origins of American Industrial Power*. New Haven, Conn.: Yale University Press, 2004.

Benkler, Yochai. *The Wealth of Networks: How Social Production Transforms Markets and Freedom*. New Haven, Conn.: Yale University Press, 2006.

Blackstone, Sir William. *Blackstone's Commentaries: With Notes of Reference to the Constitution and Laws of the Federal Government of the United States and of the Commonwealth of Virginia*. 5 vols. Edited by St. George Tucker. Philadelphia: W. Y. Birch and A. Small, 1803.

Bland, A. E., et al. *English Economic History*. 2d ed. London: G. Bell and Sons, Ltd., 1915.

Blumin, Stuart M. *The Emergence of the Middle Class: Social Experience in the American City, 1760–1900*. New York: Cambridge University Press, 1989.

Boorstin, Daniel J. *The Mysterious Science of the Law: An Essay on Blackstone's Commentaries, Showing How Blackstone, Employing Eighteenth-Century Ideas of Science, Religion, History, Aesthetics, and Philosophy, Made of the Law at Once a Conservative and Mysterious Science*. Boston: Beacon Press, 1958.

Boucicault, Dion. "The Octoroon." In *Selected Plays by Dion Boucicault*, edited by Andrew Parkin, 135–90. Washington, D.C.: Catholic University of America Press, 1987.

Boyd, William K. *The Story of Durham, City of the New South*. Durham, N.C.: Duke University Press, 1927.

Brayer, Elizabeth. *George Eastman: A Biography*. Baltimore: Johns Hopkins University Press, 1996.

Bridenbaugh, Carl. *The Colonial Craftsman*. New York: New York University Press, 1950.

Brinkley, Douglas. *Wheels for the World: Henry Ford, His Company, and a Century of Progress, 1903–2003*. New York: Viking, 2003.

Bronner, Simon J. *Consuming Visions: Accumulation and Display of Goods in America, 1880–1920*. New York: Norton, 1989.

Brundage, James A. *The Medieval Origins of the Legal Profession: Canonists, Civilians, and Courts*. Chicago: University of Chicago Press, 2008.

Bryan, Vernanne. *Laura Keene: A British Actress on the American Stage, 1826–1873*. Jefferson, N.C.: McFarland & Company, 1993.

Brylawski, B. Fulton, and Abe Goldman, eds. *Legislative History of the 1909 Copyright Act*. 4 vols. South Hackensack, N.J.: F. B. Rothman, 1976.

Bugbee, Bruce. *The Genesis of American Patent and Copyright Law*. Washington, D.C.: Public Affairs Press, 1967.

Burlingame, Roger. *Inventors behind the Inventor*. New York: Harcourt, Brace, 1947.

———. *March of the Iron Men, a Social History of Union through Invention*. New York: C. Scribner's Sons, 1938.

Calvert, Monte A. *The Mechanical Engineer in America, 1830–1910: Professional Cultures in Conflict*. Baltimore: Johns Hopkins University Press, 1967.

Carr, William H. A. *The du Ponts of Delaware*. New York: Dodd, Mead, 1964.

Catton, Bruce. *The Civil War*. New York: Houghton Mifflin, 1987.

Chandler, Alfred D., Jr. *The Visible Hand: The Managerial Revolution in American Business*. Cambridge, Mass.: Harvard University Press, 1977.

Chandler, Alfred D., Jr., and Stephen Salsbury. *Pierre S. du Pont and the Making of the Modern Corporation*. New York: Harper & Row, 1971.

Chesbrough, Henry W. *Open Innovation: The New Imperative for Creating and Profiting from Technology*. Cambridge, Mass.: Harvard Business School Press, 2003.

Cheyney, Edward P. *An Introduction to the Industrial and Social History of England*. Rev. ed. N.p., 1920.

Clark, Christopher. "Social Structure and Manufacturing before the Factory: Rural New England, 1750–1830." In *The Workplace before the Factory: Artisans and Proletarian, 1500–1800*, edited by Thomas Max Safley and Leonard N. Rosenband. Ithaca, N.Y.: Cornell University Press, 1993.

Colby, Gerard. *Du Pont: Behind the Nylon Curtain*. Englewood Cliffs, N.J.: Prentice-Hall, 1974.

Collins, Douglas. *The Story of Kodak*. New York: Harry N. Abrams, 1990.

Commons, John R. *Legal Foundations of Capitalism*. New York: Macmillan, 1924.

Commons, John R., David J. Saposs, Helen L. Sumner, E. B. Mittelman, H. E. Hoagland, John B. Andrews, and Selig Perlman. *History of Labour in the United States*. New York: Macmillan, 1918.

Conlin, Joseph R. *Big Bill Haywood and the Radical Union Movement*. Syracuse, N.Y.: Syracuse University Press, 1969.

Coolidge, John. *Mill and Mansion: Architecture and Society in Lowell, Massachusetts, 1820–1865*. 1942. 2d ed., Amherst, Mass.: University of Massachusetts Press, 1993.

Cowan, Ruth Schwartz. *A Social History of American Technology*. New York: Oxford University Press, 1997.

Crawford, Mary C. *The Romance of the American Theatre*. Boston: Little, Brown, 1913.

Crawford, Richard. *The American Musical Landscape*. Berkeley: University of California Press, 1993.

Curtis, George T. *A Treatise on the Law of Patents for Useful Inventions in the United States of America*. Boston: C. C. Little and J. Brown, 1849.

———. *A Treatise on the Law of Patents for Useful Inventions: As Enacted and Administered in the United States of America*. 3d ed. Boston: Little, Brown, 1867.

Davis, Kenneth C. *Don't Know Much about the Civil War: Everything You Need to Know about America's Greatest Conflict but Never Learned*. New York: William Morrow, 1996.

Dawley, Alan. *Class and Community: The Industrial Revolution in Lynn*. Cambridge, Mass.: Harvard University Press, 1976.

Drone, Eaton S. *A Treatise on the Law of Property in Intellectual Productions in Great Britain and the United States*. Boston: Little, Brown, 1879.

Dubofsky, Melvyn. *"Big Bill" Haywood*. Manchester: Manchester University Press, 1987.

Du Pont, B. G. *E. I. du Pont de Nemours and Company: A History, 1802–1902*. New York: Houghton Mifflin, 1920.

Durden, Robert F. *The Dukes of Durham, 1865–1929*. Durham, N.C.: Duke University Press, 1965.

Dutton, Harold I. *The Patent System and Inventive Activity during the Industrial Revolution, 1750–1852*. Manchester: Manchester University Press, 1984.

Dutton, William S. *Du Pont: One Hundred and Forty Years*. New York: Charles Scribner's Sons, 1942.

Ehrenreich, Barbara. *Fear of Falling: The Inner Life of the Middle Class*. New York: Harper Perennial, 1990.

Eliot, George. *The Impressions of Theophrastus Such*. Edited by Nancy Henry. Iowa City: University of Iowa Press, 1994.

Elkins, Stanley, and Eric McKitrick. *The Age of Federalism: The Early American Republic, 1788–1800*. New York: Oxford University Press, 1993.

Estreicher, Samuel, and Gillian Lester, eds. *Employment Law Stories*. New York: Foundation Press, 2007.

Evans, William. *A Treatise upon the Law of Principle and Agent in Contract and Tort*. Chicago: Chicago Legal News, 1879.

Fawkes, Richard. *Dion Boucicault*. New York: Quartet Books, 1979.

Fiss, M. Owen. *Troubled Beginnings of the Modern State, 1888–1910*. New York: Macmillan, 1993.

Fox, Richard W., and T. J. Jackson Lears. *The Culture of Consumption: Critical Essays in American History, 1880–1980*. New York: Pantheon Books, 1983.

Freund, Ernst. *The Legal Nature of Corporations*. Chicago: University of Chicago Press, 1897.

Friedman, Lawrence M. *Contract Law in America: A Social and Economic Case Study*. Madison: University of Wisconsin Press, 1965.

———. *A History of American Law*. New York: Simon & Schuster, 1973.

Frow, John. *Time and Commodity Culture: Essays in Cultural Theory and Postmodernity.* New York: Oxford University Press, 1997.

Fry, Sir Edward. *A Treatise on the Specific Performance of Contracts: Including Those of Public Companies.* Philadelphia: T & J. W. Johnson, 1858.

Fuller, Edmond. *Tinkerers and Genius: The Story of the Yankee Inventors.* New York: Hastings House, 1955.

Fuller, Lon L. *Legal Fictions.* Stanford, Calif.: Stanford University Press, 1967.

Galambos, Louis. "The American Economy and the Reorganization of the Sources of Knowledge." In *The Organization of Knowledge in Modern America, 1860–1920,* edited by Alexandra Oleson and John Voss, 269–82. Baltimore: Johns Hopkins University Press, 1979.

Gibb, George Sweet. *The Saco-Lowell Shops: Textile Machinery Building in New England, 1813–1949.* Cambridge, Mass.: Harvard University Press, 1950.

Gibbons, David. *Rudimentary Treatise on the Law of Contracts for Works and Services.* London: John Weale, 1857.

Gilfillan, S. C. *The Sociology of Invention: An Essay on the Social Causes of Technic Invention and Some of Its Social Results; Especially as Demonstrated by the History of the Ship.* Chicago: Follett Publishing, 1935.

Gilmore, Grant. *The Death of Contract.* Columbus: Ohio State University Press, 1974.

Glickstein, Jonathan A. *American Exceptionalism, American Anxiety: Wages, Compensation, and Degraded Labor in the Antebellum United States.* Charlottesville: University of Virginia Press, 2002.

Godson, Richard. *A Practical Treatise on the Law of Patents for Inventions and of Copyright.* 2d ed. London: W. Benning, 1844.

Goodman, Andrew. *Gilbert and Sullivan at Law.* Rutherford, N.J.: Fairleigh Dickinson University Press, 1983.

Gother, John. *Instructions for Masters, Traders, Labourers, &c.* London, 1699.

Graham, Margaret B. W., and Bettye H. Pruitt. *R&D for Industry: A Century of Technical Innovation at Alcoa.* New York: Cambridge University Press, 1990.

Gray, John C. *Restraints on the Alienation of Property.* 2d ed. Boston: Boston Book Company, 1895.

Greenhood, Elisha. *The Doctrine of Public Policy in the Law of Contracts, Reduced to Rules.* Chicago: Callaghan & Company, 1886.

Gregory, Frances W. *Nathan Appleton: Merchant and Entrepreneur, 1779–1861.* Charlottesville: University of Virginia Press, 1975.

Haber, Samuel. *Efficiency and Uplift: Scientific Management in the Progressive Era, 1890–1920.* Chicago: University of Chicago Press, 1964.

Hamilton, Alexander. *Report on Manufactures.* Vol. 1 of *Reports of the Secretary of the Treasury,* 78–133. Washington, D.C.: Blair & Rives, 1837.

Hamilton, Alexander, James Madison, and John Jay. *The Federalist Papers.* New York: New American Library, 1961.

Handlin, Oscar, and Mary F. Handlin. *Commonwealth: A Study of the Role of Government in the American Economy: Massachusetts, 1774–1861.* 2d. ed. Cambridge, Mass.: Belknap Press, Harvard University Press, 1969.

Harley, J. B. *The New Nature of Maps: Essays in the History of Cartography*. Edited by
Paul Laxton. Baltimore: Johns Hopkins University Press, 2001.

Hartz, Louis. *Economic Policy and Democratic Thought: Pennsylvania, 1776–1860*.
Cambridge, Mass.: Harvard University Press, 1948.

Haywood, William D., and Frank Bohn. *Industrial Socialism*. Chicago: Charles H. Kerr,
n.d.

High, James L. *A Treatise on the Law of Injunctions: As Administered in the Courts of the
United States and England*. Chicago: Callaghan, 1873.

———. *A Treatise on the Law of Injunctions*. 4th ed. Chicago: Callaghan, 1905.

Hindle, Brooke. *Emulation and Invention*. New York: New York University Press,
1981.

Hindle, Brooke, and Steven Lubar. *Engines of Change: The American Industrial
Revolution, 1790–1860*. Washington, D.C.: Smithsonian Institution Press, 1986.

Hindmarch, W. M. *A Treatise on the Law Relative to Patent Privileges for the Sole Use of
Inventions and the Practice of Obtaining Letters Patents for Inventions*. Harrisburg, Pa.:
I. G. M'Kinley and J. M. G. Lescure, 1847.

Hogan, Robert G. *Dion Boucicault*. New York: Twayne Publishers, 1969.

Holdsworth, William. *A History of English Law*. 2d ed. London: Methuen & Company,
1926.

Horwitz, Morton J. *The Transformation of American Law, 1870–1960: The Crisis of Legal
Orthodoxy*. New York: Oxford University Press, 1992.

Hounshell, David A. *From the American System to Mass Production, 1800–1932: The
Development of Manufacturing Technology in the United States*. Baltimore: Johns
Hopkins University Press, 1984.

Hounshell, David A., and John K. Smith Jr. *Science and Corporate Strategy: Du Pont
R & D, 1902–1980*. New York: Cambridge University Press, 1988.

Hovenkamp, Herbert. *Enterprise and American Law, 1836–1937*. Cambridge, Mass.:
Harvard University Press, 1991.

Hughes, Thomas P. *American Genesis: A Century of Innovation and Technological
Enthusiasm, 1870–1970*. New York: Viking, 1989.

Hurst, James W. *Law and the Conditions of Freedom: In the Nineteenth-Century United
States*. Madison: University of Wisconsin Press, 1956.

———. *The Legitimacy of the Business Corporation in the Law of the United States,
1780–1970*. Charlottesville: University of Virginia Press, 1970.

Hurt, James. "Dion Boucicault's Comic Myths." In *When They Weren't Doing
Shakespeare: Essays on Nineteenth-Century British and American Theatre*, edited by
Judith L. Fisher and Stephen Watt, 253–65. Athens: University of Georgia Press,
1989.

Hyde, Alan. *Working in Silicon Valley: Economic and Legal Analysis of a High-Velocity
Labor Market*. Armonk, N.Y.: M. E. Sharpe, 2003.

Ingersoll-Rand Company. *The Story of the Hoover Dam*. New York: Ingersoll-Rand,
1932–36.

Israel, Paul. *Edison: A Life of Invention*. New York: John Wiley & Sons, 1998.

———. *From Machine Shop to Industrial Laboratory: Telegraphy and the Changing*

Context of American Invention, 1830–1920. Baltimore: Johns Hopkins University Press, 1992.

Jacoby, Sanford M. *Employing Bureaucracy: Managers, Unions, and the Transformation of Work in American Industry, 1900–1945.* New York: Columbia University Press, 1985.

James, Portia P. *The Real McCoy: African-American Invention and Innovation, 1619–1930.* Washington, D.C.: Smithsonian Institution Press, 1989.

Jefferson, Joseph. *The Autobiography of Joseph Jefferson.* New York: Century Company, 1890.

Jefferson, Thomas. *Jefferson Cyclopedia; A Comprehensive Collection of the Views of Thomas Jefferson Classified and Arranged in Alphabetical Order under Nine Thousand Titles Relating to Government, Politics, Law, Education, Political Economy, Finance, Science, Art, Literature, Religious Freedom, Morals, etc.* Edited by John P. Foley. New York: Funk & Wagnalls, 1900.

———. *The Writings of Thomas Jefferson: Correspondence.* Edited by Andrew A. Lipscomb. Washington, D.C.: Thomas Jefferson Memorial Association, 1903.

Jenkins, Reese V. *Images and Enterprise: Technology and the American Photographic Industry, 1839 to 1925.* Baltimore: Johns Hopkins University Press, 1975.

Jeremy, David J. *Artisans, Entrepreneurs and Machines: Essays on the Early Anglo-American Textile Industries, 1770–1840s.* Brookfield, Vt.: Ashgate, 1998.

———. *Transatlantic Industrial Revolution: The Diffusion of Textile Technologies between Britain and America, 1790–1830s.* Cambridge, Mass.: MIT Press, 1981.

Joyce, Craig. "The Story of Wheaton v. Peters: A Curious Chapter in the History of Judicature." In *Intellectual Property Stories,* edited by Jane Ginsburg and Rochelle C. Dreyfuss, 36–76. New York: Foundation Press, 2006.

Kanigel, Robert. *The One Best Way: Frederick Winslow Taylor and the Enigma of Efficiency.* New York: Viking, 1997.

Kasson, John F. *Civilizing the Machine: Technology and Republican Values in America, 1776–1900.* New York: Penguin Books, 1977.

Kent, James. Vol. 2 of *Commentaries on American Law.* 14th ed. Boston: Little, Brown, 1896.

Khan, B. Zorina. *The Democratization of Invention: Patents and Copyrights in American Economic Development, 1790–1920.* New York: Cambridge University Press, 2005.

King, Andrew J., ed. *The Papers of Daniel Webster: Legal Papers.* Vol. 3, *The Federal Practice.* Hanover, N.H.: University Press of New England, 1989.

Kline, Ronald R. *Steinmetz: Engineer and Socialist.* Baltimore: Johns Hopkins University Press, 1992.

Koether, George. *The Building of Men, Machines, and a Company.* N.p., 1971.

Labatt, C. B. "Enticement and Harboring of Servants." In *Commentaries on the Law of Master and Servant, Including the Modern Laws on Workmen's Compensation, Arbitration, Employers' Liability, etc.,* 2d ed., edited by C. B. Labatt, 8015–94. Rochester, N.Y.: Lawyers Co-operative Publishing Company, 1913.

Lamoreaux, Naomi R., and Kenneth L. Sokoloff. "Inventors, Firms, and the Market for Technology in the Late Nineteenth and Early Twentieth Centuries." In *Learning by*

Doing in Markets, Firms, and Countries, edited by Naomi R. Lamoreaux, Daniel M. Raff, and Peter Temin, 19–60. Chicago: University of Chicago Press, 1999.

Landes, David S. *The Unbound Prometheus: Technological Change and Industrial Development in Western Europe from 1750 to the Present*. New York: Cambridge University Press, 1969.

Laurie, Bruce. *Artisans into Workers: Labor in Nineteenth-Century America*. New York: Noonday Press, 1989.

Lawrence, Arthur. *Sir Arthur Sullivan: Life-Story, Letters, and Reminiscences*. London: James Bowden, 1899.

Layton, Edwin T. *The Revolt of the Engineers: Social Responsibility and the American Engineering Profession*. Baltimore: Johns Hopkins University Press, 1986.

Leach, William. *Land of Desire: Merchants, Power, and the Rise of a New American Culture*. New York: Pantheon, 1993.

Lears, T. J. Jackson. *Fables of Abundance: A Cultural History of Advertising in America*. New York: Basic Books, 1994.

Licht, Walter. *Industrializing America: The Nineteenth Century*. Baltimore: Johns Hopkins University Press, 1995.

Linder, Marc. *The Employment Relationship in Anglo-American Law: A Historical Perspective*. Westport, Conn.: Greenwood Press, 1989.

Lipson, Ephraim. *The Economic History of England*. 7th ed. London: A. and C. Black, 1937.

Macdonald, Anne L. *Feminine Ingenuity: Women and Invention in America*. New York: Ballantine Books, 1992.

MacKaye, Percy. Vol. 1 of *Epoch: The Life of Steele MacKaye, Genius of the Theatre, in Relation to His Times and Contemporaries*. New York: Boni & Liveright, 1827.

MacLeod, Christine. *Inventing the Industrial Revolution: The English Patent System, 1660–1800*. New York: Cambridge University Press, 1988.

Maine, Henry. *Ancient Law*. 1866. Reprint, New Brunswick, N.J.: Transaction Books, 2002.

Maitland, F. W. *Equity*. London: Cambridge University Press, 1909.

Martin, Robert S. "United States Army Mapping in Texas, 1848–1850." In *The Mapping of the American Southwest*, edited by Dennis Reinhartz and Charles C. Colley, 37–56. College Station: Texas A&M University Press, 1987.

Marzio, Peter C. *The Democratic Art: Pictures for a 19th Century America, Chromolithography, 1840–1900*. Boston: David R. Godine and Amon Carter Museum of Western Art, 1979.

Mason, Alpheus T. *William Howard Taft, Chief Justice*. Reprint. Lanham, Md.: University Press of America, 1983.

McConachie, Bruce A. *Melodramatic Formations: American Theatre and Society, 1820–1870*. Iowa City: University of Iowa Press, 1992.

McKelvey, Blake. *Rochester: The Quest for Quality, 1890–1925*. Cambridge, Mass.: Harvard University Press, 1956.

McMahon, A. Michal. *The Making of a Profession: A Century of Electrical Engineering in America*. New York: IEEE Press, 1984.

Mechem, Floyd R. *A Treatise on the Law of Agency Including Not Only a Discussion of the General Subject, but Also Special Chapters on Attorneys, Auctioneers, Brokers and Factors.* Chicago: Callaghan, 1889.

Mees, C. E. Kenneth. *From Dry Plates to Ektachrome Film: A Story of Photographic Research.* New York: Ziff-Davis Publishing, 1961.

Meyer, David R. *Networked Machinists: High-Technology Industries in Antebellum America.* Baltimore: Johns Hopkins University Press, 2006.

Mill, John S. *On Liberty.* London: Longman, Roberts & Green, 1869.

———. "On Liberty." In *Utilitarianism; On Liberty; Considerations on Representative Government,* edited by Geraint Williams. London: J. M. Dent, 1993.

Miller, Tice L. "The Image of Fashionable Society in American Comedy, 1840–1970." In *When They Weren't Doing Shakespeare: Essays on Nineteenth-Century British and American Theatre,* edited by Judith L. Fisher and Stephen Watt, 243–52. Athens: University of Georgia Press, 1989.

Mills, C. Wright. *White Collar: The American Middle Classes.* New York: Oxford University Press, 1953.

Mokyr, Joel. *The Lever of Riches: Technological Creativity and Economic Progress.* New York: Oxford University Press, 1990.

Monmonier, Mark S. *Drawing the Line: Tales of Maps and Cartocontroversy.* New York: Henry Holt, 1995.

———. *Rhumb Lines and Map Wars: A Social History of the Mercator Projection.* Chicago: University of Chicago Press, 2004.

Montgomery, David. *The Fall of the House of Labor: The Workplace, the State, and American Labor Activism, 1865–1925.* New York: Cambridge University Press, 1987.

———. *Workers' Control in America: Studies in the History of Work, Technology, and Labor Struggles.* New York: Cambridge University Press, 1979.

Morris, Richard B. *Government and Labor in Early America.* New York: Columbia University Press, 1946.

Mowery, David C., and Nathan Rosenberg. *Paths of Innovation: Technological Change in Twentieth-Century America.* New York: Cambridge University Press, 1998.

———. *Technology and the Pursuit of Economic Growth.* New York: Cambridge University Press, 1989.

Nedelsky, Jennifer. *Private Property and the Limits of American Constitutionalism: The Madisonian Framework and Its Legacy.* Chicago: University of Chicago Press, 1990.

Nelson, Daniel. *Managers and Workers: Origins of the Twentieth-Century Factory System in the United States, 1880–1920.* 2d ed. Madison: University of Wisconsin Press, 1995.

Nelson, William E. *Americanization of the Common Law: The Impact of Legal Change in Massachusetts Society, 1760–1830.* Athens: University of Georgia Press, 1994.

Neumeyer, Fredrik, with John C. Stedman. *The Employed Inventor in the United States: R & D Policies, Law, and Practice.* Cambridge, Mass.: MIT Press, 1971.

Noble, David F. *America by Design: Science, Technology, and the Rise of Corporate Capitalism.* New York: Knopf, 1977.

Orren, Karen. *Belated Feudalism: Labor, the Law, and Liberal Development in the United States.* New York: Cambridge University Press, 1991.

Parsons, Theophilus. *The Law of Contracts.* 6th ed. Boston: Little, Brown, 1873.

Paul, Arnold M. *Conservative Crisis and the Rule of Law: Attitudes of Bar and Bench, 1887–1895.* Gloucester, Mass.: Peter Smith, 1976.

Pettitt, Clare. *Patent Inventions—Intellectual Property and the Victorian Novel.* New York: Oxford University Press, 2004.

Phillips, Willard. *The Law of Patents for Inventions: Including the Remedies and Legal Proceedings in Relation to Patent Rights.* Boston: American Stationers' Company, 1837.

Phin, John. *Trade "Secrets" and Private Recipes: A Collection of Recipes, Processes and Formulae That Have Been Offered for Sale by Various Persons at Prices Ranging From Twenty-Five Cents to Five Hundred Dollars.* New York: Industrial Publication Company, 1887. (Available at the Hagley Museum and Library, Wilmington, Delaware.)

Pocock, J. G. A. *The Machiavellian Moment: Florentine Political Thought and the Atlantic Republican Tradition.* Princeton, N.J.: Princeton University Press, 1975.

Pomeroy, John N. *Specific Performance of Contracts: As It Is Enforced by Courts of Equitable Jurisdiction in the United States of America.* 3d ed. Albany, N.Y.: Banks & Company, 1926.

———. *A Treatise on Equity Jurisprudence as Administered in the United States of America: Adapted for All the States and to the Union of Legal and Equitable Remedies under the Reformed Procedure.* 5th ed. Rochester, N.Y.: Lawyers Co-operative Publishing Company, 1941.

Prindle, Edwin J. *Patents as a Factor in Manufacturing.* Baltimore: Waverly Press, Engineering Magazine, 1908.

Prude, Jonathan. *The Coming of Industrial Order: Town and Factory Life in Rural Massachusetts, 1810–1860.* New York: Cambridge University Press, 1983.

Pursell, Carroll. *The Machine in America: A Social History of Technology.* Baltimore: Johns Hopkins University Press, 1995.

Rae, John. "The Application of Science to Industry." In *The Organization of Knowledge in Modern America, 1860–1920,* edited by Alexandra Oleson and John Voss, 249–68. Baltimore: Johns Hopkins University Press, 1979.

Reeve, Tapping. *The Law of Baron and Femme: Of Parent and Child, Guardian and Ward, Master and Servant and of the Powers of the Courts of Chancery: With an Essay on the Terms Heir, Heirs, Heirs of the Body.* 3d ed. Albany, N.Y.: W. Gould, 1862.

Reich, Leonard S. *The Making of American Industrial Research: Science and Business at GE and Bell, 1876–1926.* Cambridge: Cambridge University Press, 1985.

Richards, Thomas. *The Commodity Culture of Victorian England: Advertising and Spectacle, 1851–1914.* Stanford, Calif.: Stanford University Press, 1990.

Riggs, John B. *A Guide to the Manuscripts in the Eleutherian Mills Historical Library; Accessions through the Year 1965.* Greenville, Del.: Eleutherian Mills Historical Library, 1970.

Ristow, Walter W. *American Maps and Mapmakers: Commercial Cartography in the Nineteenth Century*. Detroit: Wayne State University Press, 1985.

Rorabaugh, W. J. *The Craft Apprentice: From Franklin to the Machine Age in America*. New York: Oxford University Press, 1986.

Rose, Mark. *Authors and Owners: The Invention of Copyright*. Cambridge, Mass.: Harvard University Press, 1993.

Ross, Marlon B. "Authority and Authenticity: Scribbling Authors and the Genius of Print in Eighteenth-Century England." In *The Construction of Authorship: Textual Appropriation in Law and Literature*, edited by Martha Woodmansee and Peter Jaszi, 231–58. Durham, N.C.: Duke University Press, 1994.

Rossman, Joseph. *The Psychology of the Inventor: A Study of the Patentee*. Washington, D.C.: Inventors Publishing Company, 1931.

Roy, William G. "The Organization of the Corporate Class Segment of the U.S. Capitalist Class at the Turn of This Century." In *Bringing Class Back In: Contemporary and Historical Perspectives*, edited by Scott G. McNall, Rhonda F. Levine, and Rick Fantasia, 139–63. Boulder, Colo.: Westview Press, 1991.

Saint-Amour, Paul K. *The Copywrights: Intellectual Property and the Literary Imagination*. Ithaca, N.Y.: Cornell University Press, 2003.

Saxenian, Annalee. *Regional Advantage: Culture and Competition in Silicon Valley and Route 128*. Cambridge, Mass.: Harvard University Press, 1994.

Schouler, James. *Law of the Domestic Relations: Embracing Husband and Wife, Parent and Child, Guardian and Ward, Infancy, and Master and Servant*. Boston: Little, Brown, 1905.

Schumpeter, Joseph. *Capitalism, Socialism, and Democracy*. 3d ed. New York: Harper & Row, 1950.

———. *The Economics and Sociology of Capitalism*. Edited by Richard Swedberg. Princeton, N.J.: Princeton University Press, 1991.

———. *The Theory of Economic Development; An Inquiry into Profits, Capital, Credit, Interest, and the Business Cycle*. Translated by Redvers Opie. Cambridge, Mass.: Harvard University Press, 1934.

Scranton, Philip. *Endless Novelty: Specialty Production and American Industrialization, 1965–1925*. Princeton, N.J.: Princeton University Press, 1997.

———. *Figured Tapestry: Production, Markets, and Power in Philadelphia Textiles, 1885–1941*. New York: Cambridge University Press, 1989.

Sellers, Charles G. *The Market Revolution: Jacksonian America, 1815–1846*. New York: Oxford University Press, 1991.

Selznick, Philip. *Law, Society, and Industrial Justice*. New York: Russell Sage Foundation, 1969.

Short, John R. *Representing the Republic: Mapping the United States, 1600–1900*. London: Reaktion Books, 2001.

Sinclair, Bruce. *A Centennial History of the American Society of Mechanical Engineers, 1880–1980*. Toronto: University of Toronto Press, 1980.

———. *Philadelphia's Philosopher Mechanics: A History of the Franklin Institute, 1824–1865*. Baltimore: Johns Hopkins University Press, 1974.

Slater, Don. *Consumer Culture and Modernity*. Malden, Mass.: Blackwell, 1997.

Smith, Charles M. *A Treatise on the Law of Master and Servant: Including Therein Masters and Workmen in Every Description of Trade and Occupation*. Philadelphia: T. & J. W. Johnson, 1852.

Stahl, Matthew Wheelock. "Reinventing Certainties: American Popular Music and Social Reproduction." Ph.D. dissertation, University of California, San Diego, 2006.

Stanley, Amy Dru. *From Bondage to Contract: Wage Labor, Marriage, and the Market in the Age of Slave Emancipation*. New York: Cambridge University Press, 1998.

Steinfeld, Robert J. *Coercion, Contract, and Free Labor in the Nineteenth Century*. Edited by Christopher Tomlins. New York: Cambridge University Press, 2001.

———. *The Invention of Free Labor: The Employment Relation in English and American Law and Culture, 1350–1870*. Chapel Hill: University of North Carolina Press, 1991.

Steinmetz, Charles P. *America and the New Epoch*. New York: Harper & Brothers, 1916.

Story, Joseph. *Commentaries on Equity Jurisprudence*. 1st English ed. Edited by W. E. Grigsby. London: Stevens and Haynes, 1884.

Surrency, Erwin C. *A History of American Law Publishing*. New York: Oceana Publications, 1990.

Taylor, Frederick W. *The Principles of Scientific Management*. 1911. Reprint, New York: Norton, 1967.

Taylor, Tom. *Our American Cousin: The Play That Changed History*. Edited by Welford D. Taylor. Washington, D.C.: Beacham Publishing, 1990.

Thompson, E. P. *The Making of the English Working Class*. London: Penguin, 1963.

Thompson, Holland. *The Age of Invention: A Chronicle of Mechanical Conquest*. New Haven, Conn.: Yale University Press, 1921.

Thompson, Seymour D. *Commentaries on the Law of Private Corporations*. San Francisco: Bancroft-Whitney, 1895.

Tiedeman, Christopher G. *A Treatise on State and Federal Control of Persons and Property in the United States: Considered from Both a Civil and Criminal Standpoint*. St. Louis: F. H. Thomas Law Book Company, 1900.

Tilley, Nannie M. *The Bright Tobacco Industry, 1860–1929*. Chapel Hill: University of North Carolina Press, 1948.

Tocqueville, Alexis de. *Democracy in America*. 2 vols. New York: Knopf, 1945.

Tomlins, Christopher L. "Law and Power in the Employment Relationship." In *Labor Law in America: Historical and Critical Essays*, edited by Christopher L. Tomlins and Andrew J. King, 71–98. Baltimore: Johns Hopkins University Press, 1992.

———. *Law, Labor, and Ideology in the Early American Republic*. New York: Cambridge University Press, 1993.

———. *The State and the Unions: Labor Relations, Law, and the Organized Labor Movement in America, 1880–1960*. New York: Cambridge University Press, 1985.

Trebilcock, Michael J. *The Common Law of Restraint of Trade: A Legal and Economic Analysis*. Toronto: Carswell, 1986.

Tyner, Judith A. "Images of the Southwest in Nineteenth-Century American Atlases." In *The Mapping of the American Southwest*, edited by Dennis Reinhartz and Charles C. Colley, 57–77. College Station: Texas A&M University Press, 1987.

Usselman, Steven W. "Patents, Engineering Professionals, and Pipelines of Innovation." In *Learning by Doing in Markets, Firms, and Countries*, edited by Naomi R. Lamoreaux, Daniel M. Raff, and Peter Temin, 61–102. Chicago: University of Chicago Press, 1998.

———. *Regulating Railroad Innovation: Business, Technology, and Politics in America, 1840–1920*. New York: Cambridge University Press, 2002.

Veblen, Thorstein. *The Theory of the Leisure Class: An Economic Study of Institutions*. New York: Vanguard Press, 1932.

Von Hippel, Eric. *Democratizing Innovation*. Cambridge, Mass.: MIT Press, 2005.

Wacquant, Löic J. D. "Making Class: The Middle Class(es) in Social Theory and Social Structure." In *Bringing Class Back In: Contemporary and Historical Perspectives*, edited by Scott G. McNall, Rhonda F. Levine, and Rick Fantasia, 39–64. Boulder, Colo.: Westview Press, 1991.

Walkowitz, Daniel J. *Working with Class: Social Workers and the Politics of Middle-Class Identity*. Chapel Hill: University of North Carolina Press, 1999.

Walterscheid, Edward C. *To Promote the Progress of Useful Arts: American Patent Law and Administration, 1798–1836*. Littleton, Colo.: F. B. Rothman, 1998.

Ware, Caroline F. *The Early New England Cotton Manufacture: A Study in Industrial Beginnings*. Boston: Houghton Mifflin, 1931.

West, Nancy M. *Kodak and the Lens of Nostalgia*. Charlottesville: University Press of Virginia, 2000.

Wharton, Francis. *A Commentary on the Law of Agency and Agents*. Philadelphia: Kay & Bro., 1876.

White, G. Edward. *The Marshall Court and Cultural Change, 1815–1835*. New York: Macmillan, 1988.

Wilentz, Sean. *Chants Democratic: New York and the Rise of the American Working Class, 1788–1850*. New York: Oxford University Press, 1984.

Wilson, Christopher P. *White Collar Fictions: Class and Social Representation in American Literature, 1885–1925*. Athens: University of Georgia Press, 1992.

Wilson, Mitchell. *American Science and Invention, a Pictorial History: The Fabulous Story of How American Dreamers, Wizards, and Inspired Tinkerers Converted a Wilderness into the Wonder of the World*. New York: Simon & Schuster, 1954.

Wise, George. *Willis R. Whitney, General Electric, and the Origins of U.S. Industrial Research*. New York: Columbia University Press, 1985.

Wood, Gordon S. *The Creation of the American Republic, 1776–1787*. Chapel Hill: University of North Carolina Press, 1969.

———. *The Radicalism of the American Revolution*. New York: Vintage, 1991.

Wood, Horace Gay. *A Treatise on the Law of Master and Servant: Covering the Relation, Duties and Liabilities of Employers and Employees*. San Francisco: Bancroft-Whitney, 1877, 1886.

Woodmansee, Martha, and Peter Jaszi, eds. *The Construction of Authorship: Textual Appropriation in Law and Literature*. Durham, N.C.: Duke University Press, 1994.

York, Neil L. *Mechanical Metamorphosis: Technological Change in Revolutionary America*. Westport, Conn.: Greenwood Press, 1985.

Zunz, Olivier. *Making America Corporate, 1870–1920*. Chicago: University of Chicago Press, 1990.

Zussman, Robert. *Mechanics of the Middle Class: Work and Politics among American Engineers*. Berkeley: University of California Press, 1985.

ARTICLES

"Affairs in Massachusetts." *New York Times*, September 30, 1867, 8.

"Affairs in Massachusetts." *New York Times*, October 23, 1867, 2.

"Affairs in Massachusetts." *New York Times*, November 13, 1867, 2.

Allen, Robert C. "Collective Invention." *Journal of Economic Behavior & Organization* 1 (1983).

"Amusements." *New York Times*, March 30, 1881, 5.

Ayres, Ian, and Robert Gertner. "Majoritarian vs. Minoritarian Defaults." 51 *Stanford Law Review* 1591 (1999).

Ballam, Deborah A. "The Development of the Employment at Will Rule Revisited: A Challenge to Its Origins as Based in the Development of Advanced Capitalism." 13 *Hofstra Labor & Employment Law Journal* 75 (1995).

Barton, William B. "A Study in the Law of Trade Secrets." 13 *University of Cincinnati Law Review* 507 (1939).

Bay, Helmouth. "Air Trails Maps: A Chapter in the Early History of Aeronautical Charts." 15 *Surveying and Mapping* 322 (1955).

Beer, John J. "Coal Tar Dye Manufacture and the Origins of the Modern Industrial Research Laboratory." 49 *Isis* 123 (1958).

Blake, Harlan M. "Employee Agreements Not to Compete." 73 *Harvard Law Review* 625, 632–38 (1960).

Bourdieu, Pierre. "What Makes a Class? On the Theoretical and Practical Existence of Groups." 32 *Berkeley Journal of Sociology* 1 (1987).

Bracha, Oren. "The Commodification of Patents, 1600–1836: How Patents Became Rights and Why We Should Care." 38 *Loyola of Los Angeles Law Review* 177 (2004).

"Breach of Copyright: The Important Case of Lawrence v. Dana." *New York Times*, September 22, 1869, 5.

Brooke-Smith, James. "Mediating Invention at the End of the Nineteenth Century." Paper delivered at Con/Texts of Invention Conference, Case Western Reserve University, April 2006.

Brown, John K. "When Machines Became Gray and Drawings Black and White: William Sellers and the Rationalization of Mechanical Engineering." 25 *Industrial Archaeology* 29 (1990).

Burk, Dan. "Intellectual Property and the Firm." 71 *University of Chicago Law Review* 3 (2004).

Carpenter, Charles E. "Validity of Contracts Not to Compete." 76 *University of Pennsylvania Law Review* 244 (1928).

Bibliography

Cheever, Dwight B. "The Rights of Employer and Employee to Inventions Made by Either during the Relationship." 1 *Michigan Law Review* 384 (1903).

Clark, Walter. "Charles Edward Kenneth Mees: 1882–1960." 7 *Biographical Memoirs of Fellows of the Royal Society* 173 (1961).

"Commentaire sur les Elements du Droit International et sur l'Histoire des Progres du Droit des Gens de Henry Wheaton." Review of the French edition of *Elements of International Law,* by Henry Wheaton. *American Law Review* 409 (June 1881).

Dietz, Frederick C. Review of *A History of Mechanical Inventions,* by Abbott Payton Usher. 35 *American Historical Review* 399 (1930).

"D'Oyly Carte and Mr. Evans." *New York Times*, February 17, 1886, 1.

Dreyfuss, Rochelle C. "Collaborative Research: Conflicts on Authorship, Ownership, and Accountability." 53 *Vanderbilt Law Review* 1162 (2000).

"Eastman Kodak Says Ex-Employee Leaked Trade Secrets to 3M." *Wall Street Journal*, November 21, 1997, 1.

"*Eldred v. Ashcroft*: How Artists and Creators Finally Got Their Due." 2003 *Duke Journal of Law & Technology* 14 (May 2003).

"Elements of International Law." Book review. *American Law Review* 185 (October 1866).

Epstein, S. R. "Craft Guilds, Apprenticeship, and Technological Change in Preindustrial Europe." 58 *Journal of Economic History* 684 (1998).

Farley, Christine. "The Lingering Effects of Copyright's Response to the Invention of Photography." 65 *University of Pittsburgh Law Review* 385 (2004).

Feinman, Jay M. "The Development of the Employment at Will Rule." 20 *American Journal of Legal History* 118 (1976).

Fidler, Ann. "'Till You Understand Them in Their Principal Features': Observations on Form and Function in Nineteenth-Century American Law Books." 92 *Papers of the Bibliographical Society of America* 427 (1998).

Fisher, William W., III. "Geistiges Eigentum—ein ausufernder Rechtsbereich: Die Geschichte des Ideenschutzes in den Vereinigten Staaten." In *Eigentum im internationalen Vergleich,* edited by Hannes Siegrist and Davis Sugarman (Vandenhoeck & Ruprecht, 1999), 265–91. Translated in William W. Fisher III, "The Growth of Intellectual Property: A History of the Ownership of Ideas in the United States," 22 and n. 105 (1999). ⟨http://cyber.law.harvard.edu/people/tfisher/ iphistory.pdf.⟩

Fishman, Joel. "The Digests of Pennsylvania." 90 *Law Library Journal* 481 (1998).

———. "The Reports of the Supreme Court of Pennsylvania." 87 *Law Library Journal* 643 (1995).

Fisk, Catherine L. "Authors at Work: The Origins of the Work-for-Hire Doctrine." 15 *Yale Journal of Law and the Humanities* 1 (2003).

———. "Credit Where It's Due: The Law and Norms of Attribution." 95 *Georgetown Law Journal* 49 (2006).

———. "Removing the 'Fuel of Interest' from the 'Fire of Genius': Law and the Employee-Inventor, 1830–1930." 65 *University of Chicago Law Review* 1127 (1998).

———. "Working Knowledge: Trade Secrets, Restrictive Covenants in Employment, and the Rise of Corporate Intellectual Property, 1800–1920." 52 *Hastings Law Journal* 441 (2001).

Fiske, Stephen. "Dramatic Feuilleton." *Art Amateur*, January 1884, 27.

———. "Dramatic Feuilleton." *Art Amateur*, October 1884, 94.

———. "Dramatic Feuilleton." *Art Amateur*, April 1885, 99.

"Founder of Two Theatres." *New York Times*, February 26, 1894, 1.

Fox, Paulette S., Note. "Preserving the Collaborative Spirit of American Theater: The Need for a 'Joint Authorship Default Rule' in Light of the *Rent* Decision's Unanswered Question." 19 *Cardozo Arts & Entertainment Law Journal* 497 (2001).

Gellman, Robert M. "Twin Evils: Government Copyright and Copyright-Like Controls Over Government Information." 45 *Syracuse Law Review* 999 (1995).

"General Mention." *New York Times*, March 30, 1881, 5.

Goldstein, Patrick. "The Big Picture: Hollywood Deals with Piracy, A Wary Eye on CDs." *Los Angeles Times*, September 9, 2003, E1.

Gorman, Seth F. "Who Owns the Movies? Joint Authorship under the Copyright Act of 1976 after *Childress v. Taylor* and *Thomson v. Larson*." 7 *UCLA Entertainment Law Review* 1 (1998).

Hale, Robert. "Coercion and Distribution in a Supposedly Non-Coercive State." 38 *Political Science Quarterly* 478 (1923).

Handler, Milton, and Daniel E. Lazaroff. "Restraint of Trade and the Restatement (Second) of Contracts." 57 *New York University Law Review* 669, 721–24 (1982).

Hannigan, John E. "The Implied Obligation of an Employee." 77 *University of Pennsylvania Law Review* 970 (1929).

"Hazel Kirke in the Court." *New York Times*, April 15, 1882, 8.

"Hazel Kirke in the Courts." *New York Times*, September 18, 1881, 9.

"The Historiography of American Technology." 11 *Technology and Culture* 1 (1969).

Hobart, Charles W. "The Cascade Tunnel and the Man That Made It." 13 *Magazine of Western History* 534 (1991).

Holmes, O. W. "The Path of the Law." 10 *Harvard Law Review* 457 (1897).

Holton, James L. "John Wootten: Locomotive Pioneer." 44 *Historical Review of Berks County* 97 (Summer 1979).

Homburg, Ernst. "The Emergence of Research Laboratories in the Dyestuffs Industry, 1870–1900." 25 *British Journal for History of Science* 91 (1992).

Hounshell, David A. "Interpreting the History of Industrial Research and Development: The Case of E. I du Pont de Nemours & Co." 134 *Proceedings of the American Philosophical Society* 387 (1990).

Hughes, Thomas P. "Emerging Themes in the History of Technology." 20 *Journal of Technology and Culture* 697 (1979).

Hyde, Lewis. "Frames from the Framers: How America's Revolutionaries Imagined Intellectual Property." *Research Publication* (2005). ⟨http://cyber.law.harvard.edu /publications⟩.

"Joseph Hatton's Reading." *New York Times*, October 17, 1880, 2.

Joyce, Craig. "The Rise of the Supreme Court Reporter: An Institutional Perspective on Marshall Court Ascendancy." 83 *Michigan Law Review* 1291 (1985).

Khan, B. Zorina, and Kenneth L. Sokoloff. "The Early Development of Intellectual Property Institutions in the United States." 15 *Journal of Economic Perspectives* 233 (2001).

———. "'Schemes of Practical Utility': Entrepreneurship and Innovation among 'Great Inventors' in the United States, 1790–1865." 53 *Journal of Economic History* 289 (1993).

King, Timothy. "Patronage and Market in the Creation of Opera before the Institution of Intellectual Property." 25 *Journal of Cultural Economics* 21 (2001).

Klebnikov, Paul. "A Traumatic Experience." *Forbes*, January 18, 1993, 83.

Kleinfeld, N. R. "How 'Strykeforce' Beat the Clock." *New York Times*, March 25, 1990.

Konefsky, Alfred S. "As Best to Subserve Their Own Interests: Lemuel Shaw, Labor Conspiracy, and Fellow Servants." 7 *Law & History Review* 219 (1989).

Lamoreaux, Naomi R., and Kenneth L. Sokoloff. "The Geography of Invention in the American Glass Industry, 1870–1925." 60 *Journal of Economic History* 700 (2000).

———. "Long-Term Change in the Organization of Inventive Activity." 93 *Proceedings of the National Academy of Sciences of the United States of America* 12686 (1996).

Langbein, John H. "Chancellor Kent and the History of Legal Literature." 93 *Columbia Law Review* 547 (1993).

Lange, David. "At Play in the Fields of the Word: Copyright and the Construction of Authorship in the Post-Literate Millennium." 55 *Law & Contemporary Problems* 139 (1992).

Laski, Harold J. "The Personality of Associations." 29 *Harvard Law Review* 404 (1916).

Lawrence, W. B. "Letter of William Beach Lawrence." *North American Review*, January 1867, 309.

Lee, Jane C., Comment. "Upstaging the Playwright: The Joint Authorship Entanglement between Dramaturgs and Playwrights." 19 *Loyola of Los Angeles Entertainment Law Review* 75 (1998).

Letwin, William L. "The English Common Law Concerning Monopolies." 21 *University of Chicago Law Review* 355 (1954).

"A Literary Controversy: An Interesting Case of Alleged Plagiarism." *New York Times*, November 2, 1866, 8.

Loux, Andrea C., Note. "The Persistence of the Ancient Regime: Custom, Utility, and the Common Law in the Nineteenth Century." 79 *Cornell Law Review* 183 (1993).

Lubar, Steven. "The Transformation of Antebellum Patent Law." 32 *Technology & Culture* 932 (1991).

MacLeod, Christine. "Negotiating the Rewards of Invention: The Shop-Floor Inventor in Victorian Britain." 41 *Business History* 17 (1999).

"The Madison-Square Theatre: Mr. MacKaye's Improvements in the Stage Mechanism." *New York Times*, February 1, 1880, 5.

Manchester, Harland. "The World of Rand McNally." *Saturday Review of Literature*, January 21, 1950, 35.

McCurdy, Charles W. "The Roots of 'Liberty of Contract' Reconsidered: Major Premises in the Law of Employment, 1867–1937." *Supreme Court Historical Society Yearbook* 20 (1984).

Mees, C. E. Kenneth. "The Organization of Industrial Scientific Research." 97 *Nature* 411 (1916).

———. "A Photographic Research Laboratory." 5 *Scientific Monthly* 481 (1917).

———. "Secrecy and Industrial Research." 170 *Nature* 972 (1952).

Merges, Robert P. "The Law and Economics of Employee Inventions." 13 *Harvard Journal of Law & Technology* 1 (1999).

Metzmeier, Kurt X. "Blazing Trails in a New Kentucky Wilderness: Early Kentucky Case Law Digests." 93 *Law Library Journal* 1 (2001).

"'The Mikado' Again in Court." *New York Times*, January 31, 1886, 1.

"Movable Theatre Stages." *Scientific American*, April 5, 1884, 207.

Nader, John. "The Rise of an Inventive Profession: Learning Effects in the Midwestern Harvester Industry, 1850–1890." 54 *Journal of Economic History* 397 (1994).

"New York Water Supply." *Scientific American*, June 4, 1887, 351.

Nockleby, John, Note. "Tortious Interference with Contractual Relations in the Nineteenth Century: The Transformation of Property, Contract, and Tort." 93 *Harvard Law Review* 1510, 1514–15 (1980).

"Note to Article V.: Mr. Dana's Notes on Wheaton's Elements of International Law." *North American Review* 626 (October 1886).

Obituary of Henry C. Sergeant. *New York Times*, February 1, 1907, 9.

Patterson, L. Ray, and Craig Joyce. "Copyright in 1791: An Essay Concerning the Founders' View of the Copyright Power Granted to Congress in Article I, Section 8, Clause 8 of the U.S. Constitution." 52 *Emory Law Journal* 909 (2003).

"Plans for the Poe Entertainment." *New York Times*, January 27, 1881, 8.

"Plays and Actors." *New York Times*, March 20, 1881, 7.

Pocock, J. G. A. "Virtue and Commerce in the Eighteenth Century." 3 *Journal of Interdisciplinary History* 119 (1972).

Porter, Patrick G. "Origins of the American Tobacco Company." 43 *Business History Review* 59 (1969).

Pound, Roscoe. "Liberty of Contract." 18 *Yale Law Journal* 454 (1909).

———. "The Progress of the Law, 1918–1919." 33 *Harvard Law Review* 420 (1920).

Prindle, Edwin J. "Patents as a Factor in a Manufacturing Business." 32 *Engineering Magazine* 407 (October 1906).

"Proposed New Copyright Law." *Chambers's Edinburgh Journal* 104 (April 21, 1838).

"The Religious Editor: He Tries Steele MacKaye's New Patent Theatre Chair, and Don't Like It." *National Police Gazette*, December 22, 1883, 6.

"Rev. G. S. Mallory's Death." *New York Times*, March 3, 1897, 12.

"The Right of Private Property." 3 *Michigan Law Journal* 215 (1894).

Scherer, F. M. "The Evolution of Free-Lance Music Composition, 1650–1900." 25 *Journal of Cultural Economics* 307 (2001).

Schiller, A. Arthur. "Trade Secrets and the Roman Law; The Actio Servi Corrupti." 30 *Columbia Law Review* 837 (1930).

Siegel, Stephen A. "John Chipman Gray and the Moral Basis of Classical Legal Thought." 86 *Iowa Law Review* 1513 (2001).

Sokoloff, Kenneth L., and David Dollar. "Agricultural Seasonality and the Organization of Manufacturing in Early Industrial Economies: The Contrast Between England and the United States." 57 *Journal of Economic History* 288 (1997).

Stahl, Matthew. "Authentic Boy Bands on TV? Performers and Impresarios in *The Monkees* and *Making the Band*." 21 *Popular Music* 307 (2002).

Steffen, Charles G. "Changes in the Organization of Artisan Production in Baltimore, 1790–1820." 36 *William & Mary Quarterly* 101 (1979).

"The Success of Hazel Kirke." *New York Times*, October 11, 1881, 4.

Surrency, Erwin C. "Law Reports in the United States." 25 *American Journal of Legal History* 48 (1981).

Tobacco, November 17, 1893, 4.

Tomlins, Christopher L. "The Ties That Bind: Master and Servant in Massachusetts, 1800–1850." 30 *Labor History* 193 (1989).

Turney, Wayne S. "James Steele Mackaye (1842–1894)." ⟨http://www.wayneturney.20m.com/mackayesteele.htm⟩.

VanderVelde, Lea S. "The Gendered Origins of the *Lumley* Doctrine: Binding Men's Consciences and Women's Fidelity." 101 *Yale Law Journal* 775 (1992).

Wilde, Oscar. "The Portrait of Mr. W. H." *Blackwood's Edinburgh Magazine* 146 (1889).

Wisby, Johannes H. "Compressed Air." *Los Angeles Times*, November 19, 1899, A10.

Wise, Jim. "A Man with Big Ideas: Visionary Richard Harvey Wright Invented a Company That Sent Products to the Moon." *Durham* (N.C.) *Herald-Sun*, January 18, 2004, E1.

Witt, John F. "Rethinking the Nineteenth-Century Employment Contract, Again." 18 *Law & History Review* 627 (2000).

Woodward, R. S. Book review of *Invention, the Master-key to Progress*, by Bradley A. Fiske. 27 *American Historical Review* 541 (1922).

Workman, Henry C. "Rights of Employers and Employees in Inventions Made by the Latter." 20 *American Bar Association Journal* 538 (1934).

Yu, Peter K. "Intellectual Property and the Information Ecosystem." 2005 *Michigan State Law Review* 1, 3, n. 12. (2005).

AMERICAN CASES

Adair v. United States, 208 U.S. 161 (1908).

Addyston Pipe & Steel Co. v. United States, 85 F. 271 (6th Cir. 1898).

Addyston Pipe & Steel Co. v. United States, 175 U.S. 211 (1899).

Aetna-Standard Engineering Co. v. Rowland, 493 A. 2d 1375 (Pa. Super. Ct. 1985).

Agawam Woolen Co. v. Jordan, 74 U.S. 583 (1868).

Alden v. Dewey, 1 F. Cas. 329 (C.C.D. Mass. 1840) (No. 153).

Alger v. Thacher, 36 Mass. (19 Pick.) 51 (1837).

Allgeyer v. Louisiana, 165 U.S. 578 (1897).

American Cyanamid Co. v. Ladd, 225 F. Supp. 709 (D.D.C. 1964).

American Tube-Works v. Bridgewater Iron Co., 26 F. 334 (C.C.D. Mass. 1886).

Appleton v. Bacon, 67 U.S. 699 (1862).

Armistead v. Chatters, 71 Miss. 509, 15 So. 39 (1893).

Aronson v. Orlov, 116 N.E. 951 (Mass. 1917).

Aspinwall Manufacturing Co. v. Gill, 32 F. 697 (C.C.D.N.J. 1887).

Atwill v. Ferrett, 2 F. Cas. 195 (C.C.S.D.N.Y. 1846) (No. 640).

Balzac v. Porto Rico, 258 U.S. 298 (1922).

Banner Metals, Inc. v. Lockwood, 3 Cal. Rptr. 421 (Cal. Dist. Ct. App. 1960).

Barnes v. Ingalls, 39 Ala. 193 (1863).

Barron v. Collins, 49 Ga. 580 (1873).

Beal v. Chase, 31 Mich. 490 (1875).

Binney v. Annan, 107 Mass. 94 (1871).

Binns v. Woodruff, 3 F. Cas. 421 (C.C.D. Pa. 1821) (No. 1424).

Blakeney v. Goode, 30 Ohio St. 350 (1876).

Blanchard v. Eldridge, 3 F. Cas. 624 (C.C.E.D. Pa. 1849) (No. 1510).

Bleistein v. Donaldson Lithographing Co., 188 U.S. 239 (1903).

Board of Trade of Chicago v. Christie Grain & Stock Co., 198 U.S. 236 (1905).

Bonsack Machine Co. v. Elliott, 73 F. 834 (2d Cir. 1896).

Bonsack Machine Co. v. Hulse, 57 F. 519 (C.C.W.D. Va. 1893).

Bonsack Machine Co. v. S. F. Hess & Co., 68 F. 119 (4th Cir. 1895).

Bonsack Machine Co. v. Smith, 70 F. 383 (C.C.W.D.N.C. 1895).

Boosing v. Doorman, 103 N.E. 1121 (N.Y. 1913).

Boston Glass Manufactory v. Binney, 21 Mass. (4 Pick.) 425 (1827).

Boucicault v. Fox, 3 F. Cas. 977 (C.C.S.D.N.Y. 1862) (No. 1691).

Bourlier Brothers v. Macauley, 15 S.W. 60 (Ky. 1891).

Bright v. State, 4 Ga. App. 333, 61 S.E. 289 (1908).

Brooks v. Byam, 4 F. Cas. 261 (C.C.D. Mass. 1843) (No. 1948).

Bryan v. State, 44 Ga. 328 (1871).

Burney v. Ryle, 17 S.E. 986 (Ga. 1893).

Burr v. De La Vergne, 7 N.E. 366 (N.Y. 1886).

Burrow-Giles Lithographic Co. v. Sarony, 111 U.S. 53 (1884).

Butler v. Galletti, 21 How. Pr. 465 (N.Y. Sup. Ct. 1861).

Callaghan v. Myers, 128 U.S. 617 (1888).

Cameron Mach. Co. v. Samuel M. Langston Co., 115 A. 212 (N.J. Ch. 1921).

Carte v. Evans, 27 F. 861 (C.C.D. Mass. 1886).

Carter v. Ferguson, 12 N.Y.S. 580 (N.Y. Sup. Ct. 1890).

Chae Chan Ping v. United States, 130 U.S. 581 (1889).

Chambers & Marshall v. Baldwin, 91 Ky. 121, 15 S.W. 57 (1891).

Chapman v. Ferry, 12 F. 693 (C.C.D. Ore. 1882).

Charles River Bridge v. Warren Bridge, 36 U.S. (11 Pet.) 420 (1837).

Chew Heong v. United States, 112 U.S. 536 (1884).

Cincinnati Bell Foundry Co. v. Dodds, 10 Ohio Dec. Reprint 154 (Super. Ct. 1887).

Clark Paper & Manufacturing Co. v. Stenacker, 165 N.Y.S. 367 (Sup. Ct. 1917).

Clark v. West, 86 N.E. 1 (N.Y. 1908).

Colliery Engineer Co. v. United Correspondence School Co., 94 F. 152 (C.C.S.D.N.Y. 1899).

Comstock v. Lopokowa, 190 F. 599 (C.C.S.D.N.Y. 1911).

[332] Cont'l Windmill Co. v. Empire Windmill Co., 6 F. Cas. 366 (C.C.D.N.Y. 1871) (No. 3142).

Cort v. Lassard, 22 P. 1054 (Or. 1889).

Crowe v. M&M/Mars, 577 A.2d 1278 (N.J. 1990).

Deming v. Chapman, 11 How. Pr. 382 (N.Y. Sup. Ct. 1854).

Dempsey v. Dobson, 39 A. 493 (Pa. 1898).

Dempsey v. Dobson, 34 A. 459 (Pa. 1896).

Dental Vulcanite Co. v. Weatherbee, 7 F. Cas. 498 (C.C.D. Mass. 1866).

De Witt v. Brooks, 7 F. Cas. 575 (C.C.S.D.N.Y. 1882) (No. 3851).

Dickson v. Dickson, 33 La. Ann. 1261 (Louisiana 1881).

Dixon v. Moyer, 7 F. Cas. 758 (C.C.D. Pa. 1821) (No. 3931).

Dorr v. United States, 195 U.S. 138 (1904).

Downes v. Bidwell, 182 U.S. 244 (1901).

Duckett v. Pool, 34 S.C. 311, 13 S.E. 542 (1891).

Dyer's Case, Y. B. 2 Hen. 5, fol. 5, Michaelmas, pl. 26 (Eng. 1414).

E. I. du Pont de Nemours Powder Co. v. Masland, 216 F. 271 (E.D. Pa. 1914).

E. I. du Pont de Nemours Powder Co. v. Masland, 222 F. 340 (E.D. Pa. 1915).

E. I. du Pont de Nemours Powder Co. v. Masland, 244 U.S. 100 (1917).

E. Jaccard Jewelry Co. v. O'Brien, 70 Mo. App. 432 (1897).

Eastman Co. v. Reichenbach, 20 N.Y.S. 110 (Sup. Ct. 1892).

Eastman Kodak Co. v. Powers Films Prods. Inc., 179 N.Y.S. 325 (App. Div. 1919).

Edward Thompson Co. v. Am. Law Book Co., 119 F. 217 (C.C.S.D.N.Y. 1902).

Eenkhoorn v. New York Telephone Co., 497 N.Y.S. 2d 303 (N.Y. City Ct. 1986).

Empire Steam Laundry v. Lozier, 130 P. 1180 (Cal. 1913).

Eustis Manufacturing Co. v. Eustis, 27 A. 439 (N.J. Ch. 1893).

F. W. Dodge Co. v. Construction Information Co., 66 N.E. 204 (Mass. 1903).

Fong Yue Ting v. United States, 149 U.S. 698 (1893).

Fuller & Johnson Manufacturing Co. v. Bartlett, 31 N.W. 747 (Wis. 1887).

Fulton Grand Laundry Co. v. Johnson, 117 A. 753 (Md. 1922).

Gayler v. Wilder, 51 U.S. (10 How.) 477 (1850).

Gemco Engineering & Manufacturing Co. v. Henderson, 84 N.E. 2d 596 (Ohio 1949).

George A. Kessler & Co. v. Chappelle, 77 N.Y.S. 285 (App. Div. 1902).

Goodyear v. Day, 10 F. Cas. 677 (C.C.D.N.J. 1852) (No. 5566).

Grand Union Tea Co. v. Dodds, 128 N.W. 1090 (Mich. 1910).

H. B. Wiggins Sons' Co. v. Cott-A-Lap Co., 169 F. 150 (C.C.D. Conn. 1909).

H. W. Gossard Co. v. Crosby, 109 N.W. 483 (Iowa 1906).

Hackett v. A. L. & J. J. Reynolds Co., 62 N.Y.S. 1076 (App. Term. 1900).

Hahn v. The Concordia Society of Baltimore City, 42 Md. 460 (1875).

Hamilton Mfg. Co. v. Tubbs Manufacturing Co., 216 F. 401 (C.C.W.D. Mich. 1908).

Hammerstein v. Mann, 122 N.Y.S. 276 (App. Div. 1910).

Hammerstein v. Sylva, 124 N.Y.S. 535 (1910).

Ham v. Johnson, 55 Minn. 115 (1896).

Hapgood v. Hewitt, 11 F. 422 (C.C.D. Ind. 1882).

Hapgood v. Hewitt, 119 U.S. 226 (1886).

Hard v. Seeley, 47 Barb. 428 (N.Y. Sup. Ct. 1865).

Harry Hastings Attractions v. Howard, 196 N.Y.S. 228 (Sup. Ct. 1922).

Haskins v. Royster, 70 N.C. 601 (1874).

Hawaii v. Mankichi, 190 U.S. 197 (1903).

Hayes v. O'Brien, 149 Ill. 403 (1894).

Hayes v. Willio, 11 Abb. Pr. S (N.S.) 167 (N.Y. Common Pl. 1871).

Heine v. Appleton, 11 F. Cas. 1031 (C.C.S.D.N.Y. 1857) (No. 6324).

Henderson v. Vaulx, 18 Tenn. 30 (1836).

Herold v. Herold China & Pottery Co., 257 F. 911 (6th Cir. 1919).

Hewett v. Samsonite Corp., 507 P. 2d 1119 (Colo. Ct. App. 1973).

Hill v. Duckworth, 155 Miss. 484, 124 So. 641 (1929).

Homer v. Ashford, (1825) 130 Eng. Rep. 537 (C.P.).

Hoskins Manufacturing Co. v. PMC Corp., 47 F. Supp. 2d 852 (E.D. Mich. 1999).

Hudgens v. State, 126 Ga. 639, 55 S.E. 492 (1906).

Hudson v. State, 46 Ga. 624 (1872).

Huff v. Watkins, 15 S.C. 82 (1881).

Hulse v. Bonsack Machine Co., 65 F. 864 (4th Cir. 1895).

In re Debs, 158 U.S. 564 (1895).

Jarvis & Lobdell v. Peck, 10 Paige Ch. 118 (N.Y. Ch. 1848).

Jencks v. Langdon Mills, 27 F. 622 (C.C.D.N.H. 1886).

Johnson Furnace & Engineering Co. v. Western Furnace Co., 178 F. 819 (8th Cir. 1910).

Johns v. Patterson, 138 Ark. 420, 211 S.W. 387 (1919).

Joliet Manufacturing Co. v. Dice, 105 Ill. 649 (1883).

Jones v. Stanly, 76 N.C. 355 (1877).

Keeler v. Taylor, 53 Pa. 467 (1866).

Keene v. Wheatley, 14 F. Cas. 180 (C.C.E.D. Pa. 1861) (No. 7644).

Keller v. Stolzenbach, 20 F. 47 (C.C.W.D. Pa. 1884).

Kellogg v. Larkin, 3 Pin. 123 (Wis. 1851).

Kinkade v. New York Shipbuilding Corp., 122 A. 2d 360 (1956).

Kinsman v. Parkhurst, 59 U.S. (18 How.) 289 (1855).

Ladoff v. Dempster, 36 App. D.C. 520 (1911).

Langham v. State, 55 Ala. 144 (1876).

Lawrence v. Dana, 15 F. Cas. 26 (C.C.D. Mass. 1869) (No. 8136).

Lawson v. Mullinix, 64 A. 938 (Md. 1906).

Lee v. West, 47 Ga. 311 (1872).

Lester Agriculture Chemical Works v. Selby, 59 A. 247 (N.J. Ch. 1904).

Littlefield v. Perry, 88 U.S. (21 Wall.) 205 (1874).

Little v. Gallus, 38 N.Y.S. 487 (App. Div. 1896).

Little v. Gould, 15 F. Cas. 604 (C.C.N.D.N.Y. 1851) (No. 8395).

Little v. Gould, 15 F. Cas. 612 (C.C.N.D.N.Y. 1852) (No. 8395).

Little v. Hall, 59 U.S. 165 (1855).

Livingston v. Van Ingen, 9 Johnson 507 (1812).

Lochner v. New York, 198 U.S. 45 (1905).

Loewe v. Lawlor, 208 U.S. 274 (1908).

MacBeth-Evans Glass Co. v. Schnelbach, 86 A. 688 (Pa. 1913).

MacKaye v. Mallory, 6 F. 743 (C.C.S.D.N.Y. 1881).

MacKaye v. Mallory, 12 F. 328 (C.C.S.D.N.Y. 1882).

MacKaye v. Mallory, 79 F. 1 (2d Cir. 1897).

MacKaye v. Mallory, 80 F. 256 (C.C.S.D.N.Y. 1897).

Mallory v. MacKaye, 86 F. 122 (C.C.S.D.N.Y. 1898).

Mapleson v. Del Puente, 13 Abb. N. Cas. 144 (N.Y. Sup. Ct. 1883).

Matthews & Willard Manufacturing Co. v. Trenton Lamp Co., 73 F. 212 (C.C.D.N.J. 1896).

McCaull v. Braham, 16 F. 37 (C.C.S.D.N.Y. 1883).

McClurg v. Kingsland, 42 U.S. (1 How.) 202 (1843).

McGowin v. Remington, 12 Pa. 56 (1849).

Merryweather v. Moore, 2 Ch. 518 (1892).

Metropolitan Exhibition Co. v. Ward, 9 N.Y.S. 779 (Sup. Ct. 1890).

Microbiological Research Corp. v. Muna, 625 P. 2d 690 (Utah 1981).

Middlebrook v. Broadbent, 47 N.Y. 443 (1872).

Morgan v. Smith, 77 N.C. 37 (1877).

Morse Twist Drill & Machine Co. v. Morse, 103 Mass. 73 (1869).

Mudgett v. Clay, 5 Wash. 103 (1892).

Munns v. De Nemours, 17 F. Cas. 993 (D. Pa. 1811) (No. 9926).

Mutual Advertising Co. v. Refo, 76 F. 961 (C.C.D.S.C. 1896).

Myers v. Callaghan, 5 F. 726 (C.C.N.D. Ill. 1881)

National Cloak & Suit Co. v. Kaufman, 189 F. 215 (C.C.M.D. Pa. 1911).

National Tube Co. v. Eastern Tube Co., 3 Ohio C.C. (N.S.) 459 (Cir. Ct. 1902).

National Wire Bound Box Co. v. Healy, 189 F. 49 (7th Cir. 1911).

New Method Laundry Co. v. MacCann, 161 P. 990 (Cal. 1916).

Niagara Radiator Co. v. Meyers, 40 N.Y.S. 572 (1896).

O. & W. Thum Co. v. Tloczynski, 72 N.W. 140 (Mich. 1897).

Peabody v. Norfolk, 98 Mass. 452 (1868).

Peck v. Standard Parts Co., 295 F. 740 (N.D. Ohio 1920).

Peck v. Standard Parts Co., 282 F. 443 (6th Cir. 1922).

Peerless Pattern Co. v. Pictorial Review Co., 132 N.Y.S. 37 (App. Div. 1911).

Pennock v. Dialogue, 27 U.S. 1 (1829).

Peters v. Borst, 9 N.Y.S. 789 (Sup. Ct. 1889).

Philadelphia Ball Club v. Hallman, 8 Pa. C.C. 57 (Com. Pl. 1890).

Philadelphia Ball Club v. Lajoie, 51 A. 973 (Pa. 1902).

Pierce v. Fuller, 8 Mass. 223 (1811).

Pierpont v. Fowle, 19 F. Cas. 652 (C.C.D. Mass. 1846) (No. 11,152).

Plessy v. Ferguson, 163 U.S. 537 (1896).

Potter v. Holland, 19 F. Cas. 1154 (C.C.D. Conn. 1858) (No. 11,329).

Pressed Steel Car Co. v. Standard Steel Car Co., 60 A. 4 (Pa. 1904).

Press Publishing Co. v. Monroe, 73 F. 196 (2d Cir. 1896).

Rabinovich v. Reith, 120 Ill. App. 409 (1905).

Rhoden v. State, 161 Ga. 73, 129 S.E. 640 (1925).

Robb v. Green, 2 Q.B. 315 (Eng. Q.B. Div'l Ct.) (1895).

Roberts v. Myers, 20 F. Cas. 898 (C.C.D. Mass. 1860) (No. 11,906).

Root v. Borst, 36 N.E. 814 (N.Y. 1894).

Rosenstein v. Zentz, 85 A. 675 (Md. 1912).

S. W. Scott & Co. v. Scott, 174 N.Y.S. 583 (App. Div. 1919).

Salomon v. Hertz, 2 A. 379 (N.J. Ch. 1886).

Salter v. Howard, 43 Ga. 601 (1871).

Schilling v. State, 143 Miss. 709, 109 So. 737 (1926).

Schubert v. Angeles, 80 N.Y.S. 146 (App. Div. 1903).

Schumacher v. Schwencke, 25 F. 466 (C.C.S.D.N.Y. 1885).

Slemmer's Appeal, 58 Pa. 155 (1868).

Sparkman v. Higgins, 22 F. Cas. 878 (C.C.S.D.N.Y. 1846) (No. 13,208).

Standard Parts Co. v. Peck, 264 U.S. 52 (1924).

Star Co. v. Press Publishing Co., 147 N.Y.S. 579 (App. Div. 1914).

State v. Aye, 63 S.C. 458, 41 S.E. 519 (1902).

Sternberg v. O'Brien, 22 A. 348 (N.J. Ch. 1891).

Stevens & Co. v. Stiles, 71 A. 802 (R.I. 1909).

Stone v. Goss, 55 A. 736 (N.J. 1903).

Streat v. White, 35 F. 426 (C.C.S.D.N.Y. 1888).

Strobridge Lithographic Co. v. Crane, 12 N.Y.S. 898 (Sup. Ct. 1890).

Taylor Iron & Steel Co. v. Nichols, 65 A. 695 (N.J. Ch. 1907).

Taylor Iron & Steel Co. v. Nichols, 69 A. 186 (N.J. 1908).

Teese v. Phelps, 23 F. Cas. 832 (C.C.N.D. Cal. 1855) (No. 13,819).

Thomson v. Larson, 147 F.3d 195 (2d Cir. 1998).

Triumph Electric Co. v. Thullen, 225 F. 293 (D.C.E.D. Pa. 1915).

Tucker v. State, 86 Ark. 436, 111 S.W. 275 (1908).

United States v. Addyston Pipe & Steel Co., 85 F. 271 (6th Cir. 1898).

United States v. Dubilier Condenser Co., 289 U.S. 178 (1933).

United States v. Jung Ah Lung, 124 U.S. 621 (1888).

Universal Talking-Machine Co. v. English, 69 N.Y.S. 813 (Sup. Ct. 1901).

Utah Medical Products, Inc. v. Clinical Innovations Associates, Inc., 79 F. Supp. 2d
    1290 (D. Utah 1999).

Vegelahn v. Guntner, 44 N.E. 1077 (Mass. 1896).

Velsicol Corp. v. Hyman, 87 N.E. 2d 35 (Ill. App. Ct. 1949).

Vickery v. Welch, 36 Mass. (19 Pick.) 523 (1837).

W. J. Johnston Co. v. Hunt, 31 N.Y.S. 314 (Gen. Term 1892).

Wade v. Metcalf, 16 F. 130 (C.C.D. Mass. 1883).

Westervelt v. National Paper & Supply Co., 57 N.E. 552 (Ind. 1900).

Wheaton v. Peters, 33 U.S. 591 (1834).

Wilkens v. Spafford, 29 F. Cas. 1242 (1878) (No. 17,659).

William Rogers Manufacturing Co. v. Rogers, 20 A. 467 (Conn. 1890).

Winter Garden Co. v. Smith, 282 F. 166 (2d Cir. 1922).

Wireless Specialty Apparatus Co. v. Mica Condenser Co., 131 N.E. 307 (Mass. 1921).

Withington-Cooley Manufacturing Co. v. Kinney, 68 F. 500 (6th Cir. 1895).

Witkop & Holmes Co. v. Boyce, 112 N.Y.S. 874 (Sup. Ct. 1908).

Wollensak v. Briggs, 20 Ill. App. 50 (1886).

Wood v. Lucy, Lady Duff-Gordon, 118 N.E. 214 (N.Y. 1917).

Work v. Welsh, 160 Ill. 468 (1896).

Wright v. Duke, 36 N.Y.S. 853 (N.Y. Gen. Term 1895).

Ziegfeld v. Norworth, 118 N.Y.S. 1151 (App. Div. 1909).

7 U.S. Op. Atty. Gen. 656 (1856).

U.S. SUPREME COURT CASE RECORDS

Agawam Woolen Co. v. Jordan, *microformed on* U.S. Supreme Court Records and Briefs, Part II, no. 78 (Information Handling Service).

Bleistein v. Donaldson Lithographic Co., *microformed on* U.S. Supreme Court Records and Briefs, no. 117 (Information Handling Service).

Burrow-Giles Lithographic Co. v. Sarony, *microformed on* U.S. Supreme Court Records and Briefs, Part IV, no. 221 (Information Handling Service).

Callaghan v. Myers, *microformed on* U.S. Supreme Court Records and Briefs, Part IV, no. 302 (Information Handling Service).

E. I. du Pont de Nemours & Co. v. Masland, *microformed on* U.S. Supreme Court Records and Briefs, no. 210 (Information Handling Service).

Hapgood v. Hewitt, *microformed on* U.S. Supreme Court Records and Briefs, Part IV, no. 261 (Information Handling Service).

McClurg v. Kingsland, *microformed on* U.S. Supreme Court Records and Briefs, Part I, no. 7 (Information Handling Service).

Standard Parts v. Peck, *microformed on* U.S. Supreme Court Records and Briefs, (Information Handling Service).

United States v. Dubilier Condenser Co., *microformed on* U.S. Supreme Court Records and Briefs (Information Handling Service).

BRITISH CASES

Allen v. Rawson, 135 Eng. Rep. 656 (1845).

Barker and Harris v. Shaw, 1 Webs. Pat Cases 126 (n.d.).

Bryson v. Whitehead, 57 Eng. Rep. 29 (V.C.) (1822).

Cholmondeley v. Clinton, 34 Eng. Rep. 515 (1815).

Evitt v. Price, 57 Eng. Rep. 659 (Ch.) (1827).

Hill v. Thompson, 129 Eng. Rep. 427 (1818).

Horner v. Graves, 131 Eng. Rep. 284, 288 (C.P.) (1831).

Lumley v. Gye, 118 Eng. Rep. 749 (Q.B.) (1853).

Lumley v. Wagner, 42 Eng. Rep. 687 (Ch.) (1852).

Makepeace v. Jackson, 128 Eng. Rep. 534 (1813).

Minter v. Wells, 149 Eng. Rep. 1180 (N.P) (1834).

Mitchel v. Reynolds, 24 Eng. Rep. 347 (Q.B.) (1711).

Morison v. Moat, 68 Eng. Rep. 492 (V.C.) (1851).

Rex v. Arkwright, Webs. Pat. Cas. 64 (1785).

Ward v. Byrne, 151 Eng. Rep. 232, 238 (C.P.) (1831).

Yovatt v. Winyard, 37 Eng. Rep. 425 (Ex. Ch.) (1820).

LEGISLATIVE MATERIALS

American

Copyright Act, 1st Cong., 2d Sess., ch. 15. May 31, 1790, 1 Stat. 124.

The Reporter's Act of March 3, 1817, ch. 63, 3 Stat. 376.

4 Stat. 436 (1831).

Act of July 4, 1836, ch. 357.

11 Stat. 138 (1856).

13 Stat. 540 (1865).

16 Stat. 212 (1870).

Printing Act of 1895, ch. 23, 28 Stat. 601.

H.R. Rep. no. 60–1 (to accompany H.R. 28192, February 1909).

Act of March 4, 1909, ch. 320, 35 Stat. 1075.

37 Stat. 488 (1912).

The Restatement (Second) of Agency (1958).

H.R. Rep. no. 94–1476, at 59 (1976).

17 U.S.C. §§101, 105.

Sonny Bono Copyright Extension Act, Pub. L. no. 105–298, 11 Stat. 2827 (codified in
scattered sections of 17 U.S.C).

British

23 Edw. 3 (Eng. 1349). Reprinted in *English Economic History: Select Documents.* 2d ed.
Edited by A. E. Bland et al., 147. London: G. Bell and Sons, Ltd., 1915.

28 Hen. 8, c. 5 (1536). Reprinted in *English Economic History: Select Documents.* 2d ed.
Edited by A. E. Bland et al., 147. London: G. Bell and Sons, Ltd., 1915.

21 James I, c. 3 §5.

Index

Index

employees/servants, 224, 305 (n. 38); as litigants, 8; in map publishing, 232–33

Individual(s): authors as, 60, 74, 212, 214; creativity of, 211–12; cultural creation as product of, 87; inventors as, 41, 87, 109–12, 114; mythologizing of, 109

Individualism: corporate authorship and, 213–14

Industrial espionage, 16, 46, 191–92, 206

Industrialization, 75, 87

Industrial property: patents as, 37

Industrial sector: forms of intellectual property in, 12; injunctions against strikes in, 137

Ingersoll, Simon, 242

Ingersoll-Rand, 241–44

Ingersoll-Rand v. Ciavatta, 241–44

Ingersoll-Sergeant, 242

Injunctions: against strikes, 137; against working, 140, 162–71

Innovation/invention: association with firms versus individuals, 87; in consumer culture, 235; in economic development, 20, 77–78; economic efficiency of corporate control of, 4; Lincoln on nature of, 76–78; as personality trait, 110, 181; public understanding of, 176, 180; standardization of, 186–87; traditional approach to study of, 3. *See also* Inventors; Research and development facilities; Technological innovation

In re Debs, 173

Institutions, intellectual property: expansion of, 11

Instructions for Masters, Traders, Laborers &c., 25

Insular Cases, 173

Intangibles: property rights in, 9–10, 34–35, 88; as trade secrets, 208

Intellect: as alienable property, 38; connotations of term, 37

Intellectual capital: attribution as, 212

Intellectual labor: of employee-authors, 60–61, 68–69; as property, 36

Intellectual property: alienation in, 2; attribution as form of, 251–55; definition of, 12; expansion of scope of, 11–12, 137, 207–8, 235; future of, 254–55; modern regime of, 1, 253–55; versus monopoly, 36; origins of term, 36–37; terminology of, 12–17

Intention: in contracts, 80–81, 212

Interference, patent: in cigarette manufacturing, 131–32; definition of, 13

International copyright, 159. *See also* Foreign works

Inventor-managers, 246–50

Inventors: alienation from works, 2–3, 249; collaborators as, 33, 41, 87, 110, 182–83; firms as, 87, 179–80; as heroes, 109–13, 180; identification of significant contributions of, 41–42; individuals as, 41, 87, 109–12, 114; name of, on patents, 40–41, 42, 180. *See also* Innovation/invention; Patent(s)

Inventors, employee-: antebellum law on, 33, 39–44; attribution given to, 125, 209–10, 250; in cigarette manufacturing, 126–36; class identity of, 245–50; in corporations, 179–88, 241–42, 245–50; decline in inventiveness of, 241, 243–44; at Du Pont, 196–206; at Eastman Kodak, 188–96; employer control of talent of, 166–67; as entrepreneurs, 126, 136, 179–80, 209–10, 240–44; of farm equipment, 114–17; legal rights of, in 1800, 1; management of, 180–81, 248–49; in modern middle class, 245–50; moral right of, 202–3; postbellum law on, 108–36; at railroad companies, 114, 119–26; as servants, 187, 209; in theater, 155–58. *See also* Research and development facilities; Social status of inventors

[353]

Social status of inventors: corporate, 241–42, 245–50; in corporate R & D, 125, 180–81, 196, 204; in modern middle class, 245–50; upward mobility in, 174–75, 209–10, 242

Societies: and technological innovation, 89

Sokoloff, Kenneth, 180, 247

Sonny Bono Copyright Extension Act, 271 (n. 6)

Sothern, Edward, 145

South Africa: cigarette manufacturing in, 128, 133; maps of, 273 (n. 28)

Southern states: free labor in, 165–66

Specially commissioned works, 15

Specification: in patent applications, 13

Spirit of the Times, 156

Standard Dry Plate Company, 194

Standardization: of innovation, 186–87; by railroad companies, 123

Standard Parts Co. v. Peck, 183–86

Stanley Dry Plate Company, 194

Star Company v. Press Publishing Co., 170

State courts: patent ownership in, 266–67 (n. 55). *See also specific states*

State law: apprenticeships in, 28; copyright in, 15, 31; noncompetition agreements in, 16; patents in, 15, 31; trademarks in, 15, 16–17; trade secrets in, 15, 16

State of the art: in patent applications, 13, 33

Status: versus contract in employment relationship, 2, 9, 24–26, 79. *See also* Social status

Statute of Monopolies (English), 38, 266 (n. 54)

Statutory law. *See specific legislation*

Stecher (painter), 214

Steel companies, 5

Steffe, C. G., 283 (n. 38)

Steinfeld, Robert J., 26

Steinmetz, Charles P., 181

Stock ownership: employee, 200

Stone v. Goss, 278 (n. 26)

Story, Joseph: *Commentaries on Equity Jurisprudence*, 55–56, 161–62; and court reporters, 65; in origins of trade secret law, 55–58

Stowe, Harriet Beecher, 289 (n. 24)

Streat v. White, 266 (n. 53)

Strikes: injunctions against, 137

Strobridge Lithographic Co. v. Crane, 294–95 (n. 92)

Strouse, D. B., 126, 127, 131, 132

Stuart, William, 141–42, 148, 149, 152–53

Stuber, William G., 194

Sullivan, Arthur, 158–60, 217

Supervisory responsibility, 248–49

Supreme Court, U.S.: on copyright of advertisements, 37, 236–39; on copyright of court opinions, 65–66, 221–23; on copyright of photos, 216–19; court reporters for, 43–44, 63–66; on employer ownership of patents, 183–86; on freedom of contract, 168; on individuals as inventors, 110–12; on patent licensing, 42–44; on patents as monopoly versus property, 33–34; on patents in contracts, 114–17; on trade secrets, 203; vision for, and entrepreneurship, 88

Supreme Court Reporter of Decisions, 43, 64–66, 149

Surveyors: in mapmaking, 69–70

Surveys, government: as sources in map publishing, 70–71, 274 (n. 35)

Tacit assent, 223

Tacit knowledge, 90

Taft, William Howard, 98–100

Talent, employee: commodification of, 165–66; employer control of, 160–71

Taylor, Frederick Winslow: and Du Pont, 198; *Principles of Scientific Management*, 245; and rise of contracts, 82;